D0487803

FOOTBALL'S GREATEST HEROES

WEST
STANDING
ENCLOSURE

ENTER AT TURNSTILES
(See Plan on back)

ENTRANCE

H
61

EMPIRE STADIUM, WEMBLEY

ASSOCIATION FOOTBALL
INTERNATIONAL MATCH

ENGLAND v. SCOTLAND

SATURDAY, APRIL 14th, 1951

Kick-off 3 p.m.

Price 3/-
(Including Tax)

A. J. Elvin
CHAIRMAN AND
MANAGING DIRECTOR,
Wembley Stadium Limited

THIS PORTION TO BE RETAINED
(See Conditions on back)

FOOTBALL'S GREATEST HEROES

THE NATIONAL FOOTBALL MUSEUM HALL OF FAME

Robert Galvin with Mark Bushell

Over A Century of Footballing Legends

Foreword by Sir Bobby Charlton

ROBSON BOOKS

First published in Great Britain in 2005 by Robson Books, The Chrysalis Building, Bramley Road, London, W10 6SP

An imprint of Chrysalis Books Group plc

British Library Cataloguing in Publication Data
A catalogue record for this title is available from the British Library.

ISBN 1 86105 904 3

Designed by Neil Stevens
Printed in Thailand

Contents

Acknowledgements

I could not have researched this collection of profiles without the help of many former players, museum experts and libraries.

I would like to thank Mark Bushell, whose support for the project as communications manager at the National Football Museum has been a constant over the past two years, and Barbara Phelan, the editor, for her thoroughness, good humour and dedication.

Special thanks to Sir Bobby Charlton for writing the foreword for the book.

Mark Bushell earns a second mention for his contribution in sourcing photographs and images, and for writing the captions and the text for the 'Key Museum Artefact' section in each profile. A note of thanks to Kevin Moore for writing the introduction.

Compiling the research for this book was a rewarding experience, and I would like to place on record my thanks to Viv Anderson, Colin Bell, Sue Lopez, Gail Newsham, an expert on women's football, and Barbara Dean for their generous co-operation.

I am also grateful for the support given to the Museum by the Hall of Fame selection panel whose members include Sir Tom Finney, Sir Alex Ferguson, and Sir Bobby Robson.

The staff at the Museum, in particular Hugh Hornby, Peter Holme and Richard Cuthbert, have been diligent in their exhaustive efforts to fact-check the text.

And finally, love and thanks to my wife, Chris, who cheered me to the final word.

Robert Galvin

I owe a huge debt of gratitude to Rob Galvin for his patience and commitment to the project. I would also like to thank him for all his hard work during the development stages of the book. Without his perseverance and dedication this book may never have happened.

Jeremy Robson must be commended for his vision and the way in which he understood immediately what Rob and I were trying to achieve with this publication.

A special mention must be given to Craig Nicholson and all at Marksman International, whose early graphic treatments brought the book to life.

Pete Lucas Photography worked into the night, on countless occasions, to ensure that many prized objects from the Museum's collections were recorded for posterity.

A big thank you must also go to all the Museum team, particularly Hugh Hornby, Peter Holme, Kevin Moore and Richard Cuthbert who fact-checked and proofed whenever asked. Thanks also to the Museum Manager, Julie Allsop, for her support and understanding.

I would also like to thank Barbara Phelan, the editor, for the calm efficiency she applies to her job. It helped me in times of panic!

Finally, a huge thank you and loads of love to my wife, Hannah, who never fails to support me. Not once did she complain about the late-night calls and the loss of an inordinate number of weekends.

Mark Bushell

Spain
1950

Introduction

The National Football Museum launched the National Football Museum Hall of Fame in 2002, to celebrate the greatest players and managers of all time in English football. The Museum recognised that an English football hall of fame had been overdue. The achievements of many of the stars of the game had not been as fully recognised as they could have been during their lifetime. While the displays of the Museum, which opened in 2001, feature the greatest names in English football history, it was recognised that a hall of fame was the best way to honour the all-time greats.

To select those 'legends' from over a century of football's history to be inducted into the National Football Museum Hall of Fame, the Museum put together a selection panel of some of the greatest names in the game, including Sir Bobby Charlton, Sir Alex Ferguson, Sir Tom Finney and Sir Trevor Brooking.

At the first National Football Museum Hall of Fame Annual Awards ceremony in December 2002, 22 players and six managers were honoured. As a first step in the recognition of the hidden history of women's football, the Museum also inducted the greatest player in the history of the women's game. In this first year, the selection panel had over one hundred years of football history from which to make their selection. In subsequent years, smaller numbers have been inducted, to ensure that only the greatest names in the history of the game are included in the Hall of Fame. In 2003, a further nine players, including a woman player, and four managers, were inducted. In 2004, seven male players, two managers and one female player were inducted. The 2002, 2003 and 2004 Annual Awards ceremonies were attended by an outstanding array of star guests and attracted substantial media coverage. The National Football Museum Hall of Fame has become an outstanding awards event in the English football calendar.

The selection criteria for inclusion in the National Football Museum Hall of Fame are as follows: a player must have, first, either played in England for the majority of their career, or played in England for at least five seasons; and second, either have retired from playing, or be over the age of 30 (at 1 September prior to induction). A manager or coach must have either managed or coached in England for the majority of their career, or managed or coached in England for at least five seasons. The choice of who is then selected to be inducted, from a list of eligible nominations, is then down to the votes (by secret ballot) of the selection panel.

Reaction to the National Football Museum Hall of Fame by the greatest names in football has been extremely positive, as the following quotes demonstrate:

'I'm really proud to be included in the National Football Museum's Hall of Fame. It's a great honour. If you look at the names included I have to say I couldn't argue with them. They are all great players and people I would love to have played with. And I think it's great that the Museum has secured the Hall of Fame for the benefit of future generations of both footballers and supporters.' – *Sir Bobby Charlton*

'I'm overwhelmed. This is a huge honour. To join such an illustrious group is fabulous.' – *Sir Bobby Robson*

'The reason I love the Hall of Fame so much and the Museum itself, is because it gives people the chance to reflect on the history of football.' – *Sir Alex Ferguson*

The Museum is grateful for the support it has received from Littlewoods Football Pools, Northwest Regional Development Agency and The Professional Footballers' Association, without which the development of the National Football Museum Hall of Fame would not have been possible.

The National Football Museum Hall of Fame has also been supported by the development of the International Football Institute (IFI), which is a partnership between the Museum and the University of Central Lancashire, to undertake research on aspects of football, and to make this research available to the widest possible audience.

Kevin Moore

Museum Director
The National Football Museum
www.nationalfootballmuseum.com

Director
The International Football Institute
www.uclan.ac.uk/ifi

DENIS LAW
Manchester United & Scotland
Captain of Hungary
FERENC PUSKAS

THE FOOTBALL ASSOCIATION CHALLENGE CUP COMPETITION
FINAL TIE
BLACKPOOL v
BOLTON WANDERERS
SATURDAY, MAY 2nd, 1953 KICK-OFF 3 pm
EMPIRE STADIUM
WEMBLEY
Chairman and Managing Director: SIR ARTHUR J. ELVIN, M.B.E.
OFFICIAL PROGRAMME · ONE SHILLING

Foreword

Many great footballers have never been afforded the recognition that they deserve in the game. So I was delighted when I learned, in 2002, that the National Football Museum was to create a Hall of Fame to honour those players and managers who had made a lasting and outstanding contribution to English football.

Although the Museum's exhibitions tell the detailed story of the game, I believe that the Hall of Fame and its annual Gala Celebration Awards dinner are vital in highlighting the careers of some of the game's greatest names. Sadly, some of these individuals appear to have been forgotten, firmly justifying the role of the The National Football Museum and its Hall of Fame.

Rewards are few and far between in football, so to be inducted into the Hall of Fame is hugely satisfying. The huge salaries on offer to today's top players may compensate for lack of silverware but many of the Hall of Fame Inductees were not fortunate enough to have financial security by the time their careers came to a close. To be recognised by their peers in the Hall of Fame is some compensation, I'm sure, and ensures that their legacy is never forgotten.

Keane, Finney, Banks and Best are all names that trip off the tongue, but what about the less familiar names of Doherty, Wharton, Chapman and James? All well respected during their careers but less well known today. We must never forget these players and managers and how they have helped to shape the game that we know and love.

Beautifully illustrated and painstakingly researched, the information and detail in this publication will evoke some wonderful memories and explain why the Hall of Fame Inductees mean so much to so many.

I am delighted to write this foreword in support of the Hall of Fame book. The authors deserve every credit for their diligence and knowledge. All the Inductees deserve to be remembered and this publication is a fitting tribute to their efforts on the pitch or in the dugout.

Sir Bobby Charlton

President of The National Football Museum

FOOTBALL'S GREATEST HEROES

100 YARDS
Amateur
Champion.
PLAY UP
DARLINGTON
WHARTON
J. BRIGGS 8 SOMERBY ST. LEEDS

ARTHUR WHARTON (1865–1930)

Player • Inducted 2003

Arthur Wharton, the first black professional in English football, was goalkeeper for the best team in the country in the 1880s, and the fastest sprinter in the world to boot.

An all-round sportsman who also played professional cricket, Wharton played in goal in 1886–87 as an amateur for Preston North End, soon to be known universally as 'The Invincibles', and the first club openly to embrace the payment of players.

His agile, athletic performances during the late 1880s prompted calls from the media for his inclusion in the England team for the annual fixture against Scotland. The Football Association overlooked his claims, whether as a result of prejudice remains open to question.

The selectors, though perhaps sympathetic to the discriminatory racial beliefs prevalent in Victorian society during the latter half of the 19th century, may also have been concerned about Wharton's eccentric behaviour at times between the sticks. It is definitely true that crowds loved him for it.

The *Football News and Athletic Journal* once described him as a 'skylark', referring to his favourite tricks, which included grabbing the crossbar, bending it under his own weight, so that shots flew harmlessly over, catching the ball between his legs; and dumping onrushing forwards into the net.

On the positive side, Wharton was brave, skilful and very quick, as he proved by setting a world-record time of 10 seconds flat for the 100-yards dash at the AAA national athletics championships in July 1886.

In 1886–87, Wharton played in all six of Preston North End's ties in the FA Cup, helping the club reach the semi-finals. On the way, the team conceded only four goals, three of which came in the defeat to West Bromwich Albion. The Cup run turned out to be the highlight of his career. As the *Athletic News* newspaper stated after one of those Cup games: 'Wharton is, indeed, a born goalkeeper; he never loses his head, and his hands are always in readiness. His was one of the best exhibitions of goalkeeping I have seen for a long time.'

KEY MATCH

Corinthians 1 Preston North End 1, Friendly, The Oval, 12 March 1887

Arthur Wharton took his place in the back row for a rare team photo after playing in goal for Preston North End in perhaps the most important game of football ever played in England up to that time.

A crowd of 10,000 cheered the 'Professionals v Amateurs' match during the 'Jubilee Festival of Football', organised to mark Queen Victoria's 50th year on the throne.

Wharton, a member of 'the finest team in the world', according to Major Sudell, the North End secretary-manager, looked on as the two captains were presented to the Prince of Wales at half-time.

While it was thought a great honour for professionals to be involved in such an occasion, the greater significance of the day became apparent only later when the Prince, the future king Edward VII, 'graciously signified his willingness to become patron of the Football Association'. The sport, then still in its infancy, had won the backing of the Establishment, a vital step forward in terms of legitimacy.

Jack Ross, the Preston captain, won the toss and kicked off. Wharton, defending the goal at the Gasometer End, faced a forward line of Brann, Challen, Lindley, Cobbold and Bambridge, then considered the strongest in England.

Several times during the match Wharton was charged heavily, a legitimate tactic even if the player was not in possession. He was also 'hustled', again quite legally, by two or three forwards in another pre-arranged move.

All the players were praised afterwards for their efforts in what was described as 'a good game, which ended in a draw of one goal each'.

Left A 19th-century Baines Card – one of the earliest types of football collectables – featuring Arthur Wharton.

KEY MUSEUM ARTEFACT

Contrary to popular belief the weight of a football has always been virtually the same. The creation of the FA Cup in 1871 led to the need for a standardised football. However, as the early leather footballs, such as this example from the 1880s, did not benefit from man-made protective coatings, they absorbed water on the pitch and in the air. The result was that the ball's weight could often double increasing to as much as 2lb. In order to punch a wet ball any distance, Wharton would have needed good upper body strength and powerful arms, as well as being extremely brave.

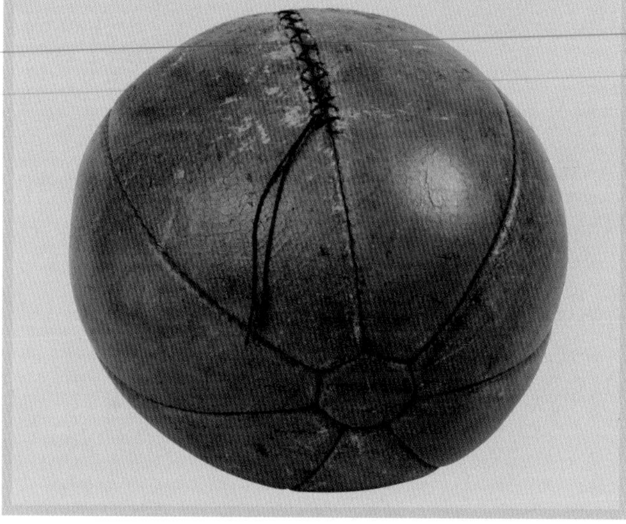

Below A Rotherham Swifts Baines card, circa1880–90. Wharton finally became a professional footballer in Rotherham, signing for Swifts' rivals RotherhamTown.

Above right A Preston North End fixture list from1885–86. It was at the end of this season that Wharton came to the attention of Preston's Secretary/Manager, William Sudell, pictured between the two players.

As the first professional black footballer, Arthur Wharton was undoubtedly treated differently because of the colour of his skin. Newspapers, for instance, routinely referred to him as a 'darkie' and occasionally questioned his intelligence. His physical and mental attributes as a player were often discussed in racial terms, reflecting the debate in Victorian scientific circles as to whether 'the Negro' was the intellectual equal of the northern European.

Whatever disadvantages he experienced, Wharton countered prejudice with a personal magnetism and appeal as a footballer who won over many reporters and the majority of supporters at several of his clubs. Later in his career, in 1896, while playing for Stalybridge Rovers in the Lancashire League, one newspaper reported that he was 'lionised' by the majority of supporters for his antics. The team even became known as 'Wharton's Brigade'.

At Stockport County, then playing in Division Two of the Football League, 'the general cry of "Good Old Wharton" came from the crowd behind the goal who had the best view of his work,' another newspaper reported. That was during Wharton's last season before his retirement in 1901–02.

Whatever disadvantages he experienced, Wharton countered prejudice with a personal magnetism and appeal as a footballer who won over many reporters.

At his peak, at Preston in 1886–67, the Northern Echo took up his cause, describing him as 'one of the most capable goal-custodians in the country', and a player who 'is undoubtedly deserving of a place in any international team'. Pushing his claims, the paper reported that Mr Reed, of Middlesbrough and Cleveland, the region's delegate to the FA Council, would also lobby on Wharton's behalf.

In 1888, the year after Wharton left Preston, the Football League was launched. The creation of the new competition, bringing together the 12 leading clubs in

“The general cry of ‘Good old Wharton’ came from the crowd behind the goal who have the best view of his work.”

– Stockport Newspaper Report

the north west of England and the Midlands, coincided with his decision to turn professional.

Wharton played for several teams in Yorkshire and Lancashire: Rotherham Town, Sheffield United, Stalybridge Rovers, Ashton North End, Stalybridge Rovers again, and, finally, Stockport County.

His brief stint with Sheffield United enabled Wharton to make his one and only appearance in Division One of the Football League, a 2–0 defeat against Sunderland in February in 1895.

Wharton worked all year round, playing football during the winter and earning additional money as a professional sprinter or cricketer in the summer months. His contacts in athletics helped him to win a contract at Sheffield United; Tim Bott, his backer as an athlete, was a director of the club and the official team manager.

Wharton even took over a pub in the city. But he had the misfortune of being at the club at the same time as Bill ‘Fatty’ Foulke, a giant of a goalkeeper who went on to play for England, restricting his opportunities in the first team. As a result, Wharton, now nearing 30, rejoined Rotherham Town, a Division Two club.

Wharton had been born into the ruling class in Ghana in 1865. In his teens, he was sent to England to train as a Methodist minister. Religion bored him, however, and he opted instead for a sporting life at the age of 17. Sadly, after retiring as a player, he slid into poverty. For the last 15 years of his working life, he was employed as a colliery haulage hand, before dying of cancer in 1930, aged 65.

He was buried in a third-class grave. The site remained unmarked until a memorial was erected in 1997, in honour of his unique place in the history of the game.

TALKING POINT

Arthur Wharton occasionally played in matches at centre-forward. As a means of self-preservation it was not a bad idea. Goalkeeping was a dangerous occupation in the 1880s. Under the laws of the day when he began playing football, forwards were allowed to shoulder charge the goalkeeper whether he was in possession of the ball or not.

Obstruction of the goalkeeper was another standard ploy. One attacker would simply barge straight into him in a bid to give a team-mate a better chance of scoring. The risk of injury to the custodian was high.

At five feet 11 inches tall and weighing 12 stone, Wharton had the physical attributes needed in what was a very tough game and perhaps the physical threat to the goalkeeper explains one of his more unusual habits: Wharton was known to stand at the side of the goal, out of the way of barging forwards, often in a crouched position, while an opposition attack developed. Only when the goal was under direct threat did he leap into action. Some observers marvelled at his agility; others thought his play ‘amateurish’.

Another law allowed for the custodian to handle the ball anywhere in his own half. In addition to his great asset – his speed out of goal – one of Wharton’s other tricks as a goalkeeper was an ability to punch the heavy ball of the day prodigious distances. According to contemporary reports, many of Wharton’s clearances with his fist carried 20–30 yards.

Above This 1884 New Toy Game of Football is the oldest football board game in the world. It was manufactured in Preston just two years before Wharton joined the club. The two teams probably represent Preston North End and Blackburn Rovers.

Above left *Men Famous In Football* was produced in 1904, two years after Wharton finished his career. While others became legendary figures, his story remained largely unknown until 1997.

HERBERT CHAPMAN (1878–1934)

Manager • Inducted 2003 • 4 Division One Championships • 2 FA Cups

In making Arsenal the most famous and successful football club in the world, Herbert Chapman defined the role of the modern team manager. His legacy, like his memorial bust, can still be seen at Highbury.

London had yet to celebrate a championship success when Chapman arrived at Highbury in 1925. Mediocre, debt-ridden, and lacking mass support, Arsenal hardly looked likely saviours for the capital. A decade later, Arsenal were the dominant power in England, let alone London.

At the time of Chapman's death from pneumonia, at the age of 55, in 1934, a second successive title was within sight, to add to an earlier FA Cup win and League Division One Championship. The team he built won three more trophies in the 1930s.

He had put Arsenal on the map, literally. In 1932, in a public relations coup, Chapman persuaded the local rail company to re-name the London Underground station close to Highbury after the club. Chapman was the first manager to win the championship with two different clubs – a feat unequalled for four decades – following successive titles at Huddersfield Town in the mid-1920s. Determined to lure him south from his native Yorkshire, Arsenal made Chapman the highest paid manager in football.

From the outset he insisted that selection and all other team matters must be left to professionals. 'Football today is too big a job to be a director's hobby,' he wrote. 'Herbert was definitely the governor,' George Male, the team captain said. 'The board didn't stand a chance.' And Chapman had the unswerving support of the players.

Cliff Bastin, the Arsenal winger, spoke of Chapman's 'aura of greatness', his power of inspiration and foresight. 'He should have been prime minister,' Bastin wrote in 1950. 'He might have been but for the lack of opportunities entailed by his position in the social scale.'

KEY MATCH

Arsenal 2 Huddersfield Town 0, FA Cup final, Wembley, 26 April 1930

Herbert Chapman drew upon all his experience and imagination as a manager to help his players win the first honour in the club's 50-year history.

The odds appeared against him: underdogs Arsenal, a middle-of-the-table side in Division One, faced Huddersfield Town, the most dominant side of the previous decade.

Worried that inexperience and nerves might be a factor, Chapman brought with him a portable gramophone and a selection of cheery records. 'We had the players whistling popular tunes as they got changed,' he recalled. First, distract them; then put them in a positive frame of mind.

The job of shadowing Alex Jackson, Huddersfield Town's 'Flying Scotsman', was given to Eddie Hapgood. In attack, Chapman put his faith in youth in defiance of conventional thinking: at the age of 18 years and one month, Cliff Bastin became the youngest player to appear in a final.

In May 1925, on arriving at Highbury, Chapman said it would take five years to build a winning team; five years on almost to the week, he made good that promise.

Left Herbert Chapman, shown here in 1931, made Arsenal the best side in the country in the early 1930s, winning both the FA Cup and Division One title.

KEY MUSEUM ARTEFACT

After the death of Herbert Chapman, in January 1934, his assistant Joe Shaw took control of team matters at Arsenal. Having successfully defended their title, Shaw was rewarded with this Championship medal made out of solid gold. In the late 19th century, medals were not always presented and sometimes players had the choice of a medal, pocket watch or even money! This medal is of typical heraldic, English design, being circular in shape and incorporating a ball motif. The introduction of European competitions in the 1950s saw the development of more abstract shapes and designs.

Right A Northampton Town ceramic pot from the 1920s. During his career, Chapman was a registered player with a number of clubs including: Rochdale, Grimsby Town, Swindon Town, Sheffield United, Notts County and Tottenham Hotspur. He joined Northampton Town on three separate occasions.

Below The reverse of Joe Shaw's 1934 League Division One Championship medal showing the detailed engraving.

Herbert Chapman arrived at Highbury in 1925, the same year that the football authorities changed the offside law. Arsenal responded positively to both developments.

Chapman alone grasped the significance of the law change. The shape of the game had fundamentally changed now that forwards had more space to work in. Gradually, he implemented new tactics to take best advantage.

Other clubs also introduced a 'stopper' centre-half, but Chapman went further. 'He changed the function of every position vitally, except that of goalkeeper,' Bernard Joy, the Arsenal defender, said.

Most importantly, one inside-forward dropped into a deeper position. The team defended in greater numbers and for longer periods, and then hit the opposition with swift counter-attacks. It was deliberate and highly effective against teams accustomed to an end-to-end, all-out attack.

Herbert Chapman backed his own judgement with a willingness to spend record sums in the transfer market.

'A team can attack for too long,' Chapman said. 'The quicker you get to your opponent's goal, the fewer obstacles you find.

'If you have a good goalkeeper and a good stopper centre-half, all I need is the two best wingers and the best centre-forward there is. It doesn't matter what the rest are like.'

There was more to it than that, of course. Previously, wingers had to beat the full-back to the by-line and cross. Cliff Bastin and Joe Hulme were told to cut inside more often and shoot. Arsenal also had Alex James, a great inside-forward. His quick, accurate distribution to the wings from deep positions was vital. Other teams copied Chapman, but they did not have

the same quality of players in key positions, and for that Arsenal also had Chapman to thank.

Herbert Chapman backed his own judgement with a willingness to spend record sums in the transfer market. In 1928, Arsenal paid Bolton Wanderers £11,500 for David Jack, the England inside-forward. The following year, Chapman returned north to sign Alex James from Preston for a fee of £8,750.

Chapman also had an eye for potential. Joe Hulme, reputedly the fastest winger in British football, arrived in 1926, while Cliff Bastin was spotted at the age of 16, playing for Exeter City. Between 1929 and 1935, the pair scored 190 League goals, an unprecedented return from the wings.

Arsenal initiated team meetings every Friday lunchtime. Players were encouraged to offer an opinion, another break with custom. There was even a table-top pitch and plastic models to demonstrate tactics. The manager, however, always had the last word. No one was allowed to challenge his authority. When a trainer shouted instructions from the bench, a responsibility Chapman reserved for himself, he was promptly sacked. Players who failed to follow his orders were quickly moved on.

The rewards for those who fulfilled his requirements were great: Chapman insisted on the best hotels, medical and dressing-room facilities for his players. To ensure continuity, his methods were applied throughout the club. The reserves won the London Combination five seasons in a row.

The manager, however, always had the last word. No one was allowed to challenge his authority.

Fundamentally, Chapman made Arsenal great by placing greater emphasis on defensive skills, while devising tactics that fully exploited the side's attacking potential. A strapping centre-half, a skilful play-maker, speedy wingers who could shoot and a burly centre-forward: the basic pattern of English football was set for a generation.

TALKING POINT

Herbert Chapman offered a glimpse of the future when he took charge of the England team on a one-off basis for their first international against Italy in Rome in 1933.

It was the first time a club manager had been granted such a responsibility, albeit on a temporary basis. Powerful forces within the Football Association who opposed the involvement of professionals made sure that the experiment was not repeated.

In Italy, Chapman organised the schedule, gave a team talk, and stood on a chair by the touchline urging on the players. Rather embarrassingly, he also misplaced the dressing-room key at half-time. The game ended 1–1.

He did not, however, select the team; the FA selectors would not give up that power completely until 1963.

Chapman favoured radical change, advocating the 'startling idea' of a squad system. 'I would like the England selectors to bring together 20 of the most promising young players for a week under a selector, coach and trainer. The result would be astonishing.'

His suggestion, as he predicted, was ignored. Progress was on the way, however. Stanley Rous, who began work as FA Secretary in 1934, appointed a permanent England manager 12 years later.

Left This 1930s' Arsenal lapel badge is made from lead and is hand-painted in the club colours, showing the club shirt's distinctive white sleeves.

Above left *Herbert Chapman on Football* was published after his death in 1934 and is based on the articles that he contributed to the *Sunday Express*. Chapman understood the importance of the media and recognised the opportunities they offered. The first ever radio broadcast of a football match was the Arsenal v Sheffield United game on 22 January 1927.

LILY PARR (1905–1978)

Player • Inducted 2002

Lily Parr, 'the most brilliant female player in the world', according to one newspaper, provided the biggest draw card for tens of thousands of supporters who regularly watched women's football at the height of its popularity as a spectator sport.

There was such a clamour to see Parr in action for Dick, Kerr Ladies, the leading women's team in England, that officials had to close the turnstiles at Goodison Park in Liverpool. The attendance of 53,000 is still a record for the women's game in England.

'Taking sex and age into consideration, there is probably no greater football prodigy in the country than Miss Parr, the outside-left of the famous Dick, Kerr Ladies,' the *Reporter* newspaper stated in 1921.

During the 1920s, when interest in the team peaked, Dick, Kerr Ladies featured on cinema newsreels and their match reports appeared regularly in major newspapers.

In her first season, at the age of 14, Parr scored 43 goals. She played on until her mid-40s, but throughout her career she was renowned for the strength of her shooting, her 'great kicking power', as one American newspaper put it in 1922.

The previous year, the Preston-based team played 67 games in aid of charity all over Britain, watched by a total of 900,000 people. In its 48-year existence, the team raised £175,000.

On Boxing Day in 1920, a capacity crowd turned up at Everton to watch them play St Helens Town. Newspaper reports stated that thousands were locked out. 'It was a genuine interest, rather than some kind of novelty,' Gail Newsham, the author of *In a League of Their Own*, said. 'The spectators turned up to watch what they expected to be a good game of football, and Lily was the star attraction.'

KEY MATCH

Dick, Kerr Ladies 4 St Helens Town 0, Goodison Park, 26 December 1920

Lily Parr gave an outstanding performance at outside-left in front of a crowd of 53,000 in Liverpool.

Dick, Kerr Ladies were leading 1–0 at half-time when the team made a tactical change that altered the course of the match. Alice Kell, the team captain and full-back, was switched to centre-forward.

It was Parr's job as a winger to get as many crosses into the penalty area for the centre-forward to chase. In the second half she did just that and Kell scored a hat-trick as a result.

As a local side, St Helens Ladies enjoyed much support in the massive crowd at Goodison Park and, remarkably, about 10,000 to 14,000 people were locked out, unable to gain admission. There was so much congestion outside the ground that the players had to have a police escort to get them safely to the changing rooms. But the large attendance meant that the game raised £3,115 for charity.

Dick, Kerr Ladies remained an attraction for football followers throughout the club's existence. In the 1950s the team was still able to draw crowds of 5,000 to their games, Gail Newsham, a historian of women's football, said.

Left Lily Parr of Dick, Kerr Ladies and England scored over 1,000 goals in her career.

KEY MUSEUM ARTEFACT

Lily Parr wore these boots during the Dick, Kerr Ladies tour of the United States in 1922. It was the first time that Parr and her team-mates had seen certain electrical appliances, such as washing machines, that were not widely available in England. The trip lasted for nine weeks and during their stay the team played nine matches, winning four, drawing two and losing three. However, many of their games were against men's teams. Lily Parr was considered the star of the team by the American press and was often referred to as the best female player in the world.

From the start of her career as a teenager, Lily Parr was renowned for having the strongest shot of any woman footballer. Although she was praised for her overall play and reading of the game it was her shooting at goal that excited spectators and earned her headlines in the newspapers.

There is one story that has become associated with her: while playing a game at Chorley in Lancashire, she was approached by a professional male goalkeeper who challenged her to put the ball past him while he stood in goal.

Apparently, the goalkeeper had watched the young Lily shooting at goal during the warm-up before a charity game involving Dick, Kerr Ladies. 'You might look good against other women,' he told her, 'but you would have no chance against a man in goal.'

There was such a clamour to see Parr in action for Dick, Kerr Ladies, the leading women's team in England, that officials had to close the turnstiles at Goodison Park in Liverpool. The attendance of 53,000 is still a record for the women's game.

Above right A medal from the 1930s, one of many that Lily Parr won while playing for Dick, Kerr Ladies.

Right This 1921 newspaper cartoon illustrates events that occurred in the away game at Sheffield. During that year, Dick, Kerr Ladies played 67 games in front of 900,000 spectators.

Never one to shirk a challenge, Lily invited him into the goal. The keeper managed to block her first shot, but at some cost. The force of the heavy ball had broken his arm, so the story went.

Parr was said to have smiled to herself as she heard the man shout to his friends. 'Get me to the hospital as quick as you can, she's gone and broken my flamin' arm!'

Tom Finney, the Preston and England winger, refereed several matches involving Dick, Kerr Ladies during the 1950s. 'Their standard of play was very good,' he said.

At the time there were no organised women's leagues – all the games were friendly fixtures – and the team was in demand for games throughout Britain and the continent. They toured France in 1920 and the United States two years later.

Results confirmed their status as the best women's team in the country. During the 48 years the team was together, Dick, Kerr Ladies played 828 games, winning 758, drawing 46 and losing only 24 times, an average of one defeat every two years.

Parr was made an honorary life member of the amateur club when she retired from football in 1951, at the age of 45. Following her war-time stint as a munitions worker in the Dick, Kerr factory in Preston, she worked as a nurse at a hospital just outside the then town. As an amateur, and the most important member of the team, she needed to take a lot of time off work.

'For many years the team enjoyed a fame that has never been equalled by a women's football team since. It is a remarkable story,' Gail Newsham said.

N° 18. Le Numéro : 50 Centimes. Jeudi 4 Novembre 1920

LE MIROIR DES SPORTS

PUBLICATION HEBDOMADAIRE ILLUSTRÉE, 18, RUE D'ENGHIEN, PARIS

UNE JOUEUSE ANGLAISE, LYONS, SHOOTE AU COURS DU MATCH FÉMININ FRANCO-ANGLAIS DE FOOTBALL

La première partie de football, jouée en France entre deux équipes féminines anglaise et française, a eu lieu dimanche dernier au Stade Pershing et s'est terminée par un match nul : 1 but à 1. Elle fut disputée avec beaucoup d'entrain

TALKING POINT

The Football Association had an ambivalent attitude towards women's football when Lily Parr was playing the game.

Dick, Kerr Ladies originally drew players from the women working in a munitions factory during World War I. The team enjoyed universal support for its efforts on behalf of charity. The Ladies' first ever game, on Christmas Day in 1917, attracted 10,000 to Deepdale, the home of Preston North End, and raised £600.

At the end of hostilities, the team stayed together. Although the side continued to earn money for good causes, there was increasing concern in the men's game that the ongoing popularity of Dick, Kerr Ladies and other women's teams was drawing custom, and potential income, from professional Football League clubs.

In 1921, the Football Association acted, introducing a draconian set of restrictions. Women footballers were no longer allowed to play on any Football League ground and any referee who took control of a women's match would be barred from officiating in the men's game.

In order to carry on, women's teams played some of their matches at the grounds of rugby clubs and the ban from Football League grounds continued to affect the England women's team until 1978.

Despite the ban, the crowds still came. 'Dick, Kerr Ladies attracted several thousand spectators to some games right up to 1965, before the team was disbanded because of a shortage of players in the 1950s,' Gail Newsham, a historian of women's football, said.

Above left A French newspaper shows Minnie Lyons equalising for Dick, Kerr Ladies in their 1–1 draw with a French representative team during their tour of the country in 1920.

Left Lily Parr is pictured holding the ball on this postcard from the early 1920s. Due to their exploits overseas, Dick, Kerr Ladies were considered as representatives of England.

DIXIE DEAN (1907–1980)

Player • Inducted 2002 • 16 caps • 2 Division One Championships • 1 FA Cup

William Ralph Dean – the great and incomparable 'Dixie' Dean – holds a secure place in the history of football on the strength of his extraordinary scoring feats during one dramatic season.

In a mere 39 games in 1927–28, Dean scored a record-breaking 60 goals for Everton in Division One. At the age of 21, he had achieved a degree of recognition and acclaim previously beyond the reach of any footballer. It is inconceivable that his record will ever be broken.

Even members of the Royal family were said to know of 'Dixie'. His waxwork likeness was put on display at Madame Tussauds, and the great American baseball player Babe Ruth went out of his way to meet him on a visit to England.

Between 1923 and 1939, Dean scored 473 goals in 502 League, FA Cup, representative and international matches. Twice, in 1927–28 and 1931–32, he was leading scorer in Division One. On both occasions, Everton were champions.

Fittingly, albeit by chance, he was the first player to wear the number nine shirt at Wembley. The Football Association chose the FA Cup final in 1933 for a trial of numbered shirts. Everton were allocated numbers one to 11. Dean, typically, scored in the 3–0 win over a Manchester City side in shirts numbered 12–22.

In his prime, Dean's value was almost incalculable. Arsenal offered a blank cheque, but Everton still said no. Dixie had no intention of leaving, anyway, having turned down a contract tripling his basic wage to play in the United States.

'Dixie was the greatest centre-forward there will ever be,' Bill Shankly once said. 'He belongs to the company of the supremely great, like Beethoven, Shakespeare and Rembrandt.'

KEY MATCH

Everton 3 Arsenal 3, Division One, Goodison Park, 5 May 1928

The stage was set for Dixie Dean to achieve greatness. Everton were already confirmed as champions, so only one question remained: could he score the hat-trick he needed to break the League record of 59 goals in a single season.

Before the kick-off, the referee, Mr Harper, perhaps caught up in the atmosphere, gave Dean a hearty handshake. By five past three Mr Harper had signalled two Everton goals, both scored by Dean.

The first was a trademark header; the second, a penalty he had earned himself, drawing a defender into a rash tackle. 'I intended to place the penalty in the corner,' he later recalled. 'It went between the 'keeper's legs. It wasn't one of my better kicks.'

It would be another agonising 75 minutes before the dramatic conclusion. Arsenal conceded a corner. 'It came in absolutely perfectly for me from the left,' Dean recalled, 'I ran from outside the area to head it into the net.'

Dixie appeared to be the calmest man inside the ground. 'That was it, the record. I just bowed, but the crowd went wild,' he said.

Several Arsenal players, including the goalkeeper he had just put the ball past, understood the magnitude of the moment. Ignoring their professional instincts they, too, shook Dean's hand.

Minutes later the game ended. Dixie Dean had made history, even if his exploits read more like the stuff of fiction.

Left Dixie Dean runs out at Arsenal's Highbury Stadium before a Division One league game in 1927.

KEY MUSEUM ARTEFACT

This Everton autograph book from the 1920s shows that supporters were collecting signatures right from the early days of the 20th century. Indeed, signed photographs were issued by the great amateurs of the 1880s and 1890s. This particular book features the signature of Samuel (Sam) Chedgzoy, who played for Everton from 1910 until 1925. He was a team-mate of Dean's for just one season, in 1924–25. Chedgzoy helped to change the rules of the game when, due to lack of clarity in the laws, he dribbled the ball straight from a corner to score a goal. The laws were immediately changed, limiting a player to one touch of the ball when taking a corner.

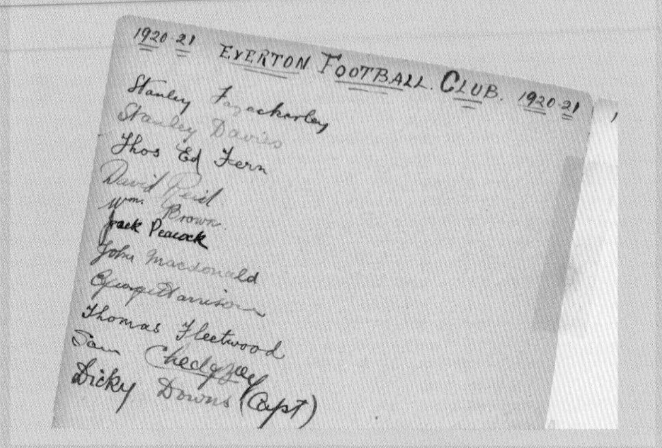
1920-21 EVERTON FOOTBALL CLUB. 1920-21
Stanley Fazackerley
Stanley Davies
Thos Ed Fern
David Reid
Wm Brown
Jack Peacock
John Macdonald
George Harrison
Thomas Fleetwood
Sam Chedgzoy
Dicky Downs (Capt)

At international level, Dixie Dean scored 18 goals in 16 appearances for England. He would be an automatic choice for only two years, but even that represented an achievement, given the fickleness and haphazard ways of the selectors. In his penultimate international Dean scored a goal in a 7–1 thrashing of Spain. He ended that season, 1931–32, as leading goalscorer in Division One. It made no difference to the 'hopelessly amateur' selectors, as an official history of the Football Association describes them.

Dean shaped the fortunes of Everton for a decade. Put simply, if Dean was fit, the team prospered. The opposite was also true. When Everton were relegated, in 1929–30, Dean missed a large chunk of the season because of injury. He returned the next season, as did Everton.

Everton Football Club Co., Ltd.

Telegraphic Address: "Football," Liverpool.
Telephone: Aintree 2263.
Secretary: Theo Kelly.
Manager: C. S. Britton.

Registered Office: Goodison Park, Liverpool, 4.

6th August 1949

Dear Keith,

I am very pleased to hear that you will be able to come through on Tuesday next.

There is a good train from Preston at 8-40 A.m. arriving in Liverpool at 9-45 a.m., which will allow you ample time to reach Goodison Park at about 10 a.m.

Looking forward to seeing you

Yours sincerely,

Right This letter to Keith Mitten of Everton from 1949 is dated 12 years after Dean had finished his Everton career. It illustrates the formal way in which players were treated by their club. Before telephones were widely used, the only means of communicating with players was by post.

As he aged, the injuries took a toll. In his 30s, as both he and his scoring rate slowed, Everton slid into mediocrity. In total, Dean underwent 15 major operations.

> **"I'd have played for Everton for nothing."** – *Dixie Dean*

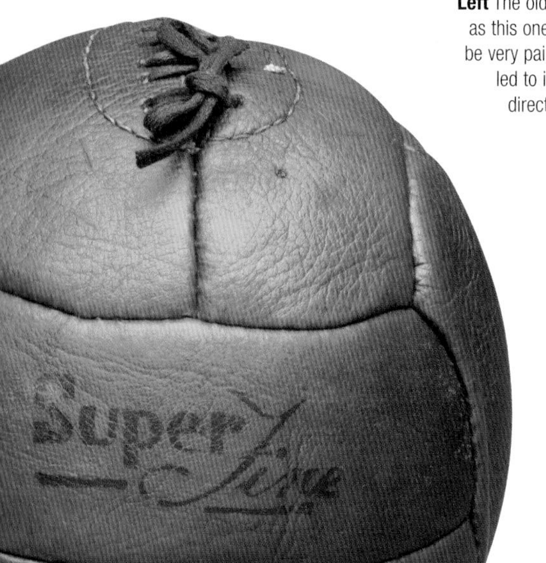

Left The old lace-up footballs, such as this one from the 1920s, could be very painful to head. They often led to injuries if the lace made direct contact with a player's forehead.

In 1924, he had a testicle removed after being kicked in the groin – deliberately, Dean always maintained – by his marker. But for his natural strength, developed lugging milk crates around the streets of his native Birkenhead, Dean may never have achieved greatness. In 1926, two years before he broke the record, he fractured his skull, jawbone and knee in a motorcycle accident. Initially, doctors feared for his life; they then said he would never play again. But Dean confounded medical opinion. When, 16 weeks later, he made his comeback for Everton reserves, 30,000 people turned up to see him.

A generous, extrovert and larger-than-life character, Dixie Dean became an icon on Merseyside at a time of great economic hardship. Before matches, he would often walk the short distance from his club-house to the ground in his slippers, chatting to supporters. Once there, he was known to buy tickets for unemployed men out of his own pocket.

Fiercely loyal to a club that he had supported since childhood, Dixie joined

Everton from Tranmere Rovers at the age of 17 for a then record fee for a Division Three player of £3,000 in 1925. He had already rejected offers from several other clubs. 'I'd have played for Everton for nothing,' he once said.

By the mid-1930s Dean was the undisputed leader of a team full of experienced internationals. Everton, a conservative club, had not yet employed a manager, and so Dean devised tactics and advised directors on selections. So, when he was unexpectedly dropped and then sold soon after, in 1938, his sudden departure stunned the city. He left Everton without fanfare, the victim, he always said, of a club official. The other players were not even informed until later.

Three decades later, Everton made some amends for this treatment of a loyal and exceptional club servant, organising a testimonial in 1964. Bill Dean died, aged 73, in March 1980, after watching Everton play Liverpool at Goodison Park. On hearing the news, Joe Mercer, a former team-mate, asked: 'Where else?' A statue was erected at the ground as a permanent memorial in 2001.

Before matches, he would often walk the short distance from his club-house to the ground in his slippers, chatting to supporters.

TALKING POINT

Matt Busby once described Dixie Dean as 'the greatest ever practitioner of the heading art'. Bill Shankly said: 'When he connected with one it frightened people.'

At five feet ten and a half inches, Dean often gave away several inches in height to defenders. However, a prodigious leap – it was reported that he could jump onto a billiard table from a standing position – allied to anticipation and a fearless nature, more than compensated.

Dean had taught himself how to head as a boy. Making use of a slanted roof, he threw the ball up, heading the ball when it dropped at a target goal painted on a wall.

'Footwork is the key,' he once instructed a young Tommy Lawton, soon to be his successor at Everton, 'You must always keep your feet moving in anticipation. It's all about timing.'

Forty of his 60 goals in 1927–28 were said to have been scored with his head. 'He could out-head any defender or any number they could pack into the area,' Busby said. 'When the ball came over, it was sheer panic.'

Right An England cap from the 1927–28 season. Although Dean scored an incredible 349 goals in 399 League games for Everton, he was only capped on 16 occasions.

Left Almost half a century after Dean had finished his Everton career, he still featured on the front covers of official club publications, such as this one from 1985.

ALEX JAMES (1901–1953)

Player • Inducted 2005 • 8 caps • 4 Division One Championships • 2 FA Cups

As the owner of the most famous baggy shorts in football, Alex James did more than any other player to make Arsenal great during the 1930s.

The statistics say it all: before James arrived in 1929 the club had won nothing, despite a heavy investment in the transfer market; over the ensuing seven years Arsenal won four championship titles and reached three FA Cup finals.

'It is impossible to underestimate James' contribution to the successful Arsenal side of the 1930s,' the official club history states. 'He was simply the key man.'

From his deep-lying, inside-forward position, James was the creative hub of the team, collecting the ball from defenders, then spraying passes to either of the Arsenal wingers, Joe Hulme or Cliff Bastin.

James was signed for a fee of £8,750 from Preston North End. While at Deepdale, a cartoonist drew him wearing oversized shorts in a caricature, probably to accentuate his short stature. James played up to the image. 'They keep my knees warm,' he said. As a boy, Tom Finney idolised James. 'I began wearing ridiculously baggy shorts as well,' Finney said.

James hated to waste energy. His motto was: 'Let the ball do the work.' Others could do the chasing. Managers tolerated it all because of his exceptional ability.

'No one like him ever kicked a ball,' George Allison, the Arsenal manager said. 'He simply left the opposition looking on his departing figure with amazement.'

The Scot added to his reputation in 1928 as one of the 'Wembley Wizards' who humiliated England 5–1 at Wembley. Two years later, he helped Arsenal win the FA Cup for the first time. The Times reported that 'the skill and bold tactics of James that turned the scale in favour of his side'.

Arsenal honoured James by naming him captain for the FA Cup final in 1936, at the end of his penultimate season in the game. James collected the trophy following a 1–0 win over Sheffield United.

KEY MATCH

England 1 Scotland 5, Home International Championship, Wembley, 31 March 1928

The selection of Alex James generated a degree of criticism in his homeland. 'Does he not play his football in England?' a few disapproving reporters asked rhetorically. He was too small, anyway, like all other Scotland forwards, the papers argued.

It was a different story, though, after the game. James, the Preston North End forward, was now lionised with all the other 'Anglos' as one of the 'Wembley Wizards'.

James scored twice in a match that has since entered folklore north of the border. For his first goal he shrugged off the challenge of a defender before volleying a shot past Hufton, the England goalkeeper, from 25 yards out. His second goal, Scotland's fourth, was a snap shot. The other three Scotland goals were scored by Alec Jackson, the tallest of the Scotland forwards at five feet seven inches.

On a wet afternoon in front of 80,000 spectators, James was the central figure as the Scots 'strung passes together like beads on a string', according to an official history of the Football Association. The England players, bigger, heavier and more direct, looked cumbersome in comparison.

'The success of the Scots was primarily another demonstration that Scottish skill, science and trickery will prevail against the less attractive and simpler methods of the English style,' the *Glasgow Herald* newspaper commented. For Scots, it was a stunning and symbolic victory, and James had played his part.

Left Alex James is pictured holding the FA Cup after Arsenal's 1–0 victory over Sheffield United at Wembley on 25 April 1936.

KEY MUSEUM ARTEFACT

This ornate badge, with enamel decoration, would have been worn at the FA Cup final in 1932 by one of the stewards. Stewards wore highly decorative badges to distinguish themselves in the crowds. The ball motif on the badge is similar to those found on Football Association and Football League medals. Alex James had scored a goal in Arsenal's 2–0 FA Cup final victory over Huddersfield in 1930, but missed the 1932 final against Newcastle United through injury. The game is best remembered for the controversial United equaliser, which Jack Allen scored after Jimmy Richardson crossed a ball from the by-line that had clearly gone out of play. Newcastle went on to win 2–1.

Alex James was the pivotal figure in the attacking 'W' formation devised by Herbert Chapman in the late 1920s. Rivals soon copied the system but, lacking a playmaker of James' ability, none could make it work as effectively.

The tactics evolved following a change to the offside law in 1925. Most clubs, including Arsenal, introduced a 'stopper' centre-half in response; Chapman went one step further, dropping the inside-forwards deeper to create a loose 3–4–3 formation.

The additional numbers in midfield allowed Arsenal greater control of the ball. Once in possession, it was up to James, above all, to make good the tactical plan, by initiating fast raids down the flanks.

Alex James spent a turbulent eight years at Highbury. Success came but initially he had to contend with the hostility of supporters who turned on the expensive signing when he struggled for form in his first season at the club.

Arsenal revolutionised wing-play: instead of hugging the touchline, Bastin and Hulme cut inside more often, as Chapman ordered. No longer merely creators, the wingers were expected to score goals, too. James also perfected a pass inside the full-back for them to run onto. The system worked because of his skill and their exceptional finishing ability. In 1932–33 alone, the wingers scored 53 goals between them.

One set move illustrated how the 'triangle' worked. James would hit a long pass into space on the right wing for the speedy Hulme to chase. His cross was often

Below A ticket for the 1937 FA Cup final. James left Preston North End for Arsenal frustrated by lack of success and life in Division Two. His decision to move club was vindicated by the fact that Preston did not gain promotion until 1934. In 1937, a year after James retired, Preston finally made it to an FA Cup final.

EAST STANDING ENCLOSURE

ENTER AT TURNSTILES (See Plan on back) D 8

ENTRANCE

Empire Stadium, Wembley

The Football Association Cup Competition

Final Tie

SATURDAY, MAY 1st, 1937

Kick-off 3 p.m.

Price 2/6 (Including Tax)

A. J. Elvin

MANAGING DIRECTOR, Wembley Stadium Limited.

THIS PORTION TO BE RETAINED (See Conditions on back)

Right This image shows the Arsenal and Cardiff teams running out at Wembley before the 1927 FA Cup final. Arsenal lost 1–0 and they signed up James in 1929, for £8,750, as manager Herbert Chapman rebuilt the team.

deliberately hit beyond Jack Lambert, the centre-forward and skilled decoy, to Bastin, who then dribbled on goal or shot.

Arsenal dropped deeper, and defended for longer, then hit teams with fast counter-attacks, tactics ideal for away games. It was a blueprint for success. Between 1929–30 and 1934–35 Arsenal won only 40 fewer points on their travels than they did at Highbury.
Alex James spent a turbulent eight years at Highbury. Success came but initially he had to contend with the hostility of supporters who turned on the expensive signing

From his deep-lying, inside-forward position, James was the creative hub of the team.

when he struggled for form in his first season at the club.

The barracking 'almost broke the heart of one of the finest players it has been my pleasure to see', Chapman said. 'It was the meanest thing I have ever seen.'

James came through the ordeal, gradually convincing supporters of his importance to the side. Ever the pragmatist, Chapman nurtured this talent, allowing him preferential treatment. James could lie-in until noon on match days, a freedom denied other players; the manager also turned a blind eye to his late-night partying.

James made no secret of his pursuit of self-interest. He was 'no crusader' fighting for his 'oppressed brothers'. Off the field, he said, 'It must be each man for himself.' The rules dictated as much, and those rules 'were not invented by professional footballers', James said.

It often put him at odds with Arsenal. As captain, James failed to attend an official banquet to celebrate the championship win of 1932–33. He lost the captaincy after that. On another occasion, he was dropped after refusing to travel to Belfast for a game.

Throughout it all, though, James had been indispensable. As he, Bastin and Hulme faded as players, so did Arsenal as a team. When he retired in May 1937, the remnants of the side originally built by Chapman had only one more title left in them. The golden era – the era of Alex James – was over.

TALKING POINT

Alex James was one of the first footballers to make a determined effort to cash in on his fame. He needed to: the social life he embraced in London didn't come cheap.

On his arrival in the capital in 1929, James realised that his name carried considerable commercial value. A well-paid job at a department store and a ghosted newspaper column soon supplemented his Arsenal wage.

James was unusual as a professional footballer in terms of the company he kept: his circle included jazz musicians, movie actors, golfers and boxers. None of his showbusiness and sporting friends, however, were subject to a maximum wage regulation. The income James received for his expertise and box-office appeal was a fraction of theirs.

In order to fund the lavish lifestyle he aspired to, James effectively went on strike in 1931, deliberately refusing to sign a new contract. It meant forfeiting wages over the summer, but the benefit, he calculated, outweighed the cost.

It is not known whether he sought to pressure Arsenal into making 'under-the-table' payments, but his 'strike' certainly demonstrated his independence. Free of contractual ties to the club, he was able to explore commercial deals without constraint.

After securing extensions to his agreement with Selfridges and his newspaper client, James duly re-signed. Unfortunately, it was a rare display of business acumen. James later invested heavily in a pools company that went bust, one of several failed ventures. He did not save, nor invest in his own home and, when he died in 1953, he was virtually penniless.

Below A Hornby scale model of an LNER class B17 railway engine from the 1930s named 'Arsenal'. Many engines were named after famous football clubs throughout the 1930s and 40s.

Above left The footwear of the 1920s and 30s, as evidenced by these boots, offered high ankle protection but that together with their stiff leather made mobility for players particularly difficult. With his famous baggy shorts and his flapping shirt-sleeves, it's a miracle that James could move at all.

PETER DOHERTY (1913–1990)

Player • Inducted 2002 • 16 caps • 1 FA Cup

Peter Doherty was the most valuable footballer of his day, a brilliant creative talent and visionary who led Northern Ireland as a manager to the quarter-finals of the 1958 World Cup in Sweden.

'I've had five clubs during my career,' Doherty said. 'Four of them senior English clubs, and the sum total of fees paid on my transfer is greater than that paid for any other first-class player.'

Joe Mercer, the England international, said: 'Of all the opponents I faced, I particularly remember Doherty, who was unplayable in his day. He was built like a greyhound, very fast and elusive but with stamina, too. He had a Rolls-Royce engine in him.' And Billy Wright, the England captain, once nicknamed Doherty 'Peter the Great', describing him as 'one of the outstanding inside-forwards in the world'.

Doherty won the Division One title with Manchester City in 1936–37, scoring 30 goals, and the FA Cup with Derby County in 1946. In between times, his club and international career was interrupted by war. He later played for Huddersfield Town and Doncaster Rovers as player-manager.

As a scout later in life, he recommended Kevin Keegan, then an unknown at Scunthorpe United, to Liverpool. Respecting his judgement, Bill Shankly acted on the advice.

At international level, Doherty won 16 caps for Northern Ireland. At the end of the match against England at Goodison Park in 1947, jubilant supporters carried him from the field. His last-minute header earned a 2–2 draw, the first time the Irish had avoided defeat in 13 meetings. 'Peter pulled the strings for them that day,' Wright said.

KEY MATCH

Derby County 4 Charlton Athletic 1 (aet), FA Cup final, Wembley, 27 April 1946

Much to his relief, Peter Doherty put his side on the path to victory in extra time by restoring Derby County's lead in a game described as the most entertaining Cup Final ever.

One minute into extra time, Derby took the lead at 2–1. 'Our centre-forward Jack Stamps went through on the left and the Charlton goalkeeper Sam Bartram did well to parry his centre; but he couldn't hold the ball and I had a comparatively easy job to score,' Doherty said.

The clever inside-forward had feared that he would be attributed with scoring the own goal that brought Charlton back into the game just before the end of normal time. At a free-kick, the ball had deflected into the net off his shin, but Charlton's Bert Turner, who took the shot, was in fact credited with the goal in the record books.

In a season when FA Cup ties up to the semi-final were played over two legs, home and away, Doherty's goal set Derby on the way to their first major honour since becoming Division Two champions in 1915.

Two of Derby's other goals were scored by Stamps, who had been told by doctors he would never play again after being injured in the war at Dunkirk.

'It was a great Final, said by many to be the best seen at Wembley until that time. Our superiority was clearly marked before it became necessary to play extra time,' Doherty said.

Left Peter Doherty, June 1945. He played for Blackpool, Manchester City, Derby County, Huddersfield Town and Doncaster Rovers between 1933 and 1952.

KEY MUSEUM ARTEFACT

The original FA Cup was manufactured in 1871 for the first final in 1872. The trophy was won by Aston Villa in 1895 and on their return to Birmingham the club put it on display in the window of William Shilcock's sports shop. The trophy was stolen overnight and was never recovered. The FA had an identical copy made for the 1896 Cup final. When Manchester United won the trophy in 1909, they immediately commissioned a replica to present to one of their directors. The FA, realising that they had no copyright control over the design, withdrew the cup in 1910 and had this new trophy made for the 1911 Cup final. Peter Doherty won the Cup with Derby County in 1946.

Right Due to its distinctive panels this leather football from the 1940s and 50s was known as a T ball. It was manufactured by William Thomlinson's company, Greban. In the 1946 Cup final the ball famously burst in the last five minutes of normal time.

Lauded for his vision as an inside-forward, Peter Doherty was a visionary off the field, too. An early advocate for coaching, he also campaigned vociferously for improved working conditions and training methods for players. Bitter experience lay at the root of his actions.

In 1933, Blackpool sold Doherty against his will. 'My personal feelings counted for next to nothing in the transaction,' he wrote later. 'I might as well have been a bale of merchandise.' Then, at the outbreak of the Second World War and the consequent cancellation of League fixtures, the clubs ripped up the players' contracts. 'Without a scrap of consideration or sentiment, our means of livelihood were simply jettisoned,' he said.

Manchester City, as the holders of his registration, could still dictate when and where he played. The club repeatedly used this power to prevent him playing as a guest elsewhere, denying him a match fee. 'I bitterly resented City dictating to me in this way,' he said.

Doherty was equally scathing about the training and coaching regimes at most clubs. 'Altogether too much emphasis is placed on lapping,' he wrote in 1947. 'Ball practice should figure prominently and often in all training schemes.'

> **"[Peter Doherty] was unplayable on his day. He was built like a greyhound, very fast and elusive but with stamina, too."**
>
> *– Joe Mercer*

Instead of endless laps, Doherty suggested volley-ball, 'to promote jumping, timing and judgement'; basket-ball, 'to encourage split-second decision-making and finding space'; and walking-football, 'to build up calf muscles'. It was revolutionary stuff at the time. 'Most training at clubs is a slow form of torture,' he wrote. 'We need more variation.'

Peter Doherty was able to put his theories into practice, with some success, as the player-manager of Doncaster Rovers and then manager of Northern Ireland.

As one of the first player-managers in the game, he revived interest in Doncaster, leading the club to promotion to Division Two following his appointment by the club in 1949.

Success was achieved through some unorthodox means. In those days the number on the shirt always related to a set position: number two was the right-back, and so on. On a number of occasions, Doherty sent out his players with the 'wrong' numbers on their backs. Even such a simple ploy confused opponents.

His most notable success came during a seven-year stint as manager of Northern Ireland. 'We had a tremendous respect for him,' Danny Blanchflower, the captain said, 'With his burning enthusiasm he urged us all to the extremes of our ability.'

In November 1957, he led his country to a rare and famous victory at Wembley, their first victory over England for 30 years. The following year, the Irish reached the last eight in the World Cup. 'Peter brought an understanding, a vitality and a leadership to the players, transforming the spirit of the team almost overnight,' Blanchflower said.

'Doherty identified a core group of players and he stuck by them through thick and thin, building a club spirit,' Billy Wright, the England captain said.

TALKING POINT

Northern Ireland presented Peter Doherty with a number of unusual problems and challenges as their manager at the World Cup in Sweden in 1958.

When FIFA required him to furnish a preliminary list of players, the Irish FA wrote back to point out that there weren't '40 men remotely under consideration'. In the end, only 17 players were sent to Sweden, not the 22 allowed under the rules.

Inevitably, the lack of strength of depth caught up with them. Northern Ireland had to field several half-fit players in the quarter-final defeat against France. Tommy Casey, the right winger, played despite having eight stitches in his right leg.

Worse, their organisation was inadequate: training was delayed on one occasion because the FA officials 'went fishing in our tracksuits', one player said.

The players were also unhappy about the amount of time spent travelling by bus, particularly one journey of more than three hours' duration after a game. Exhausted, muscles aching, the players arrived at their hotel in the early hours. 'The arrangements were diabolical,' said Jimmy McIlroy, the inside-forward.

Above left Irish International Cap, 1937. Awarded to Peter Doherty for his participation in the international matches against England and Scotland in 1936 and 1937.

Above This rattle was used by Derby supporter Jack Radford to alert people of suspected gas attacks during World War II. He painted it black and white and took it to the 1946 Cup final where Doherty's Derby County beat Charlton Athletic 4–1.

Above Derby supporter Jack Radford used this bell to give air raid warnings, it was also taken to the Cup final in 1946.

TOMMY LAWTON (1919–1996)

Player • Inducted 2003 • 23 caps • 1 Division One Championship

Tommy Lawton, the owner of the most distinctive head of hair in football, was the automatic choice as England centre-forward for a decade. Recognised by selectors for his all-round ability, he was recognisable by everyone else for his distinctive looks.

At his peak in the late 1940s, Lawton was the central figure in the most celebrated of all England forward lines: Matthews, Mannion, Mortensen and Finney supplied the chances, but Lawton was the undisputed leader, the fulcrum, of the attack.

Alex James, the Arsenal inside-forward, described Lawton as 'the lightest mover of any big man who played football'. Joe Mercer, the England wing-half, said, 'He must surely have been the greatest technical centre-forward of all time.'

Lawton was feted for his heading. Many of his contemporaries rated him the greatest ever in the art, surpassing even Dixie Dean, once his hero and mentor at Everton. 'With Tommy I could guarantee he would make contact with nine out of ten crosses,' Stanley Matthews said.

For Billy Wright, the England captain, one goal stood out above all others: a first-time shot 'that barely rose four inches from the ground' against Italy in 1948. 'No hesitation, no nerves, just the work of a truly great player, a natural goal-scorer.'

Lawton earned in the region of £3,000 a year at the height of his career, making him, it is claimed, the first ever footballer in the top tax rate. But along with the early fame and fortune, football would eventually bring him pain and heartache.

KEY MATCH

Chelsea 3 Moscow Dynamo 3, Friendly, Stamford Bridge, 13 November 1945

Moscow Dynamo rated Tommy Lawton so highly that they assumed his transfer to Stamford Bridge had been ordered by the English authorities in order to ensure a victory for Chelsea in this prestigious friendly. But it was only by chance that Lawton arrived from Everton for a record fee shortly before the Soviets opened their tour of Britain.

Londoners were desperate to see the new signing and the mysterious Soviets in action. As a result, there was a lively black market in tickets for the midweek game. Interest was so high, the streets round the ground were congested hours before kick-off.

Eighty-five thousand people eventually poured in, with many fans spilling onto the greyhound track surrounding the pitch. The vast crowd, a ground record, were not disappointed, either in Lawton or Moscow Dynamo, the focus of much pro-Soviet sentiment in post-war Britain.

Lawton found the net for Chelsea, who led 2–0 at half-time. Then Moscow Dynamo, wearing their dashing all-blue strip and bearing gifts of flowers before kick-off, took over. 'They flashed the ball from man to man and waited for the opening.' Lawton recalled.

Years later, Lawton insisted that the Russians' third, equalising goal was blatantly offside. 'I screamed at the referee, but he told me he had to give it for diplomatic reasons.'

Left England's Tommy Lawton rises above an opposition defender in England's 8–2 defeat of Holland at Leeds Road in Huddersfield on 27 November 1946. Lawton scored four of his side's goals.

KEY MUSEUM ARTEFACT

The Third Division was formed in 1920 with the elected clubs coming from the south of England. In 1921, in order to accommodate the large number of clubs in the north of the country, the Third Division was renamed Third Division (South) and the Third Division (North) was founded. Tommy Lawton shocked the football world when he joined Notts County of the Third Division (South) in 1947. At 28, he was at the peak of his career. He notched 90 goals in 151 League games with County and helped them secure this trophy, the Southern Section Shield, when they became Third Division (South) Champions in 1950.

Above right Lawton was still England's first-choice centre-forward when he joined Notts County. He wore this shirt against Scotland in 1948. England won the game, played in Glasgow, 2–0.

Left Tommy Lawton playing for Burnley in 1937.

Tommy Lawton learned how to shoot at Burnley, his first club. As a teenager, he was ordered to do laps of the pitch at Turf Moor. The perimeter was dotted with 'Burnley's Beers Are Best' adverts, and Lawton was told to shoot at each letter B in turn. Miss one target, and he had to go back. The choice was his: either shoot low and straight, or be stuck out there for hours.

At the age of 16 years and 174 days, Lawton became the youngest centre-forward ever to play League football. Entrusting the coveted number nine shirt to so inexperienced a player was seen as a remarkable display of faith by Burnley.

It proved a sound decision. On the day after signing as a professional on his 17th birthday in 1936, Lawton scored a hat-trick against Spurs, outwitting his marker, Arthur Rowe, the Spurs and England centre-half.

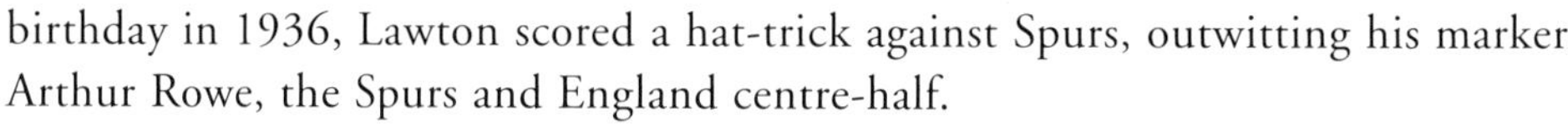

Everton had seen enough. The club paid £6,500, a record fee for a teenager, to sign Lawton the following December. He still had much to learn. Dixie Dean took one look at him in training. 'You'll be no bloody good at this heading lark 'til you move your feet more,' he told him. 'Tommy soon learned,' Dean said. 'He had just the right build for a centre-forward.'

The following season, his first full campaign at Goodison Park, Lawton was the leading scorer in Division One, with a total of 28 goals. He was leading scorer again in 1938–39, the last full season before hostilities began in Europe.

His tally of 35 goals that season helped Everton win the championship title.

His tally of 35 goals that season helped Everton win the championship title. 'It was easily the best club side I ever played in,' Lawton recalled.

An immensely popular figure at Goodison Park, Lawton made an immediate impact on Merseyside: in his first derby match at Anfield, he scored a goal in front of the Kop as Everton won 2–1.

By the end of the war, however, he had resolved to leave the club. His marriage was failing and perhaps Lawton also believed that he could earn from the game in London. In 1945, he was transferred to Chelsea. 'I should have stayed at Everton and transferred the wife,' he joked in later years.

Having already lost six prime years of his career to the war, Lawton then became something of a footballing nomad, with stints at Chelsea, Notts County, Brentford and Arsenal.

He stayed only one full season at Stamford Bridge before making the most controversial move of his career. Notts County of Division Three paid a record transfer fee of £20,000 for his signature, also promising him a job outside football to augment his income.

At 28 years of age, Lawton was in his prime. Before agreeing to the move, he sought, and received, an assurance from Stanley Rous, the FA Secretary, that his England career would not be jeopardised if he dropped down the divisions. The following season Lawton made his last appearance for England.

It was certainly good business for County: the club won promotion and crowd numbers increased almost four-fold. Sadly, for Lawton, it was also the start of his decline as a player.

After he retired as a player, Lawton's fortunes declined still further and he died almost penniless on 6 November 1996. At the funeral, his coffin was adorned with a solitary England cap.

TALKING POINT

Stanley Matthews believed that the selectors made a bad mistake when they dropped Tommy Lawton. England paid a heavy price for their misjudgement at the World Cup in Brazil in 1950, Matthews said.

Lawton, who won his last cap in the draw against Denmark in Copenhagen in September 1948, was discarded shortly after joining Notts County, then a Divison Three club.

Matthews reasoned that Lawton had played superbly and he had scored in England's previous international, a 4–0 away win against Italy. 'For a player to be told after the next international that he's finished at that level seemed crazy to me,' he said.

A number of England players, including Billy Wright, the captain, agreed with Matthews. Wright argued privately that the forward line that tore Italy apart in Turin had been broken up prematurely. 'The selectors were making too many changes, and England were failing in front of goal,' Wright said later.

'We weren't creating so many chances, and what chances that were created weren't put away. Apart from two goals against a mediocre Chile side, this was the case at the World Cup in Brazil. Had the 1948 forward line been kept together longer England would have been a major force.'

Left This cap was awarded to Lawton for his appearance against Northern Ireland in 1938. Lawton scored one of the goals in England's 7–0 win.

Above It was the express wish of Tommy Lawton's son, Tommy Junior, that his father's ashes be placed in The National Football Museum's permanent displays in 2003 in recognition of his father being inducted into the Museum's Hall of Fame.

STANLEY MATTHEWS (1915–2000)

Player • Inducted 2002 • 54 caps • 1 FA Cup

Record crowds flocked to grounds for a glimpse of the most famous and revered footballer in the world: Stanley Matthews, the 'Wizard of the Dribble'.

Matthews played for England over a longer period than anyone else in history. Twenty-three years after he made his international debut, he won the last of his 54 caps at the age of 42, in 1957, and even at that age, Billy Wright, the England captain, was convinced that Matthews still had something to offer his country. 'The selectors dropped him too soon,' Wright said. 'Just his name on the team sheet had given us a psychological advantage.'

By that time, Matthews was revered throughout the world. Recalling his excitement before playing against him at Wembley, in 1953, Ferenc Puskas, the Hungary captain, said, 'We were in awe of him and England. Matthews was a giant in our eyes.'

In 1956, Brazil were mesmerised and then demoralised by his skill. At the end of the game at Wembley, Nilton Santos, the great full-back and World Cup winner in Sweden two years later, shook his hand. 'Mr Matthews, you are the king,' he said.

In the middle of an international against Belgium, the other 21 players on the field stood and clapped in rhythm as Matthews jogged back into position following yet another dazzling run.

Matthews was the first Footballer of the Year in 1948, the first European Footballer of the Year in 1958 and, in 1965, he became the first active footballer to be knighted.

No player before, or since, has had such drawing power. In 1947–48, Arsenal, Sunderland, Manchester United, and Aston Villa all recorded their highest attendances of the season against Blackpool. At Everton, 72,000 turned up. The visitors from Blackpool had no hope of winning the title; they all came to see Matthews.

KEY MATCH

Blackpool 4 Bolton Wanderers 3, FA Cup final, Wembley, 2 May 1953

At the age of 38, and at the third time of trying at Wembley, Stanley Matthews finally fulfilled his great ambition: to win an FA Cup winner's medal.

To celebrate, the renowned teetotaller took a sip of champagne from the trophy. 'It was,' he recalled later, 'the first and only time I knowingly drank alcohol.'

Matt Busby once said that Matthews is the type of player who will do little of significance for three-quarters of a game but then 'destroy you in the other 15 minutes'. Bolton would come to know exactly what he meant.

When Bill Perry, the Blackpool winger, scored the winning goal in injury time, it was Matthews, the creator of the goal and the inspiration behind the comeback from 3–1 down, who was mobbed by his team-mates.

'In the last 15 minutes Matthews had the Wembley crowd for the very first time standing on the seats on the frontiers of hysteria,' recalled Sir Stanley Rous, the FA Secretary.

Inevitably, it became known as 'The Matthews Final', despite his insistence that Stan Mortensen, the Blackpool centre-forward, deserved the plaudits for his hat-trick. Mortensen was philosophical: 'Stan did his stuff when it mattered and I didn't mind him getting all the headlines.'

Left Stanley Matthews finally gets his hands on an FA Cup Winner's medal at 38 years of age. Team-mates Jackie Mudie and Stan Mortensen chair him onto the pitch after the presentation of the Cup following Blackpool's 4–3 win over Bolton Wanderers in the 1953 final.

KEY MUSEUM ARTEFACT

Many players collect mementoes throughout their career and amass significant collections of memorabilia. This unique picture, taken by one of the England party, shows Bert Sproston, followed by the legendary Stanley Mathews, entering the field of play from the changing rooms located beneath the pitch at the Olympic Stadium in Berlin on 14 May in 1938. Before the game against Germany, the British Ambassador told the players to give the Nazi salute. England humiliated the Germans 6–3 in front of 110,000 spectators.

'Fitness is confidence,' the son of boxer Jack Matthews, the 'Fighting Barber of Hanley', once said. Matthews junior neither drank, nor smoked. Famously, he was fit enough to play Division One football at the age of 50.

No matter the weather or the time of year, the daily routine was the same: up at dawn, a cup of tea, then the short drive to the beach. Once there, he did his breathing exercises, stretching and sprints. It might last anything between 30 minutes and an hour and a half; his body told him when he'd done enough.

> **" He will run defenders into the ground. He makes them look like fumbling children, and the more they curse him the more he will do it. "**
>
> *– Joe Mercer*

Later in the day, there was a four-mile run.

'If I needed to find Stanley, the first port of call was South Shore beach at 8.00 a.m.,' Jimmy Armfield, the Blackpool full-back, said. 'There he'd be, in his windcheater and flat cap, training alone.'

Once back home, Matthews had a cold shower. Breakfast was toast and cereal. For lunch it was salad and crispbread. On Mondays, he ate nothing, to 'detoxify my body'. All his training was geared to developing and maintaining his renowned acceleration over 20 yards. In his 40s, he still had the speed off the mark to get away from defenders half his age.

His dedication and highly developed self-discipline set him apart. 'Stanley trained religiously,' Alf Ramsey, his England team-mate said. 'No youngster fighting to gain a place in a League side would have worked harder.'

Stanley Matthews had a rare strength of character. In the era of the maximum wage, minimal employment rights for players, and bruising defenders, the 'Ageless Wonder' took control of his own destiny in the game.

'His mental courage is the greatest I have known,' Joe Mercer said. 'If full-backs upset him – and dozens have tried, using all kinds of methods – he will run them into the ground. He makes them look like fumbling children, and the more they curse him, the more he will do it, absolutely mercilessly.'

Right Matthews won this cap playing against Spain in the Maracana Stadium in the 1950 World Cup in Brazil.

The Brazilians had a high regard for Matthews. 'He is one of the great examples in the world of an intelligent player,' Didi, the Brazil forward, said. 'The Englishman knows himself absolutely, and how to use his strength at the right moment for positive objectives.' Pelé described Matthews as 'the man who taught us the way football should be played'.

Matthews made the game work for him. During the war he decided that he wanted to live by the sea. He made his home in Blackpool, buying a small seaside hotel. Training at Bloomfield Road, he only travelled to Stoke on match days. In 1947, he persuaded the Stoke board to sell him to Blackpool.

He was equally single-minded when it came to negotiating contracts for his media work and endorsements. He was reputedly the highest-earning player in the country.

At the age of 46, Matthews returned to Stoke City in 1961 for a nominal fee. It was money well spent: home gates trebled during his second stint at the Victoria ground. Those supporters cheered a Stoke revival, culminating in promotion to Division One in 1962–63. Fittingly, Matthews scored the goal that ensured they went up as champions. The end finally came in 1965. His strong character was a key factor in his longevity: a player who made his debut in 1932 as a contemporary of Dixie Dean bowed out in the age of George Best.

TALKING POINT

Joe Mercer knew exactly what to expect when Stanley Matthews ran at him with the ball at his feet; yet, more often than not, it made no difference.

In one game Mercer was beaten ten times by his England team-mate. 'Stan would bring the ball squarely to me so that I would never know whether he would go inside or outside,' Mercer said. 'He would lean so far that it was obvious that he had to go that way, but his balance is so perfect he could then sway away and go the other way.'

Johnny Carey, the Manchester United full-back likened the experience of marking Matthews to 'playing against a ghost'.

He developed those skills as a young boy, placing the kitchen chairs in a row in the backyard and then dribbling with the ball back and forth in between them for hour after hour, perfecting his skill and body swerve.

In the mid-1930s, when he first broke into League football, it was the custom for the winger to wait for the defender to come on to him. Only then would he try to jink round his opponent, Matthews said. 'In a reserve game, I bucked the trend. I ran straight at him,' Matthews said. 'The full-back looked absolutely dumbfounded.'

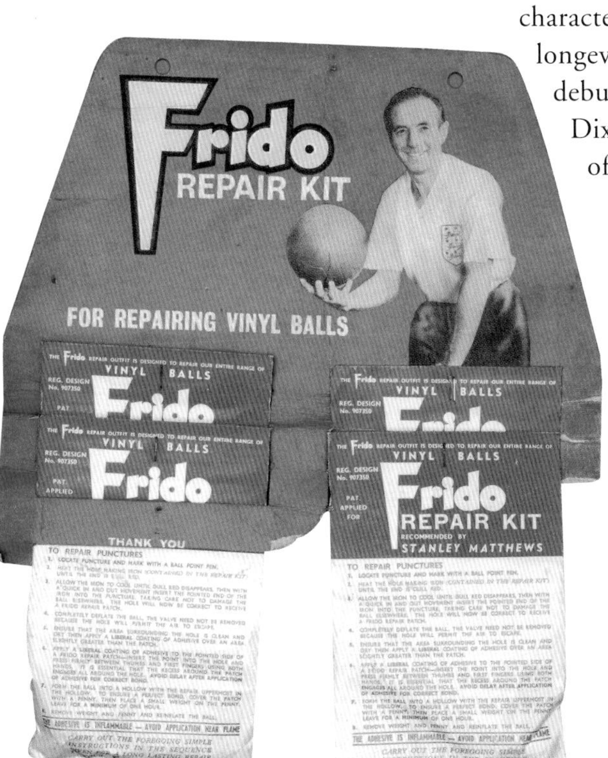

Above These matches were made to commemorate Matthews' special benefit game to celebrate his retirement in 1965. The testimonial was played against an International XI that included Alfredo di Stefano, Ferenc Puskas and Lev Yashin.

Left Matthews' celebrity led him to endorse many products, including this 1950s Frido repair kit for plastic and vinyl footballs.

Right A bone china plate, bearing the signature of Stanley Matthews, which was made by the Duchess Company in England in the 1950s.

WILF MANNION (1918–2000)

Player • Inducted 2004 • 26 caps

Wilf Mannion, the inside-forward nicknamed 'Golden Boy' during the 1940s on account of his mop of blond hair and precocious talent, was described by his England team-mate Alf Ramsey as the 'greatest soccer brain in modern football'.

Idolised by the supporters of Middlesbrough, his hometown club, Mannion was a member of the great post-war England forward line, alongside Tom Finney, Stan Mortensen, Tommy Lawton and Stanley Matthews. He won 26 caps for England between 1946 and 1951.

Stanley Matthews once said of Mannion: 'Wilf is my idea of a perfect inside partner.' Alf Ramsey said: 'He was in a class of his own as a skilful strategist.'

One of those Middlesbrough supporters who adopted Mannion as a sporting hero was Brian Clough, the future England international and Derby County and Nottingham Forest manager. 'Wilf played football the way Fred Astaire danced,' Clough recalled. But there is little doubt that, for all his talent and achievements with England, Mannion failed, sadly, to reach his potential as a footballer, for reasons largely outside his control.

As a front line soldier in the Second World War, Mannion was weakened and traumatised by his experiences in combat. On his return to Middlesbrough, he became frustrated and disillusioned during a dispute with the football authorities over what he saw as his right to play for the club of his choice.

It was said that Juventus offered him the then staggering sum of £15,000 as a signing-on fee. On a more modest scale, the citizens of Oldham organised a public fund in a bid to help the local club raise the cash for his transfer. Middlesbrough, however, refused all offers for their player while Mannion was in his prime. The club deemed him irreplaceable.

KEY MATCH

Great Britain 6 Rest of Europe 1, International Friendly, Hampden Park, 10 May 1947

The world press previewed this FIFA-celebration match as a test of British football's standing – and Wilf Mannion responded with a hat-trick in a Man-of-the-Match performance.

Mannion combined with his wing partner Stanley Matthews to mesmerise the scratch European side in front of a crowd of 135,000 at Hampden Park, generating record receipts of £30,000.

Before the game, organised to celebrate the re-admission of the four home associations to FIFA and raise much-needed funds for the international body, Mannion worked out a tactic involving fellow forwards Billy Steel and Tommy Lawton.

'It was simple, direct and effective,' Steel recalled. 'I had to get the ball in midfield and pass it down the inside-left side of the field. Lawton was to run for it, taking the centre-half with him, then flick the ball first time into the centre-forward position, where Wilf would arrive at the same time as the ball.'

The tactic worked a treat. Mannion also hit the post, despite the discomfort of playing in a pair of restrictive new boots.

Mannion, who had the responsibility of being penalty taker, was praised in the match reports, with several newspapers commenting favourably on his partnership with Matthews. It 'came of age', one football writer said.

His selection at inside-forward ahead of Raich Carter had generated great debate beforehand. Even though he stressed how much he had wanted to play, Carter was sporting enough to praise the performance of Mannion highly.

Left Wilf Mannion, the England and Middlesbrough forward, in 1947.

KEY MUSEUM ARTEFACT

This medal was awarded in Belgium, in 1946. It is inscribed: CMF Combined Services XI v B.A.O.R Combined Services XI. Like many players of his age, Mannion lost the early part of his career to the Second World War. He joined the Green Howards Regiment in 1940 and was involved in the armed forces' withdrawal from Dunkirk. He spent two years in Palestine, in the Middle East, where he contracted malaria and was nursed back to health by the future Arsenal manager Bertie Mee. Mannion's war-time experiences were not unlike those of many professional footballers of the period.

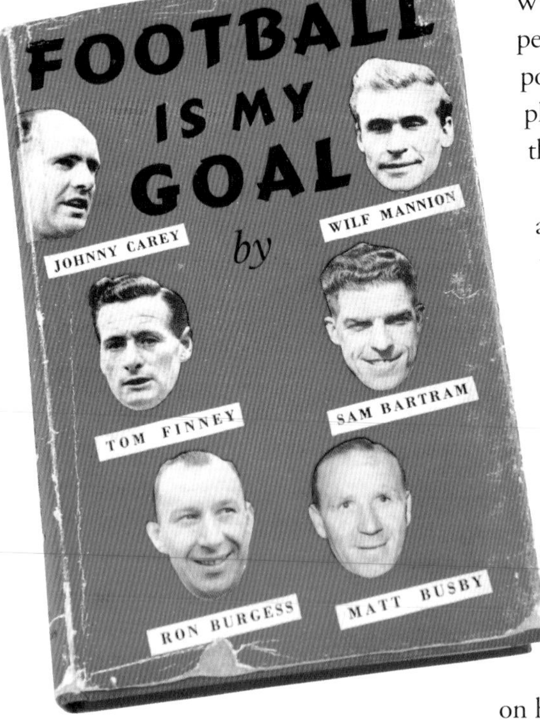

Wilf Mannion was the subject of perhaps the most notable example of poor treatment of the leading England players by the Football Association in the post-war era.

After playing an international against Scotland, Mannion stood in the third-class carriage all the way from Glasgow to Darlington. The train was full, and the Football Association had not bothered to book him a seat. His suitcase would have to do. The game generated £32,000 in gate receipts; the cost of a seat reservation was one shilling.

Mannion had a more serious problem with his club, though. He had lost five years of his career to war and on his return home, at the age of 28, he had 'the serviceman's urge to move'. Middlesbrough refused his transfer request, and the rules said he had to stay. 'Against this soccer serfdom, even the Army seemed to be a haven of freedom,' he recalled.

David Jack, the Middlesbrough manager, told reporters: 'Even if a club came to us with a cheque for £50,000 we would not transfer Mannion. Why should we let the best player in Britain go?'

In 1948, Mannion staged a one-man strike in a bid to force the issue, refusing to sign a new contract before the start of the season. It meant he was ineligible to play for England. But Middlesbrough refused to budge. If Mannion did not play for them, he would not be allowed to play for anyone else. As holders of his registration, the club had this power under the existing rules. That winter, Mannion ended his protest and returned to the side, although his sense of resentment would remain throughout his career.

England were struggling for form during the World Cup in 1958 when Walter Winterbottom, the national team manager, told football journalists: 'I would give a lot for another Wilf Mannion right now.'

> **"The most notable partnership over the past dozen years for England has been that of Wilf Mannion and Tom Finney, reaching its sublimation in the famous 10–0 win against Portugal in 1947."** – *Walter Winterbottom*

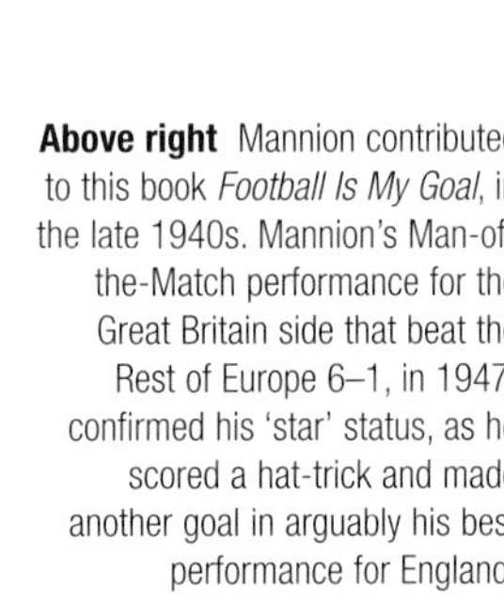

Above right Mannion contributed to this book *Football Is My Goal*, in the late 1940s. Mannion's Man-of-the-Match performance for the Great Britain side that beat the Rest of Europe 6–1, in 1947, confirmed his 'star' status, as he scored a hat-trick and made another goal in arguably his best performance for England.

Left A *Topical Times* card, such as this one featuring Mannion, was the collectable of its day. Topical Times also produced presentation books in which to collect the cards.

> **“He was the greatest of our inside-forwards since the end of the war in 1945, an artist reliant exclusively on sheer skill.”** – *Walter Winterbottom*

ENGLAND
(White Shirts Black Knickers)
1—F. V. SWIFT
Goalkeeper
(Manchester City)
2—L. SCOTT
Right Back
(Arsenal)
3—G. F. HARDWICK (Capt.)
Left Back
(Middlesbrough)
4—W. WRIGHT
Right Half
(Wolverhampton W.)
5—N. FRANKLIN
Centre Half
(Stoke)
6—H. COCKBURN
Left Half
(Manchester United)
7—T. FINNEY
Outside Right
(Preston N.E.)
8—H. S. CARTER
Inside Right
(Derby County)
9—T. LAWTON
Centre Forward
([illegible])
10—W. MANNION
Inside Left
(Middlesbrough)
11—R. LANGTON
Outside Left
(Blackburn R.)
Blue Stripe.
Linesman: N
REFEREE MR. W. WEBB (Scotland)
11—T. EGLINTON
Outside Left
(Everton)
10—A. STEVENSON
Inside Left
(Everton)
9—D. WALSHE
Centre Forward
(West Brom.)
8—P. COAD
Inside Right
(Shamrock R.)
7—K. P. O'FLANAGAN
Outside Right
(Arsenal)
6—W. WALSH
Left Half
(Manchester City)
5—C. MARTIN
Centre Half
(Glentoran)
4—J. CAREY (Capt.)
Right Half
(Manchester United)
3—W. HAYES
Left Back
(Huddersfield T.)
2—W. GORMAN
Right Back
(Brentford)
1—T. BREEN
Goalkeeper
(Shamrock Rovers)
Linesman: M
Red Stripe.
(Green Jerseys White Knickers)
IRELAND

Sadly for Winterbottom, whose side were knocked out at the quarter-final stage in Sweden, Mannion had played his last game for his country seven years earlier.

It was not only his creative skills that England missed; in the 1946–47 season, Mannion was top scorer for England with ten of the side's 30 goals that season. In the late 1950s Winterbottom rated Mannion as the 'greatest of our inside-forwards since the end of the war in 1945, an artist reliant exclusively on sheer skill'.

'The most notable partnership over the past dozen years for England has been that of Wilf Mannion and Tom Finney, reaching its sublimation in the famous 10-0 win against Portugal in 1947,' Winterbottom said.

'The two players worked together, only three or four yards apart, exchanging seven or eight passes in succession between them. On other occasions when they were selected on opposite flanks, Mannion was still able to find Finney with accurate cross-field passes.' 'Mannion could flit from one situation to the next unnoticed,' Winterbottom recalled. 'He had stunning ball-control and high deftness of touch.

'Wilf was always prepared to fit in with Finney, a clear indication of his greatness. When a super player in his own right is prepared to subordinate himself to the optimum needs of the team, he puts severe stresses on his own inclinations. But in doing it he confirms his own greatness.'

'Wilf never failed to be a pleasure to watch,' Winterbottom said.

TALKING POINT

The career of Wilf Mannion was almost certainly shortened as a consequence of the physical and mental strain he endured in combat during World War II.

An established first-team player with Middlesbrough before the war, Mannion served in the Army in France and then Italy, where he saw action as a company runner. In Sicily, his company was pinned down. 'We lost half of our men that day,' he recalled.

In 1944, his health collapsed as a result of the stress and in Palestine, he came under the care of Bertie Mee, a physiotherapist and future Arsenal manager. 'When someone gets killed next to you, I can understand you losing it. Wilf had gone from A1 to B2, the lowest grade considered capable of being rehabilitated,' Mee said.

Mannion suffered jaundice and then malaria. On one occasion he was found collapsed under a palm tree. In total, he suffered ten relapses. All interest in football seemed to have been lost.

Only gradually did he regain sufficient stamina to play for Wanderers, the Army team that entertained troops. But the strain on his mind and body had been enormous.

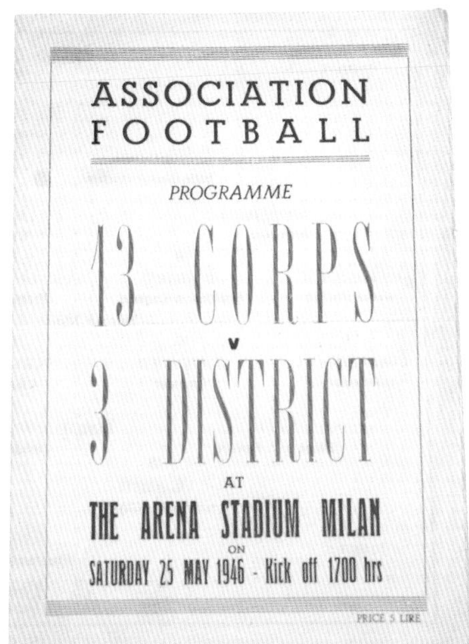

Above left A team sheet, signed by the players of both sides, from the England v Ireland match in the 1946–47 season.

Above A programme from a 1946 Armed Services match. Few professional footballers were lucky enough to join the Physical Training staff in the services, but in 1942, Mannion enjoyed a year playing football in South Africa.

WALTER WINTERBOTTOM

(1913–2002)

Manager • Inducted 2005

As a pioneering coach and outstanding teacher, Walter Winterbottom worked tirelessly in his efforts to drag English football into the modern era, encouraging players, clubs and administrators to change the way they thought about themselves and the game.

'Nobody believed in coaches at first.' Winterbottom said. 'I wanted to change the whole attitude to coaching in this country.' It was a monumental task that occupied all of his 16 years as FA director of coaching and national team manager, starting in 1946.

'Many people in the game now have no idea how much English football owes Walter,' Ron Greenwood wrote. 'He launched our coaching system and gave it impetus and status.' Bobby Robson, another of his successors as England manger, described Winterbottom as 'a prophet'.

Founder of the national coaching centre at Lilleshall in Shropshire, he wrote a ground-breaking coaching manual in 1952. The blurb on the sleeve made clear his priorities: 'Mr Winterbottom,' it stated, 'as well as being the FA's Director of Coaching is also the England team manager.'

Gradually, Winterbottom brought about radical change within the national team set-up and won a general acceptance of the value of coaching at both professional and amateur level.

He campaigned in tandem with his mentor, Stanley Rous, the Secretary of the FA and later, following his election in 1961, FIFA President. 'Walter brought entirely new ways of thinking to the game, achieving remarkable success in changing attitudes.' Rous said. 'His combination of the scholarly and practical opened up new horizons for the likes of Ron Greenwood, Dave Sexton, Jimmy Armfield, Bobby Robson and Alf Ramsey. Inspired by him, they developed into a new breed of manager.'

KEY MATCH

England 8 Mexico 0, International Friendly, Wembley, 10 May 1961

The decision made by Walter Winterbottom to change the England selection policy was justified by this crushing victory as optimism ahead of the 1962 World Cup in Chile reached a peak.

At the start of the 1960–61 season Winterbottom finally persuaded the FA selection committee of the benefits of a settled England team. No longer, he announced, would wholesale changes be made match-by-match on the basis of recent club form. 'Injury and availability permitting, we will be keeping the same side,' Winterbottom said.

Results over the season, culminating in this trouncing of Mexico, offered tangible evidence in support of his argument. Using a total of only 13 players, England had played five, won five, scoring 32 goals and conceding eight.

In the absence of Jimmy Greaves, who was suspended by Chelsea, Gerry Hitchens made his debut, and the Aston Villa forward scored with his first shot after only 90 seconds.

England operated a 4–2–4 system, with Johnny Haynes and Bobby Robson in midfield and Bryan Douglas and Bobby Charlton on the wings.

'This was Walter's reward for keeping a settled England side together,' said Robson.

Sadly, the optimism did not last. England lost form the following season, going out at the quarter-final stage at the World Cup in Chile.

Left Walter Winterbottom being interviewed for radio during training.

KEY MUSEUM ARTEFACT

This silver World Cup runners-up medal was produced for the 1962 World Cup final, between Brazil and Czechoslovakia, in Chile. Brazil ran out 3–1 winners securing their second successive World Cup. The Brazilians had beaten England, by the same scoreline, in the quarter-final in a game that proved to be one of the best in the tournament. The open, attacking football was a welcome change from the defence-ridden games of the group stages. This was to be Walter Winterbottom's final tournament, in charge of the England team, as he resigned directly after the competition.

Left This pennant was presented to England and Wolverhampton Wanderers captain, Billy Wright, before a game against Valencia of Spain for his club in 1957. Winterbottom made Wright his England captain in 90 games.

Right This football magazine, printed in 1957, features the great Manchester United side that was decimated in the Munich air crash of 1958. Walter Winterbottom's England World Cup team of that year never recovered from the loss of Duncan Edwards, Roger Byrne and Tommy Taylor in the disaster. As a player, Winterbottom made 27 appearances for United, between 1936 and 1938, before a back injury prematurely ended his career.

Walter Winterbottom found it difficult to bring about change in a professional game that he considered to be to be stuck in the past, conservative, tactically backward, and, worst of all, casual and undisciplined.

From the outset, he encouraged players to analyse the game more deeply, urging them to change the 'slapdash, unrealistic and haphazard' habits of many regarding fitness, training, diet, and match-preparation. Players had to take on greater responsibility for themselves.

> **"There cannot be many men in the game who see the theory, practice and politics of football as clearly as Walter does."**
> *– Sir Bobby Charlton*

Winterbottom stopped the post-match payment of fees in cash; instead, they were paid by cheque to encourage the use of bank accounts. England blazers were also handed out 'to encourage a team mentality'. As late as 1960, he defied a Football Association regulation by allowing players to talk to the media.

But perhaps his greatest battle came against the England selectors, whose influence and power he gradually weakened.

In the early days, Winterbottom was excluded from the room as the committee went through the ridiculous ritual of whittling down candidates, five or more at a time, position by position: 'Gentlemen, nominations for goalkeeper, please,' and so on.

Over time, Winterbottom persuaded the selectors to accept a list of only 30 names to choose from. At the next stage, he would be asked his opinion, before being asked to leave the room as the committee members made their final decision.

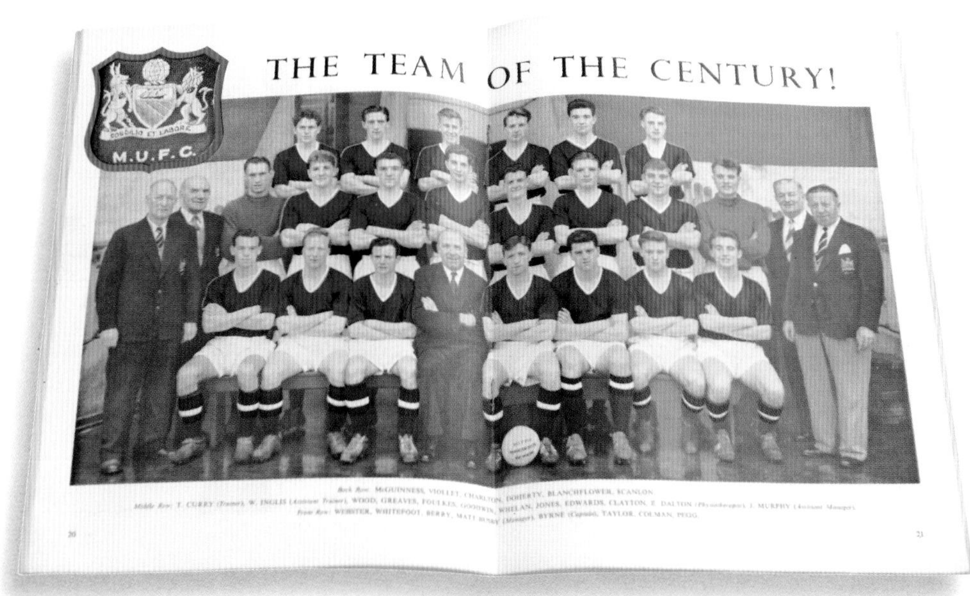

Finally, in the latter years of his time as manager, Winterbottom started the process by naming his preferred side, although the committee members could still outvote him when it came to the crunch.

'There cannot be many men in the game who see the theory, practice and politics of football as clearly as Walter does,' Bobby Charlton wrote in 1967. Jimmy Greaves said that Winterbottom had 'the shrewdest football brain in the country'.

A skilled political operator, Winterbottom took advantage of the setbacks suffered by England during his time as manager to push through his agenda. The debacle of defeat against the United States at the World Cup in 1950 was cited by Winterbottom as evidence in support of his campaign for change. Similarly, the subsequent humiliations inflicted by Hungary in 1953 and 1954 highlighted the need, Winterbottom argued, for regular and longer squad training sessions to improve understanding and team play. As for continuity, that would be improved with the introduction of an England under-23 side, he said.

Finally, a third successive failure at the World Cup, this time in 1958, prompted Winterbottom to change England's tactics and formation from the orthodox 2–3–5 to the 4–2–4 system showcased by Brazil in Sweden.

A 'chalk on his fingers' manager, as Bobby Charlton described him, Winterbottom undoubtedly earned the respect of both players and officials for his technical knowledge. Proof of that came in 1970 when FIFA invited him to head their World Cup technical committee.

Ultimately, Winterbottom bridged the gap between the 'amateur' era of elderly selectors and England players nipping out 'for a quick fag' before kick-off and the advent of the 'modern', organised game. His work prepared the way for the appointment by England of a professional club manager, a 'mud on his boots man', as Charlton put it.

Alf Ramsey, who was able to insist on full control of team selection, had no doubt about the contribution made by his predecessor. 'I had the deepest respect for Walter,' he said. 'His tactical knowledge and outlook left a lasting impression on me.'

TALKING POINT

A generation of young managers transformed English football in the early 1960s, and they all readily acknowledged the debt that they owed to Walter Winterbottom.

As they neared the end of their playing careers, Bobby Robson, Ron Greenwood, Bill Nicholson, Jimmy Hill and Billy Wright were all encouraged by Winterbottom to attend coaching courses organised by the Football Association.

These young managers introduced the training methods and tactics that revitalised League football and brought success for their clubs in Europe. Nicholson led the way by winning the European Cup-winners' Cup with Spurs in 1963. West Ham United, managed by Greenwood, brought the trophy back to England in 1965

Winterbottom had used his contacts to open doors for them in the game: Greenwood and Nicholson, for instance, gained early experience as a coach at Oxford and Cambridge universities respectively; others were offered full-time jobs on the FA coaching staff.

'Walter was an inspired teacher,' said Greenwood, who was recommended by Winterbottom for the manager's job at West Ham United in 1961. Bobby Robson was first encouraged to take up coaching in 1958 while still an England player. 'He urged me to take up coaching under guidance at Lilleshall. I owe Walter a lot for seeing that I had potential in that direction.

Above This is the original match ball from the first ever World Cup final in 1930. Uruguay, the hosts, beat Argentina 4–2 to lift the World Cup in Montevideo. Walter Winterbottom guided England to their first World Cup finals in 1950, in Brazil.

Left The magazine *Charles Buchan's Football Monthly* was quick to analyse why England had been beaten 7–1 by Hungary, in Budapest in 1954. Only six months earlier, England had suffered a 3–6 defeat at the hands of the same team at Wembley. Winterbottom was keen to adopt the Hungarian approach to coaching and match preparation and the defeats emphasised how much work had to be done at international level.

STAN MORTENSEN (1921–1991)

Player • Inducted 2003 • 25 Caps • 1 FA Cup

Stan Mortensen, the centre-forward nicknamed 'Electric Heels' for his lightning pace, scored the first – and so far, only – hat-trick in an FA Cup final at Wembley, helping his beloved Blackpool stage a stirring comeback in 1953.

The third of Mortensen's goals, a fiercely struck free-kick, levelled the score at 3–3 against Bolton Wanderers. It was then left to Stanley Matthews to make the last, decisive intervention, setting up the winning goal for Bill Perry, the Blackpool winger.

A Tynesider by birth, Mortensen arrived in Blackpool at the age of 16, and he never left, opening a postcard shop on the Golden Mile. On match days he would turn up just before kick-off, as his family lived only 40 yards from the ground.

He was intensely loyal to the club, even going so far as to auction his football medals to raise funds, and to the town. In the 1960s, he also had a brief spell managing the team.

Originally considered too slow to make the grade, Mortensen trained intensively to improve his speed after being grounded by the RAF during the Second World War. On his full England debut in 1947, he scored four goals against Portugal, followed by a hat-trick against Sweden later in the year.

Stanley Matthews always argued that the final at Wembley in 1953 should be known as 'The Mortensen Final'. Instead, it was Matthews himself who attracted all the attention. 'The papers should all have been writing about Mortie,' he said. 'To score a hat-trick at Wembley was a fantastic achievement.'

KEY MATCH

Italy 0 England 4, International Friendly, Turin, 16 May 1948

Stan Mortensen ignored the knowing looks and smiles of his team-mates. No matter how much they might suspect differently, he was adamant his goal had been no fluke.

Running onto a Stanley Matthews pass down the line, Mortensen beat two defenders, cut back, and then, from near the goal-line, he fired a curling shot into the roof of the net from a narrow angle.

Bacigalupo, the Italy goalkeeper, was stunned. He, and everyone else in the packed ground, had expected a cross. In celebration, Mortensen gave a half bow. It was the fourth minute of the game.

In the dressing room at half-time, Mortensen insisted that he had intended to shoot all along. 'We said, "Don't be crazy,"' Stanley Matthews recalled. 'But Mortie was insistent. "I aimed, I tell you."'

'My intention had been to centre the ball for Tommy Lawton,' Mortensen said later, 'but I noticed that the Italian goalkeeper had not positioned himself properly, so I shot on the run. This goal has pride of place in my England collection.'

As if to prove the point, Mortensen used his pace once more to make a second break midway through the first half. This time, after looking up again, he did pull the ball back for Lawton, who scored with a low drive.

'I don't think I have ever known a stadium go quite so deathly quiet as when Stan Mortensen scored,' Walter Winterbottom, the England manager said. 'The Italians had not lost an international for two years.'

Left Stan Mortensen scores Blackpool's second goal on the way to their 4–3 FA Cup final victory over Bolton Wanderers on 2 May 1953.

KEY MUSEUM ARTEFACT

This tangerine-coloured Blackpool shirt was worn in the 1953 FA Cup final. While the colour remains synonymous with the club, Blackpool have possibly appeared in more colours than any other team. Although they were elected to the Football League in 1897, it wasn't until 1924 that the first of the tangerine shirts saw the light of day. Initially, their players wore blue-and-white-striped shirts, which were followed by shirts of all red, red-and-white halves, red, yellow and blue stripes, all white and, finally, light and dark blue stripes. Unbelievably, it wasn't until after World War II that Blackpool finally chose tangerine.

Above right A team sheet taken from the centre of the official 1953 FA Cup final programme.

Above A scrapbook of the 1953 FA Cup final. Before television's popularity collecting newspaper cuttings was the only way to re-live a game. Because the 1953 Cup final was played in the year of HM Queen Elizabeth II's coronation, there was an unprecedented demand for televisions, resulting in over 10 million people watching the game on TV.

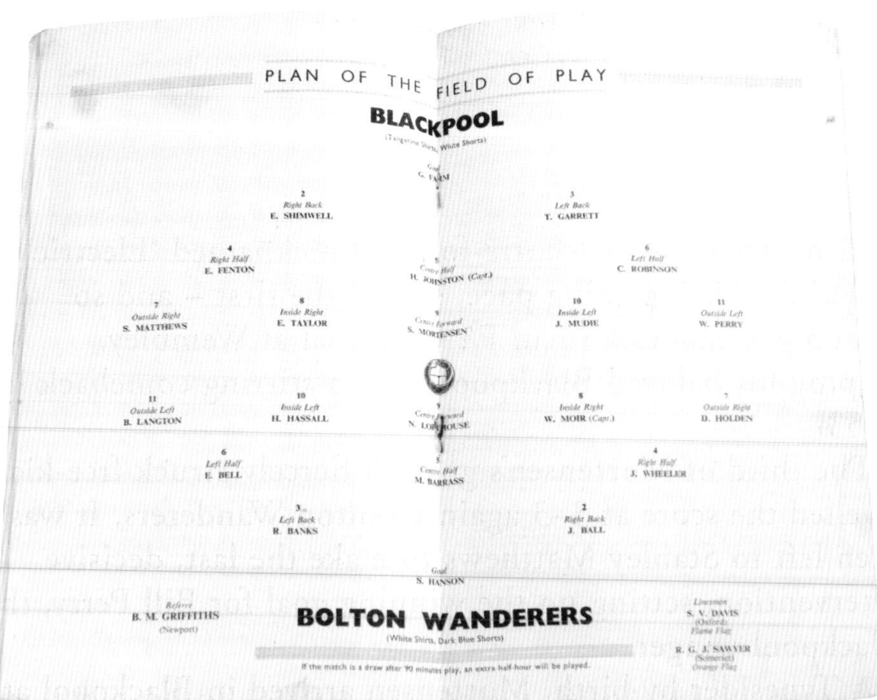
PLAN OF THE FIELD OF PLAY
BLACKPOOL
(Tangerine Shirts, White Shorts)
Goal G. FARM
2 Right Back E. SHIMWELL
3 Left Back T. GARRETT
4 Right Half E. FENTON
5 Centre Half H. JOHNSTON (Capt.)
6 Left Half C. ROBINSON
7 Outside Right S. MATTHEWS
8 Inside Right E. TAYLOR
9 Centre Forward S. MORTENSEN
10 Inside Left J. MUDIE
11 Outside Left W. PERRY
11 Outside Left B. LANGTON
10 Inside Left H. HASSALL
9 Centre Forward N. LOFTHOUSE
8 Inside Right W. MOIR (Capt.)
7 Outside Right D. HOLDEN
6 Left Half E. BELL
5 Centre Half M. BARRASS
4 Right Half J. WHEELER
3 Left Back R. BANKS
2 Right Back J. BALL
Goal S. HANSON
Referee B. M. GRIFFITHS (Newport)
BOLTON WANDERERS
(White Shirts, Dark Blue Shorts)
Linesmen S. V. DAVIS (Oxford) Flame Flag
R. G. J. SAWYER (Somerset) Orange Flag
If the match is a draw after 90 minutes play, an extra half-hour will be played.

In 395 League games for Blackpool, Mortensen scored 225 goals. There were other offers, but 'the thought of leaving Blackpool put me off'. However, his love of football, saw him happily drop down the divisions to prolong his playing career by turning out for some non-league teams. In his late 40s, he formed a team for charity matches and throughout all this, he behaved impeccably. 'I had a responsibility as a role model,' he once said.

Even when sorely tested, he did not retaliate; nor did he show dissent. In the disastrous defeat against the United States in the 1950 World Cup finals, he was convinced his shot crossed the line before being cleared, only for play to be waved on; moments later, he was rugby-tackled when clean through on goal. On both occasions Mortensen simply shrugged his shoulders and got on with it.

Stoic and brave, he thought nothing of personal sacrifice on behalf of the team. In the days before substitutions, he often played on despite injury. Already hobbling in one game, he pivoted on his injured leg to shoot against the crossbar. Blackpool needed a goal; the risk of aggravating the injury, as he did, didn't come into it.

His sportsmanship endeared him to opponents. In 1948, at the end of a thrilling FA Cup Final, won 4–2 by Manchester United, Mortensen said: 'It was a privilege to have been part of the game even though we lost.'

Five years later, with his side losing at half-time in the final, he congratulated Nat Lofthouse, a fellow centre-forward, for his feat in scoring for Bolton in every round of the competition. Mortensen completed his hat-trick in the second half. At the end of that game, Mortensen lifted Stanley Matthews on his shoulders. 'The maestro did a great deal to turn it round and it was inevitable the focus was on him,' he said.

At his peak, in 1948, Stan Mortensen finished second in the voting for the inaugural Footballer of the Year award. The winner was Stanley Matthews.

The two Stans were football's great double act, but with Matthews always taking the lead in the public imagination, no matter what Mortensen did. In 1951, 'Mortie' was the leading goal-scorer in Division One and an England match-winner, yet it was Matthews' failure to secure a Cup-winner's medal that was seen as the big story of the season. For his part Matthews endlessly praised Mortensen as a mobile forward who contributed more in build-up play than was the norm for a number nine.

Mortensen often dropped deep to initiate attacks. Once he had the ball, Matthews knew that it was his signal to begin his run down the wing, knowing his colleague had the talent to find him with a pass. Mortensen, meanwhile, was heading to the near post, using his pace to get in front of the defender. 'Stan's change in direction and speed threw his markers,' Matthews said. 'He had great ability to swivel and turn his body, and that helped him shield the ball when he received it. He wasn't the tallest of forwards but when he went for a header he seemed able to defy gravity and hang in the air for ages.

'Mortie was barrel-chested, and he had cornflake-box shoulders and legs like bags of concrete. I can't ever recall him being knocked off the ball and when he went after it, he did so with demonic enthusiasm.'

Walter Winterbottom, the national team manager, said: 'England owes much to Stan Mortensen, for his spirit, for his biting at the most meagre morsel thrown up by an attack, for his sheer invincibility. He was a lionheart.'

Left An FA Cup Winner's Medal from 1953, which was made by Fattorini & Sons Ltd, who were also responsible for designing the third FA Cup in 1911.

Right The official programme of the 1953 FA Cup final.

TALKING POINT

The England team always made great efforts to help former RAF wireless operator-air gunner Stan Mortensen when he complained of blinding headaches and insomnia.

Mortensen suffered from migraines and sleep deprivation as a result of the head injury he sustained in a fatal bomber crash during the Second World War. Both the pilot and the bomb-aimer on the combat mission were killed, while the navigator lost a leg.

Carried unconscious from the burning wreckage of the Wellington, Mortensen had a deep four-inch gash along the base of his skull. Doctors who told him he would not play football again underestimated his great physical strength. After spending a month in hospital, he spent the rest of the war grounded.

'Mortie found it difficult to get any rest,' recalled Billy Wright, the team captain. 'So a cabin was secured on the boat taking us to Ireland for an international. Our kit was placed in it, and Stanley was encouraged to get some rest in the bunk.

'The sight of famous footballers creeping into the cabin on tiptoe to see if Mortensen was comfortable made a lasting impression upon me.'

Beba

BILLY WRIGHT (1924–1994)

Player • Inducted 2002 • 105 caps • 3 Division One Championships • 1 FA Cup

Billy Wright, a player described as 'a national treasure' by *The Times* in 1959, became something of an institution in the heart of the England team, amassing a then record total of 105 caps.

Over a period of eight years, starting in 1951, England did not once take to the field without Wright in their ranks, a record run of 70 consecutive appearances. Ninety times he led England as captain, another record at the time.

'Billy had a heart of oak and was the most reliable of men,' Walter Winterbottom, the England manager said. 'I considered myself lucky to have him to call on so often.'

Between 1946 and 1959 Wright experienced defeat with England only 21 times and went six years before tasting defeat at Wembley. In 541 League and Cup games for Wolves, at wing-half and centre-half, he was never booked or sent off.

'Essentially a team player who never tried to seek personal glory, Billy turned simplicity into an art form,' Winterbottom said. After one England international *The Times* wrote: 'Billy Wright had a rare day off. He only played like one man.'

Footballer of the Year in 1952, Wright was still the captain of both England and Wolves, Division One champions, when he retired from football seven years later. In recognition of his long service to the game, the Football Association made him a Life Member. He was the first professional player to be awarded the honour.

On his retirement, *The Times* wrote: 'There were more talented and more skilful players, but what he embroidered into the fabric of our lives were the values of loyalty and industry, attributes which helped pull us as a nation through those difficult years immediately after the war.

'Billy Wright, the man, is a human being of exemplary character. Billy Wright, the footballer, was a national treasure.'

KEY MATCH

England 1 Scotland 0, Home International Championship, Wembley, 11 April 1959

On hearing the final whistle, Don Howe and Ronnie Clayton lifted Billy Wright onto their shoulders, before carrying the England captain from the field in triumph as the first man to win 100 caps.

Every Scotland player made a point of shaking the hand of the England captain. As one national newspaper reported the next day: 'Wright is admired and respected far beyond English boundaries.'

Bobby Charlton scored the only goal of the game with an acrobatic header, and England might have won by a bigger margin but for the performance of Bill Brown in the Scotland goal.

'I was inundated with messages and telegrams wishing me well,' Wright recalled. 'The German team manager Sepp Herberger came over to London specially to present me with a giant silver candlestick on behalf of the West German FA.

'From the Football Association I received a magnificent silver salver emblazoned with the flags of all the countries I had played in, and the greatest honour of all, I was invited to Buckingham Palace for a private lunch with the Queen and the Duke of Edinburgh.'

Left Billy Wright leads the England team out at the Maracana Stadium for a World Cup group game against Chile in 1950. It was the first time that England had taken part in the tournament. They won the game 2–0.

KEY MUSEUM ARTEFACT

By the 1950s, endorsing products such as these Rubstuds was becoming increasingly popular among footballers. Like many of his colleagues, Billy Wright would wear a pair of boots for as many years as he could. The leather used in boot manufacture was so hard that, in order to wear them in, players would often sit in a bath of water allowing the boots to mould to the shape of their feet. If they wanted to retain their balance in the winter months, the only option available to players was to change their studs. This was done by pulling out the old studs and nailing in a new rubber set.

As a youngster, Billy Wright collected the autographs of Stanley Matthews and Tommy Lawton, little realising that one day he would line up alongside them in the same England team.

Barely five feet tall when he joined the Molineux staff as a teenager in 1938, there was no indication that Wright would enjoy such a long and distinguished career. It was not long before he was summoned to see Major Frank Buckley, the Wolves manager. 'Sonny, you're far too small to ever make the grade,' Buckley told him. 'I'm sending you home.'

Only the intervention of the training staff persuaded Buckley to change his mind. Within half an hour Wright was back in the manager's office. 'The Major pushed his finger at my chest and said: "I'm assured that you're big where it really matters: in the heart. You can stay.'

> **"Billy Wright, the man, is a human being of exemplary character. Billy Wright, the footballer, was a national treasure."**
>
> *– The Times*

Wright played at wing-half for club and country until the summer of 1954. He had no thought of switching position until circumstances intervened. At the World Cup in Switzerland, Wright was asked to cover when the regular England centre-half was ruled out by injury. A few games into the following season, the same situation occurred at Wolves. Wright found the new role less demanding physically and he wore the number 5 shirt for the rest of his career.

The change, albeit unplanned, prolonged his career by several seasons. Eventually, however, at the age of 35, Wright realised it was time to bow out. A young Jimmy Greaves gave Wright the first hint by running rings around him in a fixture at Chelsea. Then, during pre-season training, Wright was running up a hill when he realised his legs had 'gone'. 'At that moment I decided to retire while I was still at the top in the game.'

At five feet eight inches tall, Wright was a little on the short side for a central defender. He worked hard in training to make good this potential shortcoming in the air. Jumping over hurdles from a standing position improved his spring, as did weight training to strengthen his leg muscles. A tenacious tackler despite his slight frame, Wright never shirked physical confrontation. 'I only had two things on my mind as

Above This Moscow Spartak Club pennant was presented to Billy Wright before a game in 1954. Wolves won the match 4–0 under the Molineux floodlights. Their midweek exploits against continental clubs contributed to the creation of the European Cup in 1955.

Right A banquet menu from the Gala Dinner celebrating Wright's 100th International appearance, in 1959. Wright became the first player in the world to reach such a landmark and it was fitting that it came against Scotland in a 1–0 victory.

a player: to win the ball and then to give the simplest pass I could to the nearest team-mate,' Wright once said.

Writing in 1958, Tom Finney praised his captain's reliability, rating him a better centre-half than wing-half. 'He must be challenging for the honour of the most consistent centre-half ever to play for England. Billy fully deserves the nickname Mr Dynamo. He never stops running.'

On one of the rare occasions that Wright was unable to play for England because of injury, Alf Ramsey led the side. Before his first international as captain, Ramsey received a telegram from Wright congratulating him on the honour and wishing him well.

As a captain Billy gets results by the "human touch",' Ramsey wrote in 1952. 'He has the knack of setting an example to the rest of the team, and his tackling

> **"I only had two things on my mind as a player: to win the ball and then to give the simplest pass I could to the nearest team-mate."** – *Billy Wright*

cannot be surpassed for its accuracy and perfect timing.'

Opponents praised his sportsmanship. An hour after Hungary thrashed England 6–3 at Wembley in 1953, Wright rushed from the dressing room, still dripping with water, when he spotted one of the Hungary players. 'He shook me by the hand and told me that it had been a wonderful match and that he enjoyed it very much,' Sandor Barcs recalled. 'He then said, "I congratulate you. You have a wonderful team." I was so moved. What a fantastic gesture.'

TALKING POINT

When Billy Wright married the glamorous pop singer Joy Beverley in 1958, he entered uncharted territory for a footballer: the world of media 'celebrity'.

As a single man who lived in digs until his mid-30s, Wright appeared the least likely subject for sensational headlines. His hobbies included playing dominoes and rug-making. But the romance changed everything.

When one national newspaper wrote a story about Joy's first marriage, it prompted other journalists to chase a comment for a follow-up story. The reporters thought nothing of disrupting his preparations for the upcoming World Cup. Wright was telephoned as he tried to sleep in his room at the team hotel in Sweden. The intrusion prompted an unusual reaction from Wright, normally the most reserved and polite of footballers: he swore at the callers.

'I had never been so angry in my life,' Wright recalled. It was a disgraceful invasion of privacy. I was not concerned for myself, only Joy, who was having her past raked up just because we had fallen in love.

'For one of the few times in my life I was ready to biff the reporters on the nose.'

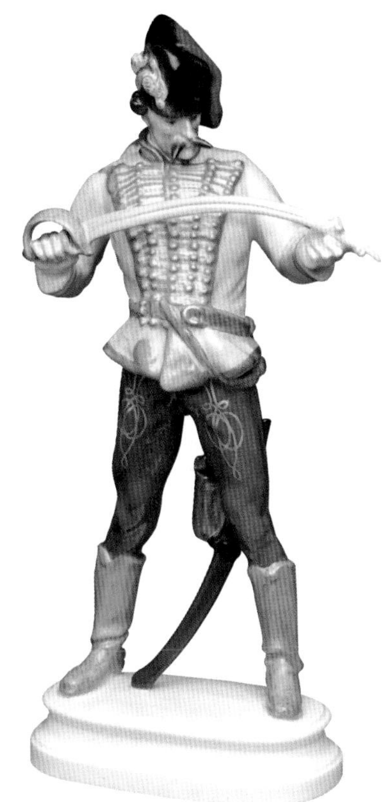

Right This ceramic hussar was presented to the Football Association by Hungary prior to their match against England in Budapest in 1954. Hungary won 7–1.

Left The cover of this book, written by Ferenc Puskas in 1955, shows him exchanging pennants with Billy Wright prior to England's shock 6–3 defeat by Hungary in 1953. Puskas was also part of the Honved side that was beaten 3–2 by Wolves at Molineux in 1954.

TOM FINNEY (1922–)

Player • Inducted 2002 • 76 caps

Tom Finney, a man described by Bill Shankly as 'the greatest player I ever saw, bar none', was the toast of international football during an illustrious England career that stretched over 12 years.

In the days of specialist positions, Finney was talented enough to play on both wings and at centre-forward for England. He scored 30 goals, a record at the time, in 76 international appearances. 'No better player than Tom has ever worn an England shirt,' Billy Wright, his captain, said.

The first player to be twice voted Footballer of the Year, in 1953–54 and 1956–57, Finney was revered throughout Europe. His performances on tour with England in 1952 prompted an Italian millionaire to offer him a fortune to join Palermo. In addition to promising him a free car and seaside villa, the Sicilian club was prepared to pay Preston substantial compensation in return for a two-year loan. Alternatively, Preston could bank £30,000 for his permanent transfer. North End refused to sell, even for a record fee; Finney was irreplaceable.

At the official banquet following England's 5–3 victory over Portugal at Goodison Park in 1951, all 11 Portuguese players stood in salute. The captain made a toast: 'To Mr Finney – the Master.' Four years earlier Finney had been the outstanding England player in a 10–0 rout of Portugal in Lisbon.

Bill Shankly once joked that Finney, his Preston team-mate, could beat his marker 'wearing an overcoat'. He had watched Finney practise his skills, using both feet, against a wall at Deepdale. When he became manager of Liverpool in 1959 Shankly introduced similar drills at Anfield.

'Tom was crafty, quick and elusive,' Shankly said. 'He could beat you on either side without breaking stride. When he had the ball, that was it, you'd never get it back. A brilliant, exceptional player.'

KEY MATCH

Portugal 0 England 10, International Friendly, Lisbon, 27 May 1947

The Portuguese changed the ball, the defender who was marking him, and the goalkeeper, but nothing they did could stop Tom Finney on his first appearance on the left wing for England.

Previously, Finney had vied with Stanley Matthews for the number seven shirt, creating a dilemma for England selectors. In Portugal, an injury to Bobby Langton, the regular left-winger, forced their hand. As an experiment, Finney switched wings.

Although he later stated his displeasure and frustration at being played out of his favoured position, Finney enjoyed himself enormously against Portugal. 'We had a beano. It was as if we could read each other's minds,' he said. 'After this, we were the talk of Europe.'

During the first half, Portugal 'lost' the heavier ball chosen by England, replacing it with a smaller, lighter one. It made no difference. With either ball at his feet Finney tormented his marker, prompting the Portugal manager to order his full-back, Cardosa, to feign injury so that a substitution could be made. Finney carried on regardless, giving the replacement defender an equally torrid time.

'At 5–0, the crowd began to take it out on Azevedo, the Portugal goalkeeper,' Finney recalled. 'The poor fellow didn't have a chance with the shots, but they showed their disapproval by giving him "the seagull screech",' Finney said. Azevedo was substituted, too.

'I shall always associate Tom with this wonderful win,' Billy Wright said. 'His nimble feet had been the despair of our opponents that day.'

Left Tom Finney holds off Rolden of Chile during England's first ever World Cup match on 25 June 1950.

KEY MUSEUM ARTEFACT

This cap was awarded to Tom Finney for representing his country against Wales and Scotland in 1957 and 1958. On occasions, England players have been given one cap to commemorate several games. More often, this has occurred when a player has taken part in a particular tournament, or tour, rather than individual games. The origins of the international cap can be found in the universities and public schools of the 1860s and 70s. Before different coloured playing kits were invented, the only way to distinguish players and teams from one another was to look at the house or school cap that they wore.

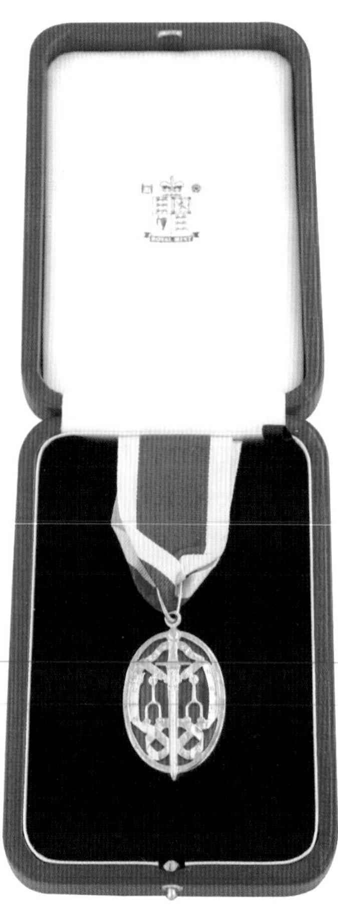

Above The KBE awarded to Sir Tom Finney in 1998.

Right This drinking instrument, in four parts, was presented by the Argentina National team. Each member of the England party received the gift when the two countries met on 9 May 1951.

Tom Finney played for Preston for 14 years, between 1946 and 1960. North End were a decent side during the 1950s, losing an FA Cup final and twice finishing runners-up in Division One.

The team relied heavily on the versatile Finney, who at one time or another occupied all five forward positions for the club. One national newspaper said he 'was half the Preston team' and, as if to prove the point, North End were relegated from Division One the season following his retirement.

If Finney didn't perform, more often than not nor did Preston. Their defeat against West Bromwich Albion in the FA Cup final at Wembley in 1954 was Finney's greatest disappointment in the game. Nerves and a mass of defenders got the better of him. 'My legs felt heavy and I was running around like I had a sandbag across my shoulders,' he said.

Finney was an established England player when Preston were relegated in 1948–49. Had he agitated for a transfer, Blackpool and Manchester United were ready to pay a record fee for his signature.

Finney had a quiet word with the chairman. Assured that the club had the means and ambition to recover, he was happy to stay. Two years later, Preston won promotion as champions of Division Two. It was the only medal he won in his career.

His loyalty to the club and the town was rewarded later in life. In 1972, he was made a Freeman of Preston. Knighted in 1998 for his work as a footballer, magistrate and civil servant, Finney's name will forever be associated with Preston North End. In recognition of his contribution to the club, a statue was erected at Deepdale in 1998. Following a name change, the ground itself can now be found on Sir Tom Finney Way.

The great 'Who's the best – Matthews or Finney?' debate divided football opinion for the best part of a decade. The paying public may have preferred to watch Matthews dribble past defenders, but many of their fellow professionals favoured the all-round skills of Finney. It was

> **“Three of four Arsenal defenders dithered like old women on a zebra crossing every time Finney had the ball.”**
> – *The Times*

not for them to decide who played for England, however. The people who did, the members of the FA selection committee, tended to favour Matthews, particularly during the decade following the war.

The national debate arose inevitably out of competition; both men played on the right wing for their respective clubs, and both of them wanted to wear the number seven shirt for England. Faced with a dilemma, and loathe to leave one of them out, the selectors switched Finney to the opposite wing, a solution he always maintained was unfair. ‘Why is it that I should always be the one to play out of position?’ he once asked. The England selectors weren’t listening; they picked Finney at outside-left in 33 of his 76 internationals for England. Late in his career, he also won three caps at centre-forward.

Although left-footed, Finney preferred playing on the right wing. From there, he was able to cut in for a shot on goal. If he went the other way, on the outside, he could cross the ball accurately with his right foot.

The opposition had no idea which way he would go. ‘Three or four Arsenal defenders dithered like old women on a zebra crossing every time Finney had the ball,’ one newspaper wrote.

Johnny Haynes said: ‘Tom is the more complete footballer. He can do more things. Also, he never flinched no matter what hard knocks he took. His skill was quite exceptional.’

Walter Winterbottom, the England manager, said that Finney averaged one goal or one ‘assist’ per match, a remarkable record for a winger. ‘When the chips were truly down he would try and try and then try a little bit harder. He was the complete team man. I could never imagine an England team without him in it in those days,’ Winterbottom said.

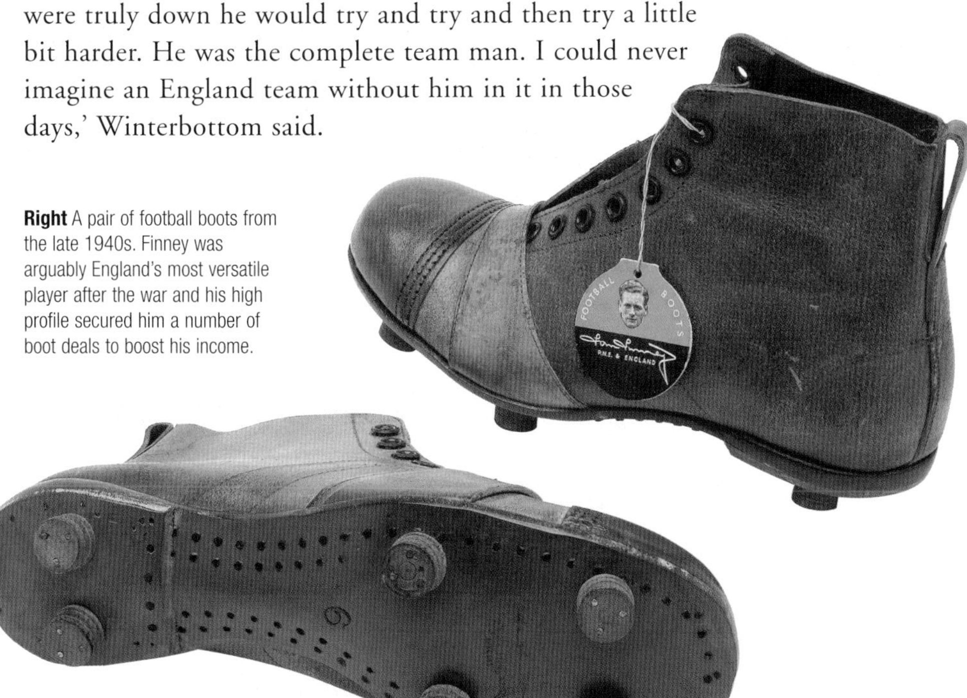

Right A pair of football boots from the late 1940s. Finney was arguably England’s most versatile player after the war and his high profile secured him a number of boot deals to boost his income.

TALKING POINT

The emotion of the day got the better of Tom Finney when he made his 433rd and final League appearance for Preston North End, his only club, on the last day of the 1959–60 season.

‘Don Bradman was out for a duck in his last Test match because he said he couldn’t see the ball for tears in his eyes. Well, that’s the way I felt for the whole of the game. It was so hard to concentrate,’ Finney later recalled.

Before the kick-off at Deepdale, the Preston North End and Luton Town players formed a circle in the middle of the pitch. As a tribute to Finney, they sang ‘Auld Lang Syne’ and ‘For He’s a Jolly Good Fellow’, accompanied by the large home crowd, numbering twice the season average.

Choked with emotion, his voice trembling, Finney addressed the crowd by microphone after the game. He concluded his speech by saying: ‘It is sad, but today is a day I will remember forever and thank you all for making it so grand.’

Cliff Britton, the Preston manager, had been playing Finney at centre-forward that season. For this, his last match, Britton allowed him to choose his own position, in recognition of his services to the club. Finney opted for outside-right, the same role he filled on his debut two decades earlier.

Above The Football Writers’ Association’s Footballer of the Year trophies of 1954 and 1957. Finney became the first player to be named Footballer of the Year twice.

NAT LOFTHOUSE (1925–)

Player • Inducted 2002 • 33 caps • 1 FA Cup

Nat Lofthouse was the last great champion of a dying breed: the traditional English centre-forward – the talismanic figurehead given the job of leading the attack, taking more than his share of knocks and scoring most of the goals.

Over a period of eight years, Lofthouse scored 30 times in 33 internationals. Since then, only Jimmy Greaves has matched that strike rate for England over a prolonged period.

Lofthouse was an old-style, robust number nine, like Dixie Dean and Tommy Lawton before him; 'a battering ram,' as he once described himself. Tom Finney was far more generous, listing his attributes as 'speed, fearlessness, a hard shot in either foot, good heading ability, and a robust frame to stand up to all the physical stuff'.

His performance in the FA Cup final of 1953 was typical: Lofthouse scored one goal, hit the post, harassed his opponents, and was almost knocked unconscious. At the end of the game, he shook the hands of the victorious Blackpool players.

Such acts of sportsmanship added to his appeal. Voted Footballer of the Year in 1953, he was elated when his conduct on the field was praised as highly as his scoring prowess.

After making his debut in 1951, he began a run of 18 successive games for England the following year. For six years, England made a point of aiming everything at his head.

His international career appeared over in 1956 when he was dropped by the selectors, despite scoring 32 goals in 36 games for Bolton.

In the wake of England's disappointing performance in the World Cup in 1958, Lofthouse was briefly recalled the following winter. 'It made no sense that Nat was left out for the World Cup in the first place,' Billy Wright, the England captain recalled. 'The old guard was gradually being stood down.'

KEY MATCH

Austria 2 England 3, International Friendly, Vienna, 25 May 1952

Nat Lofthouse earned the nickname 'Lion of Vienna' for his bravery in scoring a crucial goal that also prompted a rare display of emotion from Alf Ramsey.

With the score at 2–2, England were under intense pressure in a match billed in the press as an unofficial championship of Europe.

'Tom Finney was inside our half when he got the ball,' Lofthouse recalled. 'He drew the lone defender and plonked a long ball through for me. With defenders chasing me, I had nobody but the 'keeper to beat.'

Billy Wright looked on as the move developed. 'As the goalkeeper came out it was obvious there was going to be a collision. Nat just kept going. It was unbelievable bravery,' he said.

'It was one of the few occasions in my football life I really did feel like shouting out with joy,' Alf Ramsey, normally the most phlegmatic of full-backs, said. 'The players all but kissed him for what we felt would be the winning goal.'

Lofthouse was knocked unconscious briefly, but insisted on returning to the action despite a knee injury also sustained in the collision. Despite the handicap he still hit the woodwork with another shot.

'The courage Nat showed was typical of him. The way he insisted on coming back on lifted the heart of every Englishman in the stadium. It made us redouble our efforts to keep the Austrians out,' Ramsey said.

Left Bolton Wanderers' Nat Lofthouse challenges the Manchester United goalkeeper, Harry Gregg, for the ball during the FA Cup final on 3 May 1958. Lofthouse scored two goals in Bolton's 2–0 victory over a United side that had been decimated by the Munich air disaster.

KEY MUSEUM ARTEFACT

This embroidered, decorative pennant was presented to England before the 1952 game against Belgium at Wembley. It has been the custom since the early years of the 20th century for the captains of national teams to exchange gifts prior to kick-off. England won this particular game 5–0. Although Lofthouse had made his England debut in 1951, it was not until 1952 that he secured his position in the national side, winning seven caps during the year. He went on to score an astonishing 30 goals in 33 internationals.

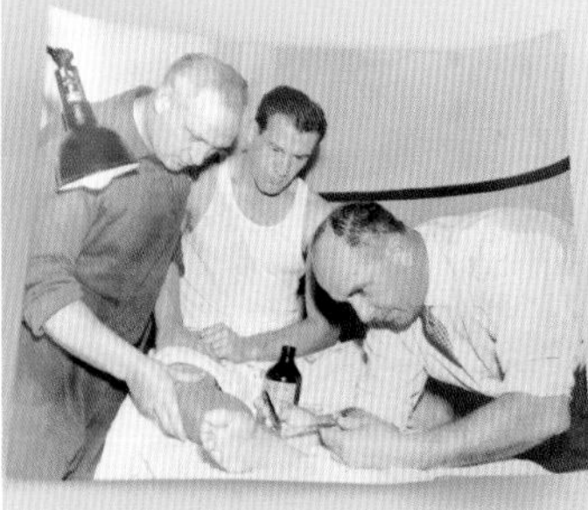

Left Lofthouse receives stitches to an ankle wound from Bolton's club doctor, Bill Ridding, as physiotherapist, Bert Sproston, looks on.

Right Nat Lofthouse made his League debut for Bolton in 1946. Such were the crowds at Bolton's FA Cup sixth-round home tie against Stoke City earlier in the year that two crush barriers collapsed, resulting in the deaths of 33 people and injuries to another 500. This letter is a response to an inquiry from an injured fan.

Nat Lofthouse was born and bred in Bolton. He signed for Wanderers as a 14-year-old amateur in 1939, and he played his last game for them 21 years later. During that time he played 503 games for the club, scoring 285 goals. The total number of appearances would have been higher but for the loss of several seasons to wartime football. As a result his league debut was delayed until 1946, when he turned 21.

The conflict shaped him as a player. 'My war-time experience toughened me up, physically and mentally,' Lofthouse recalled. Too young for military service, he worked in a coal mine. On Saturdays, he awoke at 3.30 a.m., in order to catch the tram to work an hour later. His shift below ground lasted eight hours, pushing tubs of coal. At the end of it, the team coach was waiting for him at the gate. Only then did he play 90 minutes of football.

His fitness level was rising, but his form remained stubbornly flat. At the age of 19, Lofthouse became so disillusioned with his own performances, and demoralised by the criticism of supporters, that he considered giving up the game. 'I was very limited at this time,' he recalled.

Then, suddenly, it all came together. 'Just like that,' Lofthouse recalled. 'One day you go up for the ball and, bang, it's in the net. You've been doing the same thing for months and getting nothing for it. That's how it was. No one was more

> **"My war-time experience toughened me up, physically and mentally"**
> *– Nat Lofthouse*

BOLTON WANDERERS FOOTBALL & ATHLETIC CO. LTD.

WINNERS OF THE
FOOTBALL ASSOCIATION CUP 1923, 1926, 1929.
LANCASHIRE CUP 1885-6, 1890-1, 1911-2, 1921-2, 1924-5, 1926-7, 1931-2, 1933-4.
MANCHESTER CUP 1894-5, 1905-6, 1908-9, 1920-1, 1921-2.
RICHARDSON CUP 1928-9, 1930-1.
WEST LANCASHIRE CUP 1930-1.

TELEGRAMS: "WANDERERS, BOLTON."
TELEPHONE: BOLTON 800.
SECRETARY MANAGER.
W. J. ROWLEY

GROUND & REGISTERED OFFICE:
BURNDEN PARK,
BOLTON.

March 26th 1946.

Dear Sir,

I thank you for your letter of the 20th instant and am pleased to know that you have made such satisfactory progress. May this continue until your full health is restored.

I am sorry that we failed to surmount the Charlton obstacle.

We will try again later.

With kindest regards.

Yours faithfully,

surprised than me.' On the resumption of League football in 1946, he was a first-team regular.

Nat Lofthouse served Bolton Wanders as a player, manager, executive club manager and club president. His association with the club has lasted a lifetime. Blackpool, Plymouth Argyle and Arsenal all tried, and failed, to sign him, Lofthouse said. There was also an offer from 'a foreign team' in 1952. 'I was tempted, but now I'm really and truly glad that I didn't take it up and stayed put,' he said.

The huge physical demands of playing centre-forward eventually had their effect. Injured during a summer tour to South Africa, he missed the whole of the 1959–60 season. His final game was against Birmingham City in December 1960. During the match he damaged cruciate ligaments, an injury that effectively ended his career. There was a brief attempt at a comeback, but it ended in resignation.

Football was changing. Lofthouse and the rest of the 'old guard' had played a simpler game tactically, with the centre-forward as the 'pivot' of the attack. Len Shackleton, the England inside-forward, explained it this way: 'Billy Wright won the ball and passed it to me. I gave it to Stan Matthews who ran down the wing and centred for Nat Lofthouse, who scored.'

A new 4–2–4 formation was being introduced into English football. There would still be burly, robust forwards in the game – Bobby Smith of Spurs, for instance – but the responsibility was now shared between twin forwards. The playing career of Nat Lofthouse was ending, as was the golden age of the centre-forward.

Left *Goals Galore* by Nat Lofthouse.

TALKING POINT

Nat Lofthouse had the misfortune of playing in two of the most emotionally charged FA Cup finals in history. Every neutral in the country, it seemed, wanted his team, Bolton Wanderers, to lose at Wembley in 1953 and 1958.

Lofthouse gave his side the lead in 1953 but the nation celebrated the result it wanted when Blackpool staged a late comeback to win 4–3. Stanley Matthews, the most famous man in football, had his winner's medal at last.

Five years later, in the wake of the Munich air disaster, the tide of public feeling against Bolton was even stronger. Against the odds, Manchester United, a club in mourning, had battled their way to the final.

It was all a little unfair on Bolton, who had their own romantic story: all eleven of their players were local lads, and none of them had cost more than the £10 signing-on fee. This time, Bolton and Lofthouse ripped up the script. Lofthouse scored twice, bundling the ball into the net with a shoulder charge against Harry Gregg, the Manchester United goalkeeper, for one of his goals.

'Bolton was an island surrounded by the opposition,' he recalled. 'It was unlucky, really having everybody supporting the other side on the two times we went to Wembley.

'In the second, God forbid, it was after Munich. If I hadn't been a Bolton player, I would have wanted them to win as well.'

Right A match programme from a summer tour in 1959. Many English Division One teams undertook such tours to South African countries in the late 1950s.

STAN CULLIS (1915–2001)

Manager • Inducted 2003 • 3 Division One Championships • 2 FA Cups

Stan Cullis, the 'Iron Manager', shook English football out of its post-war exhaustion and lethargy by putting the emphasis on speed of thought and action. In doing so, Cullis forged Wolves into the most powerful side in the land and the team young George Best wanted to play for when he grew up.

On his orders, the Wolverhampton Wanderers players increased the tempo of their play. 'Fast, direct attack,' Cullis instructed; and for a spell in the 1950s, the best sides in England and Europe could not contain them.

To win consistently, argued Cullis, the Wolves players had to pass the ball accurately over distance and they had to be fitter than their rivals. Above all, the ball had to go forwards; to pass the ball sideways, let alone backwards, was to shirk responsibility, the players were told.

Their positive, energetic play carried Wolves to three championship titles in the space of five years. These successes in the League were sandwiched between two FA Cup triumphs, in 1949 and 1960. Only once in nine consecutive seasons did Wolves finish outside the top three in Division One. No other side came close to matching that level of consistency during the 1950s.

In the middle of the decade, Wolves beat several of the leading club sides of Europe, including Honved of Hungary and Spartak Moscow, in prestigious midweek friendlies under newly installed floodlights at Molineux. Cullis had made a moderately successful provincial club and founder member of the Football League, a recognised force in Europe.

In England, only Manchester United rivalled them. For many youngsters, including George Best as a boy growing up in Belfast, Wolverhampton Wanderers were the most glamorous club in the country.

'Wolves in those days stood for everything that was good about British football,' Matt Busby said. 'They played with great power, spirit and style.'

KEY MATCH

Wolverhampton Wanderers 3 Honved 2, Friendly, Molineux, 13 December 1954

Standing in the dressing room at Molineux, Stan Cullis motioned the newspaper reporters towards the exhausted Wolves players. 'There they are,' Cullis told the journalists, 'the champions of the world.'

It was thirteen months since England had been humiliated 6-3 by Hungary at Wembley. Less than an hour earlier Wolves had restored a degree of confidence in English football by staging a stirring second-half comeback to beat mighty Honved, the champions of Hungary. The whole country celebrated. By the following morning the flood of letters and telegrams had begun.

'The legend of Hungarian invincibility perished forever in the Molineux quagmire,' one newspaper stated under the headline: 'Hail Mighty Wolves'.

The BBC broadcast the second half live; Wolves were 2-0 down. Fortunately for the Corporation its one camera was positioned behind the goal they were attacking.

'Our play was designed to hit continental teams with passes they weren't used to. We tried to hit long balls over their heads for forwards to run onto,' Cullis said.

Cullis made two tactical changes at half-time. 'Get the ball out to the wings quicker,' he told his players. 'Their full-backs are taking up poor positions and we must take advantage of this weakness.' Second, he ordered Bill Slater and Ron Flowers, the half-backs, to sort out Ferenc Puskas, the Honved playmaker. 'Stop trying to smother him once he's got the ball,' Cullis said. 'Let's cut off his supply of passes instead.'

'It was the greatest night in my club football career,' said Billy Wright, the Wolves captain.

Left Stan Cullis passes on some of his tactical knowledge to a number of the younger players at Wolverhampton Wanderers.

KEY MUSEUM ARTEFACT

When Stan Cullis took over as manager of Wolverhampton Wanderers, after the Second World War, he immediately became known as the Sergeant Major. His strict discipline was legendary. These aerobic clubs were used as part of his training regime for the players. The tactics that he employed for his side required that they should be at the peak of their fitness. Like many teams of the day, Wolves trained sparingly with a ball and based their sessions on stamina work. Cullis was famously quoted as saying 'I do not encourage my players to parade their ability'.

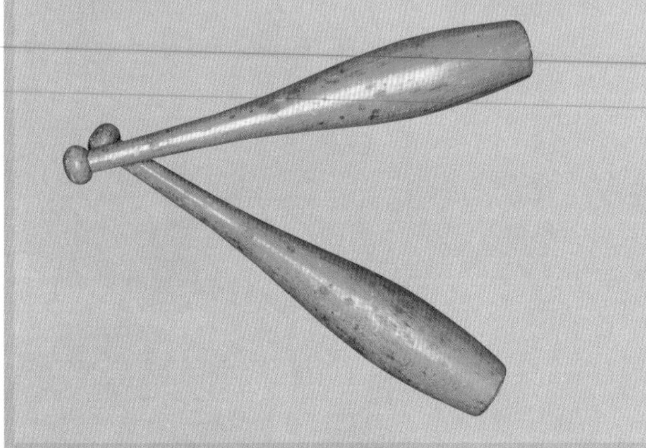

Above Football League Division One, Winner's Medal. This was awarded to Cullis in 1954, after Wolves had secured their first Championship under him.

Right A 1960 FA Cup poster. Cullis won his last trophy for Wolves in 1960 when they beat Blackburn Rovers 3–0 in the FA Cup final.

Stan Cullis took his players for training runs up a steep hill in the heathland of Cannock Chase near Wolverhampton. 'Heartbreak Hill,' Billy Wright called it. 'It was used as a barometer of our fitness,' the team captain said.

Pre-season training was punishing. Daily, the players tackled a commando-like assault course, followed by sprints up their least favourite incline. Other teams might match, perhaps even surpass, Wolves for skill, but very rarely did they equal their drive and energy.

Cullis adopted a scientific approach to training. Athletics coach Frank Morris, a former national running champion, supervised the sessions. Each player was

Other teams might match, perhaps even surpass, Wolves for skill, but very rarely did they equal their drive and energy.

given specific targets: 100 yards in 10.5 seconds, for example. Minimum times were set for other distances: 220 yards, 440 yards, 880 yards, 1 mile and 3 miles. All the players had to be able to jump a height of 4 feet 9 inches. Cullis gave his players 18 months to reach those standards. Anyone who complained was soon on his way out.

Weight training was also introduced into the fitness programme at Wolves before it was standard practice at many other clubs.

Cullis insisted that his team could play at a higher tempo than the opposition. In this way, opponents could be pressurised into making mistakes. In addition, his players were more agile and alert. 'They have to move quickly and think quickly,' he said.

Wolves played the standard tactics of the day but at a furious pace that often overwhelmed the opposition. Cullis also added a little brawn and matchless courage to the mix.

The system relied on hard-working wing-halves, speedy wingers, a brave, powerful centre-forward and

a skilful inside-forward, who could add a little subtlety and variety. Cullis found the right players to fill all the roles.

At the World Cup in Sweden in 1958, England played the Wolves half-back line of Eddie Clamp, Billy Wright and Bill Slater. The architect was Peter Broadbent, the one player Cullis allowed the freedom to dwell on the ball.

The wingers, Jimmy Mullen on the left and Johnny Hancocks on the right, hit cross-field passes to each other to unbalance defences, and Roy Swinbourne, the centre-forward and England international, was expected to get on the end of their crosses from the flanks.

Famously described as the 'Passionate Puritan' by the sportswriter John Arlott, Cullis watched games with the same intensity he expected his men to play them. Agitated, arms flying, he could not keep still. Those sitting next to him often ended up with a few bruises. 'He got carried away in games completely,' Billy Wright said.

Intensely loyal to the club, Cullis and the rest of football were shocked when Wolves sacked him in 1964, after several indifferent seasons. The decision shattered Cullis and shocked the rest of football. Years later, the club made some amends, naming the new north stand at Molineux in his honour.

In their heyday in the late 1950s, Wolves scored more than 100 goals in four successive seasons. Critics decried their flat-out, relentless, long-ball football as 'kick and rush'. Cullis did not care. 'They can say all they like. Our supporters get more entertainment from watching Wolves than any other two teams put together.'

TALKING POINT

Stan Cullis was the captain of England when he gave up the game for fear that one more blow to the head might cost him his life.

Cullis was prone to suffering severe concussion, requiring intensive medical care. The first of several hospital stays followed a collision with an Everton forward during the 1938–39 season. Knocked unconscious, Cullis was carried from the field on a stretcher.

In a war-time game, he was knocked out again when a fierce shot hit him full in the face. 'This time I was on the danger list in a Liverpool hospital for five days,' he recalled.

Doctors had been warning him for several years that another serious concussion could kill him. Finally, at the age of 30, he accepted their advice and retired. Even heading a heavy leather football could prove fatal, they told him.

His retirement was a huge loss to the national side. Cullis was the youngest-ever England captain following his appointment at the age of 22 in 1939. A combative centre-half whose career was badly interrupted by war, Cullis was praised by opponents for his calmness under pressure and passing ability. Tommy Lawton described him as the best centre-half in the game and Ferenc Puskas said he was 'a classical defender'.

Above This pennant was presented to Wolves, by Barcelona, when the two clubs met in the quarter-final of the European Cup in 1960.

Left This rattle was taken to the 1949 FA Cup final where Wolves beat Leicester City 3–1. It was the first major honour for Cullis as manager of the club.

BERT TRAUTMANN (1923–)

Player • Inducted 2005 • 1 FA Cup

The year 1956 was a memorable one for Bert Trautmann: soon after becoming the first goalkeeper to be named Footballer of the Year, he broke his neck in the FA Cup final. Unaware of the true nature of the injury, he played on in pain, winning his medal and the respect of the nation.

Barely a decade on since taking up the game as a novice, the former German soldier had established himself as the most highly rated goalkeeper in the country. 'I have never seen a goalkeeper to compare with Trautmann in the form he was in for two or three seasons before 1956,' Bobby Charlton wrote in 1967. 'The man was inhuman.'

Trautmann signed for Manchester City in 1949. In his prime, he was the only goalkeeper ever to figure in the team-talks given by Matt Busby, the Manchester United manager.

'Don't stop to think where you're going to hit it with Trautmann,' Busby implored his players. 'Hit it first and think afterwards. If you look up and work it out he will read your thoughts and stop it.'

Great saves 'were a normal part of his game', Charlton said. Saving penalties was a particular speciality: during his career he saved 60 per cent of those he faced.

Pressures off the field made his performances on it all the more remarkable. Trautmann had fought for four years against the Allies, making him an obvious target for anti-German hostility in the post-war era. Following his capture in 1945, he was interned at a prisoner-of-war camp in Lancashire, and it was here that he began playing football.

One game at Fulham in 1950 kicked off to the sound of incessant chants of 'Kraut' and 'Nazi' and ended with the applause of both his pponents and the crowd at Craven Cottage.

Years later, when asked to name two world-class goalkeepers, the great Russian 'keeper Lev Yashin rather immodestly named himself and 'the German boy who played in Manchester'.

KEY MATCH

Manchester City 3 Birmingham City 1, FA Cup, Wembley, 5 May 1956

Standing in his goal, unsteady on his feet and wincing from the pain, Bert Trautmann vaguely remembered hearing a large portion of the crowd singing a chorus of 'For He's a Jolly Good Fellow'.

It was an odd sentiment to direct at a goalkeeper who had just broken his neck. But then again, neither the crowd saluting his bravery from the terraces nor Trautmann himself had any idea of the seriousness of the situation at the time.

Trautmann had dived, head first, for the ball at the feet of Peter Murphy, an onrushing Birmingham City forward. There was heavy contact between boot and head. Trautmann made the save but then lay on the turf, stunned, for one minute.

There were 12 minutes left in a game Manchester City were winning 3–1. Their keeper, however, had also suffered concussion and barely knew where he was.

'How in this state, he contrived to make two further saves of the last-ditch variety, even he cannot explain,' H D Davies wrote later in the *Guardian*.

The first of those came seven minutes later, when the blond 'keeper was involved in a second collision. He collapsed again. Dazed, he got to his feet and played on, all the time rubbing his neck.

By making those saves, and risking a further blow to the head in the process, Trautmann had undoubtedly, if inadvertently, put his life at risk. At the final whistle he staggered, supported by a team-mate, to the Royal Box to collect his winner's medal.

Left Bert Trautmann poses for a photograph prior to the Manchester City, League Division One home game against Sunderland in 1955.

KEY MUSEUM ARTEFACT

This sculpture by Balter was a gift from the German FA to commemorate the international between Germany and England in Berlin on 14 May 1938. International gifts are exchanged at every game between two countries. A capacity crowd witnessed not only England's 6–3 victory but also the England team giving the Nazi salute. Trautmann's commitment to playing football in England after the war prevented him from playing for the German national team, as footballers plying their trade overseas were not selected at that time.

Above This pre-war painting, *The Goalkeeper* by J. Petts, perfectly illustrates the potential loneliness of a goalkeeper in front of massive crowds.

Above right Ball games have been played throughout the world for centuries. This engraving from 1630 by Matthaus Merian the Older depicts a game of pallone, an early German ball game.

Born in the north-German city of Bremen in 1923, Berndt Trautmann had a number of obstacles to overcome when he began his professional career in his mid-20s. Not only did he lack experience for his age, having played non-League football for St Helens Town, but he also had to win over team-mates and supporters given his war-time service in the German army.

Eric Westwood, the Manchester City captain and a survivor of the Normandy beach landings, publicly welcomed Trautmann in a prepared speech written by the club. Privately, however, Westwood was said to have had reservations, as did the other managers who hesitated to sign Trautmann for fear of an anti-German backlash. They had all underestimated his ability, strength of character and personal appeal. It took time, but he eventually gained acceptance in England, as the Football League officially confirmed by selecting him as a foreigner to play for their representative side.

It was a tough baptism at Maine Road, on and off the field: Manchester City were relegated in the 1949–50 season, conceding 68 goals in their 42 games. Gradually, though, Trautmann and Manchester City turned things round. Promoted at their first attempt, Trautmann then played a crucial role in keeping the club up in each of the following three seasons.

Off the field, he worked diligently on behalf of his club and adopted city, escorting visiting German trade delegations and acting as an interpreter for visiting teams and officials. In addition, Trautmann made a point of helping Jewish youth clubs.

> **“At the official Cup final banquet, I could hardly move my neck because of the pain”** – *Bert Trautmann*

He still received hate mail on occasion; but after making public the fact, he received another flood of letters, this time in his favour.

Trautmann did not apologise for his nationality, nor flinch when subjected to abuse. His outstanding ability obviously helped his cause. By the time Manchester City began two successive Cup runs to the final at Wembley, Trautmann was undoubtedly the team's star and most popular player.

Bert Trautmann left the field at the end of the FA Cup final in 1956 rubbing his neck. 'At the official banquet I could hardly move my head because of the pain,' Trautmann recalled. 'I did not let that interfere with my enjoyment, mind you.'

After the goalmouth collision, he had been treated with a sponge and cold water. Forty-eight hours later, Trautmann lay in a bed in Manchester Royal Infirmary. The diagnosis – a fractured bone in his neck - was made public on Wednesday, sparking another wave of public sympathy and support.

Trautmann was also a central figure for a ten-man Manchester City 12 months earlier. His saves prevented Newcastle United from adding to their 3–1 winning margin in the FA Cup final of 1955 following an injury to Jimmy Meadows, the City right-back.

His FA Cup winner's medal from 1956 was the only major honour Trautmann won in the game; he never played for West Germany because of a rule barring individuals playing for overseas clubs.

When Trautmann retired in 1964, three years after the abolition of the maximum wage, he was the longest-serving player on the books at Maine Road. 'I'm not big-headed but I was still the best player and they offered me £35, knowing they had given two other players £85 and £90 a week,' he recalled. 'I probably could have carried on another two years, but I was so disappointed with their wage offer.'

The Manchester City supporters were more generous: a crowd of 47,000 turned up for his testimonial in 1964. No matter his nationality, Trautmann

TALKING POINT

Bert Trautmann made good use of his experience as a boy growing up in Germany to change the way goalkeepers played the game.

Goalkeepers had long considered themselves as a last line of defence: as shot-stopper and the man who caught crosses. Trautmann added a new dimension. Once he had possession he also thought of himself as the team's first attacker.

Rather than just lob the ball to the nearest player in a blue shirt or boot it hopefully down field, he utilised skills he developed in his youth as a handball player to initiate a sharp counter-attack.

'His push-throw could send the ball 40 yards to great effect,' Bobby Charlton wrote in 1967. 'Most 'keepers have now copied this technique.'

Trautmann said: 'That was my handball experience. After making a save I moved the ball quickly. People were running into space and I delivered the ball with my hand, eliminating three, four or five opponents.'

His ability to deliver the ball quickly and accurately was a vital element of the tactics employed by Manchester City in the mid-1950s.

After Hungary thrashed England 6–3 at Wembley in 1953, Manchester City copied their tactics, converting Don Revie to a deep-lying centre-forward. Trautmann also had a key role in the system labelled the 'Revie Plan' by the newspapers.

'I played a big part in all this, because after having saved a shot or caught a cross, the ball was always on its way quickly,' Trautmann said.

Above Bert Trautmann saves spectacularly during a League Division One game against Sunderland in 1955.

Right Tipp-Kick game, 1930s. A young Bert Trautmann may well have been familiar with this 1930s' German Tipp-Kick football game. Such games were hugely popular throughout Europe in the 1930s, 40s and 50s.

MATT BUSBY (1909–1994)

Manager • Inducted 2002 •1 European Cup • 5 Division One Championships • 2 FA Cups

Matt Busby, the visionary, charismatic manager who almost lost his life in the cause of Manchester United, created an aura of style and quality around Old Trafford.

He created two truly great sides in more than two decades as manager: the 'Busby' Babes of the mid-1950s, and the European Cup-winning side of the 1960s, the celebrated team of Bobby Charlton, Denis Law, and George Best.

Busby outlined his philosophy of the game in a speech delivered in 1967 when he was made a Freeman of the City of Manchester:

'There is nothing wrong with trying to win, so long as you don't set the prize above the game,' he told the audience. 'There is no dishonour in defeat, so long as you play to the limit of your strength and skill.'

'What matters above all is that the game should be played in the right spirit, with the utmost resource of skill and courage, with fair play and no favour, with every man playing as a member of the team, the result accepted without bitterness or conceit.'

Nobby Stiles, the Manchester United and England midfield player, said. 'Matt urged us to give expression to all our talent. Regimenting isn't coaching; inspiring is coaching, he used to say.'

'You never knew what was going to happen,' Bobby Charlton said, referring to games in the mid-1960s. 'We could be lousy, but the crowds flocked in, week after week, because they were frightened they might miss the game when everything just exploded: when George dribbled past all the defenders, when Denis scored his goals, and I hit one, perhaps, from outside the box. It was a magical period.'

KEY MATCH

Benfica 1 Manchester United 4, European Cup final, Wembley Stadium, 29 May 1968

At the sound of the final whistle, Matt Busby walked slowly on to the pitch. After embracing Eusebio, he hugged Bobby Charlton and Bill Foulkes, the two players who had played in all four of Manchester United's European Cup campaigns.

The two survivors of the Munich air disaster tried to push Busby up the steps at Wembley. They wanted the manager to enjoy the acclaim of the Manchester United fans: Busby had achieved his tribute to the eight players who perished in the crash.

Busby declined their invitation. Instead, he walked quietly off the pitch. The tears came in private in the dressing room, followed by the celebrations, and a chorus of the song 'What a Wonderful World'.

Ten years earlier, in the aftermath of the crash, Busby had needed walking sticks to get to his seat at Wembley. In 1958, his patched-up team lost in the FA Cup final.

'Munich survivors Jackie Blanchflower and Johnny Berry attended our victory banquet,' Busby recalled. 'They provided an awful reminder of our perilous journey up the staircase to the sky,' as he described the club's pursuit of the European Cup.

Busby had remained true to his belief in the value of nurturing young talent. 'Eight of the side that beat Benfica were developed by the club,' he said.

One of them, John Aston, the United winger, was told beforehand to knock the ball past his marker. 'Just run at him,' Busby said. On a scouting mission he had noted that the Benfica full-back was slow on the turn. Aston was rated Man of the Match.

Left Matt Busby offers words of encouragement to Manchester United players Bill Foulkes (5) and Bobby Charlton (9) before the start of extra time in the European Cup final at Wembley on 29 May 1968.

KEY MUSEUM ARTEFACT

Technological developments in the printing industry led to more colourful magazines during the later years of the 1950s. *The United Story* combined both articles and pictures to tell the tale of Manchester United's precocious young side. Nicknamed the 'Busby Babes', after their manager, the team had won the Division One title in 1956. They repeated their success in 1957, and also progressed to the FA Cup final. This 1957 edition was produced in preparation for a possible League and Cup Double. One particular article describes the United side as the 'team of the century'.

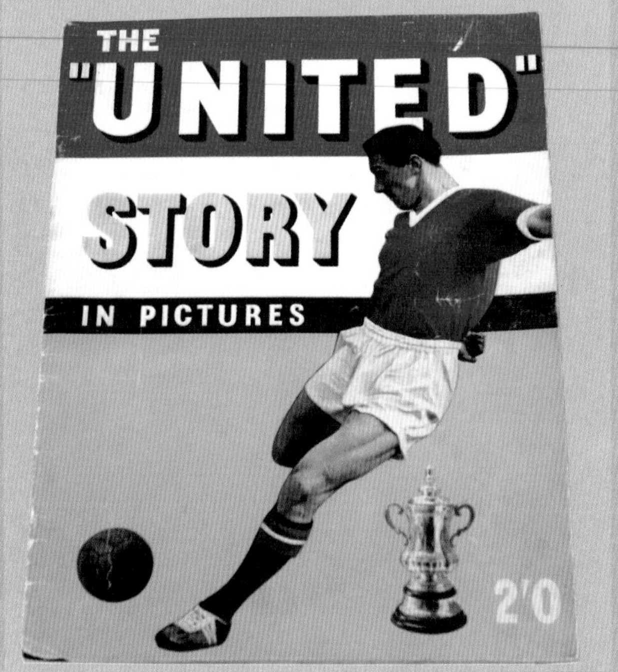

Manchester United's victory over Blackpool in the FA Cup Final of 1948 was the first major honour won by the club in 37 years, since the First Division championship success of 1910–11. Busby, a former Manchester City and Liverpool player, had been appointed manager at Old Trafford in 1945, at the age of 35.

He was one of the first 'tracksuit' managers and he broke with precedent again by insisting on absolute control of all team affairs. 'Matt will seek the board's advice, ponder over it and then go away and do precisely what he wants to,' Harold Hardman, the club chairman, said years later.

The situation in 1945 appeared desperate. The club had an overdraft of £15,000, the equivalent of the then record transfer fee, Old Trafford was bomb-damaged, forcing the team to play temporarily at Maine Road and the only place for the players to train was the car park.

Busby approached the challenge with enthusiasm and plenty of innovative ideas. 'I wanted a different kind of football club from what was normal at the time,' he recalled. 'There wasn't a human approach. I wanted to manage a team the way I thought the players wanted it.

'In those days the atmosphere in clubs was bad. The first team would hardly recognize the lads underneath. The manager sat at his desk and you saw him once a week.'

As a priority, Busby worked on another idea new to football: to find, recruit and then train the best young players in the country as a means of building a team.

During the 1950s Matt Busby scoured Britain for the best schoolboy talent. His network of scouts found Duncan Edwards in Dudley, under the noses of Wolverhampton Wanderers, while Bobby Charlton was a schoolboy star in the north east, who opted for the United in Manchester rather than Newcastle. As a result, Manchester United won the newly created FA Youth Cup five seasons in succession

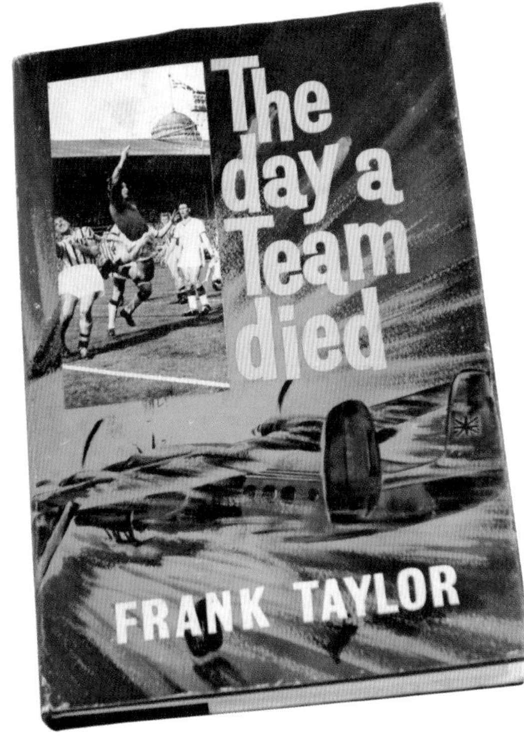

Above right This Umbro shirt was endorsed by Matt Busby in the 1950s. The colour of the shirt does not relate to Manchester United's club strip. It is unlikely, nowadays, that any manager would successfully endorse a generic kit.

Right After the Munich air crash in 1958, in which eight United players lost their lives, many books, such as this, were published detailing the team's meteoric rise to success.

To Bert
all good wishes
Matt Busby

ASSOCIATION OF FORMER MANCHESTER UNITED PLAYERS

Sir Matt Busby C.B.E., K.C.S.G.
80th BIRTHDAY CELEBRATION

Friday, 2nd June 1989

Manchester United Executive Suite
Old Trafford
Manchester

between 1953 and 1957. The legend of the 'Busby Babes' had been born.

In 1951–52, the club won the championship with an ageing side. Busby then made another bold decision: he broke up a successful, experienced, winning side to make way for youth. By the middle of the decade, the average age of the team was 22. Winners of successive titles in 1955–56 and 1956–57, Manchester United also were the first English club to compete in Europe. The club was on the rise.

When eight players, including Edwards, died in the Munich crash in February 1958, the team was chasing a triple: League, FA Cup and European Cup. Busby was the only passenger facing the front of the plane at the time of impact who survived. His injuries, however, were terrible. 'I wanted to die,' he recalled. 'Lung punctures, broken-bone manipulation, torn-flesh repairs without anaesthetics were a regular drill of undiminished horror.'

Seriously weakened, it was several years before Busby could concentrate all his energy on the task of rebuilding the club. Denis Law, Pat Crerand and Alex Stepney were bought, George Best was unearthed, and Bobby Charlton, one of the surviving 'Babes', was made the hub of the team. But by the mid 1960s Manchester United were finally ready for another crack at the European Cup.

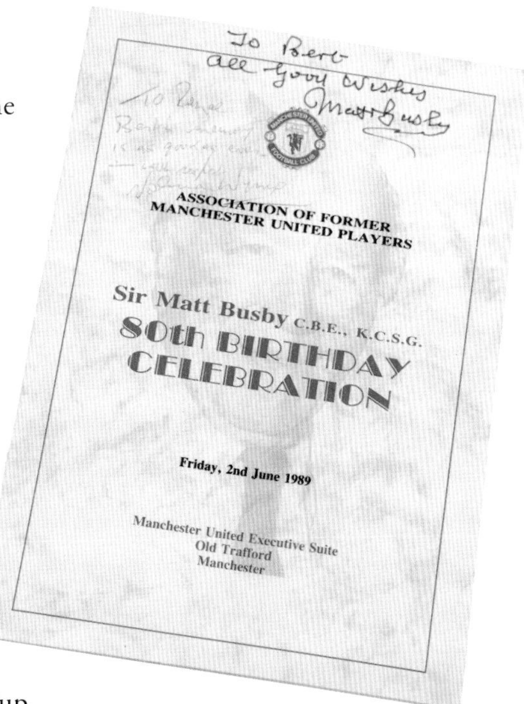

TALKING POINT

Matt Busby always argued that 'challenges should be met, not avoided', and he followed his own advice in persuading Manchester United to become the first English club to compete in the European Cup.

The Manchester United board had been strongly advised by the Football League against entering the competition, then in its second season. The club was reminded that its first duty was to the League, and then warned of the adverse consequences if this 'gimmick' caused any disruption to Division One fixtures.

'Matt was eager to enter,' said Stanley Rous, the Secretary of the Football Association at the time. 'He had been to Europe and came back telling everyone that we had to get involved or fall behind. He deserves a lot of credit for his vision.'

Chelsea had been eligible to enter the previous season but the club had agreed with the League's argument that domestic football must be paramount.

After seeking the advice of Rous, Busby successfully argued that the money raised could be spent on installing floodlights at Old Trafford and that football was increasingly an international game.

Below Matt Busby with Manchester United players (left to right) Tommy Taylor, Denis Viollet and David Pegg.

Above left Sir Matt Busby special commemorative birthday programme from 1989. Busby remained at Old Trafford as a director and as club president until his death in 1994.

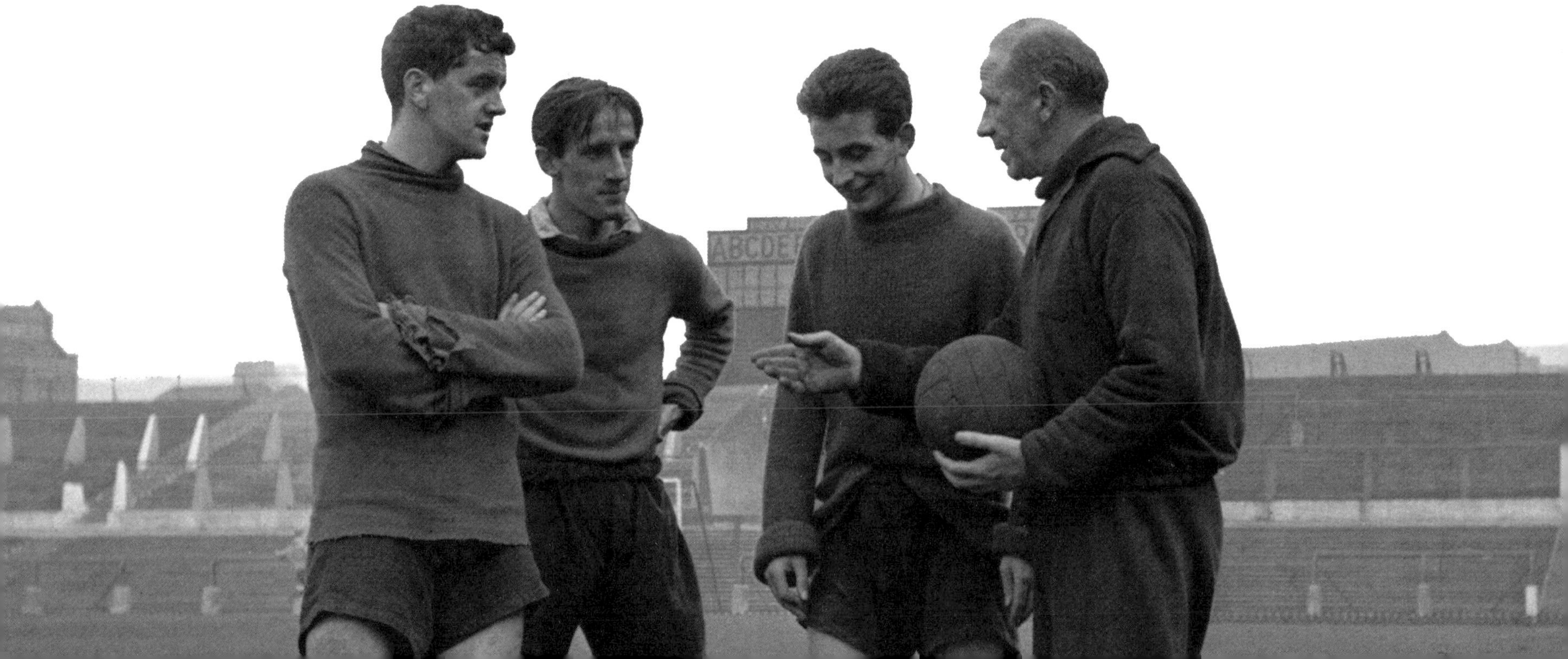

JOHN CHARLES (1931–2004)

Player • 2002 • 38 Caps

The best foreign footballer to play in *Serie A*, as voted for in a poll in the Italian media, was not Michel Platini, Ruud Gullit or even Diego Maradona; it was a proud Welshman from Swansea: John Charles.

The most valuable and versatile footballer of his era, Charles was idolised by the supporters of Juventus during his five-year stint in Turin between 1957 and 1962.

Equally effective in defence or attack, Charles was rated the best centre-half in Europe by both Denis Law and Tom Finney. 'Mind you,' Law said, 'when he plays up front, he's also one of the top three centre-forwards I've ever seen.'

Juventus paid Leeds United a world record fee of £65,000 for the then 25-year-old Charles. They had effectively bought two players in one. Twice he was voted Footballer of the Year in Italy. 'John is a mythological character in Italy,' Bruno Garzena, a Juventus team-mate said. 'He wasn't a normal footballer; he was an extraordinary one. Even now, he is still considered a god in Turin.'

In his first season in Italy, Charles led Juventus to the championship, scoring 28 goals in 34 games, making him the leading goalscorer in the top division. Over the next four seasons, Juventus added two more League titles and two Italian Cups. In total he scored 93 goals in 150 League games.

John Charles died of cancer and was buried in Leeds. On his last visit to Turin, he made an emotional return to Juventus, four decades after his last game for the club. As he walked round the ground, with tears in his eyes and a black and white scarf around his neck, 40,000 fans chanted his name.

KEY MATCH

Wales 2 Hungary 1, World Cup group game, Solna, Sweden, 17 June 1958

John Charles needed all his renowned self-discipline when he took a battering for the cause as Wales achieved their finest moment in international football by qualifying for the quarter-finals of the World Cup.

Released at the last moment for the tournament in Sweden by his Italian club Juventus, Charles attracted the attention of the Hungary defenders.

'John had scored with a header in an earlier pool game and the Hungarians had clearly prepared their tactics with him in mind. During the game he was subjected to some savage treatment by the Hungarians,' said Ivor Allchurch, the Wales inside-forward. By half-time Charles had been virtually kicked out of the game.

The overwhelming favourites for this game and World Cup finalists four years earlier in Switzerland, Hungary were so focused on the threat posed by Charles that they found themselves surprised by the class of Allchurch and the pace and skill of the Spurs wingers Cliff Jones and Terry Medwin.

Ten minutes into the second half, Allchurch equalised with a volley. Then Grosics made a mess of a clearance, allowing Medwin a simple goal. 'We refused to lie down,' said Allchurch. 'John was magnificent in the example he set.'

To put the result into context: Wales had achieved a feat beyond England, whose four encounters with Hungary between 1953 and 1962 all ended in defeat.

Left The Hungarian goalkeeper, Gyula Grosics, jumps for the ball with John Charles, playing for Wales, during their World Cup group game in Sweden on 17 June 1958.

KEY MUSEUM ARTEFACT

John Charles joined Juventus in 1957, after scoring 150 goals in 297 League appearances for Leeds United. He had starred for the club in both Divisions One and Two. Juventus paid Leeds £65,000 to take him to Turin. This Juventus shirt features the 'Scudetto' badge worn by the Italian League Champions. Even in hot, humid countries shirts were made from heavy, woollen materials. Originally, Juventus wore pink shirts but changed to black and white after the wrong shipment of shirts was delivered to the club from their suppliers in England.

John Charles posed a dilemma for managers. They had to choose where to play him: centre-forward or centre-half.

His record in attack for Leeds United is impressive: Charles scored 164 goals in 318 games, yet it was not until his fifth season at the club that he switched to centre-forward from centre-half. In 1956–57, in only his second season up front, he scored 38 goals, making him the leading goalscorer in Division One and the major Italian clubs took note.

After they had signed him, Juventus adopted their tactics to make best use of his versatility. Charles often played in both attack and defence in the same match. Once Juventus went ahead – and Charles was often the goalscorer – he would drop back to help protect the lead.

Juventus wanted him to extend his stay in Italy beyond five years. 'I could have stayed, playing centre-half, which is the easiest job in football,' Charles said. 'But I didn't want to overstay my welcome.'

Charles signed as a professional at the age of 17. He owed much of his versatility as a footballer to his early education at Elland Road. Major Frank

> **"Easily the best centre-half I have ever seen."** – *Tom Finney*

Buckley, the manager, played him at left-half, right-back, centre-half, inside-forward and, finally, centre-forward. The Major also insisted that all players, Charles included, were two-footed.

Short of money, Leeds refused to release Charles to a rival English club when they were forced to sell him in 1957. He did not agitate for a transfer. 'Leeds was my team,' Charles said. 'I loved the place.'

John Charles was renowned for his immense physical strength and exemplary behaviour. He was nicknamed 'The Gentle Giant' for good reason.

Above John Charles scores from close range for Leeds United in the 1957 Division One clash against Tottenham Hotspur at White Hart Lane. This picture is taken from his book, *King of Soccer*.

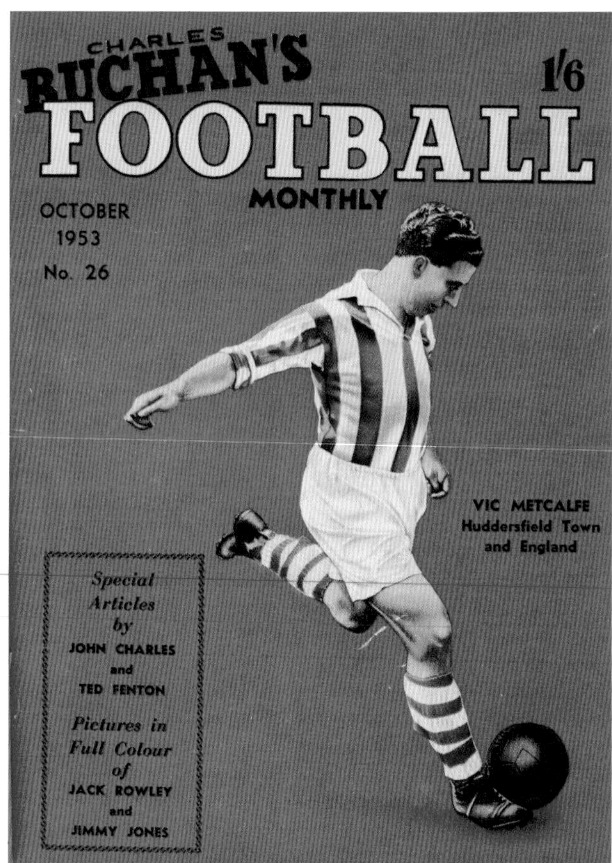

Above right A 1953 edition of *Charles Buchan's Football Monthly*. By the age of 21, Charles was regularly contributing to the most famous football annuals of the day.

'You had no fear of playing against him because you knew that it was going to be a fair game,' Denis Law recalled. 'Whoever came out on top, well, that was it. It was fair.' Jack Charlton said: 'John never, ever did anything nasty.'

In his Leeds days, when an opposition centre-forward broke Jack Charlton's nose in an aerial challenge, Charles dropped back to centre-half as cover. 'The same forward just bounced off John when they went up for a header,' Norman Hunter, a team-mate that day, recalled. Bruno Garzena was taken aback when 'this giant of a man' walked into the dressing room at Juventus. 'A defender would grab his shirt,' he recalled, '[and] John would just drag him along like a tow-truck.'

Even rival Torino fans liked him for his character and sportsmanship. 'In a derby match I bumped into a fellow and hurt him accidentally,' Charles said. 'I was on my way to goal. I stopped and kicked the ball out so he could get treatment.'

> **"You had no fear of playing against him because you knew that it was going to be a fair game."** – *Denis Law*

Gordon Banks never forgot their first meeting. Chesterfield Reserves were playing Leeds. Banks had only a handful of games behind him; Charles was returning from injury. 'He walked up to me, and he said, "Now, don't worry, son. You do your best our here today. I won't hurt you."

'As a 16-year-old I would have been a pushover for him, but he played it fair and he played it straight.'

TALKING POINT

John Charles wrote a guide for British footballers on how to survive as a foreign 'import' in Italian football, but many of the players who followed in his footsteps ignored his advice.

'In England, footballers were ordinary working men; in Italy they're royalty,' he said. 'I'd been a half-pint-of-shandy man; now I was drinking the finest red wines and eating pasta, which I'd never tasted before.'

It was a culture shock. The football was much more defensive, the rewards for winning were much higher, and discipline was stricter. Italian clubs fined players heavily for breaking rules and demanded more of their time.

On the strength of his own experience, Charles advised ex-pat British players who came to Italy to 'toe the line'. Protesting about the defensive style of the football and the restrictive club rules, as Jimmy Greaves and Denis Law did during their brief stint in Italy, was a waste of energy, he said.

'Playing in Italy is just like going into one of the Services. If you try to kick against everything then you are in for a miserable time. You must tell yourself you are getting well paid and put up with the strictness and soul-destroying defensive football. Then you will have a fine time.'

Above Hereford pennant, 1980s. Charles joined Southern League Hereford United in 1966. He took over as player/manager in December 1967. Although he left the club in 1971, many of his players were in the team that famously defeated Newcastle United in an FA Cup third round replay in 1972.

Left The book, *King of Soccer* by John Charles.

DUNCAN EDWARDS (1936–1958)

Player • Inducted 2002 • 18 Caps • 2 Division One Championships

Duncan Edwards was the youngest player to represent England. Stanley Matthews, the oldest man to win a cap, described the 'Busby Babe' as the most complete footballer of the era.

'You could play him anywhere and he would slot into that position as if he'd been playing there season after season,' Matthews wrote. 'When the going gets rough, Duncan is like a rock in a raging sea.'

A month before Edwards died, at the age of 21, from injuries sustained in the Munich air crash of February 1958, Matt Busby, the Manchester United manager, described him as 'the best all-round player in Britain, if not the world'.

'When he first came to Old Trafford I tried to find fault with Duncan,' Busby recalled in 1974, 'but I couldn't find one. He was never really a boy; in football terms, he was always a man.' At 16, Edwards was six feet tall and weighed more than 13 stone.

His England debut came at the age of 18 years and 183 days against Scotland in 1955. He had already played for the Under-23s at the age of 16, by which time he'd already been a Manchester United regular for a year.

Billy Wright was taken aback at the maturity Edwards displayed on his debut against Scotland. Afterwards, Walter Winterbottom, the England manager, told his captain that day, 'Billy, I think we've uncovered a gem.'

Edwards' favourite position was left-half, from where he could both attack and defend. Exceptionally versatile, he also played at inside-forward for England and both centre-forward and centre-half for Manchester United.

At the time of his death he had already won nine England schoolboy caps, three FA Youth Cup medals, two Division One championship medals, an FA Cup loser's medal, and 18 full caps. It was taken as read that he would lead England into the next decade and possibly beyond. 'I am convinced that Duncan would have been a fixture in the England team well into the 1970s,' Busby said. 'Whatever was needed in a player, he had it.'

KEY MATCH

West Germany 1 England 3, International Friendly, Berlin, 26 May 1956

The German newspapers nicknamed Duncan Edwards 'Boom Boom' after watching his barnstorming display – and memorable individual goal – against the World Cup holders. 'He has a Big Bertha shot in his boots,' the papers said.

'The name of Duncan Edwards was on the lips of everybody who saw this match. He was phenomenal,' Billy Wright said. 'There have been few individual performances to match what he produced in Germany. He tackled like a lion, attacked at every opportunity and topped it all off with a cracking goal.

'Duncan was still only 20, and he was already a world-class player. We had beaten the world champions in their own backyard,' Wright said.

England were under pressure as Edwards brought the ball out of defence. His surging run took him past several defenders. He then unleashed a shot from 25 yards, some distance out, given the heavier footballs of the day.

Edwards perfected his shooting during long hours of practice at Old Trafford, where he marked a target on a whitewashed wall. For hour after hour, he would relentlessly strike the ball at the same spot, varying the pace but always seeking to maintain accuracy.

Hugo Meisl, the manager of Austria, watched Edwards in action against West Germany. 'Duncan could win a match alone, and won many games that way,' he said.

Left Duncan Edwards trains at Old Trafford on 5 January 1954 after being selected to play for England's Under 23 team at the age of just 17.

KEY MUSEUM ARTEFACT

The 'Rock and Roll' era of the 1950s was a time when the youth of the country was finding a voice. The Busby Babes were not only a great side but were also particularly media-friendly. Manchester United's youthful stars with their good looks and slicked-back hair appeared to be made for colourful publications such as this *Red Devils* magazine of 1957. The cover features Duncan Edwards, Mark Jones, Roger Byrne and David Pegg, all of whom lost their lives a year later in the Munich air crash.

Duncan Edwards died in a Munich hospital in the early hours of 21 February 1958. He fought for life for 15 days with the same tenacity with which he played his football. Edwards suffered massive internal injuries in the crash. The doctors flew a kidney machine from Stuttgart, but to no avail. His body was slowly poisoned.

So badly broken was his thigh, it is unlikely that he could have played again. Frank Taylor, an injured journalist, recalled the words of one of Edwards' closest friends: 'Maybe it was better this way. The doctor said, had he lived, he might have had to spend the rest of his life in a wheelchair. Duncan couldn't have stood that.'

At the time of his death he had already won nine England schoolboy caps, three FA Youth Cup medals, two Division One championship medals, an FA Cup loser's medal, and 18 full caps.

Edwards lived for football. As a first-team player he often asked to play in the youth team with his mates. 'Duncan would have played every day of the week if he could,' Jimmy Murphy, the Manchester United assistant manager, said. His appetite for the fray was unquenchable. In 1956–57, Edwards played 95 games for his club, the Army and England.

Lying in hospital, he had occasional bursts of consciousness, during which he would shout for a gold watch presented to him by Real Madrid. It was found in the wreckage and strapped to his wrist. A calm then befell him.

At other times he would mutter, semi-conscious, to Murphy about the next game on the fixture list. 'What time is the kick-off against Wolves, Jimmy?' he kept on saying. 'I mustn't miss that one.'

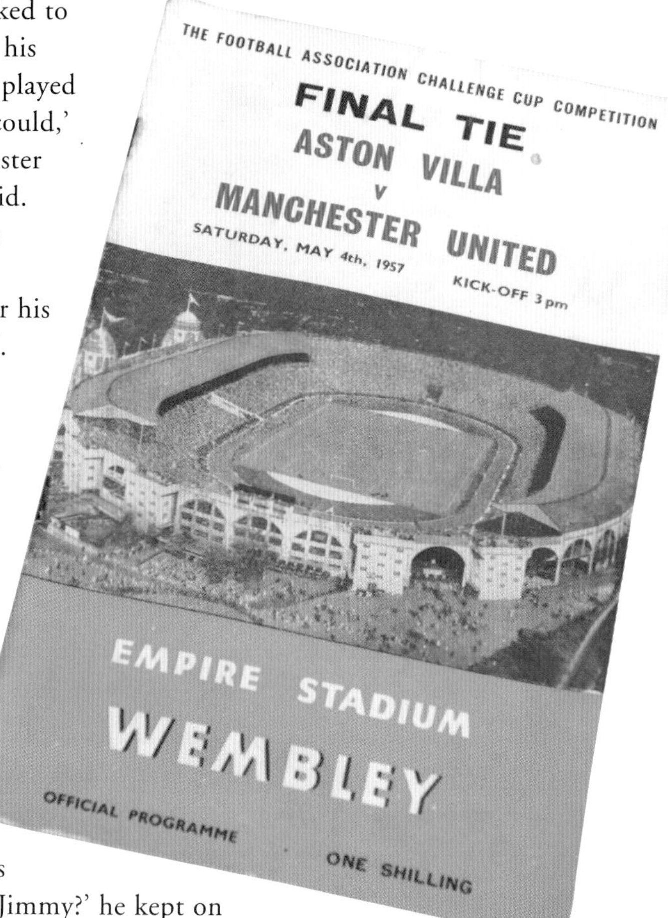

Right The official programme from the 1957 FA Cup Final. Manchester United's patched-up side somehow made it to the final before losing to Bolton Wanderers.

According to Bobby Charlton, Duncan Edwards was 'simply the greatest footballer of all time'. But Charlton, a fellow 'Busby Babe', also spoke of his team-mate as 'my great friend'.

As young men they were often inseparable and, at the age of 18, Charlton did his National Service with Edwards. As part of their duties, they shifted ammunition about. 'It was great for our fitness,' Charlton recalled.

The two lads also shared the privations of life on the staff at Old Trafford and in digs. 'Money was tight with me,' Charlton said, 'Once, Duncan gave me a new shirt which he said was too small for him. I don't think it was really, but it was a very welcome addition to my sparse wardrobe.'

Edwards loved to play practical jokes, even on the senior England players. 'A leg-pulling rascal off the pitch, but everyone loved him.' Billy Wright said. 'Duncan always had this infectious boyish enthusiasm as he ran down the tunnel before games.'

TALKING POINT

Jimmy Murphy, the assistant to Matt Busby, had a simple and winning tactic when he took charge of the Manchester United youth team. Before games he would give his usual team-talk: 'Give the ball to Duncan,' he told the other players.

Manchester United were about to play an FA Youth Cup tie against Chelsea at Stamford Bridge and Murphy decided it was time for a change.

Murphy feared that the players habit of looking first to Edwards had become too ingrained. 'Remember, lads, this is a team game,' he told them. 'Don't automatically pass it to Duncan. Try to express yourselves a bit. Go for another option if it's on.'

At half-time, the United players came trooping back into the dressing room. They were losing 1–0, a rare experience for a club that dominated the competition during the mid 1950s. Murphy spoke again: 'Right, lads, remember what I told you before the game. Well, forget that. When you get the ball, give it to Duncan.'

The players followed Murphy's instructions. Manchester United won 2–1, with Edwards scoring both of the goals.

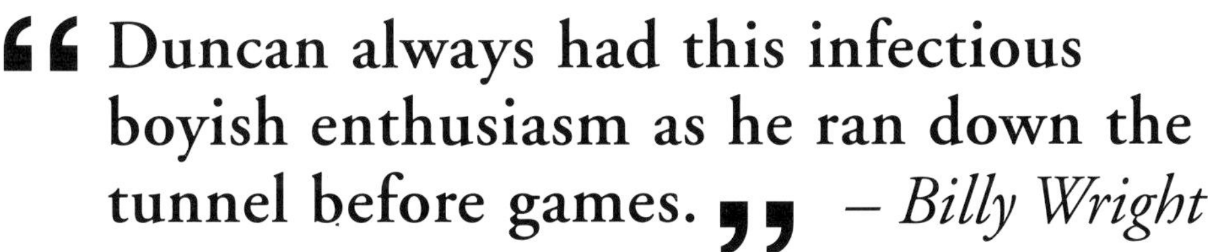

"Duncan always had this infectious boyish enthusiasm as he ran down the tunnel before games." – *Billy Wright*

At the funeral, 5,000 people stood outside the church in his native Dudley. Three years later St Francis's Church was full again for the dedication of a stained glass memorial depicting him in action as a player. All the survivors of the crash attended the service, conducted by the Bishop of Worcester.

In 1993, 35 years after Edwards' death, his then 83-year-old mother, Anne, said, 'People still haven't forgotten. Strangers come up and tell me: "He were a real good 'un was your Duncan."'

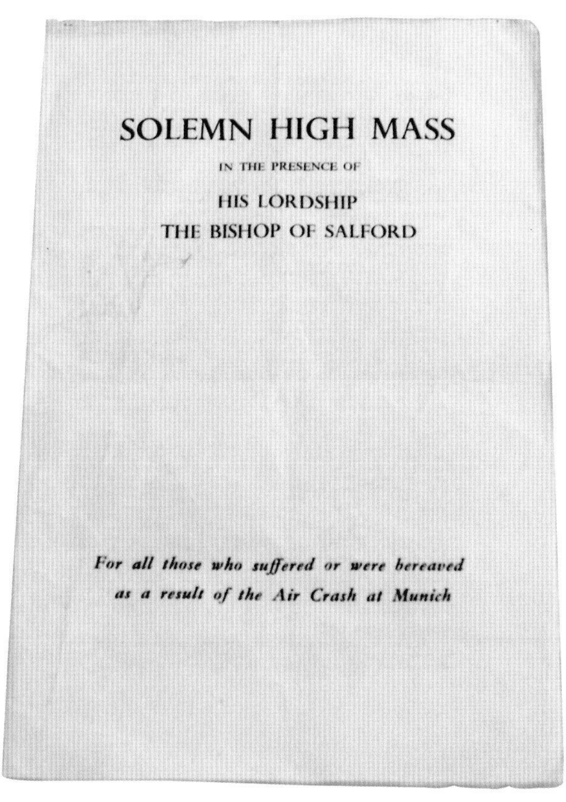

SOLEMN HIGH MASS

IN THE PRESENCE OF

HIS LORDSHIP

THE BISHOP OF SALFORD

For all those who suffered or were bereaved as a result of the Air Crash at Munich

Above A football signed by the Manchester United side of 1957.

Right A memorial programme produced after the Munich air disaster.

BILL NICHOLSON (1919–2004)

Manager • Inducted 2003 • 1 Division One Championship • 3 FA Cups
1 UEFA Cup • 1 European Cup Winners' Cup • 2 League Cups

Bill Nicholson overcame the disappointment of scoring with his first touch in international football and then never playing for England again to achieve glory as the manager of Tottenham Hotspur.

In his first three years as manager, Nicholson introduced new methods in training, devised innovative tactics and invested shrewdly in the transfer market to create the great Double-winning side of 1960–61.

The 'Super Spurs' team reached its zenith in the autumn of 1960 during a run of 11 successive wins at the start of the season, according to Danny Blanchflower, the team captain.

Following the 6–2 win over Aston Villa on 24 September, one newspaper wrote of 'the majesty and rich theatre of their enchanting brand of football'.

The following week, Wolverhampton Wanderers, the FA Cup winners and Division One runners-up the previous season, were thrashed 4–0 at Molineux. 'Spurs are the finest English club team I've ever seen,' Stan Cullis, the Wolves manager, said afterwards.

Tottenham amassed a record-equalling 66 points in 1960–61, and more than two million people went through turnstiles across the country to watch them do it.

In Nicholson's first season in charge, Spurs finished 18th, but over the next 13 years the club only once finished outside the top ten in Division One.

As a player, Nicholson won a championship medal with Tottenham in 1950–51. A dynamic, tireless right-half, he made his debut for England against Portugal in 1951. It was to be his only cap; he had the misfortune of being reserve to the remarkably consistent Billy Wright.

Summing up his philosophy, Nicholson said: 'It is better to fail aiming high than to succeed aiming low.'

KEY MATCH

Tottenham Hotspur 2 Leicester City 0, FA Cup final, Wembley, 6 May 1961

The disappointed Leicester City players paid tribute to the great Spurs side built by Bill Nicholson by forming a guard of honour outside the players' tunnel at the end of the game.

The Tottenham players and their gruff, avuncular manager earned widespread praise after their victory at Wembley. After the game, Matt Gillies, the Leicester manager, promised Nicholson his support when Spurs played in the European Cup the following season. 'You are worthy of the Double,' he said.

Nicholson had worked tirelessly to prepare his players for the final. Tottenham were the overwhelming favourites, and the manager knew that the pressure of expectation might prove a handicap.

In a bid to keep the players relaxed, Nicholson decided against taking the squad away during the week; he wanted them at home, following their normal routine. On Friday night, they all went to the cinema to watch the war film *The Guns of Navarone*.

On the day itself, Dave Mackay thought his colleagues were unusually quiet in the dressing room. 'True to form, Bill had a word with each of us. He then suggested, so that we might get accustomed to the unique Wembley atmosphere, that we went out again to inspect the pitch and get a feel for the pace of the ball,' Mackay said. 'Our manager had again shown a thoroughness in his approach which has played a major part in our success.'

Left Bill Nicholson celebrates a 2–1 victory over Sheffield Wednesday at White Hart Lane on 17 April 1961. The win secured the Division One Championship for Spurs.

KEY MUSEUM ARTEFACT

Thanks to the increasing popularity of television the wonderful achievements of Bill Nicholson's Spurs sides were brought to a much wider audience. Although 10 million viewers tuned in to see the Coronation Cup final of 1953, between Blackpool and Bolton Wanderers, it was during the 1960s that televisions, such as this 1950s and 60s EKCO model, became affordable for the masses. In 1964, the football highlights programme *Match of the Day* was launched on BBC2. Hosted by Kenneth Wolstenholme, the show helped to create the 'armchair' football fan.

The 'Super Spurs' team reached its zenith in the autumn of 1960 during a run of 11 successive wins at the start of the season.

Above Before the invention of television, players only appeared in pictures. This 1907 cartoon of Tottenham's Herbert (Bert) Middlemiss was produced by the cartoonist RIP. The original drawing was possibly used for a cigarette card.

Above right League ladders produced for the comic *Valiant* in 1962.

It took Bill Nicholson three years to win the Double, but his ambition to dominate English football during the 1960s was frustrated in cruel and tragic circumstances. By the middle of the decade, the Tottenham half-back line, the creative and physical engine room of the team, had been struck down by death, injury and retirement.

'The heart was ripped out of Spurs in a painful way,' Jimmy Greaves recalled, 'a black cloud of despondency enveloped the club.'

In July 1964, John White, the Scotland international who was described by Greaves as 'the eyes of the side, a player who dismantled teams with passes no one else could see', died after being struck by lightning while playing golf.

Then, over a period of nine months from December 1963, Dave Mackay, the combative left-half, had already been sidelined after breaking his leg in December 1963. In his comeback match, he suffered another fracture. 'Dave was sidelined for more than a season,' Jimmy Greaves said. 'The heart of the team went missing as a result.

In April 1964 Spurs suffered another setback when Danny Blanchflower announced his retirement. At the age of 38, it was finally the end of the road for the 'captain and brains of the team', as Greaves described him. And the following season, in another round of heavy blows, Greaves himself succumbed to a bout of hepatitis, while Maurice Norman, the centre-half, had his career ended by a double fracture of his leg.

'Bill did extremely well to deal with all the setbacks,' Greaves said. 'We still had some memorable moments later on, but we never touched the peaks of the side of the early sixties.'

Bill Nicholson was the leading figure in the vanguard of young managers who preached a new gospel of coaching in the early 1960s. He shifted the emphasis away from the traditional high-tempo, long-ball game perfected by Wolves in the mid to late 1950s in favour of a more

After taking his FA coaching badge, Nicholson assisted Walter Winterbottom, the England manager, at the World Cup in Sweden in 1958.

deliberate, short-passing game. While Wolves tended to build their attacks down the wings, Spurs looked to work the ball more through the middle.

After taking his FA coaching badge, Nicholson assisted Walter Winterbottom, the England manager, at the World Cup in Sweden in 1958. His defensive strategy prevented Brazil, the eventual winners, from scoring in a group game. It was the only time the South Americans failed to score in the tournament.

Back at White Hart Lane, Nicholson overhauled training methods, introducing specific weight-lifting regimes with the aim of improving stamina.

In a change of emphasis, the players concentrated on tactical preparations during pre-season training. Set pieces and patterns of play were devised and practised, and Nicholson introduced 'ghost football' – training games in which the players went through set moves without a ball.

'We worked for five or six hours a day, mixing runs and road walks with five-a-side games, practice matches and ball work,' Dave Mackay said. 'We couldn't wait for the season to start.'

An innovative thinker, Nicholson was ahead of his time as a coach. 'I introduced the best training schedules, the sort of organised training which all clubs brought in during the 1960s and 1970s,' he said.

While working with individuals on particular aspects of the game, Nicholson also wanted to change the group mentality. He rejected the 'flat-out for 90 minutes' approach then prevalent in the game. 'The intense pressure must come in spells,' he said. 'My players are intelligent enough to know now when just such a spell is on. It is then that they should score enough goals to win.'

TALKING POINT

Bill Nicholson lived almost all of his adult life in a modest terraced house close to White Hart Lane. It meant a shorter journey to work, allowing him more time for his obsession: managing Tottenham Hotspur.

Over 38 years at White Hart Lane, as first player and then manager, Nicholson was renowned for his commitment and dedication. 'Bill is the one who turns on the lights in the morning and turns them off at night,' joked one rival manager.

'Football in general, and Spurs in particular, were his life,' recalled Pat Jennings, the Spurs goalkeeper. 'You would find Bill at White Hart Lane on a Sunday morning if you were injured and went in for treatment.'

Nicholson was unhappy with players who asked for a rest or time off. 'He might not say anything but he will look grim, as if you're taking the bread out of his mouth,' Danny Blanchflower, the Spurs captain, said. 'No matter how hard you might work or how many hours you put in, you know that he is doing a lot more than you.'

Above If supporters were unable to afford a television, then listening to the commentary on a radio such as this KB model of the 1950s and 60s allowed them to follow their team.

Above left One of the many books written about Nicholson's magnificent Double winning team of 1961.

NEWS

JOHNNY HAYNES (1934–)

Player • Inducted 2002 • 56 Caps

Johnny Haynes, a perfectionist hailed by Jimmy Greaves as 'the greatest passer of the ball I've ever seen', left the nation stunned when he became the first player in English football to be paid £100 a week.

Fulham made the offer of a five-fold pay rise as a means of keeping Haynes at Craven Cottage in the face of determined efforts by Milan to lure the England captain to Italy in early 1961. The pay offer reflected Haynes' status as the highest-profile player in the game. Advertisers understood his value: Brylcreem signed him up as their sporting representative in succession to Denis Compton, the England cricketer and Arsenal winger.

In April 1961, following the abolition of the maximum wage, Fulham made good their promise. Haynes signed the new contract.

'I'd sooner have the job of marking any other footballer in the world than Johnny Haynes,' Dave Mackay, the Spurs and Scotland player said. 'I have tried close-marking him and getting in quick tackles, but it didn't stop him. In one match, I decided to lay off to see, but he was even more deadly.'

Haynes specialised in the accurate through-ball to the feet of an advancing striker. In the England team that was Jimmy Greaves. 'There has rarely been such a dominant figure for England as Johnny,' Greaves said. 'Nearly every forward move was masterminded by him.'

By the time the squad arrived in Chile for what would be a disappointing World Cup campaign in 1962, England's reliance on Haynes was obvious to all, including the opposition. Asked how his team would play against England, Hungary coach Baroti told reporters: 'Simple: number 10 takes the corners, number 10 takes the throw-ins; number 10 does everything. So what do we do? We put a man on number ten. Goodbye, England.' And so it proved.

KEY MATCH

England 9 Scotland 3, Home International Championship, Wembley, 15 April 1961

Johnny Haynes was chaired off the field on the shoulders of his team-mates, after orchestrating the most comprehensive defeat of Scotland in history.

'We paraded the great Haynesie around the Wembley pitch as if he was the FA Cup at the end of the match in which he touched perfection,' recalled Jimmy Greaves.

This match marked a pinnacle in international football for Haynes, whose appreciation of the instinctive, off-the-cuff play of Greaves was fundamental to England's attacking play.

'I had a very good understanding with Jimmy,' Haynes recalled. 'Sometimes I didn't even have to look up when I hit a long pass. I just knew that Jimmy would be on the end of it.'

'We would have beaten anybody that day,' Haynes said. Greaves scored a hat-trick, and Haynes added two more from the inside-left position.

The match proved a point for Walter Winterbottom, the England manager, whose successful lobbying for the earlier release of players by the clubs was seen to be vindicated.

At the end of the game, Haynes collected the British International Championship Trophy from the Queen.

Left Johnny Haynes during a training session at Fulham in 1955.

KEY MUSEUM ARTEFACT

As chairman of the Professional Footballers' Association (PFA), Jimmy Hill campaigned against the maximum wage, operated by the Football League, that restricted a player's earnings. In the summer of 1960, the PFA, backed by its members, threatened to strike in order to free themselves from the restricted wages of £20 a week. Jimmy Hill sat in this chair whilst fighting his media campaign to gain the support of the general public. In 1961, the League finally agreed to abolish the maximum wage. Almost immediately, Johnny Haynes' salary was raised by Fulham chairman Tommy Trinder.

Johnny Haynes made his England debut in the 2–0 win against Northern Ireland in Belfast in October 1954. Billy Wright, the England captain, was immediately impressed.

'Johnny was just 19, and it was unusual at that time for the selectors to put their faith in youth,' Wright recalled. 'But he already looked an assured and confident player, someone who could hit accurate 40-yard passes with either foot.'

The selectors, 'acting like headless chickens', according to Wright, didn't agree with his assessment. They made sweeping changes for the next international, dropping Haynes, who only returned to the side the following year.

Once recalled, Haynes was played out of position, at inside-right, in England's 3–0 win over Northern Ireland at Wembley in November 1955. 'I was delighted to see him back,' Wright said. 'There was no question that he was the most accurate passer of a football in the League.

'I almost used to purr when watching Johnny play his beautifully disguised reverse passes with either foot. He was a footballing master.'

"I almost used to purr when watching Johnny play his beautifully disguised passes with either foot. He was a footballing master." – *Billy Wright*

In 1958–59 Haynes proved his value as an attacking player, scoring 26 goals in 34 League matches for Fulham, the only club he played for during his career.

Then, in 1962, at the height of his fame, he was involved in a serious car accident that put him out of the game for almost a year and effectively ended his international career. He was 28, and he had captained his country 22 times. 'Basically, if he was fit during my time in charge, he played,' said Walter Winterbottom, the England manager.

In April 1961, AC Milan made a bid of £100,000 for Johnny Haynes. Fulham turned it down: 'He is not for sale,' said Tommy Trinder, the club chairman.

Above right A poster from the 1962 World Cup.

Above This placemat was produced to commemorate the 1962 World Cup finals in Chile. Haynes made his final appearance for England in the tournament. His last 22 caps for his country were gained as captain.

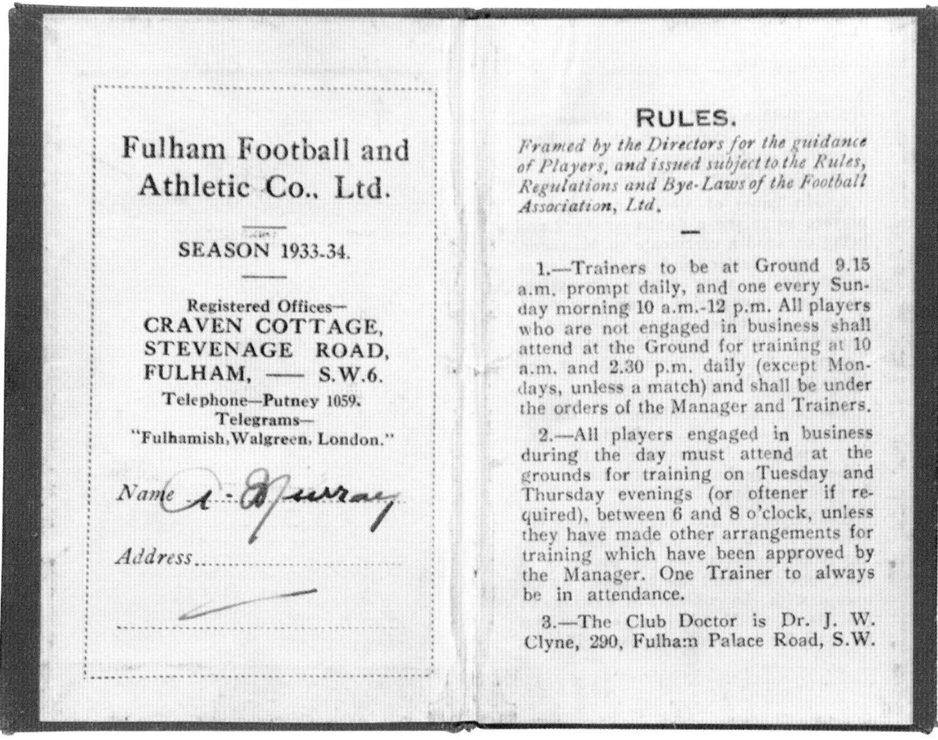

Fulham Football and Athletic Co., Ltd.

SEASON 1933-34.

Registered Offices—
CRAVEN COTTAGE,
STEVENAGE ROAD,
FULHAM, — S.W.6.

Telephone—Putney 1059.
Telegrams—
"Fulhamish, Walgreen, London."

Name A. Murray

Address

RULES.

Framed by the Directors for the guidance of Players, and issued subject to the Rules, Regulations and Bye-Laws of the Football Association, Ltd.

1.—Trainers to be at Ground 9.15 a.m. prompt daily, and one every Sunday morning 10 a.m.-12 p.m. All players who are not engaged in business shall attend at the Ground for training at 10 a.m. and 2.30 p.m. daily (except Mondays, unless a match) and shall be under the orders of the Manager and Trainers.

2.—All players engaged in business during the day must attend at the grounds for training on Tuesday and Thursday evenings (or oftener if required), between 6 and 8 o'clock, unless they have made other arrangements for training which have been approved by the Manager. One Trainer to always be in attendance.

3.—The Club Doctor is Dr. J. W. Clyne, 290, Fulham Palace Road, S.W.

TALKING POINT

'My burning ambition now is to captain England in the finals of 1966 at home, and to be the captain of the winning team.'

Johnny Haynes had just experienced the disappointment of England's elimination in the quarter-finals of the World Cup in Chile. He was determined that four years later the outcome would be different. But within a matter of months, in August 1962, he was badly hurt. His dream, like his leg, was shattered in a car crash in Blackpool. At 28, and with 56 caps to his name, he was in the prime of his career as an international player.

He would not return to League action with Fulham until late in the 1962–63 season. But even after such a lengthy lay-off, he continued to be troubled by a persistent knee problem.

By the time Haynes had recovered fully, Alf Ramsey, the England manager, had abandoned the tactics best suited to Haynes' passing game. The car accident had forced Ramsey to act. Haynes' time as an England player had passed.

The previous winter, as rumours had spread about the Italians' interest, Trinder, a famous comedian, said: 'Haynes is an entertainer like I am, and if the maximum wage is ever abolished, I will pay him what he is worth, which is £100 a week.' A few days after the bid from Milan, the wage restrictions in English football were lifted. Trinder had little option but to offer what was a five-fold increase in salary to his captain. 'I signed the contract straight away,' Haynes said.
'I love London, I am captain of England and I feel I owe the game something,' Haynes said at the time.

Milan had offered a salary of £10,000 a year plus bonuses. 'I was not trying to be patriotic or noble about it. I felt that if Fulham made me an offer reasonably close to what I thought I was worth, I would accept it. I knew I could earn quite a lot of money commercially in England.'

'Also, I believed that, however successful I was in Italy, I would still at the end of it all be a foreigner.'

Haynes stayed at Fulham for the rest of his career, turning down a move to Spurs in 1964, much to the disappointment of Jimmy Greaves, his one-time England team-mate.

But there was one more twist to the story: 'I was the first player to be paid £100 a week, but Fulham did not increase my wages by a penny to the day I retired in 1970,' Haynes said.

THE EVENING NEWS, WEDNESDAY, APRIL 13, 1960

Appeal To Ministry The Only Answer, Says Jimmy Hill

LEAGUE REBUFF PLAYERS

But No Strike Call From PFA

By VICTOR RAILTON

THE rulers of the Football League took another free-kick at the Professional Footballers' Association to-day when they rejected the players' claims for the abolition of the maximum wage, shares of transfer fees, and a review of conditions.

The League also said they do not consider an industrial dispute exists between the players and their employers, as stated in the PFA letter of March 22.

'A Dispute'

Anything, But . . .

The Knee can K.O. Hill

DAILY MAIL, Thursday, April 14, 1960

No-strike Soccer players plan last-ditch fight

by ROY PESKETT

FOOTBALL LEAGUE players will not strike—even though their wage demands have been rejected outright and 750 footballers are likely to be sacked by their clubs this summer.

This was made clear to me last night by the two leaders of the Professional Footballers' Association, secretary Cliff Lloyd and chairman Jimmy Hill.

CLIFF LLOYD "No strike action"

JIMMY HILL Going to the Ministry

Uphold

Drastic

SNUFFED OUT

F.A. executive?

Above Fulham rulebook, 1933/34. Rulebooks such as this were issued to every player in the Football League by their club, up until the 1960s.

Right This scrapbook belonging to Jimmy Hill, from 1960, shows newspaper cuttings referring to the threatened strike by PFA members.

DANNY BLANCHFLOWER

(1936–1998)

Player • Inducted 2003 • 56 caps • 1 Division One Championship 2 FA Cups • 1 European Cup-winners' Cup

'Mind you, football is not really about winning, or goals, or saves or supporters. It's about glory. It's about doing things in style, doing them with a flourish. It's about going out to beat the other lot, not waiting for them to die of boredom. It's about dreaming of the glory of the Double.'

Danny Blanchflower made Tottenham Hotspur believe it was their destiny to win the Double, a feat considered by many at the time to be beyond any football team. In 1960–61, under his captaincy, Spurs became the first club that century to win the League championship and the FA Cup in the same season.

Cliff Jones, a winger in the Double-winning side, said: 'Danny was so far ahead of his team in his thinking that people would allow him to get on with things that struck them at first as a bit odd, but generally, his ideas worked out to the good.'

Blanchflower played in all 42 games that season. At the age of 34, he was voted the best player in the country by one newspaper. When the title had been won, the Tottenham supporters poured on to the pitch at White Hart Lane and began chanting: 'We want Danny! We want Danny!'

For four years he had insisted that it was possible, and that Spurs were the team to prove it. By July 1960, he was convinced. At training he addressed his team-mates. This, he told them, would be 'a season of destiny for Tottenham Hotspur'.

'At pre-season training I was impressed with the team: its individual ability, its teamwork and its whole personality,' he said. 'But I knew that it couldn't be done with a weak heart. The team would really have to believe.'

His influence on the team was enormous. In April 1964, Blanchflower announced his retirement. 'A light has gone out at White Hart Lane,' Jimmy Greaves said.

KEY MATCH

Atletico Madrid 1 Tottenham Hotspur 5, European Cup-Winners' Cup final, Rotterdam 15 May 1963

Danny Blanchflower listened to the team-talk given by Bill Nicholson with a growing sense of unease. Spurs were about to make history as the first English club to play in a European final, but there was a tense atmosphere in the dressing-room.

Years later Pat Jennings, the Spurs goalkeeper, said that one of Nicholson's very few weaknesses was his habit of occasionally over-praising opponents. And here he was again, outlining, one by one, the threat posed by the Spaniards, the Cup holders.

Seeing the first hints of apprehension on the faces of his team-mates, Blanchflower knew he had to act. So, once Nicholson had left the room, the Irishman spoke out. 'They're probably having a team meeting right now,' Blanchflower told his team-mates, 'and somebody is saying, "They've got this big six-foot three-inch fellow in Bobby Smith and Cliff Jones can catch pigeons." Hard men? When Maurice Norman takes his teeth out, he frightens me. And Jimmy Greaves invents ways of scoring goals.'

The psychology worked. Freed from tension, the Spurs players gave a scintillating performance. 'It was in Rotterdam that people told us that we played like Real Madrid,' Nicholson said.

'What Spurs did is the start of a new age of football in Britain which could have its confirmation in the World Cup of 1966,' one Spanish newspaper commented.

Blanchflower recalled: 'I carried the Cup high because I felt we had truly earned it.'

Left Danny Blanchflower arrives for pre-season training with Spurs in August 1962.

KEY MUSEUM ARTEFACT

World Cup posters, such as this one from 1958, have been a feature of the tournament since its inception in 1930. Much football art of the early 20th century consisted primarily of pen-and-ink sketches and caricatures that were often featured in newspapers. World Cup posters helped to develop a much more progressive, continental style of graphic design. This one advertised the tournament in which Blanchflower starred for Northern Ireland, who performed heroically, beating Czechoslovakia in a play-off to progress to the quarter-finals, where they eventually lost 4–0 to France.

Right Blanchflower published *Danny Blanchflower's Soccer Book* in 1962. As one of the key players in the 1961 Double winning side, Blanchflower began to enjoy commercial success off the field.

> "I had never seen a captain so ready to face up to his responsibility."
> – *Jimmy Greaves*

Danny Blanchflower knew his own mind. He once refused, live on camera, to appear on *This is Your Life*. No one had done that before. On the subject of captaincy, he was equally forthright. 'You cannot lead from the middle of a pack,' he always argued.

Although his captaincy was later recognised as a crucial factor in Spurs' success, Blanchflower had a harsh lesson in the realities of the job. In 1958–59 he was sacked.

It all came to a head when he changed tactics during a game that Spurs were losing. It had worked before; this time it didn't. Tottenham lost. Under pressure, the manager, Jimmy Anderson, stripped Blanchflower of the captaincy. Fortunately for Blanchflower, Peter Doherty, the manager of Northern Ireland, showed more faith in his judgement. 'He always backed me as captain,' Blanchflower said. The partnership gelled: together, they took the Irish to the quarter-finals of the World Cup in 1958.

A change of culture at Spurs took a little longer. Bill Nicholson was appointed manager in 1958. The following season Blanchflower was restored as captain, with full authority.

'If there is a problem that Bill and I have not foreseen, I act on my own judgement,' Blanchflower said at the time. 'I believe in trying the unorthodox when the orthodox isn't working.' 'I had never seen a captain so ready to face up to his responsibility,' Jimmy Greaves said. 'It takes common sense to spot the move and then courage to carry it out. That is great captaincy.'

Danny Blanchflower made Spurs tick as an attacking force. Jimmy Greaves attributed much of his success as a goalscorer in the early 1960s to the creative talent of the team's right-half.

'Danny's play suits me right down to the ground,' Greaves said at the time. 'When we have possession he is constantly looking for the gap for a 30-yard pass down the middle. That is just the kind of pass I like, the one that gives me the chance of a quick dash on goal.'

Cliff Jones said: 'Danny had excellent vision and passing ability. He had beautiful balance. He was always on his feet. He was never on his backside unless someone put him there.'

As with the captaincy, however, Blanchflower had to overcome a setback before fully demonstrating his value to Spurs as a player. Voted Footballer of the Year in 1958, he had returned from the World Cup in Sweden mentally and physically exhausted. The following season Tottenham sank into a relegation battle. Bill Nicholson needed to steel the defence, so he dropped Blanchflower, the team's most creative player.

His point made, Nicholson soon restored Blanchflower. He was even given added responsibility as team leader, and Spurs gradually improved. They were on their way. A vital component of the Double-winning side was in place.

'In a poor side Danny can be an expensive luxury,' Bill Nicholson said. 'That is why he was dropped, for then we had a poor team. In a good side he's a wonderful asset through his unorthodox approach and ball skill.'

TALKING POINT

Opinionated and forthright, Danny Blanchflower did not hesitate to speak out against what he considered injustice. He was not slow to criticise those in positions of authority, even if they were paying his wages.

His willingness to offer a forthright opinion on controversial issues made him unpopular with some managers and directors. Sports editors, in contrast, loved his outspoken ways. They queued up to employ him as a columnist and pundit.

In the early 1950s, during his time at Aston Villa, he was a regular guest on a weekly radio programme. He made the most of the platform, criticising the training methods at Villa Park and the refusal of the football authorities to abolish the maximum wage.

In one of his columns for the Birmingham Evening Mail, he wrote: 'Our training schedules at Villa should have been changed a long, long time ago. I want to see more use of the ball in training. It is teamwork that counts and this is often overlooked.' Villa responded by eventually off-loading him to Spurs.

Throughout the 1960s, he also railed against negative play, describing the tactics of Internazionale, winners of the European Cup in 1964, as 'a cold, predictable plan to destroy the opposition'. Winning by any means wasn't enough. 'Where is the glory in that?' he asked.

Top An Aston Villa vesta, or match-holder, from 1897. Blanchflower moved to Aston Villa in 1950 where he made 148 League appearances. Villa became only the second team to do the Double in 1897.

Left This watercolour and pencil picture of the Wembley Towers was created by H M Livens in 1923. Blanchflower enjoyed two consecutive FA Cup final victories at Wembley in 1961 and 1962. He even managed to score from the penalty spot, in the 3–1 victory over Burnley, in the second game.

Right This set of four silver presentation spoons from 1958 was manufactured in Stockholm, Sweden, prior to the 1958 World Cup.

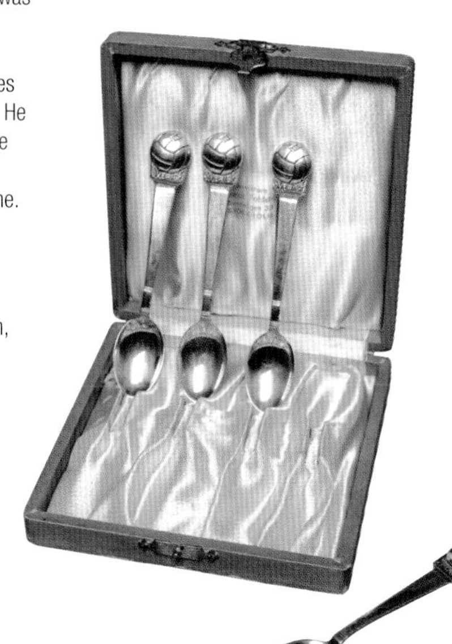

ALF RAMSEY (1920–1999)

Manager • Inducted 2002 • 1 World Cup • 1 Division One Championship

Gordon Banks spoke for all the members of the England team of 1966. 'Without Alf Ramsey,' he said, 'we would never have won the World Cup.'

Ramsey made the players believe in themselves and the way the national team played. English football, in his opinion, was the best in the world, and he made the players believe that, too.

'Alf was an excellent coach, for starters,' Banks wrote. 'His motivation and man-management skills were also outstanding.'

'He was always fair to his players and scrupulously honest, a man of unyielding integrity and absolute loyalty, and his loyalty was reciprocated by the players,' said Banks.

'He was devoted to the team ethic, and yet he always stressed that no one was indispensable. He bore no grudges and had no favourites. His knowledge was unrivalled, complemented by superb tactical acumen, yet his instructions were clear and simple.'

Alan Ball stressed Ramsey's patriotism: 'Alf made us proud to wear the England shirt,' he said.

Bobby Charlton said the players responded to Ramsey's professionalism and integrity. 'He gave you the confidence that you'd been picked because you were a good player, not because your club team was doing particularly well or because of anyone else's say-so, or because the press had been clamouring for your inclusion.

'He found a formula that made England consistent for the first time ever. Up until Alf came along anybody could beat us abroad. He stopped us being frightened of anybody, and he made us believe we were better than anybody else.'

In May 1966, the top five teams in the FIFA rankings were Portugal, Brazil, England, West Germany and Argentina. In July, England beat three of them within the space of seven days to win the World Cup.

KEY MATCH

England 4 West Germany 2 (aet), World Cup final, Wembley Stadium, 30 July 1966

The professionalism that underpinned everything Alf Ramsey stood for as a manager didn't desert him even in the moment of his greatest triumph.

There is a photograph of the England bench taken at the moment when the ball hit the back of the net for the fourth England goal, the rest of the squad and the trainers leap up in celebration of victory. At the centre of it all, amid the bedlam, sits Ramsey: calm, reflective, stony-faced even.

'I was watching Overath [West Germany midfield player] chasing back after Hurst, and admiring him for such effort and commitment in the last minute of such a match,' Ramsey later recalled. It was a compliment from one professional to another.

As Ramsey had been quick to point out before the start of extra-time, the other German players lacked Overath's stamina. 'Look at them, they're flat out,' he told his players. 'Now stand up, don't let them think that you're tired too.'

Ramsey had already delivered his best remembered line, only moments after West Germany had taken the game into extra time with a last-gasp equalizer: 'You've won it once,' Ramsey said. 'Now go out and win it again.'

He then rallied each player individually. 'When he came to me,' recalled Alan Ball, 'he just said something like: "Attack, attack, every time you can, attack."'

Although he would later be knighted for his achievement, Ramsey declined all appeals to join his players on the lap of honour. Instead, he strode, smiling and composed, to the dressing room, with the chant 'Ramsey! Ramsey!' echoing around Wembley.

Left World Cup, quarter-finals, 1966. The England manager Alf Ramsey tries to stop defender George Cohen from swapping shirts with an Argentina player after the game.

KEY MUSEUM ARTEFACT

This heavy woollen shirt and cap were worn by Arnold Kirke Smith in the first official England international match which was against Scotland in 1872. Interestingly, the 'Three Lions' badge that Ramsey was so proud of was used in the game which was played in Glasgow and which ended in a 0–0 draw. The attitude of the teams involved was somewhat different to that of the Argentina players who starred in the quarter-finals of the World Cup against England some 94 years later. While Argentina were branded as 'animals' by Ramsey, for what he perceived as their hostile behaviour, those who played in the 1872 game were independently wealthy gentlemen who would never have considered breaking the rules.

Right A 1966 England blazer badge issued by the FA to all members of the press covering the tournament.

Below The collar belonging to Pickles, the dog who found the World Cup, which had been stolen prior to the 1966 finals. In recognition of what he had done Pickles received a number of awards and the collar features one medal from the National Canine Defence League and one from the World Cup Collectors club.

Soon after his appointment, in 1962, Ramsey made an unequivocal statement about England's prospects. 'We will win the World Cup,' Ramsey said, without qualification. 'We have the players, the ability, the strength of character and temperament to win the title in 1966.'

In 1968, two years after England's triumph over West Germany at Wembley, a journalist said to Ramsey: 'You were sticking your neck out a bit, weren't you? No one expected you to commit yourself to that extent.' Ramsey replied: 'It was what I believed. I couldn't have taken the job if I didn't think we would win.'

Ramsey built his team from the back. In only his second match in charge, he gave Gordon Banks his England debut. Banks would remain his undisputed first-choice until he lost an eye in a car accident nine years later.

His defence came together one year before the tournament when Jack Charlton and Nobby Stiles both made their debuts in the game against Scotland. The same six players – Banks, full-backs George Cohen and Ray Wilson, Bobby Moore, Charlton and Stiles – stayed together as a unit throughout the World Cup. They conceded three goals in six games, a record low total in the history of the tournament.

Ramsey was now able to concentrate on attacking formations and tactics. He experimented with several systems, all pivoting around Bobby Charlton, the deep-lying number nine and the one player deemed irreplaceable by the manager.

In selecting the other forwards, Ramsey put the emphasis on hard work and flexibility.

Ramsey was the first former England player to manage the national team. He was also the first professional club manager to be put in charge.

His appointment by the football association marked a turning point in English football. Ramsey's predecessor, Walter Winterbottom, while an outstanding coach and administrator, had no such 'hands-on' experience, nor did the 'amateur' selectors. As a professional, Ramsey picked the team, and he took the responsibility for results.

He began by losing his first two matches. In the 44 games that followed, culminating in the World Cup final in 1966, England tasted defeat only four times. Overall, his record as England manager read: played 113; won 69; drawn 27; lost 17; goals for 224; goals against 99.

Only when those results began to turn against him, in the early 1970s, did he become vulnerable. He was sacked in May 1974.

Under Ramsey England regained the respect of the world as a football power. England had never gone past the quarter-finals stage at a World Cup on foreign soil before. Yet, in Mexico, in 1970, they went into the tournament as joint favourites. Brazil certainly regarded England as their most serious threat.

Ramsey believed that England's rightful place was at the top of world football. When England finished third in the European Nations Cup in 1968, Ramsey was dissatisfied. This was not good enough for England.

'England are still the world champions and third place in Europe is not our place,' he said.

Above The programme of the 1966 World Cup final.

TALKING POINT

Alf Ramsey lied about his age to improve his prospects of a career as a professional footballer, and then surprised even himself by going on to play for England.

When he was looking for a club as the Second World War neared its end, Ramsey, then aged 24, knocked two years off his age. 'In the circumstances, what Alf did was understandable,' Tom Finney, a future England team-mate said. 'All he wanted was a chance.'

Early in his career with Southampton, Ramsey lacked confidence in his own ability. Only after his transfer to Tottenham did he establish himself as an England regular at right back. He even took over as captain whenever Billy Wright was absent.

His nickname – 'The General' summed up his qualities as a defender. Obsessed by tactics and organisation, Ramsey was renowned for his calm play under pressure, qualities that compensated for a lack of pace.

'Alf was as cool as an ice-soda,' Wright said. 'I learned that nothing could disturb his perfect balance and poise; no situation, however desperate, could force him into abandoning his immaculate style.'

Above *Phew! What A Scorcher*: this acrylic painting on upholstered canvas by Chris Holwell from 1994 features an Argentina player shooting for goal.

BOBBY CHARLTON (1937–)

Player • Inducted 2002 • 106 caps • 1 World Cup
1 European Cup • 3 Division One Championships • 1 FA Cup

Bobby Charlton was the inspiration at the heart of both England and Manchester United in the two most memorable finals ever staged at Wembley.

In victory, Charlton shed tears at the end of both games. First in joy, choked with patriotic pride, following the World Cup final in 1966.

Two years later, when Manchester United finally lifted the European Cup, he cried again, this time in remembrance of the eight team-mates who perished in the Munich air disaster in 1958.

Wearing the number nine shirt for both club and country, Charlton generated a mix of fear and awe in his opponents. 'He is the central figure of every match he plays in,' Helmut Schöen, the West Germany manager said. 'A truly great player.'

In the European Cup final, the Wembley crowd witnessed the extraordinary sight of several Benfica players congratulating Charlton after he scored one of his two goals.

Charlton holds a unique position in English football as the only player to win the four major honours in the game: the World Cup, European Cup, League championship title and FA Cup. In 1966, he was voted Footballer of the Year, and the following season he added the European individual honour to his collection.

Between 1958 and 1970 he won a then record 106 caps. He is immensely proud of his England career. 'I keep all my caps in plastic bags so that they don't lose their colour,' he once said.

Charlton was admired throughout the world. Harold Shepherdson, the England trainer, observed the reaction of people overseas. 'As soon as Bobby steps off a plane or off a bus, they just start clapping. He is the most respected footballer England has ever produced.'

KEY MATCH

England 2 Portugal 1, World Cup semi-final, Wembley, 26 July 1966

After Bobby Charlton scored the second of his two goals of the game, a Portugal player walked up to shake the hand of the player who had just deprived him and his team-mates of a place in the final.

The Portugal players respected Charlton to the point of reverence. Earlier in the season he played in Manchester United's famous 5-1 win against Benfica in the European Cup, and they also remembered his two outstanding goals for England against Portugal in 1958.

'After the second goal at Wembley in the semi-final, Augusto ran over and shook my hand. I was very touched by this gesture and often think about it,' Charlton said.

Charlton put England ahead when the ball fell to him 25 yards out with Pereira, the Portugal goalkeeper, stranded out of his goal. 'In an instant I thought, "Don't blast it. Just make sure you hit it straight."'

His second goal was more typical: a fierce drive struck with perfect timing. 'I find I can read the pace of the ball at Wembley,' he said.

As late as lunchtime that day, Charlton feared he might miss the game, having awoken with a stiff neck. After undergoing heat treatment, the muscle was still troubling him when Ramsey asked him if he was fit.

'With my head at a particular angle, I replied, "I can feel it slightly, but I'm fine." After that I was determined not to let Alf down.'

Left Bobby Charlton produces a trade-mark shot at goal during this Division One game against Sheffield United at Bramall Lane in October 1967. Manchester United ran out 3–0 winners.

KEY MUSEUM ARTEFACT

The European Cup began in 1955 with the first final played in 1956. The irrepressible Real Madrid won the first five tournaments with outstanding players such as the Argentine-born Alfredo di Stefano. After Madrid's third successive final victory over AC Milan, UEFA gave them the trophy to keep in perpetuity. The second trophy to be designed is the cup we recognise today. Although Bobby Charlton got his hands on this second trophy, it has since been copied as a result of three successive wins by Ajax of Amsterdam.

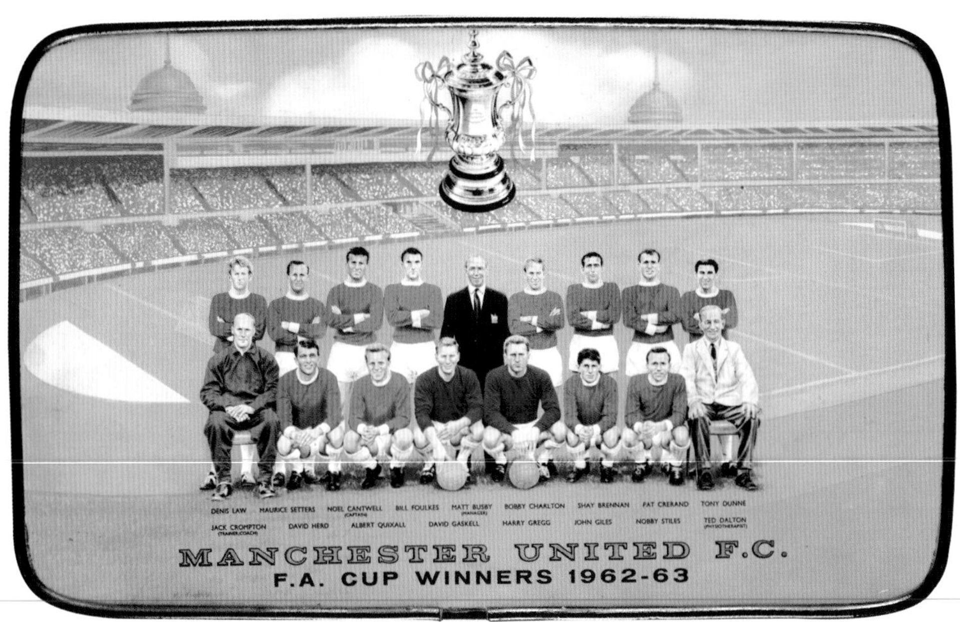

Right A Manchester United coffee table from 1963, produced to commemorate their FA Cup final victory over Leicester City.

> **"As a lad, Bobby had exceptional timing. Even with the heavier ball we used in those days he could hit a corner beyond the far post using either foot."**
>
> *– Sir Matt Busby*

Matt Busby was taken aback by the powerful play of the 15-year-old schoolboy international who chose Manchester United over the other 17 clubs desperate to sign him in the summer of 1953.

'Bobby had exceptional timing,' Busby recalled. 'Even with the heavier ball we used those days he could hit a corner beyond the far post with either foot and with scarcely any back-lift. A lot of senior players couldn't do that.'

Busby advised Charlton to alter the mix of his passing 'with a touch of the short stuff as well as the long passes' that had made him stand out in schoolboy games.

He was ordered to do individual training sessions, often on Sunday mornings at a deserted Old Trafford, with Jimmy Murphy, the Manchester United assistant manager. 'He used to drive this message into me about movement and making myself available for the return pass until I was sick of it,' Charlton recalled. 'Jimmy would say, "You've got to learn to do it instinctively", and eventually I did.'

The hard work paid off. Five days before his 19th birthday, Charlton made his first-team debut in October 1956. Two years later he was playing for his country. For years, Charlton gave away none of his memorabilia, his 'England stuff', because it was so valuable to him. There was one exception: a shirt he made available for auction. 'That was for Jimmy Murphy,' he said. 'It was a thank-you, because I learned more from him than anyone else at Old Trafford.'

The Last Lap

IT'S ALL OVER ...... Winners and losers troop off the Highbury pitch together after Manchester United's amazing 5-3 victory in the semi-final replay.

The new Busby Babes have astounded the football world by reaching the Cup Final for the second season in succession. They now meet Bolton Wanderers at Wembley on May 3rd in the first all-Lancashire final since 1953.

IT wasn't until just after 4.40 p.m. on the afternoon of Wednesday, March 26, at Highbury Stadium that we knew for certain Manchester United had performed the impossible—got through against seemingly overwhelming odds to a Wembley Cup Final for the second successive season . . .

United beat Fulham 5—3 in one of the most exciting and most high-scoring semi-final replays of all time—a replay made necessary by the 2—2 draw between the clubs in the original tie at Villa Park, Birmingham, the previous Saturday.

Let's begin at the beginning and go back to the Saturday game. High tension all round, but the Manchester United youngsters quickly suppressed their "nerves" and were a goal in front after exactly 12 minutes.

Bobby Charlton—this young survivor of the Munich crash has certainly carved his name in Manchester United history—was the scorer from a shrewd pass by ex-Blackpool forward Ernie Taylor.

Bobby's was a great shot on the volley from the edge of the penalty-box, the kind of scoring effort worthy of a great occasion. Yet United were not destined to hold the lead for long.

Jim Langley, the Fulham left-back, went through with the ball and completely foxed the United defenders as to his intentions. Finally he slammed low into the goalmouth a ball that was half a pass, half a shot, and Fulham's centre-forward Arthur Stevens was there to side-foot it home from close range.

Fulham took on a new lease of life. They saw the Wembley gates almost open for them and after a series of devastating attacks the bearded Jimmy Hill fastened on to a pass from Johnny Haynes and put Fulham in front with a crashing goal. Langley was hurt and had to leave the field for attention and while he was off the amazing Bobby Charlton did it again for United—a crackerjack of a goal scored after Pearson's shot had been blocked.

Two-all . . . the interval and, in the second half a limping Langley on the left wing.

Fulham fought pluckily; goalkeeper Tony Macedo brought off some amazing saves, but was lucky to see yet another shot from Bobby Charlton brush against his finger-tips, the ball sailing on to hit the bar and rebound to safety. Two-all it was at the final whistle. Manchester United's team at Villa Park was:

Gregg; Foulkes, Greaves; Goodwin, Cope, Crowther; Webster, Taylor, Dawson, Charlton, Pearson.

continued on page 8

From his deep-lying position in midfield, Bobby Charlton was the irreplaceable lynchpin of both the Manchester United and England attacks. In the early years of his career Charlton had played at inside-forward or winger for both his club and country, without ever settling in either role. The turning point came in 1964, when Matt Busby brought him infield in order to make the most of his exceptional shooting power. Within a year Alf Ramsey had made the same positional change; Charlton was installed as the creative pivot of the England attack for the World Cup in 1966.

He had long been the central figure at Manchester United. In the wake of the Munich disaster in 1958, Charlton became 'the foundation on which we had to rebuild over the ruins', Busby said. 'He is as near perfection as a man and player as it is possible to be.' In total, Charlton played 606 League games for United, scoring 199 goals. When he staged a testimonial in September 1972, 60,000 people packed into Old Trafford to acclaim him. It was the biggest-ever benefit game played in Britain. He retired the following April.

Charlton was equally important to the England manager. 'I knew months, even years before the World Cup that Bobby Charlton would have a number nine on his back,' Ramsey said.

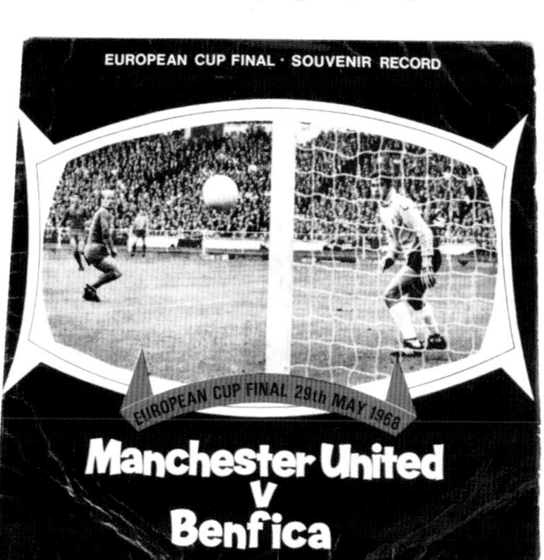

Ramsey always liked to have specialist cover for each position in his team. That way the team could stick to the same tactics if injury ruled out a first-team player. Charlton was the key. His ability to break from deep positions and threaten goal was vital to England's strategy in 1966.

Asked several years later if he had looked for a substitute in a similar mould in case injury sidelined Charlton before the tournament, Ramsey said: 'No, there wasn't one. Bobby was one of a kind.'

TALKING POINT

In the aftermath of the Munich air crash, as the nation mourned the death of a football team, the British public took Bobby Charlton to their hearts.

Charlton had been knocked unconscious in the disaster that claimed the lives of eight of his Manchester United team-mates in February 1958, but otherwise he escaped with barely a scratch.

At the age of 20, the youthful Charlton came to personify a sense of hope and renewal in the wake of tragedy. For huge numbers of people, Charlton, the survivor who was miraculously thrown clear of the wreckage, was a living representative of the other 'Busby Babes' so sadly lost.

Within weeks of the crash, he began to receive about 100 letters a day from schoolgirls; 500,000 readers of the *Eagle* comic voted him their favourite sportsman.

In May 1958, Charlton returned to Belgrade, the starting point for the fateful flight home three months earlier, to play for England against Yugoslavia. His courage in flying again so soon after the trauma earned him widespread respect.

His popularity soared. At one point Charlton led the voting for BBC TV's Sports Personality of the Year award. A reluctant public figure who felt shy in the spotlight, Charlton was said to be relieved when he narrowly lost out to motorcyclist John Surtees.

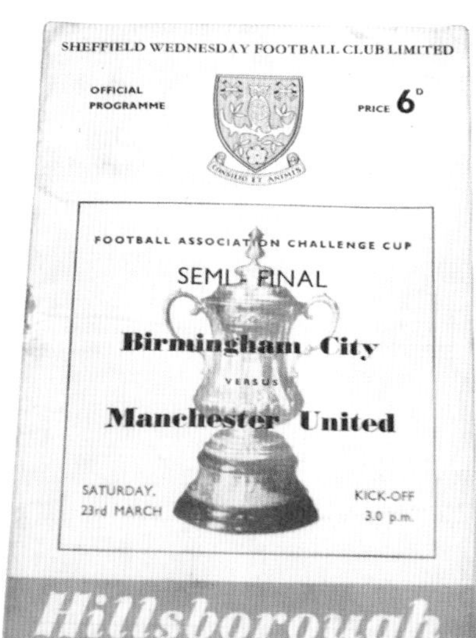

Right The 1957 FA Cup semi-final programme for the match between Manchester United and Birmingham City in which Bobby Charlton scored.

Left The cover of the 1968 European Cup final match commentary record showing Charlton scoring his first goal against Benfica.

Above left This 1958 magazine shows players leaving the field after the FA Cup semi-final replay at Highbury, home of Arsenal FC. Manchester United had just beaten Fulham 5–3 to progress to the final where they met Bolton Wanderers.

BOBBY MOORE (1941–1993)

Player • Inducted 2002 • 108 caps • 1 World Cup • 1 FA Cup
1 European Cup-winners' Cup

Bobby Moore, the only Englishman to lift the World Cup, was captain of England a record 91 times, inspiring team-mates through the example of his own unshakeable composure and self-belief.

'He did not know the meaning of the word panic,' Alan Ball recalled. 'He put the rest of the players at ease. He was the best defender, the best reader of play, and a superlative captain.'

His positive influence was evident before a ball had been kicked in the World Cup final against West Germany in 1966. 'He carried out the match ball, resting on his hip with the kind of panache that no other captain could manage,' Geoff Hurst recalled.

Alf Ramsey once described Moore as 'my general on the field who translates our strategy into reality'. One of Ramsey's earliest decisions as England manager was to promote Moore to captain; he was 22 at the time. The following year, 1964, Moore was voted Footballer of the Year, the youngest ever recipient of the award.

Ramsey told Moore: 'Whatever you do, whatever decisions you think are necessary during a game, you will have my full backing.' The two men had made a professional bond that would shape their country's fortunes for a decade, during which time Moore won a record 106 England caps.

'I was thrilled,' Moore said. 'I like being captain. I like the feeling of responsibility, that if something happens on the field I have to make a decision.'

In three successive seasons, Moore led his side up the steps to the Royal Box at Wembley to collect a trophy: the FA Cup in 1964, the European Cup-Winners' Cup in 1965 and the World Cup in 1966.

KEY MATCH

West Ham United 2 TSV Munich 1860 0, European Cup-Winners' Cup final, Wembley, 19 May 1965

Early in his career, Bobby Moore was taken to one side by Ron Greenwood, the West Ham United manager, for a quiet chat. 'Bobby,' Greenwood said, 'I'm going to build this team around you.' The fruition of that work was seen in this match of high quality and sportsmanship.

Four years later, Moore justified his manager's faith in a team performance that Greenwood always highlighted as the ultimate expression of his values as a coach. 'This was Bobby Moore's greatest game for the club,' he said. 'It was technical perfection.'

Moore explained his method: 'You don't have to go around kicking people up in the air to be a good tackler. The art is to deny a forward space and force him to knock the ball away.'

'Our defence was excellent,' recalled Greenwood, who had taken the unusual step of organising for his players to watch 1860's semi-final game against Torino. 'It takes two sides to make a great final, and the Germans were full of flair and determination. They kept at us. Moore gloried in the occasion.'

In earlier rounds Greenwood made a crucial tactical change, switching Moore into a deeper, more defensive sweeper role for away legs in earlier rounds of the competition.

West Ham made sure of victory at Wembley with a second goal in the second half when Moore floated over an accurate free-kick for Alan Sealey to convert.

Left England Captain Bobby Moore clears the ball from West Germany's Lothar Emmerich during the 1966 World Cup final on 30 July 1966.

KEY MUSEUM ARTEFACT

The first World Cup trophy, crafted for the inaugural finals in Uruguay in 1930 by the sculptor Abel Lafleur, was originally christened Victory, but by the time the final took place it had been decided to name it after the FIFA President, Jules Rimet. Originally thought to be made of solid gold, recent research suggests that, in fact, the trophy was silver with a gilt coating. When the trophy was stolen (though later returned) prior to the 1966 World Cup finals, the FA had this identical replica made for security purposes. It was substituted for the real trophy directly after the final and stood in for the original for the next four years.

Right World Cup Willie, the mascot of the 1966 World Cup, was the first official mascot of a FIFA World Cup.

In 1970, after England had played Brazil in the World Cup, Pelé described Bobby Moore as 'the greatest defender I ever faced'. One Mexican newspaper called him 'The King of world football'.

In the game against Brazil, Moore dispossessed Jairzinho with a perfectly timed challenge as the Brazil winger bore down on goal. Alan Hansen, the Liverpool defender, has since described it as the best tackle he has ever seen.

Yet Moore was not particularly quick, nor hard-tackling. Worse, still, for a central defender, he did not like to head the ball, preferring to control it on his chest or foot instead. 'I don't think he wanted to spoil his hair,' Ron Greenwood, the West Ham manager, joked.

None of this mattered. His abundant composure and technical skill, allied to an unrivalled ability to read the play, made Moore great. 'A cool, calculating footballer I could trust with my life,' Ramsey said. Jock Stein, the Scotland manager, once joked: 'There should be a law against him. He knows what's happening 20 minutes before anyone else.'

As a teenager, Moore became the youngest holder of a full coaching badge. Add to theory a willingness to graft. 'Bobby had a fanatical dedication,' Greenwood said. 'He made himself into

> **"There should be a law against him. Bobby Moore knows what is happening 20 minutes before anyone else."** – *Jock Stein*

a great player. He wanted to know everything.'

'Bobby never let me down but I knew that when the bugle sounded he would always find another 20 per cent. He grew to the meet the challenge. This is what being a top international player is all about.'

Bobby Moore won the respect and admiration of his manager and team-mates as a leader whose presence was considered essential to England's success.

At Wembley, in 1966, Ramsey demonstrated his regard for Moore to the world in a single gesture. As Moore walked towards the steps to collect the trophy, Ramsey rose from the bench, approached his captain and, smiling, gave him a

victory embrace.

The players accepted him as their spokesman. The following day, Ramsey wanted to know how they thought the £22,000 win bonus should be divided up. Moore spoke up immediately: 'It should be divided equally between every member of the squad, Alf.' The others nodded their approval.

By 1970 Moore had assumed an even more integral role as the team's talisman and figurehead. After being falsely accused of stealing and briefly locked up in a Colombian jail, Moore finally arrived in Mexico alone, just before the start of the tournament. Ramsey met him at the airport in Guadalajara.

TALKING POINT

The pass Bobby Moore made in the dying moments of the World Cup final at Wembley encapsulated him as a footballer.

As West Germany pressed for an equaliser, the ball fell to the England captain just outside his own penalty area. Jack Charlton, his central defensive partner, screamed at him to 'hoof it into the stands'. Instead, Moore controlled the ball, drawing a couple of German players. To Moore's left stood Ray Wilson but giving a short pass would only shift the responsibility and the pressure to the England full-back. Looking up, Moore saw the run made by Geoff Hurst. He then delivered an inch-perfect pass over 40 yards into space for his West Ham team-mate to collect, whose shot made the score 4–2.

'It's always been in my manner to try and play, whereas others with another type of make-up might have just tried to hit the corner flag ball in that type of situation,' Moore said later. 'The pass gave us the opportunity to get in behind them. It was the best way of finishing the game as it turned out.'

“He made himself into a great player. He wanted to know everything.”

– Ron Greenwood

Ramsey, a man rarely given to displays of emotion, scampered across the tarmac to greet Moore. 'How are you, my old son?' Ramsey asked, telling him that seeing him again was the most wonderful sight he had had since watching him lift the World Cup. 'I feel 10 years younger just putting my arms round this lad,' Ramsey told the waiting reporters.

Later, when Moore arrived at the team hotel, the entire England squad lined up outside to applaud him. 'His clothes were completely unruffled, as was the man himself,' recalled Gordon Banks.

Above Numerous items of merchandise were made to commemorate the 1966 World Cup, such as this beer mat.

Left A 1960s' West Ham United shirt, manufactured by Bukta.

Below This soap on a rope was produced by Avon to mark the 1966 World Cup.

BILL SHANKLY (1913–1981)

Manager • Inducted 2002 • 1 UEFA Cup • 3 Division One Championships • 2 FA Cups

Bill Shankly was a folk hero whose infectious enthusiasm, energy and charisma transformed Liverpool from a club mired in mediocrity into a major power in European football.

'Shanks arrived at Anfield and just changed the whole thing,' recalled Ian Callaghan, the Liverpool and England midfield player. 'When you look at the club now, it was Bill Shankly who put down the foundations.'

For 15 years, between 1959 and his shock resignation in 1974, Shankly preached the same basic message. 'We would pass the ball 20 yards to a team-mate and then support,' Kevin Keegan said. 'It was as simple as that: keeping the ball moving.'

During that time Liverpool won promotion, lifted the title three times, the FA Cup twice, and the UEFA Cup. Bob Paisley, Shankly's assistant and then successor, won the European Cup three times as manager. 'I just carried on what Bill had started,' Paisley said.

Shankly was eulogised by Liverpool supporters, and the respect and admiration was mutual. Before one game he went on the Kop with 'the boys', as he called them. He then walked into the dressing room, his shirt torn, tie undone and jacket askew to inform his amazed players.

In 1965, at the victory parade to celebrate the club's longed-for first FA Cup success, Shankly stepped forward to speak from the town-hall balcony. 'He just put up his hand and 250,000 people fell silent,' Ron Yeats, the Liverpool captain, recalled. 'He had this connection with people.'

Shankly once told Emlyn Hughes, one of his favourite players: 'When I die I only hope that people will be able to say he played the game, he was fair, he never cheated anyone. And if they can say that, I know I will be able to rest in peace.'

KEY MATCH

Liverpool 3 Internazionale 1, European Cup semi-final, first leg, Anfield, 4 May 1965, (Inter won the tie 4–3 on aggregate)

Internazionale were feared and highly disciplined European champions, but they had never been tested by the type of experience Bill Shankly served up on the first of Liverpool's great European nights at Anfield.

Shankly tapped into the energy of a packed Kop to intimidate and unnerve the Italians. 'Inter first lost psychologically and then went to pieces in play,' the *Corriere Della Sera* newspaper reported.

The Liverpool supporters were already in euphoric mood. On the previous Saturday they had chanted their delight at seeing their side lift the FA Cup for the first time. Wembley had never heard anything like it.

Shankly whipped up the energy levels at Anfield another notch with a calculated gesture before the kick-off: he instructed two injured players – Gerry Byrne, the hero of the Cup final victory, and Gordon Milne – to parade the trophy.

Amid the bedlam, the Italians came out to do their warm-up. They ran towards the Kop, 'home' territory as far as the Liverpool supporters were concerned. Inter soon got the message and retreated to the other end of the ground.

Once the game began, Liverpool tore into them. 'The moving, colourful, picturesque and electrifying support of their fans isn't enough to explain the surprising technical quality of Liverpool's game. It was a miracle, a triumph of athletic soccer,' wrote *Corriere Della Sera*.

'We've been beaten before but tonight we were defeated,' said Helenio Herrera, the Inter manager.

Left Bill Shankly leaves the field to applause after Liverpool's 0–0 draw with Leicester City has secured them the League Championship on 28 April 1973.

KEY MUSEUM ARTEFACT

This book, published in 1996, is one of the many books detailing the story of Liverpool's enigmatic manager Bill Shankly. Originally books on football were aimed solely at the adult market. Charles Alcock, Secretary of the Football Association in its formative years, produced one of the earliest annuals detailing the game. Simply entitled *The Football Annual*, it was first printed in 1868 and published yearly. It examined the teams playing the game throughout the country and, following Alcock's invention of the FA Cup, charted the success of teams in that competition. Today, both players and managers are much more astute, ensuring that books provide them with added income.

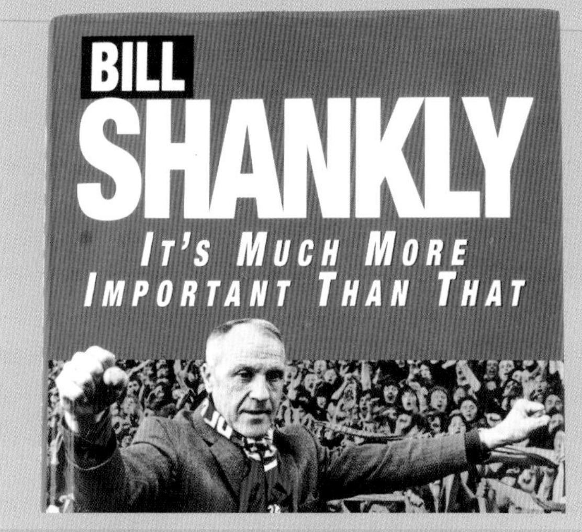

Above A 1911 Scotland shirt. Shankly only pulled on the Scotland jersey on five occasions. But for the outbreak of war, he would surely have added to his international appearances.

Right The *News Chronicle*'s 1938 FA Cup final community singing sheet. Shankly was in the Preston North End team that lost 3–1 to Sunderland, in 1937. A year later, he and Preston returned to Wembley to beat Huddersfield Town 1–0.

When Bill Shankly took up his job as manager of Liverpool in 1959 he was shocked to find that one of the toilets at Anfield had no running water. 'What an eyesore,' he thought to himself, looking round the dilapidated ground.

It was not only the stadium that was in a state of decay. In each of the previous three campaigns, Liverpool had narrowly missed out on promotion to Division One. The club had not won a major honour since 1946. Supporters were frustrated and dispirited.

'In the post-war years Liverpool were not a team of winners,' Paisley recalled. 'There was a feeling that we belonged in the middle of the table, but Bill changed that.'

Shankly was eulogised by Liverpool supporters, and the respect and admiration was mutual.

Shankly first sought stability. He assured the training staff that their jobs were safe. There was one condition: 'At this club there will be no stories about another man,' he told them.

The staff began to meet in a small room under the stand to discuss their work, a habit encouraged by Shankly. It was the start of the 'Boot Room' tradition at Anfield.

On Shankly's orders the team shed their white shorts and socks in favour of an all-red kit. 'I wanted Liverpool players to look more imposing,' he said.

Shankly had insisted on selecting the team as a condition of taking the job. The directors had to content themselves now with finding money to buy new players.

Shankly spent those funds wisely, bringing Ron Yeats, a centre-half, and a forward, Ian St John, from Scotland. All but a handful of the players he inherited were sold to pay for further reinforcements.

In the season before his arrival Liverpool were beaten in the FA Cup by Worcester City, a non-League side. By 1961–62, promotion had been won. Two seasons later, Liverpool were champions.

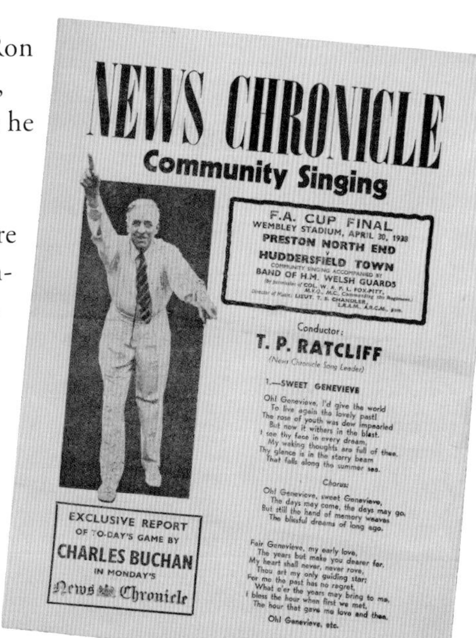

NEWS CHRONICLE
Community Singing

F.A. CUP FINAL
WEMBLEY STADIUM, APRIL 30, 1938
PRESTON NORTH END
v
HUDDERSFIELD TOWN
COMMUNITY SINGING ACCOMPANIED BY
BAND OF H.M. WELSH GUARDS

Conductor:
T. P. RATCLIFF
(News Chronicle Song Leader)

1.—SWEET GENEVIEVE

Oh! Genevieve, I'd give the world
To live again the lovely past!
The rose of youth was dew impearled
But now it withers in the blast.
I see thy face in every dream,
My waking thoughts are full of thee.
Thy glance is in the starry beam
That falls along the summer sea.

Chorus:
Oh! Genevieve, sweet Genevieve,
The days may come, the days may go,
But still the hand of memory weaves
The blissful dreams of long ago.

Fair Genevieve, my early love,
The years but make you dearer far,
My heart shall never, never rove,
Thou art my only guiding star;
For me the past has no regret,
What e'er the years may bring to me,
I bless the hour when first we met,
The hour that gave me love and thee.
Oh! Genevieve, etc.

EXCLUSIVE REPORT
OF TO-DAY'S GAME BY
CHARLES BUCHAN
IN MONDAY'S
News Chronicle

Professional footballers loved to work for Bill Shankly. He gave them self-belief, a football to kick about in training, and success as professionals.

The Liverpool players spent much of their time in training playing five-a-side. Shankly always insisted on keeping things simple.

CARLISLE UNITED A.F.C. (1921) LTD.

MEMBERS OF THE FOOTBALL LEAGUE (3RD DIVISION–NORTHERN SECTION) & N.E. LEAGUE

Colours—ROYAL BLUE JERSEYS AND WHITE KNICKERS

DIRECTORS :

G. CORRIERI (*Chairman*), P. W. SHARP (*Vice-Chairman*), W. HARRISON, T. J. HILL, J. JOHNSTONE, G. W. REED, W. I. BATEY

Telegrams : "EMERY, BRUNTON PARK, CARLISLE"
Telephone No. : 26237 CARLISLE
Secretary-Manager : F. EMERY
Hon. Treasurer : GEO. W. REED

May 1st 1957.

Registered Office :
Brunton Park,
Carlisle

Dear Keith,

You have been granted a Free Transfer, that is you are free to sign for any club after June 30th.

I shall be pleased to help you in any way I am able if you care to call and see me at the office.

Thanking you for your services.

Yours faithfully,

F. Emery

Above This letter to Carlisle United's Keith Mitten was sent by Bill Shankly's successor as manager, Fred Emery. In 1949, Shankly returned to Brunton Park as manager, 17 years after United had given him his first professional contract as a player

TALKING POINT

No matter what the weather, Bill Shankly always had the same message for the Liverpool players before the start of training.

'Just about every morning we'd go out for training,' recalled Brian Hall, the Liverpool midfield player, 'and it could be pouring with rain or blowing a gale, and Shanks would say: "Great to be alive, boys; all you need is the green grass and a ball.'

Shankly hated to miss an opportunity to play football. As a middle-aged man, during his time as manager of Huddersfield Town in the mid-50s, he would join in a kickabout on Sunday mornings with local lads on open ground near his home.

At Liverpool, he organised five-a-side games involving the other coaches and apprentice players. If they were short of numbers, Shankly would invite the bin men to have a game. It was common knowledge that the games would go on until Shankly's side was in front.

In his Preston days, one newspaper described Shankly as 'an inexhaustible' player. 'I wasn't satisfied unless I could sprint for 90 minutes, let alone play,' he said.

At his previous club, Huddersfield Town, the reserve-team players threatened to go on strike when Shankly was put in charge of the first-team training. 'We wanted a share of Bill as well,' recalled Ray Wilson, the future England defender. 'He made training ever so enjoyable. All he wanted to do was play.'

Shankly had an eye for leadership quality in others. Ron Yeats was made captain before he had played a single game. A few weeks later, after his home debut, journalists were invited 'to take a walk around our new centre-half'. Yeats recalled: 'I was a bit embarrassed but it made me feel ten feet tall.'

He also made players believe in themselves. In his early days at Anfield, as a raw 20-year-old, Kevin Keegan was told that he would go on to play for England within 18 months. Buoyed by this statement, Keegan made it with a couple of months to spare. He, in turn, was devoted to Shankly, dedicating an autobiography to his memory.

Bill Shankly died in 1981. He had touched everyone in the city. When his funeral procession drove past the Everton training ground, the players, still in muddy kit, stood in a line at the side of the road, heads bowed.

Left A Grimsby Town ceramic pot from the late 1920s. After his spell at Carlisle United, Shankly moved to Grimsby where he stayed from 1951 to 1953.

DAVE MACKAY (1934–)

Player • Inducted 2002 • 22 Caps • 1 Division One Championship • 3 FA Cups

'Dave Mackay was the physical leader of the Double-winning Tottenham Hotspur side,' Jimmy Greaves once wrote. 'He went into games as if he was a warrior going into battle.'

'Dave was the greatest player in that great side,' Greaves said, 'an individual who had just about everything: power, skill, stamina and enthusiasm. He was the best professional I ever played alongside. When he was missing we all had to work twice as hard.'

Cliff Jones, a member of the Double team of 1960–61, said: 'Once Dave Mackay settled into that number six shirt, he turned a good side into a great one.'

Bill Nicholson paid Heart of Midlothian £30,000, then a British record fee for a wing-half, to bring Mackay to White Hart Lane in 1958. He stayed for a decade, during which time Spurs won the Division One title once and the FA Cup three times, in 1961, 1962 and 1967.

By the time he captained Spurs to victory at Wembley in 1967 Mackay had, by his own admission, slowed considerably. Struggling to keep up with the pace in midfield, he was made available for transfer in 1968.

On hearing the news, Brian Clough raced down to London, unannounced. Risking rejection, Clough subjected himself to the indignity of being kept waiting at White Hart Lane for several hours, all for the chance to persuade Mackay to join him at Derby County.

Clough regarded the veteran Mackay as a potential mentor for his young side. Mackay signed; in his first season at the Baseball Ground, Derby were promoted as Division Two champions, and the veteran Scotsman was voted Footballer of the Year.

'I can't overstate the impact and influence Mackay had at the Baseball Ground,' Clough said. 'Our self-confidence soared because of him. He was the consummate, complete professional, a man of immense talent.'

KEY MATCH

Chelsea 1 Tottenham Hotspur 2, Wembley, FA Cup final, 20 May 1967

Dave Mackay was able to exorcise some painful memories when he walked up the famous steps at Wembley to collect the FA Cup.

In that moment he confounded those critics who previously wrote him off as a spent force.

As he lifted the trophy, the Spurs captain thought back to the events of 1963 and 1964, when he endured the agonising experience of twice breaking his leg in the space of nine months.

'A lot of people wrote me off when I broke my leg for a second time, and nobody is happier than me to prove them all wrong,' Mackay recalled. 'It was one of the most satisfying moments of my career when I collected the Cup.'

'Dave had a personal mission to win after having been inactive for so long, and he was driving us on like a man possessed,' said Jimmy Greaves.

Six years on from the Double, Mackay was the only surviving member of the 1961 side in the starting line-up against Chelsea.

As his pace deserted him, Mackay concentrated more heavily on his defensive duties. Against Chelsea, he rarely made attacking forays in a game Spurs dominated. 'We were never going to lose the game, and I wanted to make sure we didn't give anything away,' Mackay said.

Left Spurs captain, Dave Mackay, keeps his eye on the ball in this aerial tussle with Liverpool's Ian St John during a match in March 1968.

KEY MUSEUM ARTEFACT

This goalkeeper's shirt was worn by Scotland's goalkeeper Frank Haffey in their 9–3 humiliation by England at Wembley in 1961. Although Scotland contained a number of truly world-class players, such as Denis Law and Dave Mackay, they were no match for England on the day. Unfortunately for Haffey, the bright yellow shirt he wore clearly distinguished the goalkeeper from any outfield players. However, this had not always been the case. Until 1909, goalkeepers wore the same colour shirts as the rest of their team-mates, which often led to confusion during goalmouth scrambles.

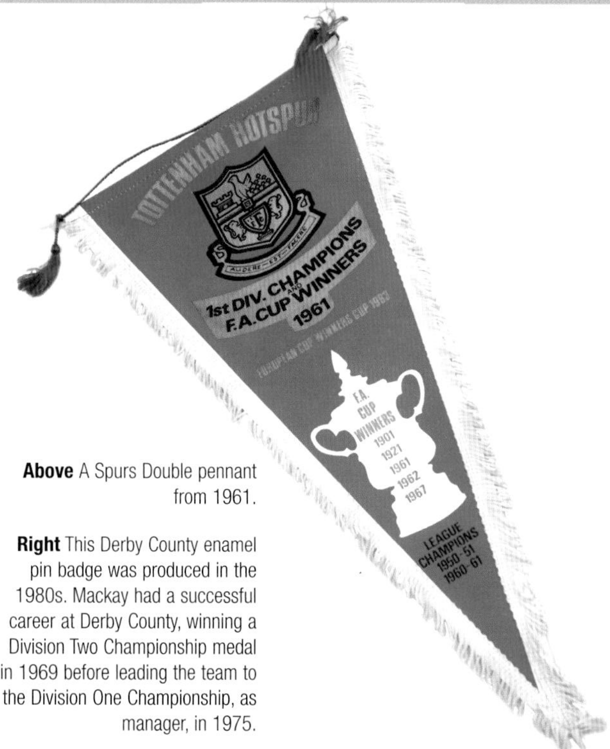

Above A Spurs Double pennant from 1961.

Right This Derby County enamel pin badge was produced in the 1980s. Mackay had a successful career at Derby County, winning a Division Two Championship medal in 1969 before leading the team to the Division One Championship, as manager, in 1975.

> **"When Dave was carried off [with a broken leg], the heart of the Double side went with him."** – *Jimmy Greaves*

The big English clubs were surprised when Hearts suddenly put their best player up for sale in 1958. Dave Mackay, the lynchpin of the Scotland half-back line, had recently fractured a bone in his foot. The newspapers were suspicious: reporters asked had fitness concerns prompted the sale? Bill Nicholson ignored all the rumours and tabled a bid.

In fact, Hearts had simply wanted the money, Mackay said later. A foot injury had been troubling him, but a regime of treatment and weight training at Spurs soon corrected the problem.

Mackay was bought to strengthen the defence, and his arrival freed the creative talent of Danny Blanchflower, his half-back partner, and Cliff Jones, the Spurs winger. 'With Dave behind him, I knew Cliff would be able to show his full potential,' Blanchflower said.

Mackay was surprised when he broke his leg on a cold night at Old Trafford in December 1963. He had expected to feel sharp pain; instead he just felt sick. It was a serious injury. Mackay would be sidelined for more than a season. 'When Dave was carried off, the heart of the Double side went with him,' Jimmy Greaves said. 'We were never the same again.'

The following September, Mackay broke his leg again in his comeback reserve match. 'It plunged all of us at the club into a mood of gloom,' Greaves said. Bill Nicholson 'was absolutely choked' on hearing the news.

'Dave was critical to the Double side,' Greaves said. 'Looking back, it was as if the team died overnight at Old Trafford. It took more than a season for its complete break-up but somehow the magic had gone.'

Dave Mackay helped Derby County reach the top, first as a player and then as manager at the Baseball Ground. Brian Clough needed all his powers of persuasion to bring Mackay to the Midlands. The player looked set to quit England altogether. He had set his mind on the job of assistant manager at Hearts.

When all else failed, Clough offered to make Mackay one of the highest paid footballers in the country. 'Done,' Mackay said immediately. Clough described the deal as 'the best bit of business I did in my entire career'. Instead of playing in midfield, Mackay was told to drop back as sweeper, the ideal position from which to bark out his orders.

'Brian went out of his way to build me up as a superman,' Mackay said. 'Even when I had a bad game others were criticised. It was good psychology, though, because I could only make the young players

> **[Buying Dave Mackay was] the best bit of business I did in my entire career.**
> – *Brian Clough*

believe in themselves if they believed in me.'

Soon after the club won promotion Mackay left to begin his management career. In October 1973, he was back. Derby County were in crisis following the departure of Clough and Peter Taylor.

Mackay first quelled a player rebellion in support of Clough, then gradually stamped his own imprint on the side that his predecessor had guided to the Division One title in 1971–72.

Derby secured their second title in four years in 1974–75. Mackay made two important signings: Bruce Rioch, a marauding midfield player, and Francis Lee, a forward. They scored 27 goals between them.

'I knew that once I got the players' full attention and concentration we would make a strong challenge for the championship,' Mackay said.

Above An England v Scotland ticket from 1951. Mackay made his international debut in 1957 whilst at Hearts. He won 22 caps and faced England on only three occasions – in 1959, '61 and '63.

Right A programme from the England v Scotland international in 1961.

TALKING POINT

When Dave Mackay went into a tackle, he 'could bruise the side of a tank', according to one of his team-mates at Hearts.

In his days at Spurs, Mackay was without rival as the strongest tackler in English football, said Matt Busby. 'Dave had juddering impact on opponents when he went for the ball. In my experience, the only player who could compare with him was the late Duncan Edwards,' Busby wrote in 1973.

'Mackay was as hard as anyone in the game but he had skill too,' said Jimmy Greaves, his Tottenham team-mate.

Mackay won possession in the tackle through a combination of strength, bravery and balance.

Mackay was renowned for his competitiveness. His voice was always the loudest in five-a-side matches, according to Danny Blanchflower. One incident above all summed him up. During a fourth-round FA Cup replay at White Hart in February 1960, Mackay was warned by the referee for going in too hard against lowly underdogs Crewe Alexandra. Spurs were winning 7–1 at the time. They won the game 13–2.

DENIS LAW (1940–)

Player • Inducted 2002 • 55 Caps • 2 Division One Championships • 1 FA Cup

Matt Busby paid a British record transfer fee of £115,000 to bring Denis Law to Old Trafford in July 1962. 'Denis would have been good value at twice the price,' Busby said.

'Denis was the sharpest striker I had ever seen, and he was also the most unselfish,' the Manchester United manager added. 'He was seconds quicker than anyone else in thought and deed. Goals that looked simple as Denis tapped them in were simple only because he got himself into position so quickly.'

Busby recognised the talent early. At the age of 16 years and 303 days, Law made his debut for Huddersfield Town. Within a matter of weeks, Busby put in his first bid for his transfer.

After watching Law play a youth game, Busby offered Bill Shankly, the then Huddersfield Town manager, £10,000, an unheard of sum for a player that age. It was, however, less than a tenth of the fee Busby would eventually have to fork out. Shankly turned him down flat.

A year later, Busby, the part-time manager of Scotland, gave Law his debut at full international level. He was the youngest player ever to represent the country.

After a brief spell at Manchester City, Law was sold to Torino for a fee of £125,000 in 1961. Within months, he was describing Italian football as 'sick, ruined by money'. Turin, he said, was like a 'prison for a footballer'.

His escape followed a chance meeting. Law was playing for the Italian League against the Football League at Old Trafford. 'I don't like playing in Italy,' Law told Busby. 'Why don't you come and buy me?'

Busby needed no encouragement. 'It was one of my best ever bits of business,' he said.

KEY MATCH

Leicester City 1 Manchester United 3, FA Cup final, Wembley, 25 May 1963

Denis Law helped fulfil a pledge made by Matt Busby in the dark days after the Munich disaster with two goals at Wembley in a display that left Gordon Banks, the opposition goalkeeper he outwitted, awe-struck in admiration.

Busby had said it would take him five years to rebuild Manchester United into a club capable of winning major honours following the tragic losses of 1958 – and this was the last chance for them to meet that deadline.

'I have never seen Law play better,' wrote Donald Saunders in the *Daily Telegraph*. 'Audacious, slippery as an eel, driven to greater and greater effort by a very Scottish determination to succeed, this volatile young man unravelled Leicester City's defensive web.'

Law had scored 23 times in 38 League appearances that season – goals which almost certainly kept a struggling side in Division One. Having narrowly avoided relegation, they were underdogs at Wembley.

Law scored his side's vital first goal. Receiving the ball with his back to goal, he turned sharply and fired a low shot past Banks. But the England 'keeper was even more impressed later in the game by 'the most staggering header' he had ever seen. 'I sensed no danger: the cross seemed yards too high for him. Yet Denis somehow met it. With amazing reflexes and power he lifted himself what appeared to be three yards off the turf. I stood transfixed on my line. I was staggered that anyone could have done that.'

Left Denis Law celebrates a goal in trademark fashion at Old Trafford.

KEY MUSEUM ARTEFACT

Law's natural agility and speed off the mark, allied to some brutal confrontations with opposition defenders, saw him suffer a series of injuries throughout his career. This physiotherapy equipment was used to stimulate muscles and improve blood circulation. The four electrodes were attached to the skin and then an electrical current was passed through the injured area. This method of recovery, known as TENS (Transcutaneous Electronic Nerve Stimulation), is still used today to ease pain.

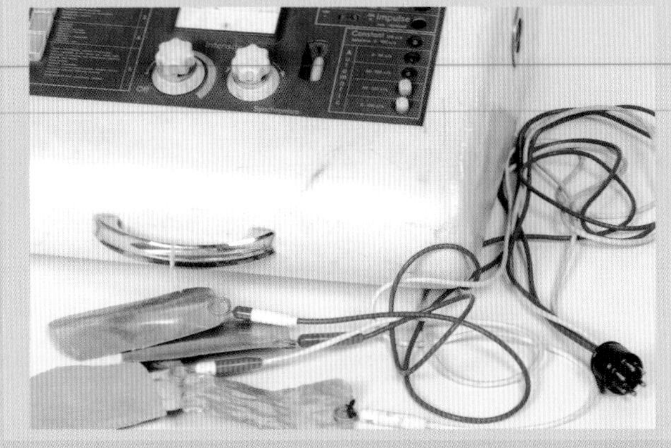

Above Denis Law missed out on a European Cup Final shirt and winners medal in 1968 due to a persistent injury. Instead, he was in hospital recovering from a knee operation. This winner's medal and shirt belonged to United goalkeeper Alex Stepney.

'Without my temperament I would be nothing as a footballer,' Denis Law said. 'It's the source of my success as well as my mistakes.'

Throughout his career Law possessed an intense will to win. 'I'm a bad loser,' he said. 'I play it hard. I have to dominate my opponent. Some people criticise such sentiments. I see them as a source of pride.'

It is hard to imagine a more unlikely looking aspiring professional footballer than Denis Law at the age of 15.

Occasionally, if he thought himself unfairly provoked, he would retaliate. He once famously chased Ian Ure, the Arsenal centre-half, around the pitch in a fury seeking retribution for a tackle. Both players were sent off.

Three times, between 1963 and 1967, Law received lengthy suspensions from the football authorities for his behaviour on the field. 'Learning to live with my temperament is my private battle,' he once said.

But there was also no doubting his bravery. 'I have seen his legs virtually cut to ribbons, with blood and cuts, and covered in bruises from kicks in a game,' Busby said.

One knock to his knee during the 1965–66 season would have unforeseen consequences. The injury was misdiagnosed and the condition of the joint steadily deteriorated. By May 1968, the pain was unbearable, forcing Law to undergo corrective surgery. He watched his team-mates win the European Cup final on television in hospital.

'Trying to kick Denis is a waste of time,' Bobby Charlton said at the time. 'It never stops him, and he is fiery enough to hit them harder than they hit him.' Dave Mackay once described Law as 'well built and hard as teak'.

It is hard to imagine a more unlikely looking aspiring professional footballer than Denis

Law at the age of 15. 'I was weak, puny and bespectacled with a dreadful squint,' Law recalled.

Andy Beattie, the Huddersfield Town manager, took one look at the boy standing in front of him, barely five feet tall, a boil on his cheek, and wearing round, standard-issue National Health glasses to correct his vision. 'The boy's a freak,' he told a colleague.

But his unlikely appearance hid a raw natural talent. An abnormally slow heart beat, instant acceleration from a standing start, and razor-sharp reflexes made young Law stand out. A diet heavy in steak and milk soon built up his strength and stamina.

Speed was the essence of Law's game. 'I had to get in front of the defender,' he said. 'It was all about getting that half-yard on my marker.' He also worked tirelessly during games. 'Training and practice bores me,' he said. 'I like to save everything for Saturday. If I don't finish a game feeling half dead I have a sense of failure.'

> **"I like to save everything for Saturday. If I don't finish a game feeling half-dead I have a sense of failure."** – *Denis Law*

The 1963–64 season was perhaps his peak. 'I was flying,' he said. 'I finished with 30 goals in as many League matches, with 15 more in Cup ties.'

Bobby Charlton described Law as 'easily the best inside-forward in Britain'. 'Denis was a bargain,' Charlton wrote. 'When he is really in form, he is virtually unstoppable.'

Above A Scotland interntional cap from 1961. Although Law made his international debut in 1959, it was not until 1974 that he appeared in his first and only World Cup finals.

TALKING POINT

On 27 April 1974, Denis Law scored his last goal at Old Trafford. His back-heel flick in the 82nd minute won a crucial derby game.

Law had a distinctive way of celebrating a goal: raising one arm and pointing his index finger to the sky. Law set the trend, according to Matt Busby. 'Before Denis, such salutes to the crowd were rare,' Busby said.

But there was no trademark celebration on this occasion. Law was playing for Manchester City, and everyone inside Old Trafford knew that his goal had condemned Manchester United to relegation.

Law had left Old Trafford against his will in 1973. At the age of 33, he returned for one season to Maine Road, where he played in 1960–61, before his £100,000 transfer to Torino in Italy.

He had not wanted to play at Old Trafford for fear of exactly this eventuality. 'United meant too much to me,' he wrote later, 'but as a professional, once I had been selected I had to play. When the goal went in, I was feeling sick. I was totally depressed and I wished that the ball had gone wide.'

Law was substituted immediately. That summer he played for Scotland in the World Cup in West Germany. He won the last of his 55 caps against Zaire in his final game as a professional. On his return home, Law retired.

'My last ever touch in League football was the goal that sent United down,' he said. 'So I left the stage, without really taking a bow.'

Above Denis Law (far left) fires in Manchester United's first goal in the 1963 FA Cup Final against Leicester City. United ran out 3–1 winners.

WELL

JIMMY GREAVES (1940–)

Player • Inducted 2002 • 57 caps • 2 FA Cups • 1 European Cup-winners' Cup

By his own admission, Jimmy Greaves posed almost no threat in the air, lacked a physical presence to unsettle his marker and did not possess an explosive shot; yet he was justly acclaimed as the greatest goalscorer of his era.

Six times in his career with Chelsea and then Tottenham Hotspur Greaves finished as the leading goalscorer in Division One. No forward of the modern era has dominated his trade to this extent.

The majority of his 357 goals in 514 League games were scored from close range and with his left foot. 'I was born with an instinctive, natural gift for sticking the ball in the net, and I wasn't interested in doing much else,' Greaves once said. 'I don't consciously scheme goals, nor take up pre-determined positions. I don't have a thunderous shot like Bobby Charlton, nor have I spent hours working out shooting angles. I just get in as close as I can and let rip.'

Bill Nicholson, the Spurs manager, once famously said that 'Jimmy could pass to the stanchions'. One newspaper likened his deft scoring style to 'closing the door on a Rolls-Royce'.

Greaves scored 44 goals, including a record six hat-tricks, in 57 appearances for England between 1959 and 1967. Johnny Haynes, the England captain in the early part of Greaves' international career, said: 'No player has ever had such cold finishing power.'

Greaves returned to English football after a brief, unhappy spell with A C Milan in November 1961. In each of the next three full seasons, Greaves finished as leading scorer in Division One.

He joined the Double-winning side for a fee of £99,999, adding a cutting edge to the attack. Dave Mackay, Johnny White and Danny Blanchflower created the openings from midfield. 'They were talented enough to read my off-the-cuff runs and instinctive play and skilful enough to make the right pass,' Greaves said. 'It was a great experience.'

KEY MATCH

Tottenham Hotspur 3 Burnley 1, FA Cup final, Wembley, 5 May 1962

The Duke of Edinburgh was surprised to see Jimmy Greaves standing before him during the presentation of the two teams before the game.

After shaking Greaves' hand, the Duke said: 'I thought you were in Italy.' Overhearing the remark, Danny Blanchflower, the Spurs captain, replied: 'No, sir, we bought him back, and he cost enough, believe me.'

Earlier in the season Tottenham had pulled off a transfer coup, spending a record fee that was set at £99,999 by Bill Nicholson, the manager, to avoid saddling Greaves with the title of 'Britain's first £100,000 player'.

On the day, Spurs won quite easily, giving the 22-year-old Greaves his first major honour. 'Our dressing room before the game was very calm,' he said. 'It's nerves that lead to scrappy play, and at Wembley we didn't have any.'

Inside the first five minutes, Greaves ran onto a flick-on by Bobby Smith, the Spurs centre-forward. Deliberately overrunning the ball in order both to confuse the defenders and to give himself space, Greaves first checked, then slotted the ball into the net.

Tottenham, like Burnley, had faltered late on in their challenge for the Division One title. In the European Cup, Spurs lost in the semi-final against Benfica. 'Even though we were bitterly disappointed, we had been hardened by the experience in Europe, and that helped us at Wembley,' Greaves said.

Left Tottenham Hotspur's Jimmy Greaves holds the European Cup-winners' Cup aloft, during the teams open-top bus tour of North London, following their 5-1 victory over Atletico Madrid in Rotterdam.

KEY MUSEUM ARTEFACT

The endorsement of products by players was nothing new to the game by the 1960s. While Jimmy Greaves was happy to tell the world that Bovril assisted his physical preparation, the star of Manchester City's FA Cup final win in 1904, Billy Meredith, attributed his fitness to Oxo. Manchester United, on the other hand, were more than happy to accept payment to tell the public that Wincarnis Popular Tonic had 'increased their powers of endurance' for their 1909 FA Cup final victory over Bristol City.

At the age of 20 years and nine months, Jimmy Greaves became the youngest ever player to score 100 goals in the Football League. Almost exactly three years later he equalled – to the day – Dixie Dean's age record for scoring the quickest 200 League goals. The lad was a phenomenon.

After making his debut for Chelsea at the age of 17, he played 169 games for the club, scoring 132 goals. At the end of his final game for the club he was carried from the field on the shoulders of supporters.

THE GREAT NEW WEMBLEY

Topping News For Sports Fans—

All 100,000 Under Cover In 1963

It Will Be World's Finest Stadium

By BILL McGOWRAN

WEMBLEY is to have a £500,000 face lift which will make it the world's finest sporting stadium. The improvements will include covered accommodation for 100,000 people under a translucent roof of fibre glass.

There will also be new restaurants and enormously improved cloakroom facilities.

Not even the massed defences in Italy could stop him. Following his transfer to Milan for a fee of £80,000 in 1961, he scored nine goals in 12 games in *Serie A*. But Greaves hated Italian football: 'An outrageous, petty, laughable world where everything was done in the name of football and the spirit of the game was battered beyond recognition.' He celebrated his return to English football during the 1961–62 season by scoring 21 goals in 22 League games for Spurs.

> **"Jimmy has a great coolness when it comes to finishing. It is a gift which can scarcely be taught. He was a natural."**
> *– Bill Nicholson*

In hindsight, his career can be divided into two halves: before and after 1965. He was never quite the same following a debilitating bout of hepatitis in November of that year. He was lighting a bonfire for his children when he suddenly felt 'as if someone had chopped my legs off'.

The illness weakened Greaves, sidelining him for three months. But the long-term consequences were more serious. 'When I came back I realised I had lost a vital half-yard of pace, and speed was vital to my game,' he said.

Meanwhile, and much to his distaste, the game was becoming increasingly defensive tactically. There were fewer chances, and though he still regarded

Above This 1953 lithographic print by Alister Grant is entitled *Snow at Stamford Bridge.* Greaves signed professional terms with Chelsea in 1957. When he joined the club, the ground had changed little since its design and construction, in 1905, by the great stadium builder Archibald Leitch.

Above right This 1961 scrapbook details the development of Wembley Stadium to protect its 100,000 spectators under one roof. Unfortunately, Greaves benefited from no such protection when he lost his place to Geoff Hurst in the 1966 World Cup finals.

One newspaper likened his deft scoring style to closing the door on a Rolls-Royce.

himself, with some justification, as the best goalscorer in the League despite the illness, his scoring rate did slow noticeably in the second half of the decade.

Joe Mercer had the greatest admiration for Jimmy Greaves because of his willingness, and courage, to do 'absolutely nothing' during a game.

'Jimmy is the greatest finisher I've ever seen,' the Manchester City manager said. 'You can't mark him. The reason: he is prepared to stand still. It takes great courage as a footballer to appear lazy, to look as if you're doing nothing. But then, all of a sudden, when the chance arises, Jimmy is gone. He had left his shadow standing.'

Bill Nicholson said: 'Jimmy's muscular reaction is fantastic, and this is why he is able to get his foot to a ball a split-second before a defender. He also has a great coolness in finishing, another gift which can scarcely be taught. Jimmy was a natural.'

At times it all seemed to be ridiculously easy. Terry Venables, a Spurs team-mate, once joined Greaves for a pre-match meal in his favourite pub before a home game. Venables ate a grilled chicken breast. Greaves ordered roast beef, Yorkshire pudding, carrots, peas, cauliflower and potatoes, roasted and boiled, followed by steamed pudding and custard. 'I gazed at him in disbelief,' Venables recalled. 'Was this any way for a professional sportsman to carry on? Evidently it was. We won 6–1 that afternoon and Jim scored five of the goals.'

Johnny Haynes was equally amazed as he watched Greaves score a hat-trick in England's 9–3 win against Scotland in 1961. 'When Jimmy plays as he did that day I find myself wondering if there has ever been a player like him in the entire history of the game,' the England captain said.

TALKING POINT

Jimmy Greaves feared the worst when Alf Ramsey approached him for a word in private on the morning of the World Cup final.

Greaves awoke that morning convinced that he would not be recalled against West Germany at Wembley. He had already packed his bags at the team hotel, ready to make his departure after the game.

'Alf didn't say much to me,' Greaves recalled. 'He just said he had decided on an unchanged team. I said, "Sure Alf. I'm sure they will win it for you."'

Greaves had not played in the quarter-final against Argentina after having four stitches inserted in a deep gash on his shin. 'It was an injury that provided the excuse for my exit from the tournament,' he later wrote.

'At the end of the semi-final I felt in my bones that Alf was not going to select me for the final. I felt sorry for myself and sick that I was out. But I was not, and have never been, in any way bitter against Alf. He did his job and England won the trophy.'

The following year he asked Ramsey not to pick him in the squad if he was not going to play. In turn, Ramsey said that he could not guarantee him a starting place. The England career of Jimmy Greaves was over.

Above *Stamford Bridge*, a watercolour painted in 1953 by Edwin La Dell. Greaves made 157 League appearances for Chelsea, between 1957 and 1960, scoring a magnificent 124 goals.

Left The 1961 European Cup-winners' Cup. Greaves helped Spurs to become the first British side to win a European trophy when he scored in their 5–1 victory over Atletico Madrid in Rotterdam in 1963.

DON REVIE (1927–1989)

Manager • Inducted 2004 • 2 Division One Championships
1 FA Cup • 2 Fairs Cups • 1 League Cup

Don Revie was ridiculed in the newspapers as a bit of a pretentious upstart when he declared: 'We are going to become a Real Madrid. One day, this club will rule in Europe.'

Behind his back, even some of his own Leeds United players were mocking him over the statement. The sniggering was hardly surprising given the circumstances. Revie had no experience yet in management, and Leeds United, a club of little pedigree, were languishing at the time in Division Two, where they had been stuck for a generation.

Revie also announced that Leeds United would be changing their colours from blue and yellow to the all-white strip made famous by Real. 'You could almost hear the laughter ringing throughout English football,' Norman Hunter, the Leeds defender, recalled.

Yet, for a brief period at least, Revie fulfilled his seemingly ludicrous promise. In the years between promotion in 1963–64 and his departure to take the England job in 1974, Leeds did, in fact, win more trophies in Europe than the Madrid aristocrats.

The younger players had reacted differently to his prophecy than had the more cynical older pros: Hunter, a future England defender, said: 'I took it as read that it would happen. I totally and utterly believed in Don Revie.'

Revie transformed Leeds into the most consistently successful team in England. For a decade they finished no lower than fourth in Division One. In addition to their two titles, in 1968–69 and 1973–74, Leeds were runners-up five times. In Europe, Leeds won the Fairs Cup twice, one more trophy than Real.

'Don's greatest asset was his intensity,' Johnny Giles, the Leeds midfield player said. 'When he took over the job he wanted to be the best manager Britain had ever known.'

His record at club level made Revie the Football Association's obvious choice as successor to Sir Alf Ramsey as England manager. Unfortunately, Revie's reputation would not survive the appointment in tact.

KEY MATCH

**Liverpool 0 Leeds United 0,
Division One, Anfield, 28 April 1969**

Billy Bremner could not believe the instruction he was being given by Don Revie. Leeds had won the club's first title, at the expense of Liverpool, their opponents on the night, and now Revie told his players to parade the trophy in front of the Kop.

None of the players wanted to do it, fearful that the gesture might backfire, but Revie insisted. He had a deep respect for Bill Shankly, the Liverpool manager, and all the club stood for, and he also wanted his own team's achievement properly acknowledged.

'As we walked towards the Kop there was a deathly silence,' recalled Norman Hunter. 'All of a sudden, a guy was hoisted up on someone's shoulders and started chanting "Champions! Champions!" It was great of the Liverpool supporters.'

In a typically disciplined performance, Leeds defended superbly at Anfield. It was the first time Revie told his team to go out with the express intention of securing a point, Hunter said.

Revie also took Bremner out of midfield and employed him as sweeper. 'We adopted spoiling tactics and worked hard at closing Liverpool down quickly,' Hunter said.

In winning the title, Leeds amassed a record 67 points, losing only twice. Revie said: 'Bill Shankly came into the dressing room to say a few words. "You didn't fluke the title or pinch it. You deserved it. You're a wonderful team."'

Left Don Revie embraces Jack Charlton after Leeds United's 1–0 victory over Arsenal in the Centenary FA Cup final on 6 May 1972.

KEY MUSEUM ARTEFACT

This shirt was manufactured by Umbro for the Centenary FA Cup final in 1972. It was worn by forward Alan Clarke who scored the only goal of the game, after 54 minutes, in Leeds United's 1–0 win over Arsenal. It gave Don Revie his one and only FA Cup as a manager. It's notable that during this period of the club's history the 'Owl' motif, so resplendent on the shirts when Leeds won the League in 1969, had been dropped. Umbro also incorporated small holes into the nylon shirts to allow the players to remain as cool as possible when playing.

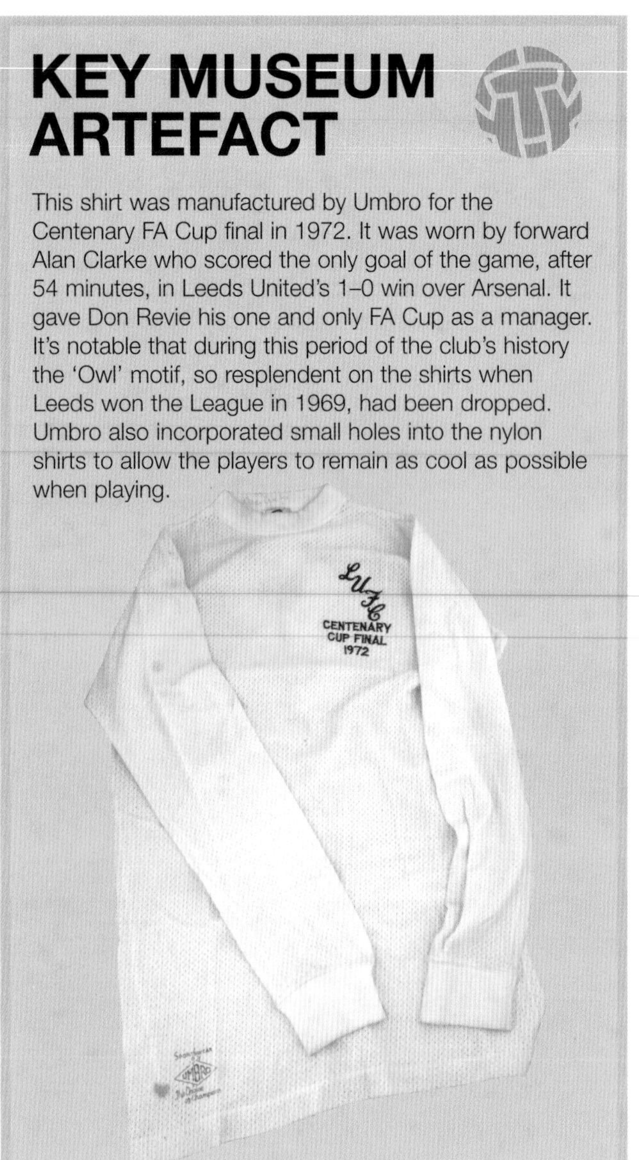

Right This scale model of Wembley was made by Calcutt, Shelly and Dorsett in 2000. Revie saw a lot more of Wembley after he agreed a five-year deal to manage the England side in July 1974. However, he found the job difficult without the daily contact with his players and he won only 14 of his 29 games in charge of England.

Soon after taking the job as Leeds United manager, Don Revie drove across the Pennines to Old Trafford on a mission to pick the brains of the man he most admired in football.

The example of Manchester United inspired Revie and Matt Busby was happy to give advice: 'Be loyal and honest to your players, never lie, and they will do anything for you in return.'

The task facing Revie in 1961 was daunting: crowds had fallen below 9,000 in what was a Rugby League stronghold; indiscipline was rife and the club's reputation in the game was poor. Several managers had previously turned down offers to work at Elland Road. Revie set about changing perceptions. He rallied supporters, demonstrated his intent by doubling the club record transfer fee and overhauled the staff. He even bought new training kit and boots.

> “You may not have heard of us now,' Revie told Eddie Gray's father, 'but we're going to be one of the biggest clubs in Britain.”

In the transfer market, Revie paid Everton £25,000 for Bobby Collins, persuading the former Scotland international to drop a division. The diminutive Collins led the team to promotion by his own fiercely competitive example.

Most significantly, he gathered together an outstanding crop of young players. Peter Lorimer and Eddie Gray were both Scotland schoolboy internationals. All three chose Leeds ahead of bigger, more established clubs. Paul Reaney, Norman Hunter, Paul Madeley and Gary Sprake also started out at Leeds.

Revie succeeded by dint of persistence, charm and salesmanship. 'You may not have heard of us now,' he told Eddie Gray's father, 'but we're going to be one of biggest clubs in Britain.' On another occasion, hearing that Lorimer might sign for a rival club, Revie drove through the night to Scotland to secure his signature.

The year 1969 was a turning point for Leeds United. After several near-misses, the club finally won the First Division championship.

'Our targets now are the European Cup and the World Club championship,' he told reporters. 'I don't think we've reached our peak yet and if we keep working at it, the best years for Leeds can still be those to come.'

Before 1969, Leeds were a disciplined, aggressive side specialising in 1–0 away wins. 'We went a wee bit over the top at times,' Bremner said. 'We weren't going to be intimidated.' Detractors accused them of cynicism and gamesmanship.

After 1969, Revie gave his players more freedom. 'We've changed our style,' he said, 'because now I believe we've got the players to win matches by scoring goals, rather than winning by keeping the opposition out.'

Bremner said: 'In about four or five games up to 1974 we came as near to perfection as you can.'

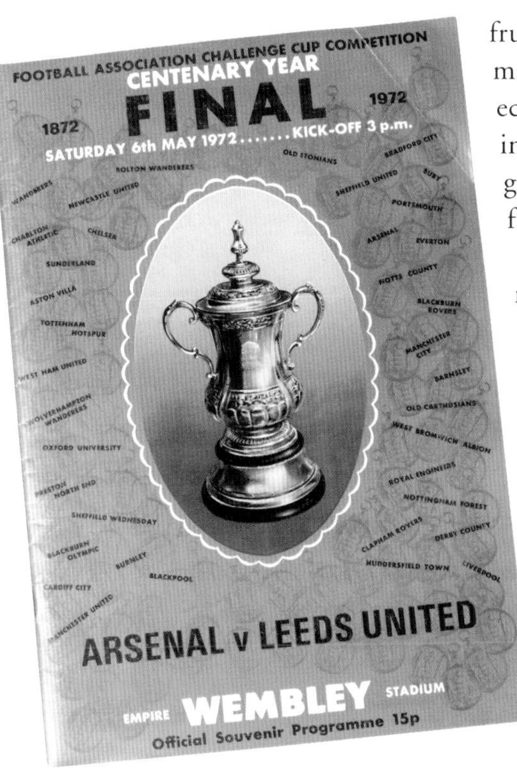

Ultimately, Revie suffered a degree of frustration and disappointment as a manager. He failed in his ambition to eclipse Manchester United as an institution; Leeds simply could not generate the necessary support and finance.

His experience as national team manager was worse. Two years after his appointment, England failed to qualify for the 1976 European Championships. Faced with the prospect of England missing out again, this time in the World Cup two years later, Revie broke his contract to accept a lucrative and secret offer from United Arab Emirates. 'I was going to be sacked anyway,' Revie said. The media vilified him for walking away in such circumstances and, to this day, his reputation has not recovered.

TALKING POINT

Don Revie enjoyed the rare distinction as a player of having a tactic named after him; but he earned greater recognition from a chance appearance in a winning FA Cup side.

Revie, who won six caps for England, was credited in the newspapers with playing a decisive role for Manchester City in the 3–1 defeat of Birmingham City at Wembley in 1956.

As a deep-lying centre-forward, it was Revie's job to anticipate the runs made by his fellow forwards and then supply them with a pass from a central position just behind the attack.

Hungary had introduced the tactic to this country with devastating effect in the 6–3 defeat of England at Wembley in 1953. When Manchester City adopted the method, the press needed a label for the tactic: as the incumbent number nine at Maine Road, Revie's name was the obvious choice, hence 'The Revie Plan'.

By 1956, however, Revie had lost his automatic place in the team. It was only as a result of a late injury to a team-mate that he earned an unexpected call-up for the FA Cup Final. He made the most of his opportunity.

Above left *Soccer's Happy Wanderer* was published in the 1950s. The title reflects the fact that Revie's playing career took him to Leicester City, Hull City and Manchester City.

Above A copy of the FA Cup final replay programme of 1970. It was the first replay to be held since 1912 and, having drawn the first game 2–2, Leeds lost this match 2–1, after extra time.

Left The FA Cup Centenary programme from 1972.

NGLAND 3 GERMANY W. 2

GEOFF HURST (1941–)

Player • Inducted 2004 • 49 caps • 1 World Cup • 1 FA Cup
1 European Cup-winners' Cup

Geoff Hurst, the original 'target man' in English football, made his name almost overnight by becoming the first and so far only player to score a hat-trick in a World Cup final.

Those three goals at Wembley – a superbly timed header, a shot on the turn with his right foot, and a thunderous drive with his left at the end of a run from the half-way line – illustrated the all-round ability of an often under-rated player.

His third goal was the last kick of the match. 'I knew I would never hit a better shot so long as I lived,' he recalled. 'The sound, the feel of the leather on leather was exactly right.'

England went into the World Cup final without an orthodox winger. As a result the ball tended to be played forwards from deeper positions. It was Hurst's job to make himself available to receive a pass. He then had to hold the ball until support arrived. Although the term had yet to enter the football vocabulary, Hurst was the 'target man'.

The hat-trick did wonders for his confidence. 'I came back from the World Cup feeling ten feet tall,' he wrote in 1967. 'I know I have skidded past opponents and scored goals this season in a way that would have been quite beyond me a year ago.'

The following season, 1967–68, Matt Busby, the Manchester United manager, tested West Ham's resolve to keep Hurst. In a telephone call made just before he left for a European Cup-tie in Gornik, in Poland, Busby offered £200,000, almost double the existing record fee. In reply, Ron Greenwood, the West Ham manager, sent a now famous telegram. It read: 'Busby, Manchester United, Gornik. No. Greenwood.'

KEY MATCH

England 1 Argentina 0, World Cup quarter-final, Wembley, 23 July 1966

The goal that made his international career, and transformed Geoff Hurst's opinion of himself as a footballer, bore the trademark: 'Made by West Ham'.

Hour upon hour of practice on the West Ham training ground at Chadwell Heath paid off when Martin Peters crossed early to the near post in a move that finally breached Argentina's disciplined defence.

'We were very innovative at West Ham,' said Hurst. 'It got so that whichever of our players found himself in that wide position, he could whip in these crosses. We worked endlessly at playing the ball in and the timing of the run to the near post.'

In his first game of the tournament, Hurst had made his mark. In that instant, he found his confidence as an England player. 'Suddenly, I was not overawed. I had a belief in myself that I'd probably not felt in my entire career before,' Hurst said.

His behaviour changed almost overnight. Previously, he had kept quiet about his preference for wearing a tracksuit in training, no matter the temperature. None of the other England players wore their tops, and he didn't want to stand out. 'I'm a hefty fellow and I liked to sweat in training. I somehow felt lighter when the real game came around. Probably this is mostly a difference in the mind, but I felt it was important.'

Finally, and for the first time, Hurst spoke his mind, telling Ramsey of his preference. 'Alf said to me, "Alright, Geoff, if it matters to you, go ahead." So I wore my tracksuit. Suddenly I felt half as fit again as I had for weeks, which helped me in the semi-final and the final.'

Left Geoff Hurst scores his third goal and England's fourth in their famous victory over West Germany in the World Cup final on 30 July 1966.

KEY MUSEUM ARTEFACT

The famous orange ball from the 1966 World Cup final remains, in 2005, the only ball to have scored a World Cup final hat-trick. Thanks to the Russian linesman Tofik Bakhramov's impartial decision, hat-trick hero Geoff Hurst secured his place in football history. The Slazenger balls for the tournament were hand-made in Yorkshire by a team of specialist craftsmen led by Malcolm Wainwright. The match ball was taken by Helmut Haller who claimed that a German tradition says that the scorer of the first goal keeps the ball and it remained in his family until it was returned to England just before the Euro 96 tournament.

Above right England had to overcome the precocious talents of Franz Beckenbauer in the 1966 World Cup final. He went on to lead the West Germans to World Cup success in Munich in 1974. This shirt was worn by him in an international against France in 1968.

Alf Ramsey had a long list of requisites for a prospective England forward: he had to be mobile, hard-working, unselfish, physically robust, and a goalscorer with all-round ability. In Geoff Hurst he found a player who fitted the bill perfectly.

Ramsey selected Hurst as his first-choice in the attack for six years between 1966 and 1972, the longest run of any forward during his time as manager.

Hurst had a powerful shot in both feet and an outstanding ability to head the ball, but it was his running off the ball that most impressed managers. 'I took it as a professional compliment when the Spurs manager Bill Nicholson sent his new signing Martin Chivers to watch me and study the way I played,' Hurst said.

'His movement off the ball was fantastic,' Ron Greenwood said. 'Sometimes he was a decoy. Other times he would just knock the ball off, one touch, and then away; sometimes he would go wide to give the attack width and create space for others.'

At more than six feet tall and 13 1/2 stone, Hurst had the ideal build to hold off defenders. 'I was always more confident that we would keep possession when I hit long passes if Geoff was in the side,' Ray Wilson said.

Alan Ball rated the performance of Hurst in the defeat against West Germany in the searing heat of Mexico as his best for England. 'No matter how much pressure you were under, you'd glance up and sure enough there'd be Geoff steaming into view, always making himself available.'

> **"His movement off the ball was fantastic. Sometimes he was a decoy. Other times he would just knock the ball off, one touch, and then away."**
>
> *– Ron Greenwood*

During the winter of 1965 Geoff Hurst was the leading goalscorer in Division One. The following autumn, during a run of 14 games, he scored 22 goals. His value to West Ham was soaring. Immediately after the World Cup, the club made him one of the highest paid footballers in the country, on a new six-year contract.

It had not always been like this. Early in his career Hurst struggled for confidence. He was as surprised as the football media when Ramsey first selected him in the England squad in 1966.

During a squad training session in the build-up to the game, Hurst was anonymous. At heart, he still felt that he did not belong in this company. He was not surprised when Ramsey overlooked him for selection, having told Hurst: 'It's up to you, you know, Geoff.'

Hurst feared that he would be omitted from the final squad of 22 for the tournament. Waiting to find out Ramsey's decision was 'pure hell', he said. Then, in one of England's final warm-up matches, Hurst gave 'the worst, most embarrassing, performance of my international career. I was convinced I had blown it'.

All that changed with his selection for the quarter-final against Argentina. A year later, in 1967, Hurst detected a sense of anticipation in the crowd when he received the ball. Defenders marking him started to ask for help more often. 'For the first time in my sporting life I had the feeling of being good at my job,' he wrote.

At the end of his career, Hurst said: 'I never considered myself a world-class player like Bobby Moore or Bobby Charlton, even at my peak, but I was comfortable in world-class company.'

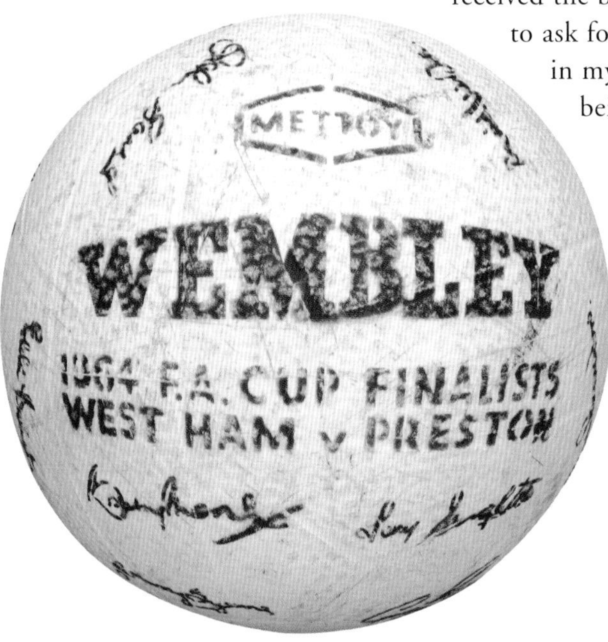

Above A 1966 World Cup Royal Mail First Day Cover posted in Preston.

Left A 1964 souvenir FA Cup final football. Geoff Hurst scored for West Ham United in their 3–2 victory over Division Two Preston North End in the 1964 Cup final.

TALKING POINT

An early report card on Geoff Hurst might have included comments such as 'terrible' and 'this boy doesn't even know where the ball is half the time'.

Hurst was barely holding his own as a wing-half at West Ham when Ron Greenwood took over as manager in 1961. At one point, Hurst almost joined Crystal Palace in Division Three.

Greenwood regarded him as 'just a big, strong, ordinary wing-half, happy when going forward but a terrible defender, particularly off the ball'.

But the coach in Greenwood also detected Hurst's potential as a forward. An injury crisis, leaving his short of strikers, during the 1962–63 season forced his hand.

'Nobody could have worked harder,' Greenwood recalled. 'Geoff increased his mobility and quickly grasped the principles of making and using space, both for himself and for others.

His progress was remarkable. In later years, Greenwood advised the football authorities to compile a film of Hurst's running off the ball for distribution to clubs as a coaching guide.

'Brave as they come, he dragged defenders out of position. The strength of his running and his ability to change direction quickly were phenomenal.'

Below A 1966 World Cup winner's medal, made of solid gold.

JACK CHARLTON (1935–)

Player • Inducted 2005 • 35 Caps • 1 World Cup • 2 Division One Championships
2 Fairs Cups • 1 FA Cup • 1 League Cup

Jack Charlton cut an unmistakable figure: whether as a defender for Leeds United and England or as the manager of the Republic of Ireland, everyone knew 'Big Jack'.

Tall, gangly, and loud, Charlton has always stood out. Even Pope John Paul II recognised him: 'Yes, I know who you are: you're the boss,' the Pontiff said on meeting him in 1990.

As a player, Charlton was a late developer. The prospect of his England debut, at the age of 29, in 1965 generated little enthusiasm. As Bobby Moore said: 'Well, Jack didn't seem to look much like an England player, but appearances can be deceptive.'

In fact, in the uncomplicated, no-nonsense and competitive Charlton, Alf Ramsey had belatedly found the ideal partner for the stylish Moore. 'You're a good tackler, Jack, and good in the air, and I need those things,' Ramsey told him.

Charlton played in 26 of the next 27 internationals, including all six World Cup matches in 1966. England lost only three of the 35 games he played, and in one of those defeats, he broke his toe.

Bill Shankly twice attempted to sign Charlton for Liverpool: 'He's the best English centre-half I've ever seen,' Shankly said. Others came to agree: Charlton was Footballer of the Year in 1967.

Over a 20-year career, Charlton made a club-record 773 appearances for Leeds, before retiring on 28 April 1973, ten days shy of his 38th birthday.

As Shankly predicted, Charlton thrived in management, guiding Middlesbrough to promotion in 1974, when he was awarded Manager of the Year before leading the Republic of Ireland to the World Cup finals in 1990 and 1994. 'He gives a straight answer to a straight question,' Shankly said, 'and that's always a good sign.'

KEY MATCH

England 2 Scotland 2, Home International Championships, Wembley, 10 April 1965

The football writers were delighted when Jack Charlton was handed his debut for England. It made good copy.

The fact that Charlton was almost 30 at the time was interesting enough, particularly in light of the fact that the World Cup was little more than a year away.

But the reporters had another angle: Jack would be a team-mate of Bobby Charlton, making them the first brothers to play in the same England side that century. 'The Press lads liked the angle even more when I passed to Bobby for him to score,' Jack said.

The brothers became closer than the media expected during the game when Bobby was drafted in as an emergency left-back following injuries to Ray Wilson and Johnny Byrne.

Substitutes were not allowed, leaving England, who led 2–1 at the time, with only nine fit players. Even with a two-man advantage, Scotland only managed one more goal.

'In a way it suited me that we had to struggle because I had to get my head down and battle and I didn't have much time to think about what I was doing,' Jack recalled.

Alf Ramsey had found his first-choice defence for the World Cup; numbers one to six that day read: Banks, Cohen, Wilson, Stiles, Charlton and Moore.

Ian St John, the Scotland forward, said Charlton had transformed himself late in his career. 'He was now playing to his strengths: in the air, in the tackle, and in his ability to read the game.'

Left Jack Charlton celebrates World Cup success by giving Alan Ball a piggy-back, around Wembley Stadium, after England's 4–2 victory over West Germany in 1966.

KEY MUSEUM ARTEFACT

This Europa Cup game from the early 1960s featured a transfer-printed tin pitch with 22 hand-operated metal players and plastic goal nets. Advertisement hoardings are also incorporated around the pitch. With the growth of European competitions from the mid-1950s onwards toys and games began to reflect the games taking place between clubs from different countries. Leeds United enjoyed a golden period in European competitions during this time. They were defeated 2–0 by Dynamo Zagreb in the 1967 Fairs Cup final, but went on to win the trophy in 1968 and 1971, beating Ferencvaros and Juventus respectively.

Jack Charlton made a poor first impression on the man who would become his manager at Leeds United, though. 'The best thing that could happen to you would be for the club to leave you out,' Don Revie told him. 'You're spoiling it for the other players with that chip on your shoulder. You'd never do for me.'

'Looking back, I did lack discipline,' Charlton said. 'I was a bit of a one-man awkward squad in my early days at Leeds.'

In the uncomplicated, no-nonsense and competitive Charlton, Alf Ramsey had belatedly found the ideal partner for the stylish Moore.

A year later, after taking over as manager at Elland Road, Revie noticed signs of a change of attitude in his centre-half. He called Charlton into his office. 'Listen Jack, I've been really impressed by your dedication and form in the past few games,' Revie began. 'You've made yourself one of the best centre-halves in the League. If you keep going like that, you'll play for England. I mean it. As long as you screw the nut all the time, not just now and again.'

The conversation proved to be the turning point for a player who had never previously thought of himself as a potential international. 'I decided to knuckle down more,' Charlton said, 'and it turned out Don was right.'

Leeds United won promotion as champions of Division Two in 1963–64, the start of a decade of consistent success for the club.

'Jack turned it round for himself,' Johnny Giles, the Leeds midfield player said. 'Once he got his attitude right, he was outstanding: always competing and getting his foot in when it mattered. His contribution in the promotion season was vital; it was the start of something good for both him and the club.'

Right The 1966 poster by the illustrator E. L. Matto features the first World Cup Mascot, World Cup Willie.

'I don't always pick the best players, you know,' Alf Ramsey told Jack Charlton, soon after giving him his England debut. 'I have a system I like to play in mind and I look for the best players to fit that pattern.

'I've watched you play Jack, and you're quite good,' Ramsey added. 'And I know you won't trust Bobby Moore.'

Charlton was taken aback slightly by this last comment. Ramsey explained his thinking: 'I know that as soon as Bobby goes upfield with the ball, you will always fill in behind him. That way, if Bobby makes a mistake, you're there to cover it.'

Ramsey always looked for players who were fully committed to the England cause. Like the manager himself, Charlton was fiercely patriotic; when he registered at hotels, for insance, he always listed his nationality as 'English', not 'British'.

Perhaps his most significant contribution for England came in the semi-final of the World Cup in 1966. 'He was embroiled in a titanic struggle for aerial superiority with the giant José Torres, the Portugal forward,' Gordon Banks recalled. Charlton won. His brother, Bobby, said: 'Jack played what I consider to be his best game for England.'

Four years later Ramsey took Charlton to the World Cup in Mexico as cover for Brian Labone, the first-choice centre-half. Charlton played in only one group game, but typically, even at the age of 35 and despite the taxing heat and altitude in Mexico, Charlton was convinced that he was still the best man for the job.

TALKING POINT

Jack Charlton was adopted as an honorary Irishman after guiding the Republic of Ireland to the World Cup for the first time in the country's history, and then repeating the trick four years later.

In recognition of his achievement the Englishman was given the freedom of the city of Dublin in 1994. He joined a select company that included George Bernard Shaw, John F. Kennedy, Nelson Mandela and Pope John Paul II.

It was the high point of his managerial career. The following year, defeat in a play-off for the European Championships prompted Charlton to stand down, after almost ten years in the job.

'His secret is that the players trust him,' Mick McCarthy, the Republic of Ireland centre-half, and his successor as manager, said. 'He's very loyal.'

In 1977, Charlton was overlooked for the job as England manager. Disappointed, he returned to club football with Sheffield Wednesday, winning promotion to Division Two in 1979–80, followed by a stint with Newcastle United. Then came the call from the Irish.

He immediately introduced a more direct style of play. 'We got a reputation for knocking the ball long, and it always annoyed me, because we don't do that,' he said. 'We put it into areas of the field which cause defenders problems. It wasn't just a case of humping everything up there and hoping.'

Irish supporters certainly had no complaints. 'Housewives used to have pictures of the Pope or JFK on the walls. Now they have replaced them with pictures of Jack,' the Republic of Ireland striker Niall Quinn said.

Above This is an original England second shirt from the 1966 World Cup final. It would have been issued as a spare and used as a replacement if the original had become damaged or dirty.

Centre This is the crossbar from Wembley that Geoff Hurst hit with the ball for his disputed second goal in the 1966 World Cup final. The wooden, elliptical-shaped bar has a steel rod running through the centre of it to give it strength.

Left A leather, laced football, such as this one from the 1950s, was commonly used until the valve football became popular in the mid-1960s. Although the white football was invented in 1951, it was not widely used until the 1970s.

GEORGE BEST (1946–)

Player • Inducted 2002 • 37 caps • 1 European Cup
2 Division One Championships

George Best, the mercurial genius of Old Trafford and the best footballer in Europe at his peak, was the game's first celebrity icon, a young lad from Belfast who counted The Beatles and Rolling Stones as friends.

Best arrived in Manchester as a shy, nervous, skinny 15-year-old in 1961. Seven years later the once homesick teenager scored the most crucial goal of a European Cup final at Wembley.

Denis Law described Best as 'a complete footballer'. Matt Busby said: 'George had more ways of beating a player than anyone I've ever seen. Every aspect of ball-control was natural to him. He would use an opponent's shins to play a one-two.'

By the age of 17, Best was a first-team regular; in 1968 he was the youngest-ever Footballer of the Year. The following year he won the same accolade in Europe and by the mid-60s he was famous across the Continent as 'El Beatle', the brilliant footballer with the pop-star good looks.

'I stepped over the line from being an athlete and became a personality or pop thing,' Best said. At the height of his popularity, he received 10,000 fan-mail letters a week.

Best played 466 League and Cup games for Manchester United, scoring 178 goals, including the precious strike that gave his team the lead in extra time at Wembley in 1968. United went on to beat Benfica 4–1. Best finished that season as the leading goalscorer in Division One with 28 goals, a remarkable return for a winger.

'I always used to say to George: "You could score 30 goals a season, if you look for Denis Law, give him the ball and go for the return,"' Jimmy Murphy, the Manchester United assistant manager said. 'But then, how can you tell a genius how to play?'

KEY MATCH

Benfica 1 Manchester United 5, European Cup quarter-final, Lisbon, 9 March 1966

Beatlemania was at its height when George Best produced the performance that both Bobby Charlton and Denis Law rate as his greatest in a Manchester United shirt.

The Portuguese newspapers dubbed Best 'the fifth Beatle', a theme taken up by *The Times* in its match report: 'With his long, dark mop of hair, he… set a new, almost unexplored beat. Best seemed quite suddenly to be in love with the ball, and the whole side followed his lead.'

The Irishman scored his side's first goal with a soaring header, then stunned the 90,000 crowd by 'gliding past three defenders like a dark ghost to break clear and slide the ball home', as *The Times* football writer Geoffrey Green memorably put it.

Benfica, trailing by only one goal from the first leg at Old Trafford, were suddenly three goals adrift after only 12 minutes. 'George just went out and destroyed them,' Matt Busby said.

The sense of shock inside the Stadium of Light was palpable: the Lisbon side had never previously lost a European tie at home.

Best understood the significance of these events. Before flying home he deliberately bought the biggest sombrero he could find. When the waiting pressmen greeted him in Manchester, they had their picture. For the first time the image of Best featured on the front as well as the back pages. Overnight, he became the first celebrity footballer.

Left George Best causes problems for the Chelsea defence at Stamford Bridge during a match in March 1966.

KEY MUSEUM ARTEFACT

George Best played in these boots – the last known remaining pair of boots to have been worn by him – during his time at Fulham, where between 1976 and 1977 he made 46 appearances for the then Division 2 club. In the 1960s, Best famously endorsed the Stylo Matchmaker boot, which pioneered a new lacing design. Rather than the laces being on the top of the boot, they were positioned at the side, giving extra comfort and offering greater accuracy when the ball was kicked. They were clearly ahead of their time, as the laces on some of the boots used by the top professionals nowadays are not located on the top of the boot or the instep.

George Best was first spotted Bob Bishop, a Manchester United scout who ran a youth club in Belfast. Bishop sent a message to Busby, saying his new find, although small and skinny, had 'an enormous ration of football gifts'.

Best practised those skills endlessly. 'Even when it was dark I'd still be there, smashing a ball against the garage doors,' Best said. 'I tried to hit the same spot. Accuracy was the key, I always thought.'

Arriving in Manchester for a trial, Best was intimidated by the city. So much so, he went straight back home the next day. Only then did he find the nerve to give professional football another go. At 15, he was small and frail for his age. On first meeting him, the landlady at his club digs thought he was an apprentice jockey.

Right from the start he showed an appetite for work. Described by Murphy as

> **"There are times when I think George Best has ice in his veins."** – *Jimmy Murphy*

'a fantastically hard trainer,' Best often practised alone, determined to make himself genuinely two-footed. A favourite drill was to try to score direct from a corner kick with his left foot. Other times he would try to hit the cross bar from the edge of the penalty area. 'By the time I was 19 or 20 most people couldn't tell which was my stronger foot,' he said.

His leaping ability and heading were helped by the fact that he played rugby at school. He also enjoyed the physical side of football. 'The manager always said that I was the best tackler at the club, which I took as a great compliment.'

'There are times when I think George Best has ice in his veins,' said Jimmy Murphy, who had seen nothing like him before. 'He was only 17 when he made his debut, and there he was before the game, sitting on his own, quietly reading the club programme.' Denis Law said, 'Really, I often think that George is completely nerveless.'

His rise was rapid. As a first-team player, Best was still eligible for the youth team in 1963–64 and he helped Manchester United win the FA Youth Cup for the first time since the heyday of the 'Busby Babes' in the mid-1950s. Best made

Above The George Best puppet from the early 1990s' satirical television programme *Spitting Image*.

Right George Best's European Footballer of the Year award from 1968.

his international debut for Northern Ireland the same season.

George Best could see possibilities on a football field that simply did not occur to other players. 'Some young players just have it so naturally that it shines out, like a beacon,' Bobby Charlton said. 'George all but missed the reserves, going straight from the youth team to the first team.'

The only criticism levelled at Best in those days concerned his tendency to over-elaborate. 'When he has eradicated this small failing I'm sure he will be numbered among the greats,' Charlton wrote in 1967.

Everyone at the club admired his courage. 'Even in the face of the most cruelly desperate tackle, George never shirks,' Denis Law said.

Eventually, however, the strain of celebrity, and the frustration he felt at playing for a team in decline while at his peak as a footballer in the early 1970s proved too much. He began drinking heavily. In May 1977, at the age of 30, after a stint playing at Fulham and overseas, Best quit top-level football.

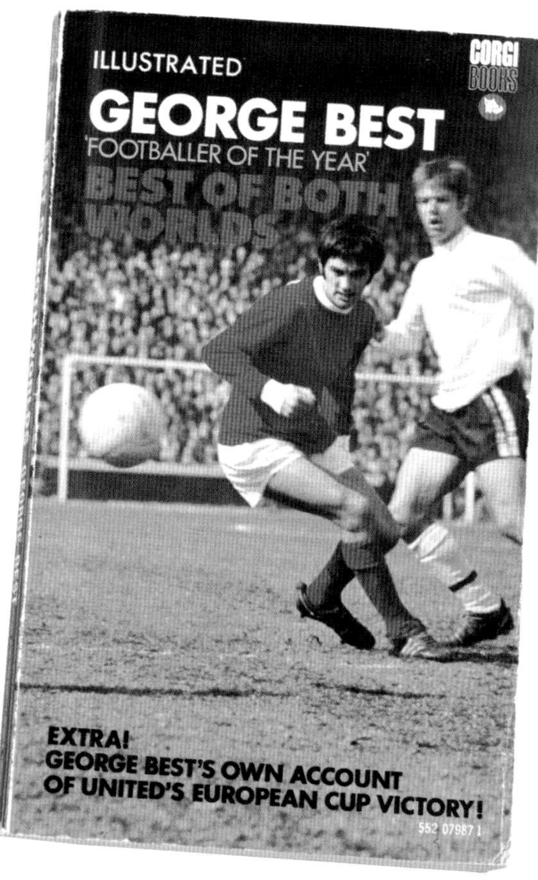

TALKING POINT

George Best had a knack for the unexpected, as Gordon Banks, the England goalkeeper, was about to find out.

Playing for Northern Ireland against England in 1971, Best combined original thinking, skill and athleticism to manufacture an audacious scoring opportunity for himself.

He had already noticed that Banks threw the ball up in the air when kicking the ball downfield. Best spotted an opportunity. Timing his move perfectly, he waited until the ball was in the air before flicking it with his outstretched leg over the goalkeeper's head.

As the ball bounced towards goal, Banks turned and frantically raced back, only to be beaten to it by Best, who had a simple tap-in into an empty net.

'No one else in the game would have even thought of trying it,' Matt Busby said. 'It was a marvellous, inspired bit of improvisation that deserved reward.'

The referee, however, did not agree. He disallowed the goal, even though Best had not touched the goalkeeper when he knocked the ball away. 'Foot up' was the only possible explanation, the newspapers speculated the next day.

'I have never stopped believing that it was a perfectly good goal,' Best said later.

Above George Best's pop-star good looks and flamboyant lifestyle provided him with countless commercial opportunities. He produced a plethora of books throughout the 1960s and 70s.

Left George Best was presented with the European Footballer of the Year award in 1968 and was the third Manchester United player to receive the accolade. Denis Law and Bobby Charlton had both been recipients, in 1964 and 1966 respectively.

BILLY BREMNER (1942–1997)

Player • Inducted 2004 • 54 caps • 2 Fairs Cups • 2 Division One Championships • 1 FA Cup • 1 League Cup

Nailed to the wall in the Leeds United dressing room at Elland Road during the 1960s was a sign. It read: 'Keep Fighting.' 'The sign hangs over my peg, appropriately, for I am the captain,' Billy Bremner said. 'I am supposed to set an example to the rest of the lads.'

Over a period of 16 years, this '10 stone of barbed wire', as *The Sunday Times* described him, did just that, inspiring the most consistently successful team in England between 1964 and 1974.

Bremner was a vital cog in the Leeds machine. When Don Revie, the manager, heard that the Scotsman might be sold, he put his job on the line in order to keep him at the club. Bremner and Revie stayed put.

The 'Keep Fighting' motto was followed literally on several occasions, particularly during the mid 1960s when the club was establishing itself in Division One. 'We were so determined that none of the élite clubs were going to get in our way,' Bremner recalled. 'We weren't star-gazers.'

Mentally, too, they fought on despite the disappointment of missing out narrowly on major honours three seasons in succession. Their remarkable resilience was finally rewarded with victory in the League Cup final in 1968.

'Now that we've won some silver at last, we'll go on to collect other trophies,' Bremner said, and he was right.

'Above all Leeds have Bremner, the best footballer in the four countries,' John Arlott wrote in the *Guardian* in 1970. 'If every manager in Britain were given his choice of any one player to add to his team some, no doubt, would toy with the idea of George Best; but the realists, to a man, would have Bremner.'

KEY MATCH

Leeds United 1 Manchester United 0, FA Cup semi-final, City Ground, 31 March 1965

Billy Bremner had the knack of scoring late winning goals in vital matches but none stirred as much feeling as this late header which took Leeds United through to the club's first ever FA Cup Final.

In the final seconds of the game, a replay, Bremner made a run to the far post to meet a deep, floated cross by Johnny Giles. With his back to goal, Bremner twisted his body to direct the ball into the top corner.

'Billy would think nothing, if Leeds were struggling in a game, of charging forward and playing almost like a centre-forward to change the situation,' Eddie Gray, the Leeds winger said. 'The high number of vital goals he scored for Leeds, particularly in big matches, speaks for itself.'

The result was of great significance to Leeds. In their first season back in Division One following promotion, they lost out in the title race to Manchester United on goal difference; but this victory, after a goalless draw at Hillsborough, was proof that they could defeat an established power on the big occasion.

Over the two games, neither side had yielded an inch. It was brutal at times. One newspaper described it as 'a sordid battle, littered with bad fouls'.

'Billy was so hard as a player,' Denis Law, the Manchester United forward, recalled. 'He had a very competitive streak, exactly the type of player you wanted in your team, given the way the physical way the game was played in those days.'

Left Bremner surveys a rather muddy field of play in the late 1960s.

KEY MUSEUM ARTEFACT

The design of the 1974 World Cup ball is possibly the most distinctive in football history. The familiar five- and six-sided, black-and-white panelled ball is now recognised the world over. Appearing in the 1974 World Cup finals, Bremner saw the first appearance of a patterned ball in the tournament's history. In the early 1900s, manufacturers of sporting equipment, such as Duke & Son of Kent, would paint names on their plain footballs with the help of a copper stencil. Often, they would name them after animals, such as the Tiger, Lion, or Zebra.

Billy Bremner had to win, no matter what the game. Defeat irritated him, even when it came to the hobbies Don Revie famously introduced as a way of avoiding boredom at the team hotel.

'I never won at bloody carpet bowls,' Bremner once complained. He couldn't help his competitive nature. 'Billy couldn't bear losing,' Norman Hunter, a Leeds team-mate, recalled. 'There were probably more arguments over carpet bowls than when we played football,' At least Bremner had better luck at bingo, the other lounge game Revie organised.

"Billy had a heart the size of Elland Road. As a midfield player, he was a free spirit who worked on instinct."

– Eddie Gray

During training sessions in the mid-1960s, the coaching staff would deliberately put Bremner and Bobby Collins, a fellow Scot and kindred spirit, on opposite sides so that five-a-side games were as competitive as possible. The two of them would often kick lumps out of each other.

'Billy played more with his heart than his head,' Eddie Gray, the Leeds winger, said. 'He had a heart the size of Elland Road. As a midfield player, he was a free spirit who worked on instinct … His speciality was the reverse pass. Billy could deliver the pass without giving any indication of his intent by his body shape when playing the ball.'

Bremner was versatile, too. When the situation demanded, Bremner would drop back occasionally to play sweeper, particular in away games. 'He was brilliant at the job,' Hunter said, 'and that just highlighted his all-round ability as a footballer.'

Billy Bremner was the first of a generation of young players to break into the Leeds United first team. Both he and they would stay

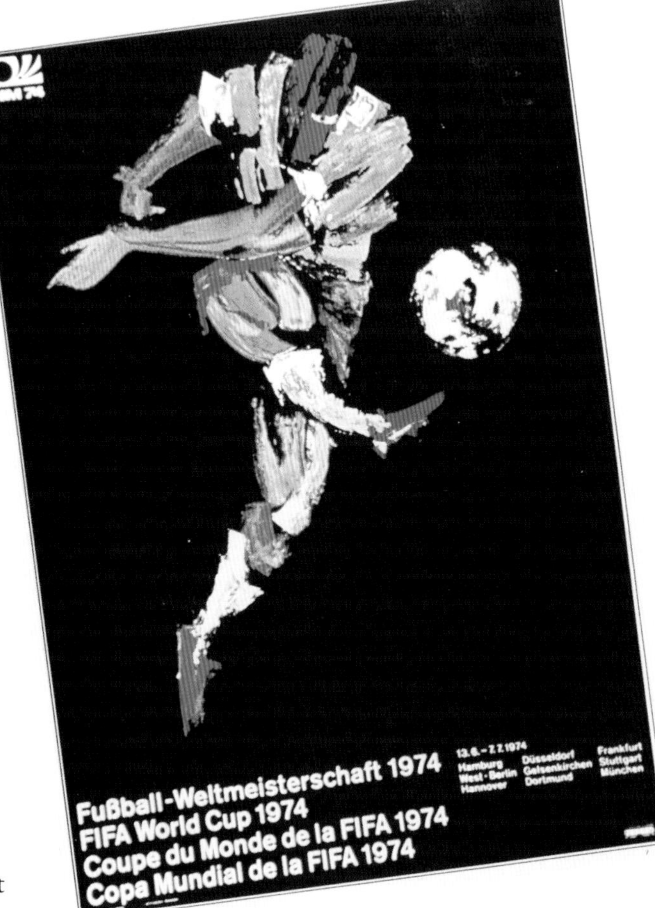

Above This plastic bust of Bremner from the 1970s was produced as part of a promotion for the Cleveland Petrol Company.

Right A 1974 World Cup poster.

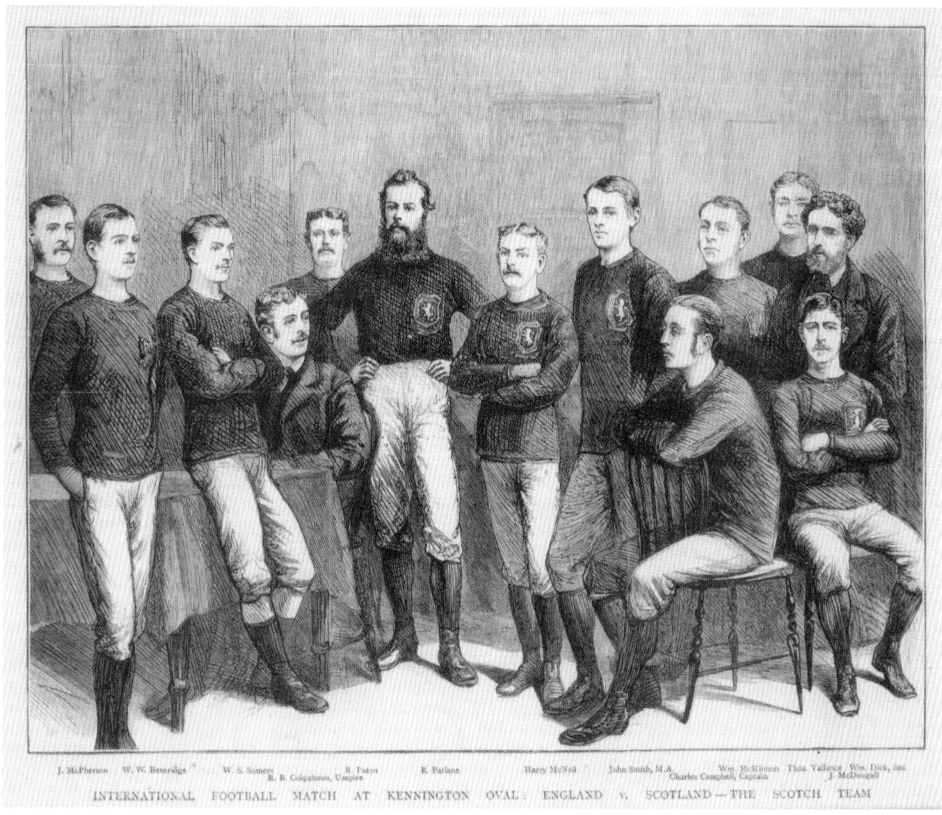

there for more than a decade. Bremner, a Scotland Schoolboy international, made his first-team debut at the age of 17. In 1959–60, he played 11 games at outside-right, alongside Don Revie, the veteran inside-forward whose playing career was then winding down.

In September 1962, Revie, now Leeds' manager, added more youth to the mix. Teenagers Gary Sprake, Paul Reaney, Norman Hunter and Peter Lorimer were all given debuts. Bremner, as the first to make the breakthrough, assumed a leadership role and Revie relied on Bremner more and more.

'Billy was very much Don's protégé,' Gray said. 'There was such an affinity between them that we used to describe Billy as Don's number two son, after the real one, Duncan.'

Increasingly, Revie would insist on his players turning out even when they were unfit. Bremner was considered particularly important to the team. 'Billy once played with a hairline fracture in his leg,' one player said.

'One time I had done my knee ligaments,' Bremner recalled. 'The following Saturday I was on the team sheet. One week for knee ligaments is impossible.

'We had a fitness test before the game and that nearly killed me. I told Don that there was no way I could play. But the boss said: "I'd rather have you with one leg than anybody else with two, to gee the other lads up." I thought that was rubbish, but that's what he said.'

TALKING POINT

Early in his career, at a time when Billy Bremner was begging to be allowed to leave Leeds United, Don Revie was putting his job on the line to keep him at the club.

In the 1962–63 season the Leeds board were seriously considering a firm bid of £25,000 from Everton for the unsettled midfield player, and when Revie heard of this he confronted the directors.

'If Billy goes, I go,' Revie told the board, 'because it is my plan to build the team around him.' He then walked out, telling his assistant, Les Cocker, to pack his bags.

No sooner had the Leeds directors backed down than Revie was handed a transfer request by Bremner, who was unhappy about being played in a position wide on the right of midfield.

'I wanted to play in the middle of the park, but Don said that I was not ready,' Bremner recalled. Dropped to the reserves over his stance, Bremner eventually came round to Revie's point of view. 'He made it clear that it was only a matter of time and that I would have a key role in the team,' Bremner said. 'He also kept stressing the team's potential for success. Finally, I took my name off the list.'

Above left A woodcut of the Scotland team of 1879. Scotland lost 5–4 to the 'auld enemy', England, in the home international match played at London's Kennington Oval that year. Bremner made his debut for Scotland as a 22-year-old against Spain in 1965

CONSTRUCTORA ARVA S.A.
MARTINI
MARTINI & ROSSI
MARTINI
KENO
URUGUAY
BRASIL
BEMVINDOS

GORDON BANKS (1937–)

Player • Inducted 2002 • 73 Caps • 1 World Cup • 2 League Cups

'If anyone had to be ill, why did it have to be him?' Those few despairing words, uttered by Alf Ramsey in the aftermath of his side's elimination from the World Cup in Mexico in 1970, summed up the importance of Gordon Banks to England.

Only days earlier Ramsey had abandoned his normal reticence on the subject of individual players to praise Banks as 'the greatest goalkeeper in the world, no doubt about it' following his performance in the group game against Brazil.

At the previous World Cup, Banks kept a clean sheet in each of England's first four matches. He remained unbeaten for 443 minutes, until Portugal scored from the penalty spot in the semi-final. In open play, he did not concede a goal until the final itself. His heroics for his country led to the rewriting of a simile – as safe as the Banks of England.

In Mexico, a stomach bug had flattened Banks before the quarter-final against West Germany. Ramsey was prepared to risk him half-fit. Barely able to run or dive, Banks passed a ridiculously easy fitness test. But a relapse left him too weak and ill to play.

After making his international debut in 1963, Banks remained the undisputed number one for ten years until the loss of an eye in a car accident forced his retirement from English football. The Footballer of the Year only the season before had won the last of his 73 caps.

A glutton for training, Banks often asked his England team-mates to stay behind to take shots at him. 'He would never let anything in,' Alan Ball recalled, 'so finally we told him that he was shattering our confidence. The next time he asked us, we just walked off. At times, he was simply unbeatable.'

KEY MATCH

West Ham United 0 Stoke City 1, League Cup semi-final, second leg, Upton Park, 15 December 1971

The weary Stoke City players stood on the edge of the penalty area, hands on hips, looking resigned to defeat, as Geoff Hurst ran up to take a penalty with only three minutes left in extra-time.

With the scores level at 2-2 on aggregate, West Ham had the chance to win the tie. Perhaps the exhausted Stoke defenders remembered the penalty Hurst had scored in the first leg at the Victoria Ground. Gordon Banks certainly did.

'He'd taken a long run up and hit the ball to my right,' Banks recalled. 'Geoff usually relied on sheer power, it looked as though he was really going to hit this one.'

Banks observed that Hurst was taking the same kind of run-up. 'I thought, "He's not going to change here.' Banks guessed right. The ball flew to his right at great pace.

'I tensed the muscles in my arm and wrist and the ball ricocheted off my hand and over the bar.'

The two-leg semi-final eventually went to a second replay. At full-time Banks, caked in mud, turned to the Stoke supporters to celebrate victory in the longest League Cup tie ever.

In the final, Banks made two late saves to protect Stoke's 2–1 lead against Chelsea, ensuring the Potteries club won its first major honour.

Left England goalkeeper Gordon Banks watches the ball arc away from goal after saving Pelé's downward header in the Group 3 World Cup game against Brazil on 7 June 1970.

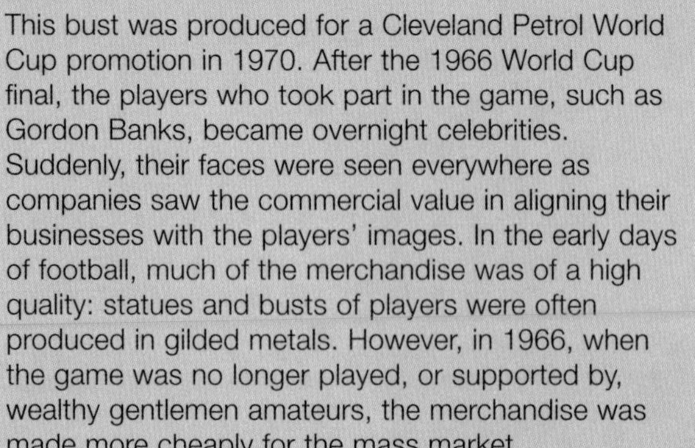

KEY MUSEUM ARTEFACT

This bust was produced for a Cleveland Petrol World Cup promotion in 1970. After the 1966 World Cup final, the players who took part in the game, such as Gordon Banks, became overnight celebrities. Suddenly, their faces were seen everywhere as companies saw the commercial value in aligning their businesses with the players' images. In the early days of football, much of the merchandise was of a high quality: statues and busts of players were often produced in gilded metals. However, in 1966, when the game was no longer played, or supported by, wealthy gentlemen amateurs, the merchandise was made more cheaply for the mass market.

Banks had the ideal physique for a goalkeeper: six feet one and 13½ stone.

There were no instruction manuals for goalkeepers and clubs did not employ specialist coaches when Gordon Banks was building his career at Leicester City in the late 1950s. So Banks set out to teach himself through a process of experiment and trial and error. 'I thought of goalkeeping as more of a science,' he recalled. 'It was all about practice, and there was definitely an element of hit and miss. It was, in the main, uncharted territory.'

On Sunday mornings he reported for extra training. 'I devised my own training schedules, working on agility, positioning, strength, reactions and focus,' he said.

In match situations he made a concerted effort to improve his reading of situations. 'I wanted to be able to anticipate my opponent's intended cross or pass by adjusting my position quickly, so making him think again,' he said.

Banks had the ideal physique for a goalkeeper: six feet one,13½ stone, and strong upper body strength, the inadvertent result of his time as a lad lugging bags of coal around for a job.

He began his career inauspiciously, conceding 122 goals in the Chesterfield reserves in the 1954–55 season. Against players his own age, his record was more impressive: in 1956–57 lowly Chesterfield surprised the bigger clubs by progressing to an FA Youth Cup final against the 'Busby Babes' of Manchester United. Banks could not prevent his team losing, but his fine performance alerted several bigger clubs, including Leicester City.

After making the first team at Filbert Street, the number of goals the team conceded gradually fell, season by season, between 1959–60 and 1962–63: 75, 70, 71 and 53. His hard work paid dividends. By the end of this run he was an England player. The following season he won a League Cup winner's medal with Leicester.

left A Brazil shirt from the 1950–60s. Banks became known throughout the world after his miraculous save from Brazil's Pelé during the 1970 World Cup in Mexico.

In 1977, at the age of 39, Gordon Banks was voted the best goalkeeper playing in the United States soccer league. In 26 games for Fort Lauderdale Strikers, he conceded 29 goals. He was nearing the veteran stage now, though it wasn't his age that made his performance so remarkable, but the physical handicap he had overcome: Banks had only one eye.

On Sunday, 22 October 1972, Banks had been involved in a head-on collision while overtaking on the B5038 between Whitmore and Trentham, near his home in Staffordshire. He had just signed a six-year contract with Stoke City.

Banks was heading home to watch the highlights of Stoke's game against Liverpool the previous day. He had been infuriated by two rulings by Roger Kirkpatrick, the referee, whom Banks blamed for Liverpool's two goals. He wanted to watch replays of the incidents to see if he'd been right.

Banks retired from English football in 1973 as a result of his serious facial injury, taking a job as a coach at Stoke City. Then, four years later, came the surprise offer from the United States, where he played for two seasons.

'I was very surprised by the standard I attained at Fort Lauderdale,' he recalled. 'I realised that, with training and practice, I could readjust to my restricted vision.

'In hindsight I could have taken a year away from the game after the car accident and then given it a go back in the Football League. But after the long gap, and now those two years in the States, it was too late to try again in England.'

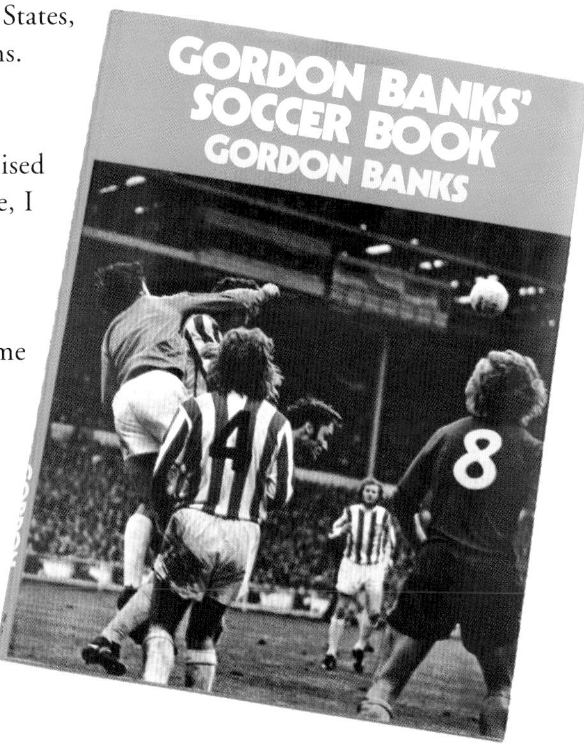

TALKING POINT

As he threw himself across goal, Gordon Banks realised that he would have to do more than just get his hand to the ball; somehow he had to get the thing over the crossbar.

'If I didn't get the ball up and away,' Banks explained later, 'Pelé would have simply followed up his header and had a simple tap-in. I knew I had to get under the ball somehow and flick it upwards, out of harm's way.

'When the cross came over I had to take up a position at the near post to cover a run by Tostao. That's why I had so far to go across to make the save.'

Pelé was so convinced his header was about to open the scoring in the World Cup group game, he shouted 'Golo!' 'It was the greatest save I have ever seen,' Pelé said later. 'It was incredible that he managed to push the ball over the bar. I have never had such a surprise on a football pitch.' The next day the Mexican newspapers nicknamed Banks 'El Magnifico'.

Banks had to contend with alien conditions in Mexico in 1970: the ball flew faster and swerved more in the thinner air, and the sunlight was so harsh that he would often lose sight of the ball.

'Before the corner Bobby Moore made me laugh when he said, "You're getting old, Banksy. You used to hold on to them."'

Above Various tickets for the 1966 World Cup. The final tie match was played late in the year – 30 July – and as a result it took place on a warm, humid afternoon in London.

Left The front cover of *Gordon Banks' Soccer Book*, 1972, features Banks punching clear during Stoke City's 2–1 victory over Chelsea in the League Cup final at Wembley.

Right This perfectly proportioned 1920s bronze statue by the Austrian sculptor Adolf Wagner von der Muhl shows the grace, agility and balance needed to be a top goalkeeper.

ALAN BALL (1945–)

Player • Inducted 2003 • 72 caps • 1 World Cup
1 Division One Championship

It was rare for Alf Ramsey to single out individuals for praise, but after the most important match in England's history, he made a point of speaking to Alan Ball. 'Young man,' Ramsey said, only minutes after the final whistle of the World Cup final in 1966, 'you will never play a better game in your life.'

Ramsey was not alone in his thinking. Bobby Charlton and Geoff Hurst were just two of the England players who nominated Ball, still only 21, as man of the match. Helmut Schöen, the West Germany manager, also praised his performance.

'If we had to pick a star,' Charlton said, 'it had to be Alan Ball, whose inexhaustible stamina was vital. His skill, control, footwork and devastating use of the ball in the final were a revelation, and he did it all against a world-class full-back in Karl-Heinz Schnellinger.'

Ball, who won 72 caps, was twice sold for record transfer fees. Soon after the World Cup, Everton paid Blackpool £110,000, a record sum between British clubs. Six years later, Everton cashed in their profit, selling him on, against his wishes, to Arsenal for £220,000, another record.

Ball was the epitome of the type of footballer Ramsey admired. Way back in 1952, Ramsey had written about the need for versatility. High in energy, Ball was prominent in a new generation of players who were capable of the multiple roles in attack and defence that Ramsey had in mind.

'It meant everything to me to play for my country,' he said. 'Alf had the same attitude, and I responded to that.' Briefly, during the Don Revie era, Ball was made England captain. 'It was such a proud moment,' he said.

KEY MATCH

Spain 0 England 2, International Friendly, Madrid, 8 December 1965

Alan Ball proved his versatility and his worth to Alf Ramsey in the run-up to the World Cup when England unveiled their new 'wingless' tactical formation to the rest of Europe.

On a bitterly cold night, Ramsey played Ball in an attacking role alongside Joe Baker in a 4–3–3 system. It was the first time Ramsey made a point of going into an international without a recognised and specialist winger.

To work, the system required players who were fit, adaptable, hard-running all-rounders, and Ball had all those attributes. Early in his career at Blackpool, he had played on both the wing and at inside-forward. Later, at Everton, he would play in the centre of midfield.

'When Alf had a role in mind he always consulted the player first and so he came to me. I jumped at the idea,' Ball recalled. 'We were to play everything in to feet with everybody joining in and that way, with our touch, it should work.'

When England attacked, five players – Ball, Roger Hunt, Baker, George Eastham, and Bobby Charlton – poured through the middle, leaving the Spain full-backs adrift with no one to mark. Baker and Hunt scored the goals.

'Spain were completely mystified by it and were utterly defeated by the end,' said Charlton.

In the stands there was a large number of international observers alongside the British and Continental football writers. 'I think this was the first time the Press thought we had a chance in the World Cup,' Charlton said.

Left Alan Ball (right) skips past Liverpool's Steve Higheway in the all-Merseyside FA Cup semi-final at Old Trafford on 27 March 1971.

KEY MUSEUM ARTEFACT

Picture cards have been produced since the late 19th century by companies such as Player's cigarettes. Initially, cards incorporated portraits of the 11 members of an FA Cup final winning team. As football became professional and crowds began to grow, there was a need to satisfy younger supporters and so collectable cards were manufactured portraying stars of the day. In the 1960s and '70s there was a huge boom in the football stickers market with brands like Panini becoming increasingly popular.

Alf Ramsey relied heavily on Alan Ball when he drew up his tactics for the World Cup final after concluding that his team could not afford specialist wingers. Ball had a dual task: to help George Cohen, the full-back, protect the right flank; and, also, whenever possible, break forward in wide positions in support of the attack. It was hugely demanding physically, yet Ball still ran Karl-Heinz Schnellinger, the German full-back, ragged.

Ball thought to himself: 'Well, I've been beating Schnellinger all afternoon, so there's no reason why I can't do it again.'

In attack, he had to be positioned in or about the edge of the penalty area whenever Martin Peters played the ball into the box from the other flank. Ball was involved in three of England's four goals. With the score at 1–1, he forced, and then took, the corner that led to Peters' volleyed goal that made the score 2–1.

Ball's influence was even more apparent during extra time. He set the tone for a period of England domination by running at the German defence almost from the kick-off; his shot was tipped over the crossbar by the goalkeeper, Tilkowski.

Ten minutes later, Ball was desperate for a breather when Nobby Stiles shaped to play a pass down the wing. Chasing after the ball, Ball thought to himself: 'Well, I've been beating Schnellinger all afternoon, so there's no reason why I can't do it again,' he recalled. Ball did just that, and from his cross, Geoff Hurst scored the third goal with a shot off the crossbar.

In the final minute, when Hurst broke away to score the fourth goal, it was Ball who raced up in support, screaming for a pass. It was the last run he had to make.

THE ILLUSTRATED LONDON NEWS

England wins the World Cup at Wembley

Clacton and Frinton: beside the same seaside

Belton House: second in a series on the great houses of England

Right A copy of the *Illustrated London News* from 1966.

Alan Ball was 17 when he made his debut for Blackpool. It could not have been a more intimidating prospect: an away fixture against Liverpool at Anfield.

It meant nothing to young Ball. 'Before the game, I'd been rightly quoted in the papers saying that the Kop didn't worry me at all.' Ball suspects that one or two Liverpool players read his comments.

'Before kick-off, one of the

Liverpool lads handed me a piece of paper, and on it I read: "Liverpool Royal Infirmary, Evening Menu." I had the last laugh, though; Blackpool won 2–1.'

His feistiness never really left him. After one international against Spain in 1965, the Spanish newspaper nicknamed him 'the poison shrimp'.

Fiercely patriotic, Ball shared Alf Ramsey's frustration when England failed to win the European Nations Cup in 1968. This, he felt, was not England's proper place. He told reporters that he threw his medal for third place out of the window afterwards.

Ball won a championship medal with Everton in 1969–70, his only major club honour. 'We played purely off-the-cuff football,' he recalled. 'The improvisations were inspired.'

He experienced defeat in two FA Cup finals, for Everton in 1968 and with Arsenal in 1972. In December 1976, he joined Southampton, helping the club win promotion to Division One in 1977–78.

His six seasons at Goodison Park marked his peak as a player. 'Alan was quite possibly the finest midfield player Everton has ever had – or is likely to have,' Howard Kendall, his team-mate said. Before leaving for Arsenal, Ball received a phone call from Bill Shankly, the Liverpool manager. 'You were great on Merseyside, son, really great,' Shankly said.

MEXICO 70
IX football world championship
may 31 - june 21

Above Mexico 1970 World Cup poster. England reached the quarter-finals of the 1970 World Cup in Mexico before being knocked out by West Germany 3–2 after extra time.

Left While England's back four had to defend against Pelé, Alan Ball had the job of containing the Brazilian overlapping full-backs in their 1970 World Cup encounter. This charcoal drawing of Pelé was made by the Jamaican artist, Ras Danieal Heartman in the 1990s.

TALKING POINT

'When I was a boy, just 17 and starting out in the professional game, people were asking me what my ambition was. I said then: "To play for England in the 1966 World Cup."'

Ball had already told his father that he would be playing international football before the age of 20. Time was pressing for Ball, if he was going to fulfil his ambition. He would not allow anyone, regardless of reputation, to slow his progress.

As an apprentice at Blackpool it was his job to clean the boots of the great Stanley Matthews. It was only five years since the veteran Blackpool winger had last played for England.

In a practice game, Ball played a ball inside the full-back in the full expectation that his winger would chase after it. Matthews just stood there, shaking his head, and pointed to his feet in an obvious message to his brash young colleague.

Ball had yet to play a first-team game, but that did not stop him shouting at the most revered footballer in the country. 'I said to him: "If the pass is on inside the full-back, you chase it and get there,"' Ball recalled.

Matthews was furious at being spoken to in such a way by so inexperienced a club-mate, Ball said. 'It was indicative of the kind of person I was becoming. Stanley was a wonderful man, but I didn't care for reputations. I was going to walk through everybody to get where I wanted to be.'

Above This Italian Canine Defence League medal was presented to the dog Pickles in 1966, after he found the World Cup which had been stolen prior to the World Cup tournament. The story made almost as much news as England's victory.

PAT JENNINGS (1945–)

Player • Inducted 2003 • 119 caps • 1 UEFA Cup • 2 FA Cups • 2 League Cups

Pat Jennings, the unflappable Irishman with the giant hands and trademark one-handed catch, won a world-record 119 caps, culminating in a farewell World Cup appearance against Brazil at the age of 41.

Jennings introduced a new style of shot-stopping during an outstanding era for goalkeeping. Bob Wilson, a predecessor in goal at Arsenal and a member of the 1971 Double-winning side, credited Jennings with developing the technique of saving shots with the feet. 'Pat's style of goalkeeping was unique in the 1970s,' Wilson recalled. 'No one had used their feet in the natural way Pat had. These days, saving with the feet is commonplace, essential, and its origin lies with him.'

Jennings, the oldest British player to appear in a World Cup finals tournament, was voted Footballer of the Year in 1972–73, during an earlier spell with Tottenham Hotspur, ahead of rivals Peter Shilton and Ray Clemence.

Sir Alf Ramsey, the England manager, recognised Jennings by picking him in a British Select XI in a match to celebrate entry into the Common Market in 1973. 'I was thrilled to get the nod ahead of Shilton and Clemence, both of whom I rate as exceptional goalkeepers,' Jennings said.

Terry Neill, the Arsenal manager, described the fee of £40,000 he paid to bring Jennings, then aged 32, to Highbury in August 1977, as 'one of the best transfer deals I made during my career as a manager'.

For his part, Keith Burkinshaw, the Spurs manager, later admitted that selling him was the worst decision of his career. Jennings went on to play more than 300 games for the Gunners in the latter part of a career that stretched over 23 years.

The affable Jennings played for both clubs in north London without ever generating the animosity of either set of supporters. When he staged a testimonial in May 1985, Spurs accepted his invitation to be the opposition.

KEY MATCH

Spain 0 Northern Ireland 1, World Cup group game, Valencia, 25 June 1982

Standing in his goal, Pat Jennings could hardly believe the events that had just unfolded in front of him. Against the odds, the Irish had beaten Spain to qualify from their group. As if that wasn't enough, the veteran keeper had kept a clean sheet.

'I thought I'd been around the football scene for too long to get emotional over the result of any match, but I've got to admit I had a lump in my throat when the final whistle sounded,' he recalled.

'Nothing in soccer has given me greater satisfaction than this victory,' he said after the tournament. 'I didn't want to leave the pitch when it was all over, and, in fact, I think I was the last player to do so after giving an on-the-spot interview to BBC Television.

Northern Ireland, who began the game as 150-1 outsiders, had to win to avoid elimination. The flights home had already been booked, just in case. The odds against them lengthened when defender Mal Donaghy was sent off.

'I wasn't overworked, but I was aware that if I conceded an early goal Spanish morale would soar sky-high and we might be overwhelmed. So I was pleased with a save I made at the feet of one of their forwards in the opening minutes.

'I have played in better sides than that one, but I have never felt so proud of a team than I did at the end of that game.'

Left Spurs goalkeeper Pat Jennings saves from Liverpool's Brian Hall, in front of the Kop at Anfield on 10 April 1973.

KEY MUSEUM ARTEFACT

This 1970s' training kit features a yellow Arsenal badge. As early as the late 19th century some clubs received permission to use their local borough's coat of arms and embroidered versions began to be sewn onto the shirt breasts. The Arsenal cannon motif recognises the club's origins and the fact that, in 1886, they went by the name of Royal Arsenal. The workers who formed the team named it after the munitions factory in Woolwich in which they worked. Pat Jennings remained a 'Gunner' for seven years after joining the club in 1977, making 237 League appearances for them and helping them win the FA Cup in 1979.

Above right A team sheet from the England v. Northern Ireland match in 1982 showing many of the Northern Ireland team who were involved in the heroic victory over Spain the hosts of the 1982 World Cup.

Right This shows a detail of the newly-designed UEFA Cup in 1972, which replaced the Fairs Cup. Jennings helped Spurs win the trophy in its inaugural year by beating Wolves, over two legs, in an all-English final.

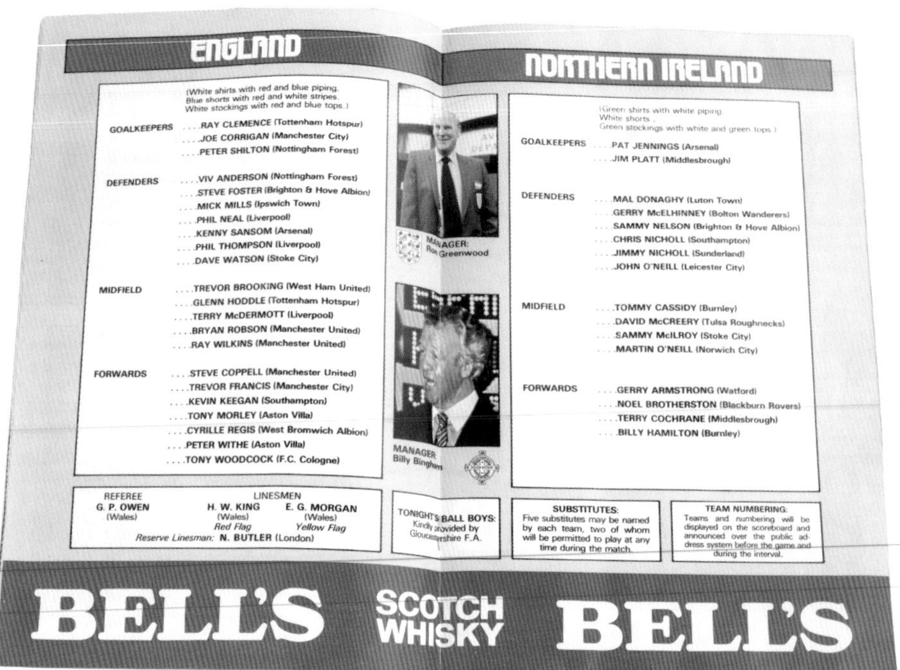

ENGLAND

(White shirts with red and blue piping.
Blue shorts with red and white stripes.
White stockings with red and blue tops.)

GOALKEEPERS
....RAY CLEMENCE (Tottenham Hotspur)
....JOE CORRIGAN (Manchester City)
....PETER SHILTON (Nottingham Forest)

DEFENDERS
....VIV ANDERSON (Nottingham Forest)
....STEVE FOSTER (Brighton & Hove Albion)
....MICK MILLS (Ipswich Town)
....PHIL NEAL (Liverpool)
....KENNY SANSOM (Arsenal)
....PHIL THOMPSON (Liverpool)
....DAVE WATSON (Stoke City)

MIDFIELD
....TREVOR BROOKING (West Ham United)
....GLENN HODDLE (Tottenham Hotspur)
....TERRY McDERMOTT (Liverpool)
....BRYAN ROBSON (Manchester United)
....RAY WILKINS (Manchester United)

FORWARDS
....STEVE COPPELL (Manchester United)
....TREVOR FRANCIS (Manchester City)
....KEVIN KEEGAN (Southampton)
....TONY MORLEY (Aston Villa)
....CYRILLE REGIS (West Bromwich Albion)
....PETER WITHE (Aston Villa)
....TONY WOODCOCK (F.C. Cologne)

MANAGER: Ron Greenwood

MANAGER: Billy Bingham

NORTHERN IRELAND

(Green shirts with white piping.
White shorts.
Green stockings with white and green tops.)

GOALKEEPERS
....PAT JENNINGS (Arsenal)
....JIM PLATT (Middlesbrough)

DEFENDERS
....MAL DONAGHY (Luton Town)
....GERRY McELHINNEY (Bolton Wanderers)
....SAMMY NELSON (Brighton & Hove Albion)
....CHRIS NICHOLL (Southampton)
....JIMMY NICHOLL (Sunderland)
....JOHN O'NEILL (Leicester City)

MIDFIELD
....TOMMY CASSIDY (Burnley)
....DAVID McCREERY (Tulsa Roughnecks)
....SAMMY McILROY (Stoke City)
....MARTIN O'NEILL (Norwich City)

FORWARDS
....GERRY ARMSTRONG (Watford)
....NOEL BROTHERSTON (Blackburn Rovers)
....TERRY COCHRANE (Middlesbrough)
....BILLY HAMILTON (Burnley)

REFEREE
G. P. OWEN (Wales)

LINESMEN
H. W. KING (Wales) Red Flag
E. G. MORGAN (Wales) Yellow Flag

Reserve Linesman: N. BUTLER (London)

TONIGHT'S BALL BOYS: Kindly provided by Gloucestershire F.A.

SUBSTITUTES: Five substitutes may be named by each team, two of whom will be permitted to play at any time during the match.

TEAM NUMBERING: Teams and numbering will be displayed on the scoreboard and announced over the public address system before the game and during the interval.

BELL'S SCOTCH WHISKY BELL'S

> **"It is not a sport for the faint-hearted and to survive you have to be able to give and take knocks without complaining."** – *Pat Jennings*

Pat Jennings learned many of the skills he drew upon to establish himself as the most highly rated goalkeeper in the country, including his distinctive one-handed catch, by playing a completely different sport.

As a teenager in Northern Ireland, Jennings played Gaelic football, a game that demands physical strength, courage, good handling skills and kicking, all vital attributes for a goalkeeper.

Soccer was banned at his school and when Jennings turned his attention to his goalkeeping, he was immediately barred from playing Gaelic football by the ruling body, which did not favour 'foreign' games.

It was immediately obvious he had made the right choice: at the age of eleven he was already playing for an under-nineteens side in his chosen sport.

In 1963, Jennings represented Northern Ireland at an international youth tournament at Wembley, attracting the interest of Bill McGarry, the Watford manager. After one season at Vicarage Road, he joined Spurs for a fee of £27,500, a sizeable sum for a goalkeeper at the time, and at the age of nineteen, on arrival at White Hart Lane, he was thrown straight into the first team.

Pat Jennings made his international debut as a teenager. Nineteen years later he finally achieved his ambition of playing in a World Cup when Northern Ireland qualified for the tournament in Spain in 1982. It was said to be the longest time anyone had waited as an international before getting the chance to play in a World Cup, a testimony to Jennings' skill, longevity, and patience.

Remarkably, Northern Ireland qualified again four years later. In his record 119th and final appearance for his country, Jennings made an emotional and sentimental farewell against mighty Brazil in Mexico on his 41st birthday.

Jennings played a crucial role in both qualifying campaigns: in eight games he conceded only three goals as the Irish booked their place in Spain; in 1986, he kept a clean sheet in the decisive game against England.

TALKING POINT

No one inside Old Trafford knew quite how to react when Pat Jennings scored the equalizing goal in the Charity Shield game in August 1967. The crowed went strangely quiet, almost in disbelief. The other Spurs players did not even celebrate.

Jennings had kicked the ball downfield in the hope of finding Alan Gilzean, the Tottenham centre-forward. The ball landed between Gilzean and Alex Stepney, the Manchester United goalkeeper, who had advanced from his goal. On the first bounce the ball sailed over Stepney's head into the top corner.

'Everything seemed to go quiet, especially at the Stretford End,' recalled Gilzean. 'I was a bit dazed and thought, "What happens now?"

Jennings said,'I wasn't even sure if the goal counted in the laws of the game, and so I didn't give any clenched-fist salute. Even the referee seemed to hesitate before deciding it must be a goal. Not one of the other Spurs players came rushing to congratulate me.'

Jennings was capable of kicking the ball a prodigious distance out of his hands, a skill he developed during his schoolboy days when played Gaelic football. 'It was a freak goal,' he said. 'I was the most surprised man in the ground.'

His saves ensured Northern Ireland qualified for the World Cup. At the final whistle, Jennings turned cartwheels on the Wembley turf in celebration.

When he walked out at Wembley in November 1985 his career was winding down; he had not played a senior match in a year. Even so he proved equal to England's best efforts in a sprightly display that belied his 40 years and helped secure the point Northern Ireland needed to qualify for Mexico.

Relying on anticipation and experience to compensate for his slowing reflexes Jennings made two outstanding saves late in the game to deny Kerry Dixon, the England forward. Those saves kept the game goalless. At the final whistle, Jennings turned cartwheels on the Wembley turf in celebration.

Above A programme from the 1982 World Cup finals in which Jennings starred for Northern Ireland.

Right The 1967 Charity Shield Plaque. The traditional opening game of the season between the League Champions and FA Cup holders saw Manchester United and Tottenham Hotspur fight out a 3–3 draw. The Spurs 'keeper, Pat Jennings, famously scored directly from clearing the ball from his own area.

COLIN BELL (1946–)

Player • Inducted 2005 • 48 Caps • 1 Division One Championship • 1 FA Cup
1 European Cup-winners' Cup • 1 League Cup

Colin Bell, the footballer nicknamed after a famous racehorse because of his extraordinary stamina, provided the energy for Manchester City's rise to prominence in the late 1960s.

Bell played 48 times for England, making him Manchester City's most-capped player, having established himself as an automatic choice in midfield for his country; but his ambition to win 100 caps would be ruined by injury.

Over a period of three seasons starting in 1967–68, Manchester City collected four major club honours. By the end of the decade, as Bell departed with England for the World Cup in Mexico, his club lay claim to having the best team in the League.

'A world-class player,' Malcolm Allison, the Manchester City manager, said. 'The City team had a beautiful balance of strength and skill, and Colin was the key piece in the jigsaw.

'He was so versatile in central midfield: he defended well, could break from deep positions, and he scored goals. He ran all day and had a real footballer's brain.' Allison was the first to nickname Bell 'Nijinsky', after the thoroughbred Derby winner.

Then, suddenly, during the 1975–76 season, it all came to an end. In a League Cup tie against Manchester United, Bell suffered a serious knee injury. 'Basically, one tackle effectively ended my career,' he said.

Bell fought doggedly to regain full fitness, making several comebacks but each time he broke down. Finally conceding defeat, he retired in 1979. 'But for the injury I believe I could have reached 100 caps,' Bell said. 'I had it in me to play at international level for another five or six years, and that would have given me enough time to reach the total.'

In 2001, Bell won more than half the votes in an official poll to determine the club's best-ever player. Following the club's move to the City of Manchester Stadium in 2003, the 14,000-seater west stand was renamed the Colin Bell Stand.

KEY MATCH

Manchester City 4 Newcastle United 0, Division One, Maine Road, 26 December 1977

Word spread around the stands and terraces of Maine Road in a matter of seconds ... 'Nijinsky is back!'

Looking down the players' tunnel, some lads had seen Colin Bell warming up, ready to come on as a second-half substitute. At that moment they knew that a City cult hero was about to make his long-awaited return from injury. 'When I came out onto the pitch there was this deafening roar,' Bell recalled. 'I will never forget the reception the City fans gave me that day.'

A goalless first half had lacked incident, except for an injury to Paul Power, the Manchester City midfield player. Power carried on until half-time, but it was obvious that he was struggling.

Tony Book, the Manchester City manager, had planned to introduce Bell for the last ten minutes or so of the game. After two years out with a serious knee injury, Bell needed to take things slowly. But now events were forcing the issue.

'It was a nothing game up to half-time,' Bell recalled, 'but in the second half the atmosphere was electric. I was choked with emotion by it all.

'I can't remember having a touch over the 45 minutes I was out there. I've been told that I hit the woodwork with a shot, but I don't recall it at all.'

Sadly, amidst the cheering, Bell knew in his heart that his knee was still a problem. 'Even in that comeback game against Newcastle I was aware it wasn't right, and that I wasn't the same player I'd been before the injury.'

Left Manchester City's Colin Bell protests against a decision in a 1970s' Division One game at Maine Road.

KEY MUSEUM ARTEFACT

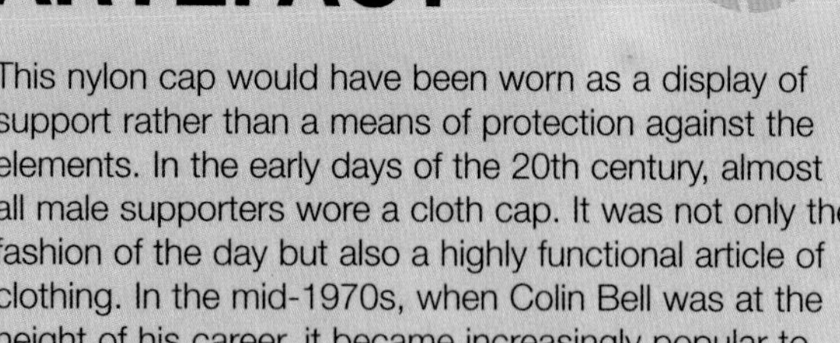

This nylon cap would have been worn as a display of support rather than a means of protection against the elements. In the early days of the 20th century, almost all male supporters wore a cloth cap. It was not only the fashion of the day but also a highly functional article of clothing. In the mid-1970s, when Colin Bell was at the height of his career, it became increasingly popular to wear silk scarves and caps that mimicked the fashions of a bygone era. But the materials used made them less than practical when watching a game during inclement weather.

Below right A Bury FC supporter's scarf from 1990. Bell signed for Bury after unsuccessful trials with Newcastle and Arsenal. He made 82 League appearances for the club before moving to Manchester City in 1966.

Malcolm Allison was desperate to sign Colin Bell, but there was a problem: Manchester City had no money in the kitty to fund the transfer fee. Allison knew that other managers were also interested, so he deliberately set out to mislead his rivals. 'When I was watching Colin, I'd say things like: "He can't play; he's no good in the air; he has a hopeless left foot" in ear-shot of other scouts.'

As soon as the funds were made available Allison did not hesitate, paying Bury a fee of £45,000 in March 1966. 'What an unbelievable bargain,' he said a decade later.

> **“Colin was everywhere that day. It was one of the finest displays of midfield play I've ever seen.”** – *Mike Doyle*

His judgement was soon vindicated. At the end of his first season, Bell scored the goal that secured promotion to Division One and the following season he was the club's leading goalscorer with 12 goals.

In 1967–68, Manchester City won the championship for the first time in 31 years. Mike Doyle, the team captain, highlighted Bell's performance in the penultimate fixture, a 3–1 win at Tottenham Hotspur, as critical. 'Colin was everywhere that day. It was one of the finest displays I've ever seen,' Doyle said. As a result, it all came down to the final day of the season. City had to beat Newcastle to guarantee the title. They did so, dramatically, with a 4–3 victory at St James' Park. Bell had scored 14 goals from midfield that season.

After winning the FA Cup in 1969, beating Leicester City 1–0 in the final, the team added the European Cup-winners' Cup the following season. The defeat of Gornik Zabrze, of Poland, in Vienna completed a memorable 'double', following their 2-1 victory over West Bromwich Albion in the League Cup final at Wembley in March.

Manchester City set their sights on establishing themselves as the best team in Europe. 'We're ambitious at Maine Road,' Colin Bell said in the summer of 1970. 'We aim to push on until we win the European Cup. I honestly believe that we're good enough now.'

A determination to reclaim what they considered to be their rightful place as 'the number one club in Manchester' fuelled the players' ambition. 'Our revenge for United taking over under Matt Busby won't be complete until that European Cup is resting comfortably in our boardroom,' Bell said.

Manchester City beat their neighbours in the semi-final of the League Cup in 1969–70. 'For us,' Mike Doyle, the team captain said, 'that victory confirmed our right to be called top dogs in Manchester.'

In 1971–72, Manchester City came close to winning the title, finishing one point behind champions Derby County. In each of the next three seasons, Manchester City finished higher in the table than United. In the middle of that run they also reached another League Cup final, this time losing 2–1 against Wolves. The loser's medal proved to be the last honour Colin Bell won in the game. The club's brief stint on top was about to end.

On 12 November 1975, during a league cup tie, Bell was involved in a tackle with Martin Buchan, the Manchester United defender. 'I tried to drag the ball

back as Martin came in to challenge,' Bell recalled, 'but it didn't work as my studs were buried in the pitch, and Buchan caught me. I don't blame anyone for what happened.'

Doyle ran over to his prone team-mate. 'I heard Colin say through clenched teeth, "It's gone, good and proper."' Bell still has a pronounced limp to this day. 'It was a terrible blow for the club and a personal tragedy for Colin,' Doyle said. 'He was the most complete inside-forward you'd ever see, coming from deep positions and making everything so easy.'

TALKING POINT

Harold Shepherdson, the England trainer at the World Cup in Mexico in 1970, was asked to name the fittest footballer in Britain. 'That's easy: it's Colin Bell,' he said.

To prove his point Shepherdson only had to cite the events he witnessed in the England training camp. 'To break up the routine and add a little interest before the start of the tournament, Alf Ramsey set aside a day for a small athletics meeting,' Shepherdson recalled. 'The whole thing was run most seriously, and all the squad tried mighty hard,' he added. 'Colin beat everybody in sight.'

There were a range of events: sprinting, running 220 yards and one mile, jumping, bench hurdles, javelin-throwing, shot-putting, long jump, pull-ups and throwing a cricket ball. In total, Bell won seven 'gold medals'.

Bobby Charlton won the 50-yard dash. 'Bobby was very quick over five to ten yards, but by the end I was catching him up. I was at my best once we got beyond 220 yards or so. I was very good at running at three-quarters maximum pace,' Bell said. 'I could go at that pace all day.'

But even the super-fit Bell, whose maximum heartbeat was recorded at 183 beats per minute, struggled in Mexico. 'As soon as I ran any distance, it was as if I had asthma. The conditions were brutal,' he said.

'Colin might easily have figured in international athletics,' Shepherdson wrote in 1973. 'He has a very strong heart and fine slow heart beat.'

Above The ball used in the 1903 FA Cup final. Bell's first League club, Bury, remain, in 2005, the highest-scoring FA Cup final winners. Having beaten Southampton 4–0 in the 1900 final they defeated Derby County 6–0 in the final of 1903.

Left This silk scarf features the Manchester City squad that won the League Cup in 1976. Bell missed the final after suffering a serious knee injury in an earlier round.

Below Silk supporters' scarf.

KEVIN KEEGAN (1951–)

Player • Inducted 2002 • 63 caps • 1 European Cup • 2 UEFA Cups
3 Division One Championships • 1 FA Cup

Kevin Keegan developed a knack for the grand finale after lifting himself from the depths of the Football League to the England captaincy by dint of sheer force of will and hard work.

Twice Keegan made his exit from a club in a European Cup final, winning one, losing the other. Then, in his final game before retirement, he waved goodbye to an adoring crowd from a helicopter as it took off from the middle of the pitch.

Keegan made an equally dramatic impression on his debut for Liverpool as a raw 20-year-old in 1971: within 12 minutes he had scored in front of the Kop and the *Match of the Day* cameras. 'A fairytale start,' he recalled.

The first Englishman to be twice European Footballer of the Year, Keegan was never dropped during his six-year Liverpool career. 'I didn't play one reserve game,' he said. 'Whenever I was injured or suspended I went straight back into the team.'

Bill Shankly paid Scunthorpe United £33,000 for Keegan, whose passing ability, refusal to admit defeat and willingness to run until he dropped mirrored his manager's own qualities as a player. 'All bustle and explosive energy,' Keegan said, describing himself.

When Kevin was with Liverpool he was, without argument, the best player in Britain,' Emlyn Hughes, the captain said. 'He was magnificent, a superb, all-round professional whose consistency was incredible.'

In 1976, Keegan captained England for the first time. Within weeks he was voted Footballer of the Year. In his acceptance speech, Keegan said: 'I am not the best player in the country by a mile, but I'm working on it.'

Years later Keegan said: 'I was never the prettiest player to watch but it was the end product that I was interested in.'

KEY MATCH

Liverpool 3 Borussia Mönchengladbach 1, European Cup final, Rome, 25 May 1977

Kevin Keegan was trusted with the responsibility of a central striking role in a revised formation for what would be his last game in Liverpool colours.

Bob Paisley, the Liverpool manager, switched from 4–3–3 to a more cautious 4–4–2 system for the encounter with the German champions, and instructed Keegan to run at the centre of the Mönchengladbach from deep positions.

Keegan was not surprised when he found himself man-marked by Berti Vogts, the West German World Cup winner, from the kick-off. Their tussle would prove decisive, and Keegan won it. Ninety minutes later, Liverpool were European champions for the first time.

'I loved the challenge because I knew that I'd have to be at my best to get the better of him,' Keegan recalled. 'He gave me a lot of respect, and in a way that gave me confidence. I was able to hold the ball up and feed other runners from midfield, where I did all my best work.'

With the score at 2–1 Keegan put the result beyond doubt eight minutes from time. Collecting the ball in midfield he made a direct run at goal. Even with the ball at his feet he kept ahead of Vogts. Once inside the penalty area, Keegan was bundled over. 'Phil Neal, as usual, slotted home the penalty,' Keegan recalled.

Left Kevin Keegan fires the ball past the German goalkeeper to score in Liverpool's 2–1 victory over Dynamo Dresden in the 1976 UEFA Cup quarter-final, second leg, at Anfield.

KEY MUSEUM ARTEFACT

English clubs dominated the European Cup through the late 1970s and early 1980s. *The European Cup 1955 –1980* was one of many books that were written to record the outstanding achievements of those who had won the trophy. Interestingly, the authors chose to use an image of Kevin Keegan, playing for SV Hamburg in their 0–1 defeat by Nottingham Forest in the 1980 final, on their front cover. Keegan, who won the trophy in his final game with Liverpool in 1977, left Merseyside for the German club in order to make his family financially secure.

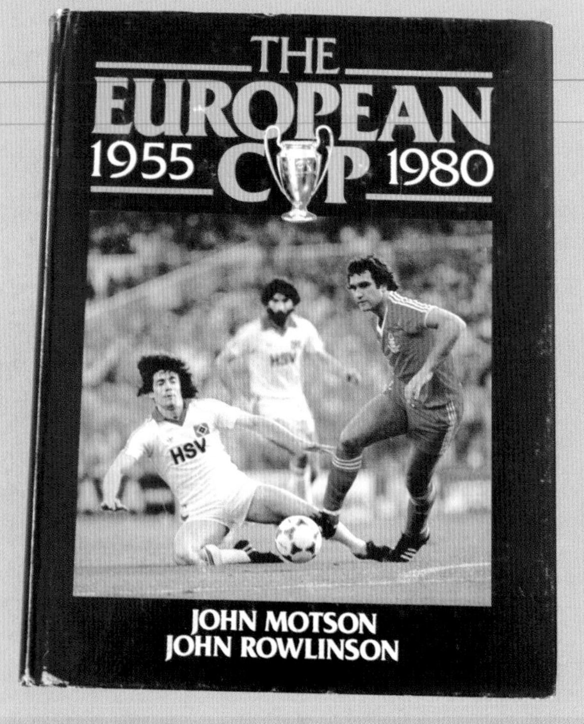

Above right By the time Kevin Keegan took part in the World Cup finals in Spain in 1982, merchandise such as this had become one of the key areas in which to generate revenue.

Right A poster from the 1982 World Cup in Spain.

It took a while for a player who began his footballing life in the lower reaches of Division Four to realise that he had a rightful place in the elite company of European football.

The penny finally dropped in 1976. Kevin Keegan had just inspired Liverpool to a 1–0 win over Barcelona in the first leg of the semi-final of the UEFA Cup. 'Sitting in the dressing room I was so impressed with the facilities. My eyes were suddenly opened to a different world in European football that I wanted to experience,' Keegan recalled.

Bayern Munich offered him the chance to fulfil his overseas ambitions, but he finally opted for SV Hamburg. The German club offered him four times his salary at Anfield.

Keegan threw himself into the challenge, learning the language and taking on the role of 'Super Kev', the face of BP, the club-sponsor, in television commercials. In his second season in Germany, Hamburg won the championship. He was also voted European Footballer of the Year for the second season in succession.

Now out of contract, Keegan was wanted by both Juventus and Real Madrid, but instead of moving on, he decided to have another crack at the European Cup with SV Hamburg, leading the team to the final, where they lost narrowly to Nottingham Forest.'The result of the final was a great disappointment, of course, but, overall, I had a great time in Germany.' he said.

After a stint with Southampton, Keegan joined Newcastle United in 1982, helping the club to promotion from Division Two in his second season. At the age of 33, he retired, departing St James' Park by helicopter. 'To add to my dramatic exit, I dropped my number seven shirt as we took off,' he said.

'Shanks told me after I had played three games for Liverpool that I'd go on to play for England within a year and a half.' Keegan, the raw recruit from Scunthorpe, could hardly believe what he was hearing.

'I remember thinking to myself, "Eighteen months! He can't be serious, surely." '

Shankly got it wrong. Keegan, it transpired, didn't need that much time. Several months ahead of schedule, he made his England debut in a 1–0 win over Wales in Cardiff in November 1972.

Two years later he was on the bench at Wembley for the fateful qualifying game against Poland. With only a few minutes remaining, and England still needing to score, the message came from Alf Ramsey: 'Kevin, get changed.'

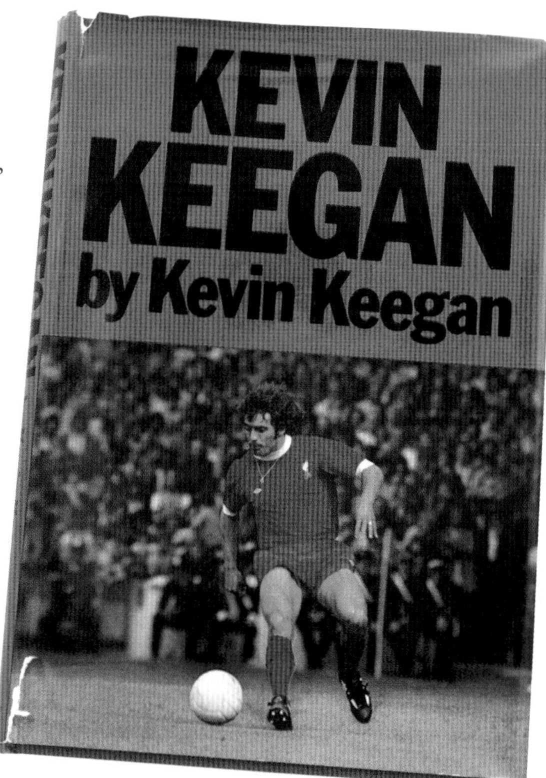

Keegan had begun taking off his tracksuit in readiness when he realised the call had not been for him, but Kevin Hector, the Derby County forward.

In 1977, Keegan scored in the 2–0 win over Italy, but England lost out on qualification for the World Cup in Argentina on goal difference. Unfortunately

> **" To add to my dramatic exit, I dropped my number seven shirt from the helicopter as we took off. "** – *Kevin Keegan*

for Keegan, his peak years coincided with a decline in the fortunes of England.

When England finally did make it, by qualifying for the World Cup finals in 1982, Keegan was cruelly sidelined by injury during the tournament in Spain. In his desperation to play, he travelled in secret for treatment on his back in Germany. On his return to Spain Keegan managed eighteen minutes as a substitute against the hosts, missed one chance, and England were out. Nor was that his last disappointment with England. He resigned as England manager in October 2000, after eighteen months in the job, which was sandwiched between stints in charge of Newcastle, Fulham and Manchester City.

'I was captain of my country in more than thirty games,' Keegan said. 'It is a source of great disappointment that the least successful part of my career should have been played out on the international stage.'

Ron Greenwood, national team manager between 1977–82, was more generous: 'Kevin was a great England player, and the man I built my team around.'

TALKING POINT

Liverpool had a reputation for giving their own particular welcome to new signings. No matter the size of the transfer fee or reputation, a player arriving at Anfield could expect to start out in the reserves, learning 'the Liverpool way' of doing things.

Kevin Keegan came to Liverpool in the summer of 1971 as a virtual unknown. Yet Bill Shankly decided there was no need for Keegan to serve an apprenticeship in Liverpool methods.

'No one goes to Liverpool and steps straight into the first team; at least, they didn't then,' Keegan recalled.

The manager recognised the skill and energy Keegan would bring to the side. 'Go out there, son, and drop grenades,' Shankly told him.

Keegan was physically prepared to play at a higher level. When Shankly first saw his physique, he compared his build to that of a professional boxer. 'I was super fit from running up and down the terraces at Scunthorpe carrying dumb-bells,' he said.

Barely out of his teens, he also had abundant self-confidence. In the week before the first game of the season, Shankly asked him which team he wanted to play for on Saturday. 'I haven't come to Liverpool to play in your reserve team,' Keegan replied. And nor did he during all his time at Anfield.

Above left Keegan was very entrepreneurial and believed that he would succeed in any field. It was no surprise when he penned his own book in 1977 and had a successful pop career in Germany.

Above A match programme from Euro '96 featuring Keegan and the legendary Dutch striker Johann Cruyff.

FOREST
EUROPEAN CUP FINAL
MUNICH 1979

BRIAN CLOUGH (1935–2004)

Manager • Inducted 2002 • 2 European Cups
2 Division One Championships • 4 League Cups

Brian Clough astonished the football world when he made an unfashionable, modest provincial club the champions of Europe in two successive seasons.

Nottingham Forest won the European Cup at their first attempt in 1979, beating Malmo of Sweden in the final, and then repeated the trick the following year, against even greater odds, by defeating Hamburg, the German champions. 'We gave Hamburg a lesson in application, determination, dedication and pride; all the things that are taken for granted in English football,' Clough said.

His achievement at the City Ground was no fluke. He had already done much the same at modest, provincial Derby County in the late 1960s and early 1970s. All his teams played neat, stylish football and they kept the ball on the deck. At both clubs, promotion was quickly followed by success in lifting the Division One championship title. Clough was the first manager to win the title with two different clubs since Herbert Chapman achieved the feat with Huddersfield Town and Arsenal during the inter-war years. Kenny Dalglish has done so since, for Liverpool and Blackburn Rovers.

Of the three managers, Clough had the least money to spend compared to rival clubs of the day.

He compensated for this relative lack of financial clout with a mastery of psychology and a genius for publicity. He kept his players mentally alert by doing the unexpected. Few other managers would have dared to prepare for a European Cup final by taking their players on a week's holiday to Majorca. Once there, he banned training and encouraged several drinking sessions. Hamburg, in contrast, opted for a conventional week in a training camp. Forest won the final 1–0.

'A player can never feel too sure of himself,' said Archie Gemmill. 'That is his secret.' Peter Shilton said. 'He had a unique style, but it certainly worked.'

KEY MATCH

Nottingham Forest 1 Malmo 0, European Cup final, Munich, 30 May 1979

Brian Clough proved the value of his unconventional methods by winning the European Cup final in 1979 after inviting the Forest players to drink a beer with him on the coach journey to the ground.

There was, of course, a reason for breaking so dramatically with conventional thinking: Clough wanted his players relaxed and their minds distracted before they took on the Swedish champions. 'Climb in, lads, but get rid of the bottles when we're near the ground,' he said.

'Better for them to have a drink than sit there bored to a stupor watching a bloody video of opponents who weren't as good as us,' Clough said later.

The Swedes were a dour, defensive side who relied on rare breaks against Forest. Clough would not be drawn into their trap. 'The manager instructed us not to be reckless when going forward,' Peter Shilton recalled.

To counter Malmo's reliance on the offside trap, Trevor Francis was deployed in midfield, with orders to join the attack late. When John Robertson began one of his weaving runs down the left flank, Francis sensed his chance. A diving header at the end of a 50-yard run gave Forest their winner.

Even though they were drained – this was their 76th game of the season – Forest retained their composure and spirit. 'We worked and complemented one another. Brian Clough's Nottingham Forest were a team in every sense of the word,' Shilton said.

Left Brian Clough returns to the City Ground to show off the European Cup to the media in 1979.

KEY MUSEUM ARTEFACT

Under Brian Clough's management, Nottingham Forest appeared in three consecutive League Cup finals, from 1978 to 1980, winning the first two. This is the programme from the 1979 final. Team sheets and programmes have been used and published since the earliest days of organised football and over the years they have become highly collectable, not only as objects detailing football history but also, through the inclusion of advertisements, as documents of social history. Particularly scarce are programmes from the pre-war period and a full set of League Cup programmes, from the early rounds to the final itself, would be highly sought after by collectors.

Brian Clough enjoyed almost all his success working in partnership with Peter Taylor. They complemented each other perfectly: Clough was brash, opinionated and unpredictable; Taylor was calm, methodical and calculated. The pair met as players at Middlesbrough and worked together in management at Hartlepool United, Derby County and Nottingham Forest.

'Nobody could touch Peter as a judge of talent,' Clough said. 'His sense of humour was also a key component of our success together.'

Taylor was also a masterful operator in the transfer market. Archie Gemmill was bought from Derby County for a fee of £20,000 plus goalkeeper Jim Middleton. Then, in 1979, Gemmill was sold on to Birmingham City for £150,000. 'What an amazing deal!' Clough said later. But Clough was also prepared to spend money and he became the first manager to pay £1 million for a player when he signed Trevor Francis from Birmingham City in February 1979, doubling the previous record.

Under Clough, Forest looked for experienced players who had yet to achieve success but who still burned with ambition. In July 1977, he signed Kenny Burns, 'an overweight striker at Birmingham City', and promptly converted him into a sweeper. Even Burns was taken aback. The following season he was Footballer of the Year.

Gary Birtles was another find. A carpet-fitter by trade, he was bought from non-league football for £2,000 and went on to play for England.

Clough recognised the contribution made by Taylor by inviting him to lead out the Forest side before the League Cup final in 1979.

Above right The Simod Cup trophy of 1988, which Nottingham Forest won in 1989 by beating Everton 4–3 at Wembley. In the wake of the ban on English clubs competing in European football, Crystal Palace Chairman, Ron Noades, helped to create the Full Members' Cup, as it was known prior to 1988. Only a handful of Division One clubs took part.

Right A book on Nottingham Forest from 1979. The front cover shows the team's victory celebrations after their European Cup triumph over Malmo in Munich that year.

Brian Clough did not lack for self-belief and confidence. Before the start of the 1968–69 season, Clough predicted during a television interview that Derby would win promotion. The previous season the club had finished fifth from bottom. At the risk of looking foolish, Clough agreed that the interview

> “I breezed straight into the board meeting at another club and told them I had come to sign one of their players. And I did.” – *Brian Clough*

should be screened at the end of the season. In May, Derby were promoted as champions.

When he was awarded the OBE in 1991, his wife joked that the letters stood for 'Old Big 'Ead'.

His self-belief lay at the root of his unorthodox behaviour. As Derby manager, he wanted to sign David Nish, the Leicester City full-back. 'I actually gate-crashed a board meeting at Leicester,' Clough recalled. 'I breezed straight in, large as life, and told them I'd come to sign to Nish.' And he did, for a British record fee of £225,000.

At the other end of the scale, Clough was prepared to wait for several hours in the reception rooms at White Hart Lane in order to sign Dave Mackay from Spurs.

His motivational team-talks could be equally unconventional. At half-time at one home game, with Forest losing, he locked the dressing room. Taken aback, the players were handed a football. 'You were rubbish,' he told them. 'Now go out there and do something to entertain the crowd for ten minutes.' Forest won the game.

He did not hesitate to confront authority when he thought the cause right. At the end of the League Cup final in 1979, he broke with custom by walking up the steps to the Royal Box. No manager had ever done that before, not even Alf Ramsey after England won the World Cup in 1966. Forest had won, and Clough decided the manager deserved some recognition.

Right A 1930s' ceramic pot from Sunderland Football Club, for whom Brian Clough scored a remarkable 54 goals in 61 League appearances before injury cut short his playing career.

TALKING POINT

Looking back on his playing career with Middlesbrough and Sunderland, Brian Clough described himself as 'the best goalscorer in Britain'. Prone as he was to hyperbole on other subjects, the statistics here support his claim. Clough scored 204 goals in 222 games for Middlesbrough and 63 goals in 74 games for Sunderland following his transfer between the clubs in 1961.

'Brian was proud that he remains the player who scored 250 goals in Football League games in the shortest amount of time,' the late Peter Taylor said of his erstwhile management partner.

All but one of those goals was scored in the then Second Division. After playing just nine first-team games, he requested a transfer from Middlesbrough, but under the transfer system at the time the club were not obliged to sell.

Clough won only two caps for England despite his outstanding record, and he failed to gain selection for the World Cup in 1958. 'It just didn't make sense,' reflected Billy Wright, the England captain.

'Two bloody caps!' Clough said years later. 'The players chosen instead of me weren't in my class.'

A cruciate ligament injury eventually forced Clough to retire as a player at the age of 29, precipitating his early entry into management.

Above Clough and his assistant Peter Taylor give instructions from the pitch-side running track during the European Cup semi-final against FC Cologne in 1979, which Nottingham Forest won 1–0.

SUE LOPEZ (1945–)

Player • Inducted 2004 • 22 caps • 8 FA Cups

A pioneer footballer, coach and then manager, Sue Lopez has made an outstanding contribution to the development of women's football during a career spanning five decades.

Lopez was the first Englishwoman to play semi-professional football as an overseas player in Italy in 1971, returning home to help establish the first-ever officially sanctioned England women's team. As an automatic choice for seven years, she won 22 caps.

In 1978, she played a major role in organising the first England women's international to be played on a Football League ground, following the rescinding of a ban on the use of such venues that dated back to 1921.

As a club player, she was the lynchpin on the left side of midfield for Southampton, the team that was almost unassailable during the 1970s, while as a coach she has brought through one full England international and 11 England youth internationals in seven years to the end of 2004–05. As a manager, she was in charge of Southampton Saints, in the National League Southern Division, between 2003–05. She remains head of women's football at Southampton.

Lopez played for Southampton in the first ten Women's FA Cup finals, starting in 1971, collecting eight winner's medals.

'I was a pioneer in the modern women's game,' Lopez said. 'It was the 1960s, and the success of the England men in winning the World Cup was another big factor, of course.'

Following her retirement as a player in 1985, she became the second woman to gain the FA Advanced Licence coaching qualification, now known as the UEFA 'A Licence'. Eight years later, in 1999, she was named *The Sunday Times* Female Coach of the Year and the following year she was awarded an MBE.

When she began playing the game in the 1960s, there were 6,000 registered women players and 300 teams in England; in 2003 that number had risen to 85,000 players and 4,200 teams. 'It's now the most popular sport for girls,' Lopez said. 'It's been an amazing change.'

KEY MATCH

England 3 Belgium 0, International Friendly, The Dell, 31 October 1978

Sue Lopez did more than drive England forward from her position on the left side of midfield. Without her equally hard work off the field, the game would not even have taken place.

Lopez helped organise the fixture, finding a sponsor to cough up £2,000 to cover expenses and fronting the media, alongside Lawrie McMenemy, the Southampton manager, at a press conference to promote the game.

'Lawrie was fantastic in terms of his support, giving up a lot of time to help us,' Lopez recalled. 'Ron Greenwood, the England manager, agreed to take part in a presentation of the teams before kick-off.'

The game, which attracted 5,500 paying customers, was the first women's match to be played on a Football League ground since 1921. The spectators saw Lopez set up the first goal with a telling pass to striker Elaine Badrock.

The game was unofficial, as the Women's FA did not come under the umbrella of the Football Association until 1993. 'Nowadays the women's national team enjoys similar resources to the men,' Lopez said. 'When I played the training kit often didn't fit and the kit itself was poor. We had no official emblem, and we sowed a badge of the England flag on the shirts.'

Left Sue Lopez displays the technique that brought her and her club unprecedented success throughout the 1970s.

KEY MUSEUM ARTEFACT

This trophy was made for the game between England and Switzerland Ladies on 28 April 1977. The game, played in The Queen's Jubilee year, took place at Hull City's Boothferry Park. Sue Lopez enjoyed the best football of her career during the 1970s. Between 1973 and 1979 she won 22 caps for her country and lifted the Women's FA Cup on eight occasions between 1971 and 1981.

Right 'Making Up For The Other Players': this is one of a set of six postcards from the early 1920s by the artist Fred Spurgin. The cards illustrate perfectly the attitudes that women football players have had to overcome.

Sue Lopez was partly inspired to take up football because of the influence of her father and the England team of 1966.

'The World Cup victory helped the women's game a lot because it inspired a lot of girls,' Lopez said. 'As for myself, I have never forgotten being taken by my grandfather to watch Southampton at The Dell for the first time.'

As an adult, she has experienced prejudice while attending coaching courses. In the 1970s and 1980s very few women took the FA badge. 'There have been times when other men on the course have raised their eyebrows a little, as if to say: "Why is she here?" But it has always been a very tiny minority, thankfully.'

During her playing career, she often featured in games against men's teams. She particularly remembers one incident: 'This bloke went right through me with a tackle. I have always thought it was a deliberate foul, and I ended up with a broken ankle.'

" I am immensely proud of the work I have done to help develop the administrative side of the game and to promote the national side. " – *Sue Lopez*

The fracture sidelined Lopez for several months, forcing her to miss selection for the first official England women's international sanctioned by the Football Association. 'I had come back from Italy to get involved with the national side, and to lose out this way was the biggest disappointment of my career.' Once fit again, she was an automatic selection for the team.

Sue Lopez sacrificed her career as a player in Italy to help consolidate the progress of the Women's FA following its inception in 1969, and to ensure her availability and eligibility to play for the national team. An inaugural member of the women's FA, Lopez assisted with administration, acting as voluntary assistant secretary for a year. In the 1980s, she took on the role of vice-chair of the ruling body, before a spell as International Officer in 1992.

She also had a hand in the crucial breakthrough in 1993 when the Football Association assumed full responsibility for the running of the women's game, absorbing the Women's FA into its own structure.

'I am immensely proud of the work I have done to help develop the administrative side of the game and to promote the national side,' Lopez said.

When Lopez retired as a player, England were one of the top eight nations in women's football. Lopez said, 'Our ranking has not changed much over the years, but the level of competition certainly has. There are so many more countries playing women's football nowadays, and the standard of performance both on and off the field has risen dramatically.' Lopez is a key figure in the story of the growth of women's football, according to the most capped female England player in history, 'Sue deserves great credit,' said Gill Coultard, who won 119 caps between 1981 and 2001. 'She fought a lot of battles against prejudice, particularly in the early days.'

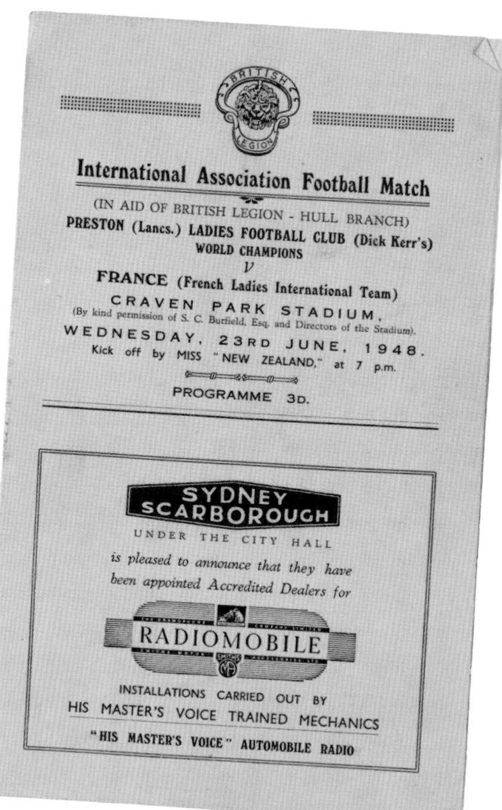

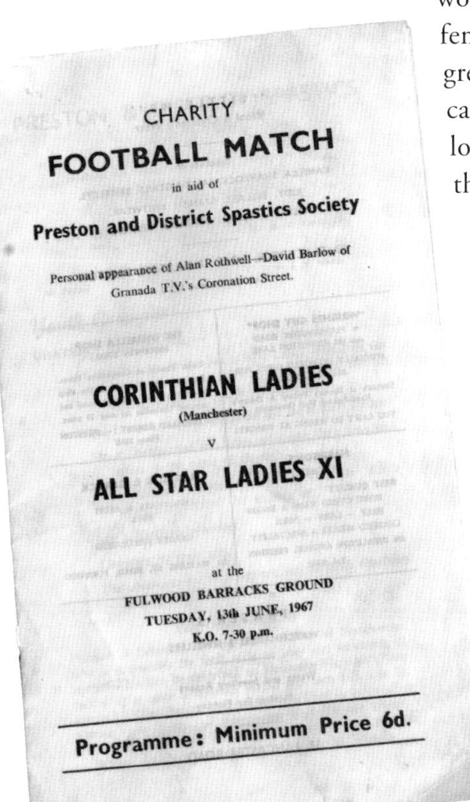

Above This 1948 match programme details the international fixture between Preston (Dick, Kerr Ladies) and France.

Left A programme from the Corinthians v All Stars match in 1967. Despite the ban on women playing football between 1921 and 1970, games were still organised regionally.

Right A Doncaster Belles' goalkeeper's shirt from 2000. While the Southampton women's football team dominated the game in the 1970s, Doncaster Belles were one of the dominant forces throughout the 1990s.

TALKING POINT

'Roma Revival with Lopez,' read the headline in *Corriere dello Sport*, the daily Italian sports newspaper in May 1971. 'It was great. The newspapers in Italy took us seriously, devoting a whole page to women's football,' Lopez recalled.

Lopez made a dramatic impact on Roma in 1971–72, her only season in Italy, after impressing scouts at an international tournament in Turin in 1969. Brought in to revitalise the former champions, Lopez scored 13 goals in 11 League matches. 'It was a fantastic experience,' she recalled.

The highlight of Lopez's stay came in a quarter-final match of the national Cup. Napoli were winning 2–0 in front of a partisan home crowd of 1,000. Playing at centre-forward she scored a hat-trick. 'Lopez lets fly at Napoli with three splendid goals,' a newspaper reported.

Roma went on to win the Cup, beating Fiorentina 1–0 in the final. Lopez made the decisive goal for her striking partner, the Austrian Monika Karner. In the League, Roma finished runners-up, two points behind champions Piacenza in the 14-team division.

'Roma gave me somewhere to live and paid all my expenses during my time over there,' Lopez said. 'We would be recognised when we walked into some restaurants. Free pizzas! It was wonderful.'

On a tour to the United States, Lopez played four exhibition matches for Roma against Southampton, the team she would help dominate English women's football over the following decade.

Liverpool

BOB PAISLEY (1919–1996)

Manager • Inducted 2002 • 3 European Cups • 1 UEFA Cup
6 Division One Championships • 3 League Cups

Bob Paisley was reluctant to take charge at Liverpool because of the doubts he had about his ability to do the job. It was a rare example of poor judgement by a shrewd man who went on to become the most successful club manager in history.

Paisley had been a loyal assistant manager at Anfield for three years before the sudden, shock retirement of Bill Shankly in 1974 thrust him into the limelight at the age of 55. It was the beginning of the most illustrious chapter in the history of the club.

'I never wanted this job in the first place, and I'm not even sure that I can do it,' Paisley told the players at his first team meeting as manager. 'I need all the help I can get from you lads. There will be no disruption to the team. Let's just keep playing the Liverpool way.'

Although impressed by his 'refreshing honesty and modesty that typified his personality', Kevin Keegan worried that Paisley might be overwhelmed by the challenge of succeeding Shankly. 'Bob surprised us all, even himself,' Keegan recalled. 'He grew into the job, sensibly sticking with the team and the tactics he had inherited from Shanks, and slowly and gradually implanting his own ideas.'

Over the next eight years Liverpool established themselves as the most powerful club in Europe, winning the European Cup three times, a feat beyond any other British manager in history, and a host of domestic honours.

'The sort of lad I am looking for as a Liverpool player will try to nutmeg Kevin Keegan in training, but will then step aside for him in the corridor,' Paisley said.

KEY MATCH

Liverpool 1 Real Madrid 0, European Cup final, Paris, 27 May 1981

Alan Kennedy stepped forward as the unlikely hero as Liverpool won the European Cup for the third time in five seasons under the management of Bob Paisley.

With the minutes ticking away in a tight game, the Liverpool left-back went on a run with the ball into the Real penalty area. 'I kept on going and no one got a tackle in, so I decided to have a pop,' Kennedy recalled. 'It was a narrow angle, but I was banking on the keeper leaving a gap at the near post.'

The ball flew into the root of the net. 'Fortunately he did think I was going to pull the ball back, or I would have been given the biggest telling-off by the manager,' recalled Kennedy.

Paisley selected Kennedy for the final even though he lacked match fitness. A cast on his fractured wrist was removed before the game. 'I knew I couldn't let the manager down,' he said.

'I'm so proud to be the manager of the first British club to win the European Cup three times,' Paisley said. 'It was a triumph for our character once again. We controlled most of the second half, and I am sure that Real don't begrudge us our victory.'

As ever, Paisley fought against complacency. His reaction to the triumph in Paris was to dismantle a side he considered past its peak. The following season, Liverpool won the championship title and League Cup double.

Left Bob Paisley celebrates yet another Liverpool championship, in 1980.

KEY MUSEUM ARTEFACT

The Barclays Manager of the Year trophy, which Bob Paisley won, was awarded from season 1965–66 until 1992–93. It was originally won by Celtic manager Jock Stein, who retained the trophy in 1967. It made its way south of the border when it was awarded to Matt Busby after his European success with Manchester United in 1968. Although several managers have won the trophy on more than one occasion, Bob Paisley dominated the award, winning it in 1976, '77, '79, '80, '82 and '83. His success mirrored Liverpool's dominance of the European game throughout this period.

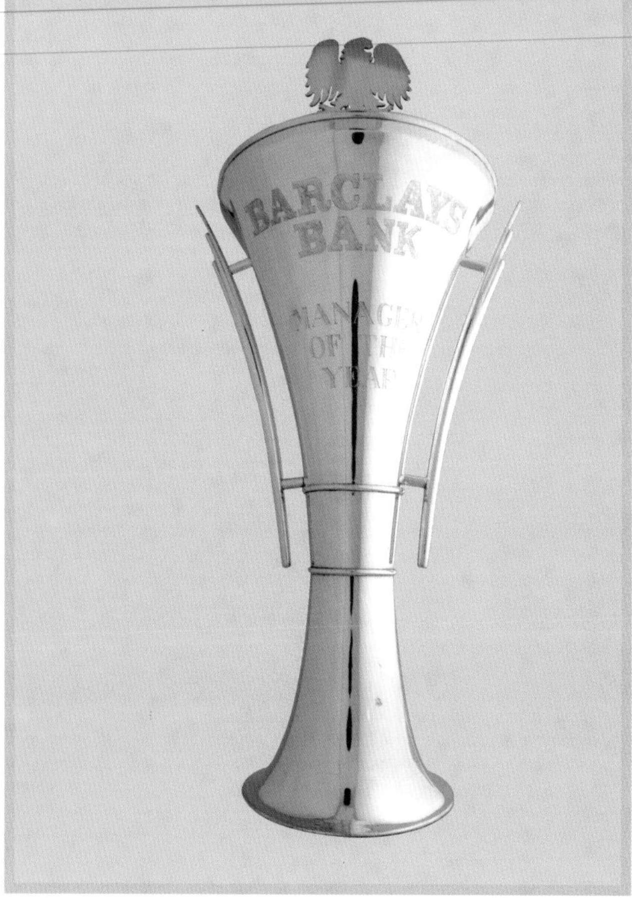

Bob Paisley devoted his working life to Liverpool Football Club. Forty-four years almost to the day after signing for the club in 1939, he walked down the tunnel at the end of his last game in charge as manager. He was 64 years of age.

The only interruption came during the war. For years the players knew him affectionately as 'The Rat', the nickname he was given after fighting in the Army as a Desert Rat in North Africa.

Born in County Durham, Paisley arrived at Anfield just before the war after winning an FA Amateur Cup medal with Bishop Auckland. He served the club as player, trainer, physiotherapist, coach and assistant manager before succeeding Shankly.

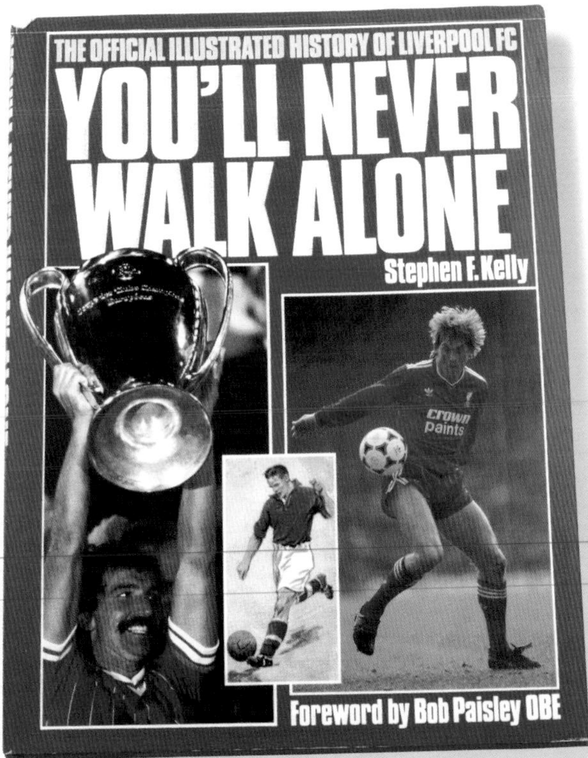

Right This 1980 book, *You'll Never Walk Alone*, chronicles Liverpool's success at both domestic and international level.

Just as he had benefited from the faith and trust shown in him by Shankly, so Paisley placed confidence in his staff. 'Bob Paisley signed me, without having seen me play, on the recommendation of his coaching staff,' Alan Hansen said. The same was true of Ian Rush, the club's leading goalscorer during the Paisley era.

> **"Bob never showed any sentiment. He just picked the best 11 players … he always said complacency was the biggest threat."** – *Alan Hansen*

Paisley differed from his predecessor in one aspect of management, however. 'Bob never showed any sentiment,' Hansen recalled. 'He just picked the best 11 players, and he always said complacency was the biggest threat.

'Possibly he learned from the Shankly era that you could be too loyal to players who were past their best. It made no difference to Bob if a player had been a magnificent servant to the club for ten years.'

Bob Paisley emerged from the shadow of Bill Shankly in 1975–76, his second season in charge, when Liverpool won the League championship and the UEFA Cup double.

'This success is down to our players doing the simple things well,' he said. 'That's the way we intend to continue, the Liverpool way.'

A decade earlier Paisley had identified how to succeed in Europe. 'We must learn from teams on the Continent that we can't go and win the ball individually, we're to win the ball collectively,' he told the players. In 1977, Liverpool became only the second English club to lift the European Cup.

Paisley described the performance against Borussia Mönchengladbach as 'one of the best ever seen' in a final. 'I hope I am not being boastful when I say I think that this is only the start. There is no team in the world that we need fear,' he said. Liverpool defended the trophy the following season.

Liverpool reached their peak in terms of their domination of English football in 1978–79. The team swept away all opposition, amassing a record total of 68 points and a goal difference of plus 69. There were 28 clean sheets, and only four goals were conceded in the League at Anfield. 'We have won the championship with a style that shows British football at its best,' Paisley said. 'It is a triumph for teamwork.'

Through it all, Paisley wore his flat caps and cardigans, a homely image that belied his single-minded determination to succeed. Matt Busby spoke of his 'inner steel and his tough, stubborn streak'.

Complacency was the constant enemy. 'This game can kick you in the teeth,' Paisley repeatedly told his players. 'If we give in to complacency, there is only one way to go, and that is down.'

Bob Paisley took a correspondence course in physiotherapy while still a player. It turned out he had a natural talent for the subject.

'Bob had a deep knowledge of injuries and how to detect and treat them,' Kevin Keegan recalled. 'He could beat qualified medical experts in diagnosing injuries, and often rightly predicted when a player was about to have injury problems.'

As trainer, physiotherapist and then coach, Paisley kept meticulous records on players' training regimes, injuries and lifestyles. Cabinets in the famous 'Boot Room' were full of 'little black books' containing all the details.

Paisley was looking for patterns that might explain why a player was struggling for form or fitness. When one player complained of a mysterious leg problem, Paisley dug a little deeper and eventually found the cause: the pedals on his new car were at a different height to the ones he was used to.

As manager, Paisley focused more on the mind than the body. 'Bob Paisley trained the players' thinking,' Alan Hansen said. 'After every season, no matter how much success we had achieved, the management line was: "Enjoy it while you can because what you have won is going to count for nothing next time".'

'There was nothing that he would not do to get the message across, and the attitude permeated every corner of the club. It became infectious. I became so hungry for medals.'

Left This Liverpool shirt was worn by Phil Neal in his testimonial game in 1985 and is signed by all the players. Neal was the regular right-back through Paisley's successful years. He also dominated the position at international level for England.

Above The Canon League Division One trophy from 1983. Although Paisley retired as Liverpool Manager in 1983, the team continued to be successful under both Joe Fagan and Kenny Dalglish and they won the League in two of the three seasons this trophy was in circulation, in 1984 and 1986.

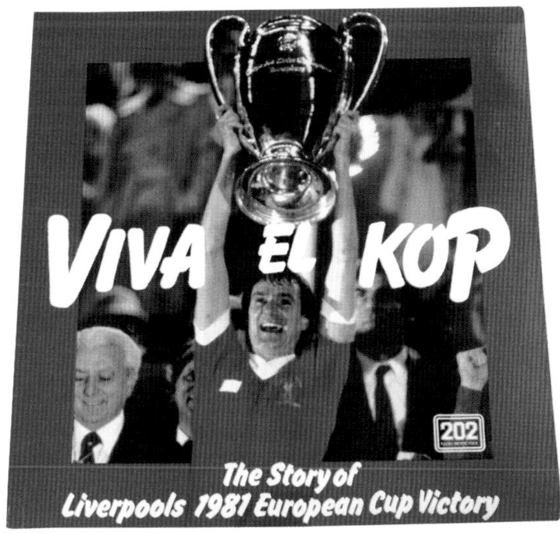

Right This LP celebrates yet another Liverpool European Cup victory and contains a commentary of the match.

PETER SHILTON (1949–)

Player • Inducted 2002 • 125 caps • 2 European Cups
1 Division One Championship • 1 League Cup

Peter Shilton made a remarkable start to his career as a goalkeeper on his way to amassing a record 125 caps for England and two European Cup winner's medals with Nottingham Forest.

His international career lasted 20 years, between 1970 and 1990; only Stanley Matthews in the modern era enjoyed greater longevity. At the age of just seventeen, Shilton had a daunting baptism at club level: succeeding the established England number one in the first team at Leicester City.

Leicester had great faith in his ability and maturity. Acting on this confidence, City cashed in their prized asset, selling Banks, a World Cup winner the year before, for £60,000, a world record fee for a goalkeeper.

'The boy's maturity and technique were outstanding,' Peter Taylor, then Forest's assistant manager, said. 'He instinctively knew the tricks of the trade at that age. Signing Peter in 1977 was a highlight of my career.'

Forest paid a record fee of £275,000. 'He was worth twice the price,' Brian Clough said. In his first season, Shilton conceded only 24 goals in 42 games, including 25 clean sheets. Forest won the title. 'We had a firm belief that if we scored, there was no way we'd lose because they wouldn't score against our defence,' Clough said.

Shilton remained fit and agile enough to play first-class football until the age of 47. In a career spanning 31 years he played a record 1,005 Football League games.

'Perfection as a goalkeeper is unachievable, I knew that,' Shilton once said. 'But it is what motivated me when I was younger. By aiming for it, I reasoned I would achieve a higher standard than anyone else.'

KEY MATCH

Nottingham Forest 1 Hamburg 0, European Cup final, Madrid, 28 May 1980

Peter Shilton had already seen enough one-way traffic in the build-up, before becoming an unbeatable last line of defence against a forward line led by Kevin Keegan.

In one of the more bizarre ideas thought up by Brian Clough and Peter Taylor, Shilton was told to practise on the grass in the middle of a traffic roundabout on the outskirts of Madrid.

The England international had been unable to find a suitable piece of ground at the team hotel for his regular training workout. 'I was always unhappy if I couldn't get a feel of the ball, to help my handling,' he said.

Clough and Taylor had a solution: a nearby traffic island. 'At first I couldn't believe it, but they were serious. So I put down two tracksuit tops, against the background noise of tooting horns from passing cars.'

Shilton also needed a pain-killing injection before the match after straining a calf muscle. 'In the circumstances, Peter gave an impeccable display,' Viv Anderson, the Forest full-back said. 'He gave the whole team confidence.'

Forest had been under pressure before John Robertson put them ahead in the first half. From then on, the onslaught simply intensified.

'I don't think I had ever been in a game where there had been so much pressure on my goal,' Shilton recalled. 'But we achieved what we set out to do, and we did it honestly.'

Left Peter Shilton throws himself across goal to pull off yet another outstanding save for Leicester City.

KEY MUSEUM ARTEFACT

Diego Maradona wore this shirt in the 1986 World Cup quarter-final clash with England. But for the genius of Maradona's second and winning goal, Shilton and England might have made it to the semi-finals of the tournament. The nylon shirt, made by Le Coq Sportif, is very light and appears to have been made rather cheaply. The badge is only sewn at the top and bottom, and the number on the reverse of the shirt had been poorly cut before being ironed onto the fabric. England's Steve Hodge exchanged shirts with Maradona in the tunnel after the game.

As a boy, Peter Shilton was prepared to stretch himself (literally!) in pursuit of his ambition to become a top-class goalkeeper.

He began training at Leicester City, his hometown club, at the age of eleven. At home, he stood under a streetlamp, for up to two hours at a time in the evening, catching a ball as it rebounded off a wall. 'It was great practice for my handling and footwork,' he said.

Fearing that he might not grow tall enough to make the grade as a goalkeeper, the young Shilton took to hanging from the banister at home. 'My mum would hang on to my legs and try to stretch me! Whether this had any effect I don't know, but I shot up from the time I was thirteen.'

Shilton studied the great goalkeepers of the time in order to learn his trade. He tried to copy the positional sense of Gordon Banks, the presence in goal of Lev Yashin, the Russian goalkeeper, and the agility and distribution of Peter Bonetti, of Chelsea.

Fearing that he might not grow tall enough to make the grade as a goalkeeper, the young Shilton took to hanging from the banister at home.

Right A Nottingham Forest card produced by Baines in the 1880s. In his 30-year career Shilton made League appearances for some seven clubs as well as appearing as a substitute for Bolton Wanderers.

'I noticed that Gordon was never caught out as the ball was struck; that Yashin projected an aura of invincibility; and that Peter was willing to take responsibility for crosses, and I wanted to bring these qualities to my game.'

Always searching for improvement Shilton found inspiration in some unusual places. In 1974, he sought the advice of a ballroom dancer, whose ideas on balance, foot movement and running found a receptive audience. 'I changed my posture, how I turned from the hips,' Shilton said. 'I threw my weight slightly forward and learned how to keep my feet light and close to the ground, moving them as if skating on ice.'

Peter Shilton was the first-choice goalkeeper for England at three successive World Cup tournaments – 1982 in Spain, 1986 in Mexico and 1990 in Italy. In 125 international appearances he conceded eighty goals.

TALKING POINT

Orient laid out the red carpet for Peter Shilton when he became the first player in the history of English football to play 1,000 League matches – 31 years after he signed as a professional for Leicester City.

Fittingly, he kept a clean sheet in a 2–0 win over Brighton, the third time he had stopped the opposition scoring in his four appearances for the club. After playing five more League games, Shilton finally hung up his goalkeeping gloves in 1997. In total, he had played in 1,391 official games.

'I never lost my appetite for the game,' Shilton said. 'Even late in my career I enjoyed testing myself in games and in training. It was always a challenge to be the best goalkeeper possible.'

No one has bettered his total of 88 appearances in the FA Cup and his total of 17 appearances in the World Cup, stretching over three tournaments, is also a record.

Shilton kept a clean sheet 66 times for England, a ratio of more than one every two games. On 14 occasions he captained his country.

In order to prolong his career he cut out alcohol from his diet in 1988, ensuring his selection by Bobby Robson for Italia '90. 'He never lost his agility or his handling in his latter years because of the work he put in,' Robson said. 'He was magnificent.'

Shilton's selection in goal covered the eras of four national team managers: Alf Ramsey, who gave him his debut in 1970, Don Revie, Ron Greenwood and Bobby Robson.

Robson, the England manager between 1982 and 1990, rated Shilton the best goalkeeper of the modern era in the world. 'I think the likes of Lev Yashin, Dino Zoff of Italy and the Brazilian Gilmar could consider themselves lucky to be classed in his company,' Robson said.

Shilton took over in goal for England following the retirement of Gordon Banks because of injury in 1973. Over the next 17 years, he had only one serious rival for the number one jersey: Ray Clemence, of Liverpool.

Ron Greenwood alternated between the two of them during his five years in charge from 1977 onwards, but, significantly, it was Shilton who got the nod at the World Cup in Spain in 1982.

There were no such doubts during the eight years when Robson was manager. Shilton was an automatic choice: 'The first name on my team-sheet,' Robson said. 'He was phenomenal for me. He was big in goal, had long arms and a good leap.'

Left Shilton and his England team-mates reached the semi-finals of the 1990 World Cup in Italy. Many thousands of fans turned up to welcome them home at the airport and inside the terminal the *Sun* newspaper presented the team with this trophy.

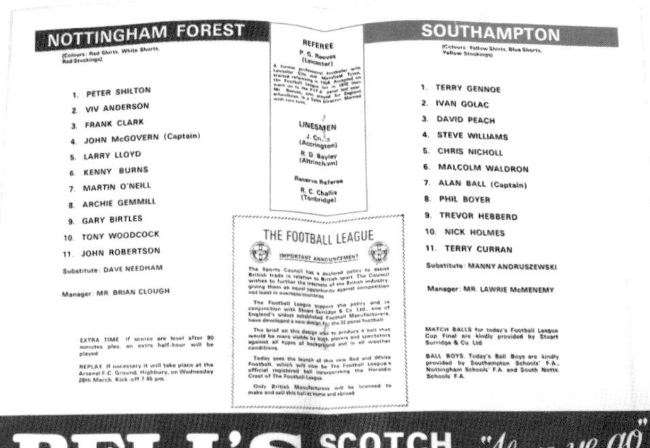

NOTTINGHAM FOREST

(Colours: Red Shirts, White Shorts, Red Stockings)

1. PETER SHILTON
2. VIV ANDERSON
3. FRANK CLARK
4. JOHN McGOVERN (Captain)
5. LARRY LLOYD
6. KENNY BURNS
7. MARTIN O'NEILL
8. ARCHIE GEMMILL
9. GARY BIRTLES
10. TONY WOODCOCK
11. JOHN ROBERTSON

Substitute: DAVE NEEDHAM

Manager: MR. BRIAN CLOUGH

EXTRA TIME. If scores are level after 90 minutes play, an extra half-hour will be played.

REPLAY. If necessary it will take place at the Arsenal F.C. Ground, Highbury, on Wednesday 28th March. Kick-off 7.45 pm.

REFEREE
P. G. Reeves
(Leicester)

LINESMEN
J. Cr[illegible]
(Accrington)
R. D. Bayley
(Altrincham)

Reserve Referee
R. C. Challis
(Tonbridge)

THE FOOTBALL LEAGUE

IMPORTANT ANNOUNCEMENT

SOUTHAMPTON

(Colours: Yellow Shirts, Blue Shorts, Yellow Stockings)

1. TERRY GENNOE
2. IVAN GOLAC
3. DAVID PEACH
4. STEVE WILLIAMS
5. CHRIS NICHOLL
6. MALCOLM WALDRON
7. ALAN BALL (Captain)
8. PHIL BOYER
9. TREVOR HEBBERD
10. NICK HOLMES
11. TERRY CURRAN

Substitute: MANNY ANDRUSZEWSKI

Manager: MR. LAWRIE McMENEMY

MATCH BALLS for today's Football League Cup Final are kindly provided by Stuart Surridge & Co. Ltd.

BALL BOYS. Today's Ball Boys are kindly provided by Southampton Schools' F.A., Nottingham Schools' F.A. and South Notts. Schools' F.A.

BELL'S SCOTCH WHISKY "Afore ye go"

Above left This book was published in 1974. Shilton made 20 of his 125 international appearances while at his first club, Leicester City, between 1970 and 1974.

Above A 1979 League Cup final programme. Forest won the League Cup, for the second season in succession, with a 3–2 victory over Southampton.

KENNY DALGLISH (1951–)

Player • Inducted 2002 • 102 caps • 3 European Cups
6 Division One Championships • 1 FA Cup • 4 League Cups

Kenny Dalglish repaid the fans on the Kop for their rapturous welcome by inspiring Liverpool to a period of unprecedented success, first as a player and then as manager.

Dalglish faced the daunting challenge of succeeding Kevin Keegan as an Anfield idol following the Englishman's transfer overseas in 1977. When he ran out for the first time at home, the Kop gave him the loudest cheer for a newcomer in living memory.

Any doubts there might have been as to whether he was up to the challenge were soon answered. The following season Dalglish scored the winning goal in the European Cup final. Twelve months on, and Liverpool were champions again, and Dalglish was Footballer of the Year. If anything, he had made Liverpool even stronger.

Bob Paisley, the Liverpool manager, paid Celtic £440,000 for the 27-year-old Dalglish. Like his predecessor in the Liverpool number seven shirt, the Scot could play in either midfield or up front.

In 1985, as his playing career was winding down, Dalglish initiated his transition into management, succeeding Joe Fagan as Liverpool manager. In his first season in charge he won the League and FA Cup double.

'Kenny made a successful transition because he behaved like an orchestra conductor,' Paisley said. 'He brought others into play. He understood that not everyone was blessed with great skill. He had patience, both as a player and as a manager.'

Sir John Smith, the Liverpool chairman, described Dalglish as 'the best player this club has signed this century'. Tommy Smith, a team-mate, said: 'He is a football genius.'

Dalglish made a huge impression, even on the blue half of the city. Late in life, Dixie Dean, the great Everton centre-forward, described him as 'a wonderful player, such skill, so brave. Probably the best combination of goalscorer and goalmaker I've ever seen'.

KEY MATCH

Liverpool 1 Club Bruges 0, European Cup final, Wembley, 10 May 1978

Kenny Dalglish produced an exceptional piece of finishing skill to achieve his great ambition at the first time of asking with Liverpool. 'It was the bit of magic that won us the Cup,' Ray Clemence, the Liverpool and England goalkeeper said.

Dalglish left Celtic for Liverpool the previous summer with just this kind of moment in mind. 'I was convinced there was more chance of winning the European Cup final at Anfield,' he recalled. With his goal against the Belgian champions, Dalglish did more than anyone else to prove his assessment correct.

David Fairclough, a team-mate at Wembley, said Dalglish introduced a new finishing technique: chipping the ball deftly over the goalkeeper just as he tries to smother a shot by spreading himself at the forward's feet.

'It was something that Kenny designed,' Fairclough said. 'It's become a common-used shot now, but he was probably the innovator. Kenny weighed up the situation and came up with the answer.'

Kevin Keegan, watching the game on television, initially thought Dalglish had taken the ball too deep. 'The angle looked too tight, but he then conjured up a goal of pure class,' Keegan said.

Immediately after scoring the decisive goal in the 65th minute, Dalglish famously leapt an advertising hoarding by the side of the pitch in celebration, before running to the Liverpool supporters behind the goal.

The previous summer he had decided to leave Celtic after concluding that Liverpool offered him a better bet for success in the European Cup. With his goal at Wembley, he had done more than anyone else to prove his assessment correct.

Left Kenny Dalglish gracefully fires in a volley for Liverpool against Manchester City.

KEY MUSEUM ARTEFACT

Developments in revenue generation during the 1980s saw each of the divisions of the Football League being renamed after a sponsor. Each successive sponsor has produced their own unique trophy! From 1987 until 1993, Division One was sponsored by Barclays Bank. Kenny Dalglish won the Barclays League Division One trophy as Liverpool manager in 1988 and 1990. George Graham's Arsenal won it in 1989 and 1991, whilst Leeds United, under Howard Wilkinson, were the last team to win it before the introduction of the Premiership. in 1992.

Above A scarf worn by a Liverpool supporter at the FA Cup semi-final between Liverpool and Nottingham Forest, in 1989. The day was the blackest in Dalglish's career, as 96 Liverpool supporters lost their lives, the result of a crush in the Leppings Lane End of Hillsborough Stadium in Sheffield.

Right This architect's scale model for Chelsea's proposed main stand at Stamford Bridge, which was produced by Darbourne & Drake in 1972, marked the start of the stadium's redevelopment. The stand was completed in 1974. It was here that Kenny Dalglish scored Liverpool's winner to secure the Double in his first season as player-manager in 1986.

Emlyn Hughes played alongside Kenny Dalglish for Liverpool and against him as a defender with England. It was obvious which situation he preferred. 'Kenny is almost impossible to mark,' Hughes said.

Hughes, the Liverpool captain, praised the intelligence of Dalglish as a footballer. 'His thinking during a game is both incisive and decisive,' he said. In 1981, Paisley said: 'Kevin Keegan was quicker, but Kenny runs the first five yards in his head.' Ray Clemence said Dalglish was 'three or four moves ahead of everyone else'.

> **"He had this rare quality of being able to know where the other players were without even looking, and to find them with a perfect pass."** – *Bob Paisley*

'What made him unique was his vision,' Paisley added. 'He had this rare quality of being able to know where the other players were without even looking, and to find them with a perfect pass.'

During his time as Scotland manager, Alex Ferguson described Dalglish 'as the best bum player in the game', referring to his strength in the lower body and ability to shield the ball from a defender.

David O'Leary, the Arsenal defender, said: 'Trying to take the ball off Kenny once he's got it, is almost impossible. He crouches over the ball, elbows poking out. Commit too soon, and he will spin and go past you.'

'One certainty is that that no defender frightened him,' Ferguson recalled. 'Because Kenny was so skilful, his courage as a player was seldom stressed, but he had the heart of a lion.'

In his 30s, Dalglish switched to a deeper role in midfield. Ian Rush, the Liverpool striker, who was the leading scorer in Division One in 1983–84, with 32 goals in 1983–84, said: 'I just made the runs knowing the ball would come to me from Kenny.'

Kenny Dalgish earned the continuing respect of the people of Liverpool for his dignified and compassionate behaviour in the aftermath of the Hillsborough tragedy of 1989.

The morning after 95 Liverpool supporters died in the crush behind the goal at the venue for the FA Cup semi-final, Dalglish contacted his players. 'What is called for now is dignity,' he told each of them. 'We need to set an example.' That evening the players attended a special mass at the Catholic Cathedral.

As a teenager Dalglish had been a Celtic player at the time of the Ibrox disaster in January 1971, when 66 fans died on Stairway 13 at the end of an 'Old Firm' match. He also witnessed the loss of life at the European Cup final between Liverpool and Juventus in 1985, when 39 Italians were crushed at Heysel Stadium.

In the weeks following the Hillsborough disaster, Dalglish and the players visited the injured in hospital and consoled the bereaved families. One mother requested that Dalglish visit her comatose son in hospital before his life-support machine was switched off.

'We were just trying to help people,' Dalglish said. 'They have always helped us as supporters, and we supported them when they needed us.' An impromptu shrine of flowers and scarves was created at Anfield. 'The saddest and most beautiful sight I have ever seen,' he said.

But the emotional toll of these events eventually took its effect. In 1991, Dalglish suddenly resigned, citing the 'intolerable pressure' he experienced on match days.

TALKING POINT

Kenny Dalglish is only the third manager in history to win the championship title with two different clubs.

His achievements with Liverpool and Blackburn Rovers put Dalglish in the same bracket as Herbert Chapman [Huddersfield Town and Arsenal] and Brian Clough [Derby County and Nottingham Forest].

Dalglish scored the winning goal against Chelsea at Stamford Bridge on the final Saturday of the league season in 1985–86 and then selected himself in the FA Cup final in which Liverpool came from behind to beat Everton 3–1. He was the first player-manager to appear at Wembley.

As player-manager at Anfield, Dalglish managed an additional feat beyond even Chapman and Clough: winning the League and Cup double.

Dalglish made significant changes at Liverpool: instead of a policy of continuity in team selection, he introduced an element of uncertainty, only announcing his line-up just before kick-off. 'Kenny hated complacency above all else, and this certainly kept us on our toes,' Alan Hansen said.

To win the Double, Liverpool had slugged through the back end of the season playing 19 games without defeat, an achievement that earned Dalglish the award as Manager of the Year. It was the first of three titles to come to Anfield during his five years in charge.

After taking a break from the game, Dalglish returned to football to guide Blackburn Rovers to the Premier League title in 1994–95, followed by stints at Newcastle United and Celtic.

Above A Liverpool FA Cup final shirt. Liverpool won the FA Cup twice under Kenny Dalglish. They beat their Merseyside neighbours Everton on both occasions – 3–1 in 1986, and 3–2 (aet) in 1989.

Left Dalglish won the Canon League Division One Trophy as a player with Liverpool in 1984 and again, as their manager, in 1986.

BOBBY ROBSON (1933–)

Manager • Inducted 2003 • 1 FA Cup • 1 UEFA Cup

By guiding England to their best performance in a World Cup final on foreign soil Bobby Robson helped lift the reputation of English football in troubled times, in what he knew would be his last act as national team manager.

After leading England to within two penalty kicks of the final of Italia '90, Robson enhanced his standing on the Continent by winning honours for PSV Eindhoven, Porto, and Barcelona.

At various times during the 1990s Arsenal, Everton, Celtic, Benfica, Nigeria and Saudi Arabia all made efforts to hire Robson. Eventually, after nine years working overseas, he decided upon a sentimental return to his native north-east, where he lifted Newcastle United out of the doldrums, winning a place in the Champions League.

During his eight turbulent years in charge of the national team, beginning in 1982, England reached the quarter-finals of the World Cup in Mexico in 1986 and the last four in Italy four years later, the country's best result since winning the tournament as hosts in 1966. England also won the FIFA Fair Play award.

His time in charge coincided with a succession of crises in English football: tragedy at Hillsborough and Bradford and a fatal outbreak of hooliganism at Heysel that led to a ban on English clubs in Europe. Throughout it all, Robson led England with a calm authority, despite being subject to bouts of media and public vilification unprecedented in their intensity.

The insults plumbed new depths following the failure to qualify for the European Championships in 1984 and intensified still further four years later when the team reached the tournament in West Germany only to lose all three group games.

A man of great loyalty and integrity, Robson took a significant pay cut to take the England job. Even during the worst of the press campaigns, he did not consider resignation, not even when Barcelona made the third of several lucrative offers to become their manager.

'He departed the England job with dignity, and grey hair,' a Football Association spokesman said.

KEY MATCH

England 1 West Germany 1, World Cup semi-final, Turin, 4 July 1990

During extra time Bobby Robson thought to himself: 'We look the more likely winners here.' His optimism would only make the subsequent agony of defeat in the penalty shoot-out all the more painful. 'The experience left me scarred, mentally scarred; the disappointment was so acute,' he said later.

Having seen Argentina defeat Italy the day before, Robson believed – rightly, as it proved – that this second semi-final would decide the winner of the World Cup. 'This is the most important game you will ever play,' he told his players beforehand.

Robson made one change, bringing in Peter Beardsley for an unfit John Barnes. He also kept faith with the sweeper system introduced in the group game against Holland.

Only when England went behind did Robson revert to an orthodox back four, taking off Butcher in order to introduce Trevor Steven on the right. It was a cross from that side of the pitch that set up Gary Lineker for the equaliser to Andy Brehme's freak goal.

At the end of normal time, with the score locked at 1–1, Robson reminded his players that they had already won twice – against Belgium and Cameroon – in extra time, but it was not to be this time.

In the first-ever shoot-out contested by England, Germany proved stronger. England were out. That night Robson told his players: 'Everyone is immensely proud of you.'

Left Bobby Robson embraces Paul Gascoigne at the end of England's 3–2 victory over Cameroon in the World Cup quarter-final match on 1 July 1990.

KEY MUSEUM ARTEFACT

The UEFA Cup replaced the Fairs Cup in 1972. The first Fairs Cup final had been played in 1958. The competition was designed for the top sides from each participating country who had failed to win their own Championship. Spurs became the first winners of the competition when they beat Wolves in an all-English final. Robson's great Ipswich side won the trophy in 1981, beating the newly crowned Dutch champions AZ 67 Alkmaar 5–4 on aggregate. Ipswich were full of quality and gained a 1–2–3 in the PFA Player of the Year poll. John Wark won the award, closely followed by Frans Thijssen and Paul Mariner.

Affable, shrewd and popular, Robson earned his reputation at Ipswich Town, winning the FA Cup in 1978 and the UEFA Cup in 1981, the same season that the club narrowly missed out on the Division One championship.

With Robson at the helm the modest Suffolk club achieved a level of consistency over a period of 13 years, from 1969 to 1982, that was bettered only by Liverpool. 'The only way you will leave this club with our blessing is to become manager of England,' Patrick Cobbold, the Ipswich Town chairman, once told him.

In 1973, Ipswich signed Robson on a ten-year contract. It was the first deal of its kind. 'A staggering offer that gave me financial security,' Robson said.

Robson kept Ipswich at the forefront of change in terms of the introduction of overseas players. At the same time, Tottenham generated headlines by signing Osvaldo Ardiles and Ricky Villa from Argentina, Ipswich made a major move in the European market.

On a pre-season tour of Holland, Robson spotted Arnold Mühren. In August 1978, he signed the left-footed midfield player from Twente Enschede for £150,000. He returned the following February to pay £220,000 for Frans Thijssen. Both transfers were funded from the £450,000 proceeds of the sale of Brian Talbot to Arsenal.

Robson kept Ipswich competitive though this type of skilful manipulation of the transfer market, and by developing its own talent, as proved by two successive FA Youth Cup wins in the mid-1970s. 'England was about the only job that could have prised me away from Ipswich. I had a winning team and a terrific quality of life,' Robson recalled.

Above This England rosette was produced for the 1982 World Cup. It features the England mascot Bulldog Bobby. Although Ron Greenwood was manager of England at the time, it seems as though the FA hierarchy already knew who the next England manager would be.

Right This advertisement was produced to promote England merchandise prior to the 1982 World Cup finals in Spain. It was promised that profits from the goods would be ploughed back into the FA Youth Trust charity.

Bobby Robson stayed on in Italy following England's exit from the World Cup in 1990 to receive a trophy that reflected positively on his philosophy as a manager.

In the aftermath of the World Cup final in the Olympic Stadium in Rome, Robson was presented with the FIFA Fair Play trophy for England's sportsmanship and good conduct. It was an important factor in the lifting of a ban on English clubs from European football imposed in the wake of the Heysel disaster in 1985.

'It is a magnificent achievement for England,' Robson said, 'when you consider the intensity of

> **“It was a joy working with England at the World Cup in Italy … It was an experience I would never swap.”**
> *– Bobby Robson*

England’s seven games in the tournament and the fact that we played three periods of extra time and still finished with fewer cautions than any other country.’

England had committed the fewest number of fouls during the tournament: one every 6.79 minutes; and received the fewest cautions of any of the 24 competing nations: six out of a total of 174 doled out.

And, by common consent, England had been involved in the most dramatic finish of any game during the tournament – the last-gasp win in extra time against Belgium; the most exciting game – coming from behind to defeat Cameroon in the quarter-final and the most titanic struggle – the semi-final against West Germany. ‘It was a joy working with England at the World Cup in Italy,’ Robson recalled. ‘It was an experience I would never swap.’

The England players returned to a rapturous, heroes’ welcome in England. After all the setbacks and insults, Bobby Robson had finally been vindicated in his last act before leaving the job.

TALKING POINT

Bobby Robson played in one World Cup finals tournament for England and would have kept his place four years later but for an injury that ruled him out just before the team arrived in Chile. He would never play for his country again.

‘The World Cup in 1962 was a calamity for me,’ Robson recalled. ‘I was injured, cracking an ankle bone in a warm-up match in Peru on the way out, and I lost my place to a young Bobby Moore. That was it for me.’

At the peak of his international career, in the early 1960s, Robson formed the defensive half of England’s midfield in the new 4–2–4 formation, in partnership with Johnny Haynes, a former team-mate at Fulham.

After a spell at West Bromwich Albion, starting in 1956, Robson returned to Fulham.

By 1966, as he neared the end of his playing career, Robson still harboured hopes of an England recall as a reserve central defender. ‘I knew I could do a job,’ Robson recalled. Alf Ramsey, however, decided against adding to Robson’s total of 20 caps.

Left This 1933 cigarette card features a scene from a top Dutch league game between Ajax and ADO. After Robson’s spell as England manager, he became coach at PSV Eindhoven. He immediately won back-to-back Dutch championship titles in 1991 and 1992.

VIV ANDERSON (1956–)

Player • Inducted 2004 • 30 caps • 2 European Cups
1 Division One Championship • 3 League Cups

Viv Anderson, the winner of two European Cup winner's medals, won 30 caps after making the vital breakthrough as the first black footballer to play for England.

He regards his selection for England in the friendly international against Czechoslovakia at Wembley in November 1978 as, above all, a cause for professional satisfaction. 'I had progressed through the England system and Forest were doing well, so I had earned my chance. At the time all I thought about was doing my job and trying to impress the manager enough to get selected again,' Anderson recalls. 'It is only looking back that I realise the importance of it all, and the responsibility I was carrying.'

It is not every player, after all, who receives a 'Good Luck' telegram from the Queen before playing his first game for England. At the age of only 22, Anderson won universal praise for his conduct as a role model.

During his career with Nottingham Forest, Arsenal, Manchester United and Sheffield Wednesday, Anderson was voted the best right-back of the 1970s in a poll of managers. George Graham, of Arsenal, went further, describing him as 'exceptional going forward, and one of England's finest post-war full-backs'.

Nicknamed 'Spider' on account of his long legs, Anderson made his mark when Forest emerged as a major force after scraping promotion from Division Two in 1976-77. The League championship was won at the first attempt on the back of an undefeated run of 26 games and a defence that let in only 24 goals in the league.

Anderson also played in Forest's successive European Cup finals, in 1979 and 1980. First, Malmo and then Hamburg were beaten 1–0: a combined total of 180 minutes of football without Forest conceding a goal.

KEY MATCH

England 1 Czechoslovakia 0, International Friendly, Wembley, 29 November 1978

Elton John sent a telegram to Viv Anderson before the game wishing him well on his international debut. Leading politicians also expressed their support.

'Winning that first cap may have been a small step for him in his career but it was a huge leap forward for black footballers in this country,' Ian Wright wrote in 1997.

Nineteen years earlier, on a bitterly cold night at Wembley, the selection of Anderson at right-back for the international friendly was the major talking point of an otherwise forgettable match.

'The newspapers had been building up the significance of the game for weeks,' Anderson recalled. 'I tried to ignore it all as best I could and concentrate on my own performance.'

The Czechs lined up without a recognised left-winger, freeing Anderson to break forwards in support of Steve Coppell when England had possession.

Anderson started the move for the England goal scored by Steve Coppell, the Manchester United winger. 'Overall, I thought I had a decent game. I wasn't outstanding, but I didn't let anyone down either.'

Anderson had graduated through the England Under-21 and 'B' sides before winning a full cap.

'Kevin Keegan, Trevor Brooking and Ron Greenwood, the England manager, all told me before the game that I was there because of what I'd done with Forest,' Anderson said.

Left Viv Anderson makes one of his trademark overlapping runs against Bristol City, in a Division One fixture at the City Ground in Nottingham in 1978.

KEY MUSEUM ARTEFACT

This League Cup final programme, featuring a portrait of Viv Anderson, was distributed at Wembley Stadium on 17 March 1979. Almost 92 years earlier to the day, England's first black professional footballer, Arthur Wharton, ran out for Preston North End in a showpiece game against the Corinthians in London. Their game, played on 12 March 1887, was contested at the Oval, the famous cricket ground. Whilst Anderson's career has a detailed photographic record, little material relating to Wharton still exists. Wharton and his team-mates drew 1–1 in front of the Prince of Wales, whilst Anderson helped to secure Nottingham Forest's second League Cup victory by beating Southampton 3–2.

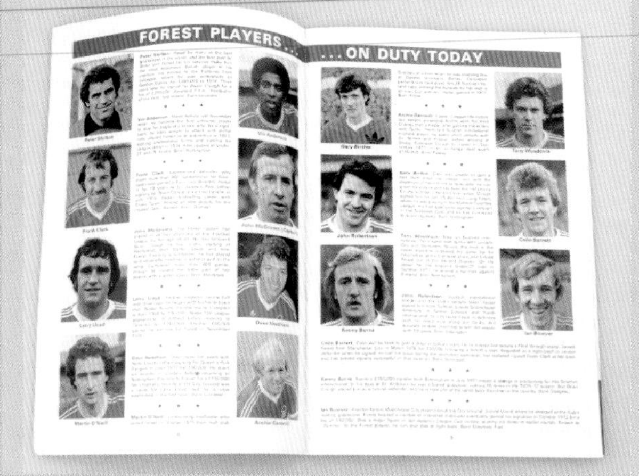
FOREST PLAYERS... ...ON DUTY TODAY

Viv Anderson was a young first-team hopeful when Brian Clough took charge at the City Ground in 1976. His education in the peculiar ways of the game's most eccentric manager began immediately.

His first experience was being dropped for the next match without explanation. 'I feared I was out,' Anderson recalled. He had, in fact, suffered cramp in the previous game and Clough was taking no risks.

Once he proved his fitness, Anderson established himself as a regular, alongside Larry Lloyd, Kenny Burns and Frank Clark, who were brought in by Clough to complete the back four.

The Forest fans recognised his contribution. In a poll conducted in 1997, 96 per cent of supporters voted Anderson the best right-back in the club's history.

Defenders were fined by Clough if they played a square-ball across their own penalty area, or if he saw them commit a bad foul, even if the referee didn't. 'Each individual was expected to know what he had to do,' Anderson said. 'Fall short of those requirements, and you were either dropped or sold.' Clough mostly left the defenders to sort out their own problems. 'We screamed at each other a bit,' Anderson said, 'but it worked very well for three or four years.'

Forest gained a reputation for resilience, particularly away from home, during a record unbeaten run of 42 League games between November 1977 and December 1978.

Their play in the European Cup final against Hamburg in 1980 was the epitome of their methods. 'We were under siege,' Anderson said, 'but our concentration and discipline never lapsed.'

The Forest fans recognised his contribution. In a poll conducted in 1997, 96 per cent of supporters voted Anderson the best right-back in the club's history.

George Graham, the Arsenal manager, paid Forest a fee of £250,000 to bring Viv Anderson to Highbury in 1984. The contrast in management styles and tactics could hardly have been greater.

For eight years under Clough, Anderson had been encouraged to take responsibility for his own decisions on the field; now he was being drilled by Graham, the arch-disciplinarian and method manager.

Above This piece of African batik art from the 1990s depicts a modern match in Uganda. Anderson has been a role model to many and his achievements have ensured that the English League is a fitting platform for players from different ethnic backgrounds.

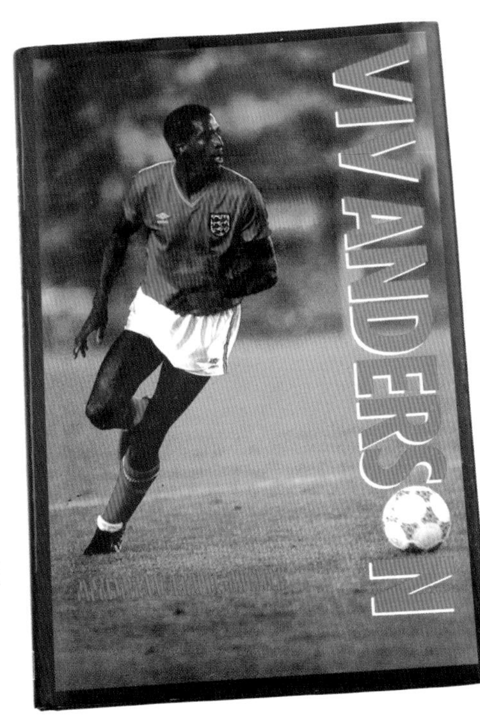

Right *Viv Anderson* by Andrew Longmore

'I worked much harder at Arsenal in terms of organisation,' Anderson recalled. 'There was much greater emphasis on working as a unit.' Graham spent hours perfecting zonal marking. The players had to hold onto a rope strung across the pitch in order to ensure they kept their shape.

The methods worked: in each of his three seasons at Highbury, the team's defensive record improved. From 27 September 1986 onwards, the team was undefeated for a club record 22 games, conceding 11 goals. At the end of the season Anderson won a League Cup winner's medal.

Such consistent performances alerted Alex Ferguson, who made Anderson his first signing as manager of Manchester United in 1987. Ferguson wanted to add experience and physical presence to a side he considered too 'lightweight' to compete for honours.

'His resolute professionalism at right-back and bubbly, contagious enthusiasm in the dressing room were worth a lot more than the £250,000 we paid for Viv,' Ferguson recalled.

Throughout this time Anderson had been adding to his collection of England caps, without ever being a regular choice: 'I was unable to win an extended run in the side of nine or ten games unfortunately, but I am delighted with my total of 30 appearances.'

TALKING POINT

'Viv Anderson did a great deal for black players in this country,' Ian Wright, the Arsenal and England forward said in 1997. 'I really admire him for coming through what he did.

'In his day it was almost constant abuse at every ground, and he was more isolated because there were far fewer black players around in the 1970s and 1980s.'

In 1984, Anderson was one of three England players subjected to racist abuse from a group of fellow passengers and suspected extreme right-wing activists during the flight home from a tour of South America.

An early experience shaped his attitude and response to racism. Before an away game at Carlisle, Brian Clough, the Forest manager, instructed Anderson to warm-up for 20 minutes on the pitch.

'As I did my exercises people were shouting abuse and throwing things,' Anderson recalled. 'I was back down again in the dressing room inside five minutes.

'I told the manager what had happened. He immediately ordered me back on the field: "Get out there. If you want a career in this game you cannot worry about what other people think."

'Sub-consciously I took in the lesson,' Anderson said. 'I knew then that I had to concentrate on my own game. I also realised just how much I wanted to make it.'

Above left This photograph from 1887 includes a very rare image of Arthur Wharton, the first black professional footballer in England, who can be seen standing fourth from the left on the back row. It was taken before Preston's game against the Corinthians in 1887.

Below This ceramic jug was made in commemoration of Sheffield Wednesday's 2–1 win over Wolves in the 1896 FA Cup final. Anderson captained the Hillsborough club in only their third Wembley FA Cup final when they played Arsenal in 1993.

HOWARD KENDALL (1946–)

Manager • Inducted 2005 • 2 Division One Championships • 1 FA Cup
1 European Cup-winners' Cup

Howard Kendall has the distinction of winning a championship title as both a player and a manager with the same club, a feat that has made him a lifelong idol to Everton supporters. The feeling of appreciation is mutual. 'You can have love affairs with other football clubs,' Kendall once said, 'but for me with Everton, it's a marriage.'

Kendall was a young prodigy. Captain of the England youth team, he was the youngest player to appear in an FA Cup final, at the age of 17 years and 345 days, in 1963–64. 'Preston North End lost the match, but found a star,' read the newspaper headlines.

Harry Catterick, the Everton manager, won the race to sign Kendall in 1967, after agreeing to pay Preston £85,000, a record fee for a wing-half. Three years later, Kendall won a championship medal; the next time the trophy came to Goodison Park, in 1985, Kendall was manager, in the first of his three spells in charge of the club.

'An unshakeable bond had formed during my playing days,' Kendall said. 'Everton was in my blood. The fascination for the club never wavered.'

In 1984–85, Everton were European Team of the Year in recognition of their achievement in winning the championship title and the European Cup-winners' Cup. Exhausted by their exertions against Rapid Vienna in Rotterdam, Everton lost in the FA Cup final three days later, in the second of their three consecutive Cup final appearances.

Kendal was an automatic choice as Manager of the Year in 1985. He won the award again in 1987 after Everton claimed their second championship title in three seasons.

'Howard created a fantastic, fluent side,' Andy Gray, the Everton striker said. Unbeaten for nearly five months in all competitions, Everton won the championship in great style in 1984–85, finishing 13 points clear at the top despite losing several games once the title had been secured.

KEY MATCH

Everton 3 Bayern Munich 1, European Cup-winners' Cup semi-final, second leg, Goodison Park, 24 April 1985

Walking into the dressing-room at half-time, Howard Kendall immediately realised the extent of the challenge facing him. 'We were totally shell-shocked by the events of those first 45 minutes,' Andy Gray, the Everton striker, recalled.

'I knew right away that I had to rally the players,' Kendall said. He had seen Bayern Munich, the Bundesliga leaders, score a vital away goal, to lead 1–0 on aggregate. 'All a bit deflating,' as Neville Southall, the beaten goalkeeper, put it.

Everton had to score twice in the next 45 minutes or they would be out. On a brighter note: at least in the second half they would be attacking the Gwladys Street end, where the most vocal and boisterous of their supporters stood.

Gray and his fellow Scot Graeme Sharp would play critical roles, Kendall decided.'Keep getting the ball forward to Andy and Sharpy,' Kendall told the team. 'Keep playing at a pace Bayern don't like. I guarantee you that the Gwladys Street will suck one in.'

Kendall later recalled: 'The tension at half-time was so palpable that you felt you could almost reach and touch it. But I was convinced that if we were patient and showed character the Germans would eventually crack.'

He was right. Gray, Sharp and Trevor Steven, the wide midfield player, scored the goals that took Everton through on a tumultuous night. 'I will never forget that second half,' Gray said. 'We had real power as a team and we showed that against Bayern.'

Kendall did a jig of delight on the touchline at the end. 'What a magnificent night,' he said. 'It is my most precious memory in football.'

The following morning the Kendall children woke up to find their dad, bleary-eyed, sitting in front of the television. 'I stayed up all night watching re-runs of the game on video.'

Left Howard Kendall is introduced to HRH The Duke of Kent before the FA Cup final at Wembley on 18 May 1985.

KEY MUSEUM ARTEFACT

After the FA Cup final of 1991, the FA decided to replace the original trophy made in 1911. Due to wear and tear, it had become badly damaged and the silver had become almost translucent. Several replicas were made and are now used by the FA for presentation at the FA Cup final and for promotional purposes across the country and on television. As manager of Everton, Howard Kendall took the club to three consecutive FA Cup finals from 1984 to 1986.

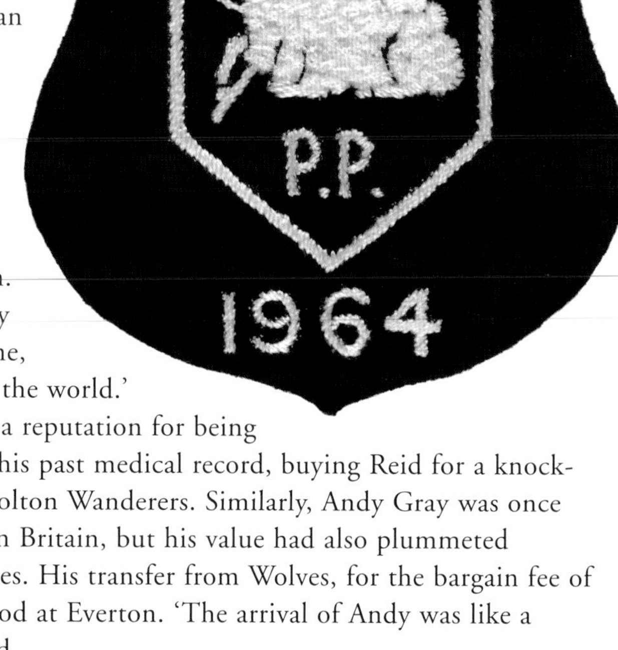

The Everton side of 1984–85 was a mix of home-grown talent, inexpensive signings from the lower divisions, one-time Liverpool reserves and two seasoned pros who had a history of injury problems.

Starting from scratch in 1981, Howard Kendall proved to be an outstanding judge of talent: nine of the players he introduced went on to win full internationals caps. In 1981, Neville Southall was an unknown at Bury, when Kendall paid £150,000 for him. 'It was my first signing, and my best,' Kendall said. 'In his prime, Neville was the best 'keeper in the world.'

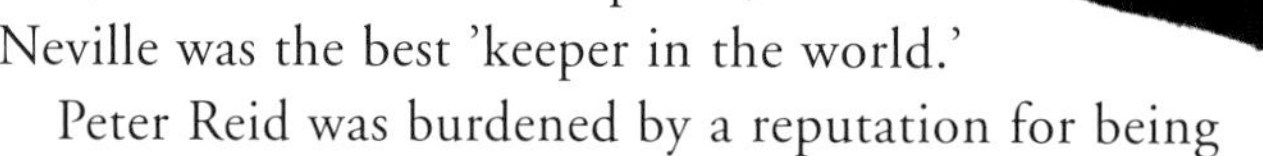

Peter Reid was burdened by a reputation for being injury-prone. Kendall ignored his past medical record, buying Reid for a knock-down price of £60,000 from Bolton Wanderers. Similarly, Andy Gray was once the most expensive footballer in Britain, but his value had also plummeted following a succession of injuries. His transfer from Wolves, for the bargain fee of £250,000, transformed the mood at Everton. 'The arrival of Andy was like a breath of fresh air,' Kendall said.

Howard Kendall proved to be an outstanding judge of talent: nine of the players he introduced at Everton went on to win full internationals caps.

Above right This Preston North End badge was made to commemorate the club's 1964 FA Cup final appearance against West Ham United. One was given to every employee of the club.

Above This cardboard hat was produced by the *Daily Express* for the 1964 FA Cup final and features Howard Kendall, second from the left. At 17 years 345 days, he became the youngest-ever FA Cup finalist when he played in Preston North End's 3–2 defeat by West Ham United.

To acquire Kevin Sheedy and Alan Harper, Kendall defied an informal understanding with neighbours Liverpool barring transfers between the clubs, since both players were reserves at Anfield. 'It was a quaint convention, but stupid,' Kendall said.

Other modest buys included Derek Mountfield, the Tranmere Rovers centre-back; Trevor Steven, who was switched to a wide midfield role following his transfer from Burnley, and Paul Bracewell, the Sunderland midfielder. Gary Stevens and Kevin Ratcliffe, stalwarts of the back four, came up through the ranks at Goodison Park.

For not much more than the record transfer fee at the time – £1.7 million – Kendall built an entire championship-winning side.

Howard Kendall was preparing Everton for their first assault on the European

Cup for 15 years when the club was hit by a massive blow that eventually contributed to his decision to leave Merseyside.

The ban on English clubs competing in Europe, introduced in 1985, denied Kendall and his players the chance to test themselves at the highest level. 'The whole club was left stunned,' Kendall recalled. 'We truly believed we were good enough to win the European Cup.'

Although Everton almost won the Double the following season and reclaimed the title in 1987, a gradual exodus of key players weakened the club. Eventually, that summer, Kendall, too, decided to test himself at the highest level overseas, accepting an offer from Atletico Bilbao.

When he returned from Spain in late 1989, he managed Manchester City for 11 months, before the call of Everton proved too strong. 'I still regarded Everton as my club,' he recalled. 'My first task was to save them from relegation, which I did.'

This time he spent three years at Goodison Park, before resigning in frustration over a lack of transfer funds. There would be a third, unprecedented, stint as manager for one season, 1997–98, when Everton again narrowly avoided the drop.

His popularity and standing amongst the fans at Goodison Park easily withstood those later disappointments. Recently, Kendall was officially named as 'Everton's greatest manager' in recognition of his first, six-year, spell at the club. 'I've always regarded Everton as the biggest and best club in England,' Kendall said, 'and I still do. It was a great honour to both play for and manage them.'

TALKING POINT

Howard Kendall was given an early education as to the fanatical commitment and passion for football on Merseyside when he joined Everton in 1967.

Harry Catterick noticed that his new signing owned a red sports car. 'Either get it resprayed a different colour than red, or be prepared for the worst,' the manager said. 'You've no idea what they're like in this city with their football rivalry.' Kendall heeded the advice: 'Within a few days I got another car – a blue MGB GT.'

Kendall soon won over the Everton fans, even though it took him time to settle in a new role. He had been a defender at Preston, but Catterick switched him to midfield. 'It was more demanding than I anticipated,' he said, 'but I adapted.'

'Howard had a good engine,' Alan Ball, his team-mate, recalled. 'He could pass the ball long or short and he had a masterful tackle. He was a good talker, plotting the course of a match, using his vision. He was very unfortunate not to play for England.'

With Ball and Colin Harvey, Kendall formed a famed midfield trio that is still celebrated by supporters to this day, primarily for their performances in the championship-winning season of 1969–70. Catterick described them as 'the best midfield I've ever seen in terms of spectator value, pure skill and entertainment'.

Kendall praised the team as a whole. 'We first clicked in 1968 and for the next two seasons we played some of the best football ever.'

The sale of Ball to Arsenal and a succession of injuries to Harvey were factors in the dismantling of the team in the early 1970s, a time of decline for Everton. 'It was a pity because I was at my peak as a player,' Kendall said.

Above left An Everton shirt from 1995. Kendall's love of Everton brought him three spells as manager of the club: 1981–87, 1990–93 and 1997–98.

Left Slazenger, having made the ball for the World Cup final in 1966, was the leading manufacturer of the period. By the time Kendall had secured the Championship with Everton, in 1970, the valve ball had replaced the lace-up ball.

BRYAN ROBSON (1957–)

Player • Inducted 2002 • 90 Caps • 2 Premiership titles • 3 FA Cups
1 European Cup-winners' Cup

Bryan Robson was a talismanic figure for both club and country; but his courage and commitment took a heavy toll in terms of injury, denying him the possibility of winning a record number of international caps for England.

Robson played 90 times for his country between 1980 and 1991, finishing his international career as the fifth most-capped player in history, despite suffering more than 20 fractures or dislocations of some sort during his career. Notably, for a ball-winning, aggressive midfield player, Robson was also ninth on the all-time list of goalscorers for England, with 26 goals.

An automatic choice when fit during the eight years that his namesake Bobby Robson was in charge, his value is best illustrated by the fact that he was never named as a substitute for England. On 65 occasions he captained the side.

'Lesser players have won more, but none have given as much,' Bobby Robson said. 'England were a taller, prouder team when he played. I could see no failings in him as a player. Bryan missed out on 35 caps under me alone and had he had a normal, relatively trouble-free career he would have broken the all-time British record with something to spare.'

Ron Atkinson, the Manchester United manager, made Robson the most expensive footballer in Britain when he paid West Bromwich Albion £1.5 million to bring him to Old Trafford in 1981. 'The best half-backs ever were Duncan Edwards and Dave Mackay, and Robbo is right up there with them,' Atkinson said.

'There was an aura about Bryan,' Alex Ferguson, the successor to Atkinson as manager, said. 'When I arrived here in 1986, there was a feeling around the club that winning or losing largely depended on whether or not he was playing.'

Robson did more than any other player to keep Manchester United competitive in the early Ferguson years. 'He was known as "Captain Marvel" for a good reason,' Ferguson said.

KEY MATCH

Manchester United 2 Sheffield Wednesday 1, Premier League, Old Trafford, 10 April 1993

Dragging his battered body once more into the fray, Bryan Robson turned the game on its head, leading a late comeback just as it seemed all hope of winning the title for the first time since 1967 had been lost.

With 20 minutes left, Manchester United were losing 1–0. 'As soon as Bryan came on as substitute his energy and determination made a difference,' Alex Ferguson recalled. Standing in goal, Peter Schmeichel also noticed the change. 'Robbo brought some order to the proceedings,' he said.

When the home side won a corner at the Stretford End, everyone focused on Robson. When he made a typically strong run towards goal, Ferguson – and several Sheffield Wednesday defenders – were watching him. 'At that moment he certainly carried my hopes,' Ferguson recalled. In the confusion, Steve Bruce headed the ball into the far corner of the net for the vital equalizer, as Robson charged into the defender guarding the post.

For the rest of the game Ferguson, when he could be heard above the noise of the crowd, channelled his instructions to the team through Robson.

In stoppage time, Bruce scored the winner with another header. The late involvement of Robson had proved decisive. Manchester United were now in the driving seat in the race to the championship, one point ahead of Aston Villa at the top with five games to play.

Left Soaring above the French defence, Bryan Robson scores England's second goal in their 3–1 World Cup victory over France on 16 June 1982.

KEY MUSEUM ARTEFACT

Manchester United's 1–0 victory in the replay of the 1990 FA Cup final marked Bryan Robson's third FA Cup success as United's captain. This Manchester United Adidas shirt bears the logo of their sponsor Sharp. Non-League Kettering were in fact the first English club to wear shirt advertising in 1976. They were reprimanded by the FA and ordered not to do it again. Then, in 1978, Liverpool secured shirt sponsorship and several leading clubs quickly followed their example. But broadcasters forced clubs to change their shirts for televised games. By 1990, sponsorship was an accepted part of football, though United's opponents in the final, Crystal Palace, were fined for their sponsor's logo being too big.

Bobby Robson regarded his namesake as being indispensable to England's cause at the World Cup in Mexico in 1986, even at the risk of his own future as national team manager. Robson took a massive gamble on the Manchester United midfield player when he named him for the opening fixture of the tournament, against Portugal in Monterrey on 3 June.

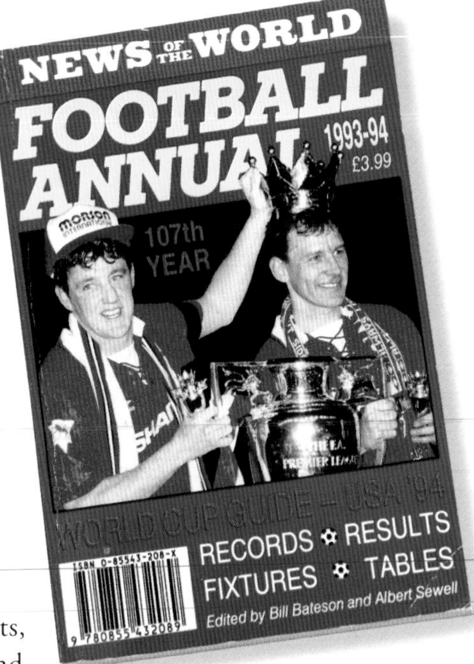

Bryan Robson had dislocated his shoulder for the third time in a warm-up game in Los Angeles, but his manager decided his inclusion was a risk worth taking. The manager acknowledged that his captain's all-action, versatile style might be hampered by the injury, but he played down his own doubts, concealing the extent of the player's injury, and the risks involved in playing him, from the media.

Two years' work and planning appeared to have been destroyed when, late in the first half, Robson fell awkwardly, and his shoulder popped out for a fourth time, ruling him out of the tournament. The media, when told the full story, was biting in its criticism of Bobby Robson.

It made no difference to the England manager. 'My heart bled for Bryan when he suffered the injury,' Robson said. 'I knew the risks involved in playing him, but I believed it was worthwhile given his importance to, and influence on, the team. Bryan was as important to England as he was to Manchester United.'

Above The front cover of this 1993–94 *News of the World Football Annual* features Manchester United's first title success in 26 years, when they won the inaugural Premier League.

Right Bryan Robson won the first of his three FA Cup winner's medals against Brighton & Hove Albion in 1983. This shirt belonged to left-back Graham Pearce and was swapped after the match.

Bryan Robson commanded a remarkable degree of respect inside the dressing room of England and Manchester United, on the strength of his leadership quality as captain and competitive nature as a player.

Alex Ferguson described him as a hero, and a competitor without equal. 'Bryan is a miracle of commitment, a human marvel who pushed himself beyond every imaginable limit on the field.

'The combination of his stamina and perceptive reading of movement enabled him, in his prime, to make sudden and deadly

> **“Bryan is a miracle of commitment, a human marvel who pushed himself through every imaginable limit on the field.”** – *Alex Ferguson*

infiltrations from midfield and score vital goals.'

Bobby Robson praised his unrelenting competitiveness and refusal to give up. 'He would hunt a rival down and get in the tackle, face to face. He challenged fairly, powerfully, correctly.'

Paul Gascoigne described Robson as the greatest midfield player in the world. 'When he was captain of England, it always felt so good knowing he was there.'

A cult figure himself at Old Trafford, Eric Cantona adopted Robson as his new idol on arrival at Old Trafford. 'An awesome player,' Cantona said. 'The fans love him. They cheer him even when he is warming up. The people don't forget those who have made them dream.'

And Roy Keane, one of Robson's successors as Manchester United captain, described him as 'the main man in the dressing room'.

'Bryan was respected to the point of awe by every other player,' Keane said. 'His courage in the face of injury or any other adversity was bottomless. When Alex Ferguson struggled in his early years at Old Trafford, Robson fought like a lion to drive the team forward. He was a great player for the club.'

Above Bryan Robson tackles Alain Giresse of France in England's opening game of the World Cup finals on 16 June 1982 in Bilbao

TALKING POINT

Bobby Robson is convinced that the absence of Bryan Robson from the World Cup semi-final against West Germany was the most significant factor in England's failure to win the trophy.

The Manchester United captain would have been an automatic selection for the England manager but for an injury that ruled out Robson during the tournament in Italy.

'We were only a whisker away from going through to the final after that penalty shoot-out against the Germans,' Robson recalled.

'I am convinced that Bryan could have made the difference; after all, he was three players in one: a tough tackling defender, a midfield player of vision, and a phenomenal goalscorer who is dominant at set plays at both ends.'

It had been the same story four years earlier in Mexico: Robson played in the first two matches of the tournament before being sidelined with a dislocated shoulder.

'Bryan suffered terribly with injuries at crucial times in his career, and I suffered with him. It left me to ponder what might have been for both of us,' Bobby Robson recalled.

Right A 1970s' West Bromwich Albion training top. Robson began his career with the 'Baggies' and, as a trainee, his diet consisted of Guinness and steak. While at the club he suffered and recovered from three broken legs.

GARY LINEKER (1960–)

Player • Inducted 2003 • 80 caps • 1 FA Cup

Gary Lineker has the distinction of being the only English player to win the FIFA Golden Boot award as the leading goalscorer in a World Cup finals tournament.

Lineker earned the accolade for scoring six goals in Mexico in 1986 as England reached the last eight. He added four more at Italia '90, including the equaliser against West Germany in the semi-final. Bobby Robson, the England manager at both tournaments, said: 'Gary was simply the best finisher I've ever seen.'

Typically, all of Lineker's goals in Mexico were scored from close range. They were all one-touch finishes too: another trademark of his play as a striker. As he said himself: 'I was what we call in the trade a box-player.'

A great goalscorer rather than a scorer of great goals, or so the saying went, Lineker realised his limitations, making the most of his natural gifts: great pace and an outstanding positional sense.

His goal for Everton in the FA Cup final in 1986 was typical: running onto a through-ball, he outpaced the defender before slotting the ball home from 12 yards out. 'No-one could match Gary for pace over 40 yards,' Howard Kendall, the Everton manager, said. In his brief stay at Goodison Park, Lineker finished the 1985–86 season as leading goalscorer in Division One and both the PFA and Football Writers' Footballer of the Year.

As an Everton player, Lineker finished on the losing side at Wembley, but he put the record straight with Tottenham Hotspur in 1991. In between those two Cup final appearances, Lineker spent three years with Barcelona following a record £2.2 million transfer in 1986.

On leaving Spain, Lineker rejected a more lucrative move to Monaco in favour of a return home with Spurs. In his first season back in England, in 1989–90, he was leading goalscorer in Division One for the third time in his career.

In 1991–92, his farewell season in English football, Lineker was voted Footballer of the Year for the second time. He then spent two years with Nagoya Grampus Eight in Japan's fledgling J-League before retiring.

KEY MATCH

Poland 0 England 3, World Cup, Monterrey, 11 June 1986

In the space of 35 minutes, Gary Lineker became the first Englishman since Geoff Hurst in 1966 to score a hat-trick in a World Cup final. It changed the course of his career and kept England in the tournament. 'When I woke up, I thought it was all a dream,' he said the next morning.

'That World Cup is the outstanding memory of my career, and if I had to pick out one game it would be the one against Poland,' Lineker said. 'Finishing top scorer in the tournament took me a huge step forward in my career.'

Lineker arrived in Mexico as an Everton player; by the time England were knocked out in the quarter-finals, he was heading to Barcelona.

All three goals were the product of keen anticipation, lightning movement and outstanding timing. All three were scored from crosses and, typically, all three were converted from close range.

Barcelona vice-president Juan Gaspart watched the match on television. 'Oh, the transfer will cost us more money now,' he said. But, as it turned out, Everton did not go back on their valuation of £2.2 million.

Lineker wore an old, patched-up pair of boots in Mexico. 'They were my lucky pair,' he said. 'They were falling to bits during the season, so I had them repaired before I left home. He was also wearing a protective cast after fracturing a bone in his wrist in a warm-up game. 'There was nothing wrong with Gary's courage,' said Robson. 'Even with the injury, I never saw him pull out of a challenge. He went where the bullets fly: in the penalty area.'

Left Gary Lineker completes his hat-trick against the Polish goalkeeper, Jozef Mylnarczyk, in the England v Poland match in the World Cup finals on 11 June 1986.

KEY MUSEUM ARTEFACT

When Gary Lineker won the Golden Boot award at the 1986 World Cup with his six goals, few could have foreseen that he would end his career in Japan. He was a new breed of player who, after securing his financial future, wanted to experience different cultures and countries. This Japanese watercolour on silk shows that ball games played with the feet, such as the game of Kemari depicted below, have a rich tradition in Asia. Kemari is derived from ancient Chinese football. After successful spells with Barcelona and Tottenham, Lineker moved to Japan to play for Nagoya Grampus Eight, immersing himself in the local culture and learning to speak Japanese.

Gary Lineker was fully aware of his limitations. Not one for flamboyance, his game was based on quickness of thought and deed, anticipation and a calculation of the odds. 'I knew my weaknesses,' Lineker said. 'I developed my own style, which basically meant that as a striker my best chances were to pounce on defenders' mistakes and to make runs into space in the hope that the ball would come to me.'

Lineker concentrated on getting a half-yard start on his marker, usually at the near-post. He would make repeated runs in the hope of the ball arriving at the right moment.

Lineker concentrated on getting a half-yard start on his marker, usually at the near-post. He would make repeated runs in the hope of the ball arriving at the right moment. In club football it happened 'about two times out of ten'. With England, 'You might get one chance a game,' he said.

Howard Kendall, the manager of champions Everton, bought Lineker from Leicester City for a fee of £800,000 in 1985. He added strength of character to the list of assets: 'If Gary misses a couple of chances, he doesn't let his head go down. He keeps going right to the end.'

Terry Venables, his manager at both Barcelona and Spurs, said: 'Very rarely does Gary shoot the ball over the bar. He wants it on target and kept low. Even if it's going wide, there's always the chance of a deflection.

Right A presentation set of enamel badges from Mexico '86, which contain the flags of each of the 24 countries who qualified for the finals.

'Gary's control is not great, but he gets himself into positions where he takes the pressure off his control. He gets himself on angles. He's learned that.'

During his stint playing in Spanish football, Lineker had to cope with man-marking. 'I had to change the angle of my runs, away from the sweeper, which was a new way of playing for me.'

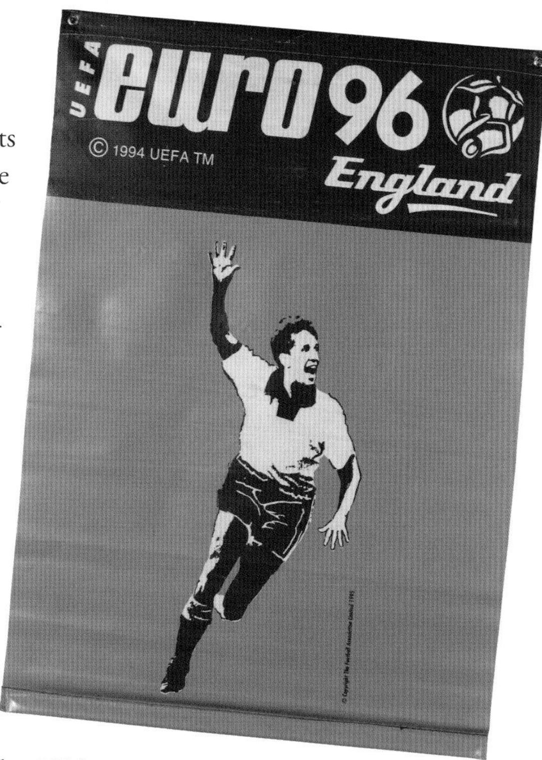

Gary Lineker finished his international career as the second-highest England goalscorer in history, one goal shy of Bobby Charlton's record total of 49.

He was leading scorer for his country at the World Cup in 1986 and 1990, and he also scored the vital equalizer that secured qualification for the 1992 European Championships in the away game in Poland in 1991.

In contrast to his great success in the World Cup, Lineker failed to score in six matches spread over successive European Championships, in 1988 and 1992. His lack of edge in Germany at least was understandable: he was diagnosed with hepatitis within days of England's exit.

In 1992, Lineker was substituted by Graham Taylor in the third group game against hosts Sweden. It was perhaps the most controversial substitution by an England manager. It didn'twork. England lost 2–1. They were out of the tournament. Soon after that, Taylor was out of a job.

It was Lineker's last appearance for his country. Going into the tournament Bobby Charlton was convinced that Lineker would break his scoring record, but England played poorly and Lineker failed to find the net.

Lineker made his debut for England against Scotland in Glasgow in May 1984. In his first 25 internationals he scored 23 goals, but his scoring rate slowed following his treatment for hepatitis.

Lineker had a knack for scoring vital goals for his country. Sixteen times Lineker scored the only goal of the game to give England victory. He was rewarded for his contribution by being named captain 18 times in the latter part of his career.

TALKING POINT

Gary Lineker was never booked or sent off during his career. His behaviour on the field, and his polite demeanour off it, as much as the 48 goals he scored for England, made him an immensely popular public figure.

Lineker even won over hard-bitten football writers. In 1992, at the end of his last press conference as an England player, the journalists gave him a standing ovation as he entered the room. A year earlier, FIFA described Lineker as 'a living example of how the spirit of fair play can be crowned with personal success'. In a rare gesture to an individual player, the world ruling body presented him with a Fair Play award. When he joined Nagoya Grampus Eight, the club explained their decision to sign him as follows: 'He is the suitable person as the first foreign player because of his good manners in soccer games.'

He skilfully charted for himself a second career in the media. He wrote, and still does, for broadsheet newspapers, hosted a BBC radio programme, spoke in an Oxford Union debate and appeared on *Desert Island Discs*. He has been a sports presenter for the BBC since 1999, most often for *Match of the Day*.

Confirmation of his status as a 'national institution' came during a court case in 1992 when a judge suggested that an amateur footballer appearing before him should watch videos of Lineker in order to learn from his behaviour.

Above A Euro '96 banner featuring an artist's impression of Gary Lineker.

Left Cartoons and caricatures are always popular and this colour postcard of the Barcelona player Vicente Piera from the 1930s by the artist Passarell bears an uncanny resemblance to Gary Lineker when he played for the club.

Left Gary Lineker's puppet from the satirical television show *Spitting Image* from the late 1980s.

crown
paints

JOHN BARNES (1963–)

Player • Inducted 2005 • 79 Caps • 2 Division One Championships
2 FA Cups • 1 League Cup

John Barnes joined a select group when he was named Footballer of the Year for the second time. Only four other players – Stanley Matthews, Tom Finney, Danny Blanchflower and Kenny Dalglish – had previously received such an accolade.

Bobby Robson, who awarded him the bulk of his 79 England caps, described Barnes as 'a match-winner' and a vital member of both his World Cup finals squads in 1986 and 1990.

His remarkable run and dribble through the Brazil defence during a friendly in Rio de Janeiro in 1984 enhanced his reputation both here and abroad. One Brazilian newspaper described it as 'the greatest goal ever scored at the Maracana Stadium'.

Most South Americans were stunned by a display of such skilful athleticism by an England winger. Not so Zico, the great Brazil striker, who was already an admirer. 'He represents the future of English football,' Zico said in 1983.

Bertie Mee, who guided Arsenal to the Double in 1971, watched his early progress at Watford. Mee looked to the past in his praise, likening Barnes' dribbling ability to that of Finney, the Preston and England winger. 'John has the same way of gliding past his marker,' Mee said. 'Like Tom, he's also two-footed, versatile and a good goalscorer.'

Barnes helped Watford to promotion from Division Two in 1981–82. The following season, Barnes made his England debut as Watford finished runners-up. One year on again he was on the losing side in the FA Cup final.

In 1987, he joined Liverpool for a fee of £900,000. In his first season, Barnes was voted Footballer of the Year, as Liverpool won the title, a 'double' feat that they repeated in 1989–90. After a decade at Anfield, Barnes went on to have stints at Newcastle United and Charlton Athletic.

KEY MATCH

Brazil 0, England 2, International Friendly, Rio de Janeiro, 10 June 1984

The first goal John Barnes scored for England was also the most memorable. He was only 20 years of age which gave him a long time to consider the consequences of his remarkable run through the Brazil defence at the famous Maracana Stadium.

'I loved the goal, of course,' Barnes recalled, 'but it created many problems for me, particularly in changing perceptions. After scoring a goal like that, I never lived up to England's expectations again.'

Receiving the ball near the touchline about 40 yards from the Brazil goal, the Watford winger started his run by cutting inside the full-back.

'A pattern developed: look around, no support, keep going, beat another Brazilian, look around, no support, keep going, beat another Brazilian,' Barnes recalled. 'I was not sure where I was until I found myself in front of goal facing the 'keeper.'

Then one final piece of skill: a sublime dummy that put Roberto Costa, the Brazil goalkeeper, on his backside, leaving Barnes in front of an empty net.

'I can honestly say that if I had seen someone to pass to I would have done,' Barnes said. 'On drifting inside from my normal left-wing position, my instinct had always been to pass first.

'The goal changed people's attitude to me,' Barnes said. 'I was expected to repeat that dribble again and again. When I didn't I was criticised. My whole England career was judged against that one goal.'

Left John Barnes brings the ball under control in Liverpool's 2–0 away win against Tottenham Hotspur, at White Hart Lane, on 28 November 1987.

KEY MUSEUM ARTEFACT

This tracksuit top was worn by a member of the Liverpool team at the 1985 European Cup final against Juventus which took place at the Heysel Stadium in Brussels. John Barnes joined Liverpool two years after this match which is sadly remembered for the appalling deaths of 39 supporters in a crush behind one of the goals. Liverpool overcame the trauma of Heysel to secure the League title in 1986. With Barnes in their side, they repeated the feat in 1988. Tragedy struck again, however, in 1989, when 96 Liverpool supporters lost their lives at the FA Cup semi-final at Hillsborough. Barnes and his team-mates showed incredible courage to progress to the final where they beat Everton 3–2.

Top The human-like, stylised, 1990 World Cup mascot was named Ciao. Its simplicity meant that it could be reproduced in a number of formats for merchandising and printing purposes.

Right Barnes played in a particularly difficult decade for English football. The disasters at Bradford, Heysel and Hillsborough resulted in plummeting attendance figures. Supporters responded by taking inflatables, such as this banana, into grounds, in an attempt to bring a smile back to the game.

Graham Taylor, the Watford manager, plucked John Barnes from the obscurity of minor non-League football. Sudbury Court, his first club, did not demand a fee for his transfer, gratefully accepting the offer of a new set of kit.

'Graham gave me the confidence to succeed,' Barnes recalled. 'He provided the momentum and discipline I needed.' Taylor also instilled self-belief. 'If I faced the most respected full-back in the world, Graham would say: "John, you are better than him. Now go out and beat him." As a young player it was great to be told things like that.'

Watford rose through the divisions playing an attacking 4–2–4 style that relied on two out-and-out, attacking wingers, and which made the most of Barnes's dribbling and crossing ability. He also had the freedom to drift inside in support of the central strikers.

'I became the only player in the history of the club to reach double figures for goals every season for six years,' Barnes recalled.

Watford rose through the divisions playing an attacking 4–2–4 style that relied on two out-and-out, attacking wingers, and which made the most of Barnes's dribbling and crossing ability.

It was not just the positive style of football and the friendly atmosphere at Vicarage Road that appealed. Barnes thrived on the challenge of playing for Watford against the biggest clubs in the country. 'I loved being part of the unheralded, unfancied side that went to places like Highbury and won at the home of mighty Arsenal,' Barnes recalled.

'Some players at the bigger clubs looked down at us,' he said. 'They tried to belittle us, calling us donkeys. All it did was motivate us. We finished second in 1982–83, which was a fabulous achievement and my most enjoyable experience in football.'

As the perennial underdogs, John Barnes and the other Watford

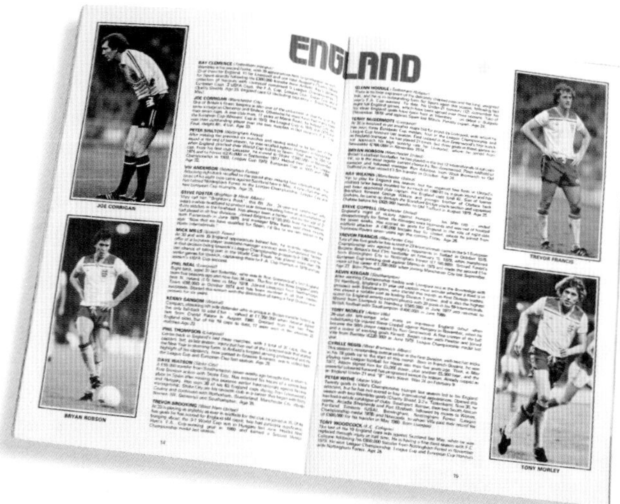

players particularly enjoyed 'trying to put one over on Liverpool'.

'I always played well against them, and I think that's why Kenny Dalglish pursued me. Often I played at centre-forward and I scored a few goals.' Dalglish finally made his move in 1987.

The Liverpool passing game suited Barnes to the ground. So much so, that he always thought of himself as a better, more effective player for Liverpool than for England. 'I often felt inhibited with England,' he said.

At his best, Barnes terrified the best defences in the world, notably in 1986 when, as a late substitute, he almost single-handedly rescued the World Cup quarter-final against Argentina. But in other England games he found himself 'marooned on the wing a lot, feeling frustrated'.

'I never saw myself as just that for Liverpool,' Barnes said. 'I was a more all-round player. In one season I scored 22 goals in 34 League games.'

Much of Liverpool's play was based around the ability of defenders to distribute the ball forward quickly and accurately. In Barnes, they found a new target. 'My first thought had been to pass the ball to the feet of Kenny Dalglish,' recalled Alan Hansen. 'But when John came to the club he became my favourite option.'

Barnes thrived on the responsibility. 'As an attacker, Liverpool's approach was marvellous because team-mates passed to me, even if an opponent was in close attendance.

'Lumping the ball forward was forbidden. Possession was to be cherished. I began to pass more than dribble. At Liverpool I improved as a footballer.'

TALKING POINT

John Barnes was number one in the eyes of many football supporters. In 1990, he reached the same exalted status in the pop charts, fronting the official England song, 'World in Motion', for the World Cup in Italy.

Barnes performed the 'rap' in the middle of the New Order composition. He also starred in the video. Yet, truth be told, he never really liked the song. 'The words were pretty meaningless. "You've got to hold and give, do it at the right time." What on earth does that mean?' he said later.

He was gradually drawn into the project, largely because of the indifferent attitude of the other England players. 'The whole squad was invited to the recording studio, but only five of us turned up – Gazza, Peter Beardsley, Chris Waddle, Des Walker and me,' Barnes recalled.

'The others ducked out because football songs traditionally had a naff reputation,' he said. Half-way through recording, the band decided to add a 'rap'. About an hour later, they asked for volunteers to perform it on record: 'It would have defied belief to have any of the three Geordies, Peter, Gazza or Chris, rapping away. That left Des Walker, who wasn't particularly good either, or me. So I did it,' Barnes recalled in his autobiography.

'Because I performed the rap, they needed me in the video, so they came up to Liverpool and spent the whole day at our training ground.'

'World in Motion' was a huge hit, but it was never his favourite football song. 'I thought Anfield Rap, the song I did with the other Liverpool players, was better,' Barnes said.

Above This 1982 match programme features the England side into which Barnes forced himself. His outstanding performances for Watford saw him make his debut against Northern Ireland in 1983 and he became a fixture in the team ahead of players like Tony Morley of Aston Villa.

Left A souvenir guide to the 1990 Word Cup.

PAUL GASCOIGNE (1967–)

Player • Inducted 2002 • 57 caps • 1 FA Cup

Paul Gascoigne was described as the most famous man in Britain in the aftermath of the World Cup in 1990. His skill enthralled football fans; and his tears in defeat had a million mums reaching for the tissues.

His popularity and commercial value became so great on his return home from Italia '90 that he licensed his own name. 'Gazza' had graduated from England footballer to business trademark.

'A sensation,' Bobby Robson said. 'He was the finest young player in the tournament.

Gascoigne cried in frustration and disappointment when he was booked in the semi-final against West Germany; in that moment he realised that he would miss the final because of suspension if England went through. 'I was devastated,' he recalled, 'and the tears just came. I resolved to give my all in whatever time there was left. So I played my heart out.'

Gascoigne wiped away the tears on his England shirt: the image that became the abiding memory of the tournament for millions of supporters back home.

His performance catapulted him onto the world stage. In 1992, Lazio paid Tottenham Hotspur £5.5 million for his transfer. The move had been delayed for more than a year while Gascoigne recovered from a serious cruciate ligament injury. He hurt his knee in making a reckless tackle during the FA Cup final in 1991. Long before his Spurs team-mates finally won the game, he was watching the action on television from his hospital bed.

A dedicated trainer, Gascoigne was respected for his work ethic by fellow professionals, and celebrated, most of the time, for his playful nature. 'He succeeds in keeping the company happy, but he is also a man who works on the field with great seriousness,' Dino Zoff, the Lazio coach, said.

Injury and alcohol abuse increasingly hampered Gascoigne as he grew older. 'I accomplished my dreams, but not my potential,' he said.

KEY MATCH

Arsenal 1 Tottenham Hotspur 3, FA Cup semi-final, Wembley, 14 April 1991

Terry Venables gave Paul Gascoigne a challenge before the game: 'Go out there today and show them you're the best player in England,' the Spurs manager said.

Gascoigne certainly gave it a go. Spurs were 2-0 up inside 11 minutes. 'That's all the time it took Gazza to put the game beyond Arsenal's reach,' Venables said. 'His performance that day was exceptional.'

Gascoigne opened the scoring with a stunning free-kick. His shot from 35 yards out beat David Seaman, the Arsenal and England goalkeeper. 'I hit the ball as hard as I could, and managed to make it swerve,' he said. Even at that distance, Seaman barely got his fingertips to it. Venables described the shot as 'phenomenal'.

Later in the half, Gascoigne played an impudent back-heel, setting Paul Allen away, and from his cross, Gary Lineker scored the second. 'We lost it in those early minutes,' George Graham, the Arsenal manager, said, reflecting on the impact Gascoigne had on the game.

There was no lack of motivation for the England player: newspapers had been full of stories linking him to a move to Lazio in Italy. The Cup, it seemed, would be his last chance to win a medal with Spurs.

He was not even fully fit. Gascoigne had recovered from a double hernia operation in four weeks, instead of the usual six. Lacking match-fitness, inevitably he tired in the second half and when he was substituted, the Spurs supporters rose to him as one.

Left Paul Gascoigne beats a defender in England's 3–2 victory over Cameroon in the quarter-final of the World Cup on 1 July 1990.

KEY MUSEUM ARTEFACT

Paul Gascoigne's outstanding performances in the 1990 World Cup in Italy brought him national and international fame. Recognition of this came when he was pronounced BBC Sports Personality of the Year that year. He became only the second footballer to win the award since its inception in 1954. England captain Bobby Moore won it after leading the country to victory in the 1966 World Cup final. There is a long tradition of nominated awards in the history of the game. Manchester City's Billy Meredith gained the most votes in *Umpire* magazine's search for the country's favourite footballer in 1904. He became football's first national star.

Above A 1990 World Cup silver salver featuring all the stadiums used in the tournament.

Right A puppet of Gazza from the television show *Spitting Image* of the early 1990s.

Paul Gascoigne always had a strong belief in his own ability. As a schoolboy he would practise his signature during lessons. 'I'm going to be a professional footballer,' he told his teachers.

Before the semi-final of the World Cup in 1990, Bobby Robson, the England manager, had a quiet word in private; he wanted to stress the scale of the challenge ahead. Gascoigne had just turned 23. 'You do realise you'll be playing against the best midfield player in world,' Robson said, referring to Lothar Matthäus of West Germany.

Gazza said, 'No, Bobby, you've got it wrong. He is.' Several weeks earlier the England players had presented Gascoigne with a birthday cake. He finished his speech by saying, 'and here I am, a legend'.

Gascoigne wiped away the tears on his England shirt: the image that became the abiding memory of the tournament for millions of supporters back home.

Gascoigne had been marked out for greatness as a potential future England player since his early days as an apprentice at Newcastle United. Jackie Milburn, the great centre-forward of the 1950s, sent Robson a message: 'We've got one here you should look out for.'

In 1984–85 Gascoigne was captain of Newcastle's FA Youth Cup-winning side. When Robson saw him in action himself for the first time, he quickly realised Milburn had been right. 'He's a little gem,' Robson said.

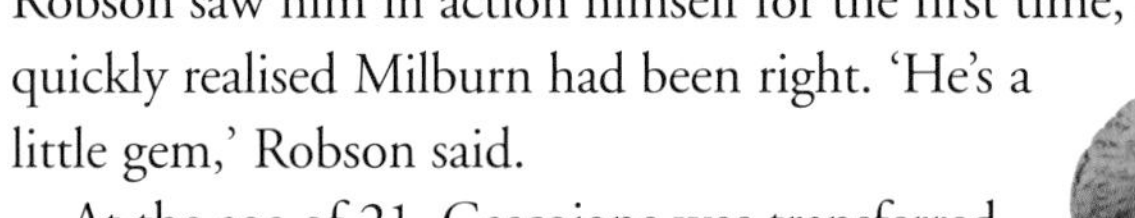

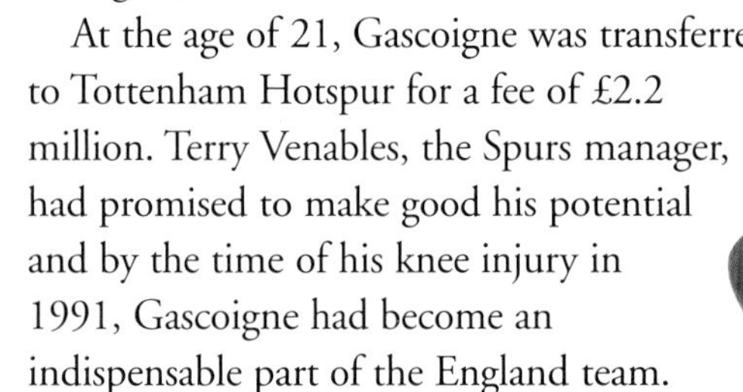

At the age of 21, Gascoigne was transferred to Tottenham Hotspur for a fee of £2.2 million. Terry Venables, the Spurs manager, had promised to make good his potential and by the time of his knee injury in 1991, Gascoigne had become an indispensable part of the England team.

The injury ruled him out of international football for two years. 'All that time we've been trying to eke out results without Paul,' Graham Taylor, the then England manager, said on his return. 'You find yourself saying, "Don't let anything else go wrong with him". He's that important to us.'

Above A ticket for the Scotland v England Euro '96 match. Gascoigne enjoyed possibly the best form of his career in these European Championships. He also scored a memorable goal in England's 2–0 victory over Scotland in the first round of the competition.

Paul Gascoigne was invited to Buckingham Palace and 10 Downing Street on his return from the World Cup in Italy in 1990. In the months that followed a judge compared him in court to the Duke of Wellington in 1815, following the Battle of Waterloo, in terms of his popular appeal.

His profile soared. Franco Zeffirelli, the Italian film director, said he loved Gascoigne's sense of humour; Osvaldo Ardiles, the Argentina international, named his dog after him; Madame Tussaud's made a waxwork figure and his puppet caricature appeared on *Spitting Image*.

'Everyone was competing for a bit of me, wanting my presence at events, my endorsements,' Gascoigne recalled. 'It was overwhelming.'

Gascoigne put his name to lunchboxes, calendars, t-shirts, keyrings, books, videos, bedroom rugs and newspaper columns. His cover of 'Fog on the Tyne' made the top ten, selling 100,000 copies. 'I enjoyed the limelight, and it was very exciting,' Gascoigne said. 'We registered the name Gazza so that people couldn't instantly rip us off.'

The celebrity status brought its rewards: a gold disc for his pop song, and the award as BBC Sports Personality of the Year in 1990. Bobby Charlton presented the trophy. 'I had a hard job keeping back the tears,' Gascoigne said.

But there was also the downside. Gascoigne often found himself besieged. 'I hid in the car boot when I was driven away from my home or White Hart Lane,' he recalled. 'The only time I feel safe now is in the middle of a football pitch. At least there I know I can escape for a couple of hours.'

TALKING POINT

Terry Venables, the England manager, described the turn and volley by Paul Gascoigne against Scotland as 'not only the best goal of Euro '96, but the best goal of the last two or three major tournaments'.

Running onto a pass from Darren Anderton, Gascoigne had feinted in order to commit the defender, flicked the ball over his opponent's head, skipped round him, and then volleyed the ball into the bottom corner.

'I just knew where Colin Hendry would be and when he would commit himself,' Gascoigne recalled. 'So I knew what to do. It felt brilliant when it all worked. I went to look like I would knock the ball past him and try to go round the outside, but I changed direction and lobbed it, and he ended up on the deck.'

Venables said the display of skill was comparable to those normally associated with the best Brazilians. 'Gazza always gives you that touch of the unexpected that the opposition don't like,' he said.

England won the group game at Wembley 2–0. 'After this goal, our opponents were making plans about how to play against him, right up to the semi-final against Germany,' Venables said.

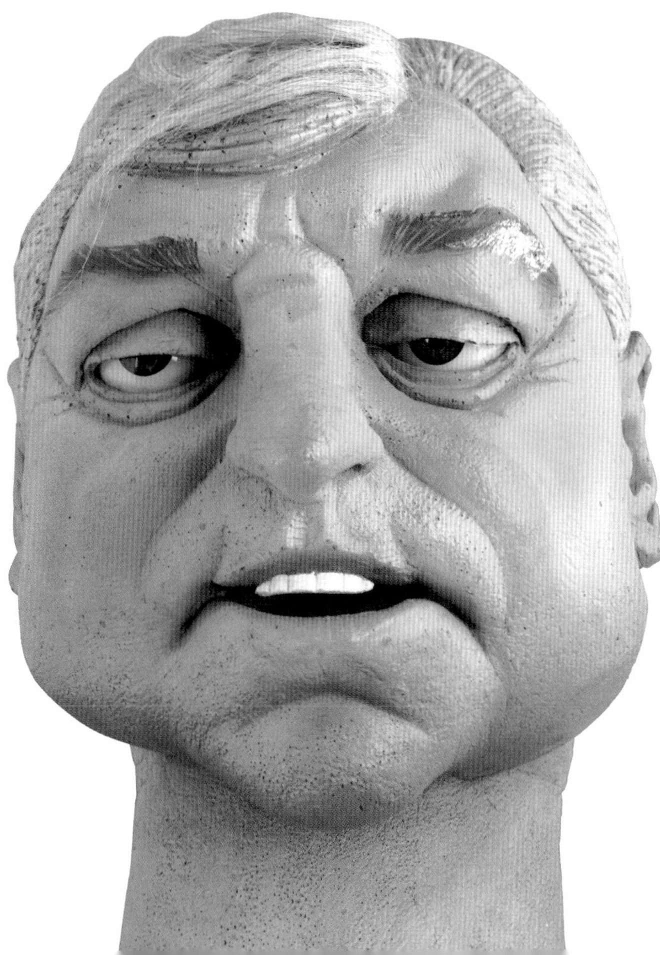

Right Terry Venables, whose *Spitting Image* puppet from the 1990s is shown here, managed Gascoigne at Spurs and Middlesbrough, as well as during his spell as England manager, and was his mentor throughout his career.

UMBRO

DEBBIE BAMPTON (1961–)

Player • Inducted 2005 • 95 Caps • 5 National League titles • 4 FA Cups • 1 League Cup

Debbie Bampton was still a schoolgirl when she made her England debut against Holland at the age of 16; and she played her last game for her country two decades later on a tour to the United States in 1997. In between times, she achieved two notable 'firsts' in the women's game.

In 1992–93 she was a member of the Arsenal side that became the first team to win the domestic treble of League championship, FA Cup and League Cup. 'As a lifelong fan of the Arsenal men's teams, it was a fantastic thrill to win these trophies in the Gunners colours,' she said.

Three years later, as player-manager of Croydon, Bampton made another breakthrough. 'I became the first woman to manage a team to the League and Cup double,' she said. 'It meant a lot to me to prove a point in this way.'

Despite being sidelined for 12 months after sustaining a serious knee injury in 1982, Bampton won 95 caps for England, scoring seven goals, and she was awarded an MBE in 1998 in recognition of her services to women's football as a player and a manager.

She played in central midfield throughout her career, with the exception of a spell as sweeper for the national team in the mid-1980s.

In 1988 Bampton joined a small exodus of British players to Italy, where she trained full-time with Trani, who finished runners-up in both the League and the Cup at the end of her only season at the club.

'I considered myself a box-to-box player,' Bampton said. 'I modelled myself on my England male counterpart Bryan Robson. Like him, I worked hard to win the ball and I was always looking to make forward runs. I was not a natural goalscorer, but I did look to set up chances for others.'

KEY MATCH

Denmark 0 England 1 (aggregate 1–3), European Championships semi-final, 28 April, 1984

'There was something special about the atmosphere in the dressing-room that day. I have never experienced anything like it before or since. We were huge underdogs but there was this absolute belief, this sense of certainty, that we would go through.'

England were preparing to face Denmark, one of the top three teams in the world, in a game that would decide who would play Sweden in the final of the European Championships. Twenty days earlier England had surprisingly won the first leg 1-0, but the Danes were still overwhelming favourites to go through.

'Denmark were the better side in that first leg,' Bampton recalled. 'Everyone expected them to win at home. Yet somehow everything just clicked for us on the day. I will always remember this sense of calm determination within the England team.'

With the score goalless in the second leg, England won a corner. Pat Chapman, the left-winger, swung over a cross. 'I met the ball with my head and it flew in for the winner,' Bampton recalled.

'I wasn't a natural goalscorer, as my record of seven goals in 95 internationals suggests; but heading was always a strong point of my game.

'It was a weakness in the women's game at one time, but I've never been frightened to head the ball. As a child I used to go out into the back garden with my dad and he would throw the ball to me. I had no idea that it would prove so useful in such an important game.'

In the final England held Sweden over two legs before losing a penalty shoot-out.

Left Debbie Bampton playing for England.

KEY MUSEUM ARTEFACT

This photograph, taken in the late nineteenth century, shows Nettie Honeyball, captain of the British Ladies Football Club. She believed that the manly game of football could also be enjoyed by women and her attitude towards physical recreation, for females, was adopted by a number of progressive girls' schools who began to develop forms of 'rationalised sport' for women. But the early pioneers of the women's game had to overcome many prejudices, not least from the medical profession of the day. In 1894 the British Medical Journal published an article calling for women to stop playing the game stating, 'We can in no way sanction the reckless exposure to violence, of organs which the common experience of women had led them in every way to protect.'

When Debbie Bampton began playing football at the age of ten, she joined in with the boys' games on the playground of her junior school in south London. It led to a succession of summonses to the headmistress's office.

'She told me time and again how unladylike it was for a girl to play a rough game like football,' Bampton recalled. 'But her words fell on deaf ears as far as I was concerned, and I carried on playing. At that time I didn't know that organised women's football even existed, and that only changed when I read a report in a newspaper one day a few years later.'

In 1992–93 she was a member of the Arsenal side that became the first team to win the domestic treble of League championship, FA Cup and League Cup.

At 14, Bampton joined Maidstone, a ladies team managed by her father, Albert, who has played a major role in her football career.

'Dad is fanatical about football, and that has rubbed off on me,' she said. 'He used to spend hours with me working on my game as I was growing up, and over the years, I have played for three clubs he has managed – Maidstone, Howbury Grange and Eastbourne Borough.'

Her stints at Maidstone and Howbury Grange came early in her career, and she was not expecting to join up with her father again until she received an unexpected appeal in 2004.

'I was 42 years of age and it had been five years since I retired officially as a player with Croydon,' Bampton said. 'I had not kicked a ball since, but then Dad asked me if I would help out with coaching the younger players at Eastbourne Borough.

'When I went along, they asked me if I would start playing again. I got the bug again straight away. I suppose it is always in the blood. My knee is still dodgy, but I managed somehow to play every game in the regional League that season.'

Above This 'Women's FA Cup Winners' plaque, from 1992, was awarded to Doncaster Belles. The following year, Debbie Bampton achieved the domestic treble as a member of the Arsenal side.

Right Gouache showing a French showgirl high kicking a coloured football, early 1920s.

Debbie Bampton fulfilled a great ambition when she joined Arsenal in 1992. It wasn't long before she had another reason to celebrate. 'In my first season with them we did the treble,' she said.

Bampton was first taken to Highbury as a five-year-old. As a supporter on the North Bank she

needed to stand on a wooden box to see the action on the pitch.

'When I had the chance to join the Arsenal Ladies I did not hesitate for a moment,' she said. 'They had just been promoted to the national League so the timing was just right for me. I was Arsenal mad, and I still am.'

In 1994–95 Arsenal came close to repeating their achievement, winning the double of League and FA Cup. 'It also proved to be my last contribution to the Gunners' cause.'

'I was still an England international and I had won a number of honours as a player,' she said. 'I was looking for a new challenge when I was approached by Croydon.

'They offered me an opportunity to become player-manager, which was an exciting prospect. The team had just won promotion to the national League, and I decided to give it a go.'

In the double season, 1995–96 Croydon defeated Liverpool on penalties in the Women's FA Cup final and won the League title on goal difference from Doncaster Belles after completing the fixture list unbeaten.

'I spent six seasons at the club as player-manager, and we won the League title three times. I kept on playing throughout my time at Croydon. By the time I finished I had achieved everything I wanted to in the game.'

TALKING POINT

Debbie Bampton did not hesitate when she was offered the chance to become a full-time professional in Italy, but it proved to be a bittersweet experience.

Bampton spent one successful season – in 1988 – with Trani in the national League before returning to England. 'I was definitely a better player for my time overseas, but I also found myself frustrated by the culture surrounding Italian football.'

Trani, a small town near Bari in southern Italy, finished that season as runners-up in the League and losing Cup-finalists, attracting crowds of up to 3,000 to home games against the likes of Milan, Napoli and Roma.

'The standard was higher than I was used to,' she said. 'That was a challenge. I had never played in a national League before.

'We trained for three hours every day. I relished that. My technique definitely improved as a result of being full-time. I felt more comfortable on the ball.'

But there was a downside. 'I didn't get on with the mentality out there,' she said. 'Everyone involved in the game was so fickle. If you're winning it's great; if not, it's a different story.'

'The money was good and all I had to pay for was my own food, but the club just wasn't reliable. Sometimes, if we lost a game, say, they would somehow forget to pay us. By the end of the season, I'd had enough.'

Several other Italian clubs offered her a contract to stay on, but it made no difference. 'I enjoyed the football itself, but I was homesick,' she said. 'It was time to come home.'

Above This scrapbook, from the 1890s, details 'Miss Honeyball's Team of Lady Football Players'.

Left The official programme from the 1992 Women's FA Cup final.

ALEX FERGUSON (1941–)

Manager • Inducted 2002 • 1 European Champions League • 1 European Cup-winners' Cup • 8 Premiership titles • 5 FA Cups • 1 League Cup (as of end-2004–05)

Alex Ferguson, the first manager in history to win the championship title three seasons in a row, bore the heavy burden of expectation at Old Trafford before restoring Manchester United to the pinnacle of domestic and European football.

Three times within a decade Ferguson led his side to the Double of league title and FA Cup, a unique feat for a manager in England. In the triumphant 1998–99 season, the European Cup was added to complete an unprecedented Treble.

'There have been some wonderful times at Old Trafford under Alex,' Bobby Charlton said. 'He has been successful, while maintaining a great tradition for attacking football at the club.'

Those good times did not arrive straight away, though. For almost seven years following his appointment in 1986, Ferguson was weighed down by history. It had been more than a quarter of a century, dating back to the days of Matt Busby, since the last championship success.

In 1992–93, the club finally broke through. 'The barrier that had defied so many talented people, world-renowned players as well as managers, had been breached,' Ferguson said. Twenty-six years of 'collective cursing and frustration', as he put it, were at an end.

Over the following decade Manchester United won the title seven more times. In 2000–01, they completed a hat-trick of championship wins, a feat no other manager has ever managed.

A one-time Glasgow Rangers centre-forward, Ferguson learned his trade at the bottom end of Scottish football. Perennial strugglers East Stirlingshire had only eight players on the books when he took over, at the age of 32, in 1974. Within three and a half months, the club was lying third in Division Two. And so it began.

KEY MATCH

Bayern Munich 1 Manchester United 2, Champions League final, Barcelona, 26 May 1999

As his players prepared to leave the dressing room at half-time, Alex Ferguson knew he had one last opportunity to influence their thinking. Ferguson chose his words carefully.

'Lads, when you go out there, just have a look at that cup. It will be about five yards away from you, but you won't be able to touch it, of course.

'I want you to think about the fact that if you lose this game, you'll have been so close to it,' he continued. 'You'll hate that thought for the rest of your lives. So just make sure you don't lose!'

He had made his last intervention in terms of motivation with what Peter Schmeichel later described as a 'shrewd and timely' speech. But Ferguson could still influence the shape of the game through his use of substitutes.

With 24 minutes left Bayern still led 1–0. So Ferguson introduced Teddy Sheringham down the left flank to give them something different to think about.

Increasingly, Ferguson noted, the Germans were tiring under the mental and physical strain of trying to contain the Manchester forwards. 'I decided it was time for a second substitution. I knew they'd have trouble with Ole Gunnar Solskjaer. He's got lightning quick reactions, and their defenders were exhausted.'

By the end of normal time, even Ferguson feared the worst. He had begun preparing a loser's speech in his mind when two goals in injury-time – scored by Sheringham and Solskjaer – won the game. At the eighth time of asking, with first Aberdeen, then Manchester United, he had finally won the European Cup.

Left Alex Ferguson celebrates Manchester United's equaliser in the 1999 Champions League final in Barcelona.

KEY MUSEUM ARTEFACT

The key to Ferguson's success at United is the way in which he has developed their youth policy. Instilling his values of work ethic, team work and flair in talented young players has seen many of his youngsters progress into the first team. A blend of home-grown players alongside more experienced professionals, such as Eric Cantona, Steve Bruce and Peter Schmeichel, saw United dominate the 1990s. No player epitomises the Ferguson way more than David Beckham. This pencil sketch of David Beckham was produced by Si Sapsford in 2000.

Above A Manchester United shirt from an early round of their 1999 European Champions League campaign.

Right A flag in Manchester United's colours bearing the name of the League's sponsor. Under Ferguson, United have won eight Premiership titles.

Manchester United were stuck just above the relegation zone when Alex Ferguson left Aberdeen to take over as manager on 6 November 1986. The team 'lacked fitness, ambition, and morale was poor,' Ferguson quickly concluded. 'Too many physical lightweights,' he said.

Ferguson began by strengthening the defence. Viv Anderson, his first signing, added experience and resilience at full-back and Steve Bruce came in as a reliable and robust centre-half.

Other problems were less easily remedied. By the third anniversary of his appointment, and with no trophy to show for his time in charge, the pressure was mounting. Frustrated supporters unfurled a banner at one home game. 'Three years of excuses; Ta-ra, Fergie,' it read.

Ferguson was unrelenting in his demands. Several former players have spoken of the 'hairdryer' treatment.

Results did not improve. 'Black December', as Ferguson came to refer to the last four weeks of 1989, was the 'lowest, most desperate point in my career'. One of the earliest lessons he had learned in management was: 'Never seek confrontation; confrontation will come to you.' And so it was at Old Trafford. A drinking culture had enveloped the club and Ferguson eventually sold two established first-team players, Paul McGrath and Norman Whiteside, as a signal of intent to others.

Ferguson was unrelenting in his demands. Several former players have spoken of the 'hairdryer treatment', a torrent of 'in-your-face' criticism delivered at close quarters. Cups, bottles and boots have been hurled in the dressing-room. Ferguson himself has expressed concern 'at the quickness of my temper and depth of my anger'.

Several players, though, have noted a mellowing in Ferguson over the years. Bryan Robson, the captain of the 1992–93 side, said: 'He is much calmer these days.'

Bobby Charlton has likened Alex Ferguson to Matt Busby in terms of their philosophy to football. 'Matt would never think about playing defensively,' Charlton said. 'He always used to say that the game must never be boring for the public, and that legacy has continued with Alex.'

The parallels in the careers of the two men, the only managers to be knighted solely for their work at club level, are striking.

Manchester United had not won the championship title for 34 years when Matt Busby took over in 1945; when Ferguson arrived at the club the supporters had already been waiting 19 years since the success of 1966–67.

Both managers won the FA Cup as their first major honour at the club: Busby in 1948; Ferguson in 1990. Both had previously finished runners-up in the League. Both men also broke up a championship-winning side to introduce a generation of young players. It was a particularly bold decision on Busby's part: back in the 1950s, 'You'll never win anything with a bunch of kids,' to use Alan Hansen's famous phrase, was even more entrenched as a way of thinking.

Manchester United reached the FA Youth Cup final two seasons in succession in the early 1990s, a throwback to the run of success in the competition enjoyed by the 'Busby Babes' in the 1950s.

Both European Cup-winning sides had a solid core of local lads and players brought up through the ranks. Ryan Giggs, Paul Scholes, Gary Neville, David Beckham and Nicky Butt were following an example set by Nobby Stiles, Brian Kidd, Bill Foulkes, David Sadler, Bobby Charlton and George Best in 1968.

'Our victory against Bayern Munich, the miracle of the Nou Camp, came on what would have been Sir Matt's 90th birthday,' Ferguson said. 'That was very important to everyone at Manchester United.'

Right An invitation to Sir Matt Busby's 80th birthday celebration. Busby was an influential figure in Ferguson's career at United and was happy to give him advice.

Left An item of merchandise featuring the Mexico '86 mascot, Pique. Alex Ferguson managed Scotland in the tournament after the sudden death of Jock Stein.

TALKING POINT

Alex Ferguson was still a player when he learned one of his favourite tricks in management from the man he revered as 'The Master'

Jock Stein, the Celtic manager, gave a valuable lesson in psychology, employing his cunning and experience in a bid to unnerve Rangers during the title race of 1967–68.

Rangers were leading the League in Ferguson's first season at Ibrox when Stein gave an interview during which he publicly 'surrendered' the title, saying: 'It is Rangers' title now, unless they throw it away.'

Timing was critical: Rangers had just suffered the double disappointment of losing a quarter-final in both the Scottish Cup and the Fairs Cup.

'I never forgot those headlines Jock instigated,' Ferguson said. Rangers surrendered the initiative, finishing two points adrift.

'The trick was instantly lodged in my memory for future use,' Ferguson said. An opportunity arose in the closing stages of the 1994–95 season.

Having spotted 'encouraging signs of nerves within the Blackburn Rovers camp', Ferguson said the League leaders 'could only throw the title away', drawing an analogy with Devon Loch, the Grand National horse. 'It was a pretty corny psychological tactic but worth a try,' Ferguson said.

Blackburn did falter, allowing Manchester United to close the gap in the run-up. Ferguson had taken the title race to the final day of the season.

ASSOCIATION OF FORMER
MANCHESTER UNITED PLAYERS

Sir Matt Busby C.B.E., K.C.S.G.
80th BIRTHDAY CELEBRATION
on
Friday, 2nd June 1989
at
Manchester United Executive Suite
Old Trafford, Manchester.

Reception 7.00pm. Dinner 7.30pm. *(prompt)*

Dress: Lounge Suit.

ARSENAL

TONY ADAMS (1966–)

Player • Inducted 2004 • 66 caps • 2 Division One Championships • 2 Premiership titles • 3 FA Cups • 1 European Cup-winners' Cup • 2 League Cups

Tony Adams, the great servant of Arsenal Football Club, is the only player to captain a championship-winning side in three different decades.

Twice, in 1997–98 and 2001–02, Adams led his team to the Double. 'An exceptional player who is highly respected because of his commitment,' Arsène Wenger said.

Adams lifted the championship trophy for the first time in 1988–89 after being appointed the club's youngest-ever captain at the age of 21. 'He is my sergeant-major on the pitch,' George Graham said. 'A colossus.'

Over a period of 19 years Adams played 421 League games at the heart of the Arsenal defence. A cult hero at Highbury, tickets for his testimonial sold out in two days.

He also played 66 times for England, including 15 appearances as captain. David Seaman, the Arsenal and England goalkeeper, said: 'He is a born leader and there's not many of those around.'

Off the field, however, an increasing dependence on alcohol blighted his private life, leading to a prison sentence for drink-driving in 1991. He publicly admitted his health problems in 1996 and set about establishing a charity to help players suffering addiction.

Perhaps the most telling compliment from a fellow professional came from Alex Ferguson, the manager of fierce rivals Manchester United: 'I can't wait for him to retire,' Ferguson wrote in 1999.

'He is the defining spirit of their team, a classic English defender – brave, reliable and capable not only of fulfilling his own responsibilities superbly but of organising and inspiring others,' Ferguson said. 'No one can be surprised at Arsenal's success while they still have him around.'

Bob Wilson, a member of the Double-winning side of 1971, said: 'The greatest of all Arsenal men, as simple as that.'

KEY MATCH

Liverpool 0 Arsenal 2, Division One, Anfield, 26 May 1989

George Graham left the final rallying call before the Arsenal players left the dressing room for the most dramatic game in the club's history to his captain, Tony Adams.

'We've come this far, lads,' Adams told his team-mates, smacking the palm of his hand as he spoke, 'and we're not letting the title slip now. They have all written us off. Now let's get out there and prove them all wrong. Let's go.'

'Tony has such a presence and self-belief that players are instantly inspired by him,' Graham said. 'He is a real man's man.'

Arsenal needed to beat Liverpool 2–0 away to win their first championship title in 18 years. Their previous seven visits to Anfield had all ended in defeat, and it had been 15 years since they managed to score two goals there.

Above all, Arsenal had to keep a clean sheet. Graham fielded three central defenders, with David O'Leary in the sweeper role behind Adams and Steve Bould.

'Everything Liverpool tried foundered on the rock of our defence,' Graham said. 'Tony was typically determined and committed.'

Adams had been pilloried and ridiculed in many newspapers earlier in the season. 'He has suffered a lot of stick, but he proved his strength of character at Anfield,' Graham said.

Arsenal famously clinched the title with a goal from Michael Thomas in injury-time. Adams collected the trophy. 'It was a very proud moment,' he recalled.

Left Tony Adams celebrates with the Division One and the Barclays Championship trophies. Arsenal had just secured the title by beating Liverpool 2–0 at Anfield on 26 May 1989.

KEY MUSEUM ARTEFACT

UEFA created the European Cup-Winners' Cup competition for those clubs who had won their own domestic equivalent of the FA Cup, in 1960–61. Birmingham City were the first English team to reach the final of a European competition. City, who lost 4–1 on aggregate to the mighty Barcelona, blazed a trail to the Inter-Cities Fairs Cup final in 1960. Tony Adams got his hands on the Cup Winners' Cup, featured below, in 1994, after Arsenal won both the League Cup and FA Cup in 1993. Arsenal were the first team to win this particular double in one season.

Tony Adams made his debut for Arsenal in November 1983 at the age of 17 years and 26 days, making him at that point the second youngest player to appear in an Arsenal shirt.

'I was so nervous I put my shorts on the wrong way round in the dressing room,' Adams recalled. 'When I came in at half-time I was told it might be an idea to change. I didn't play particularly well, and the team lost, but it was a start.'

He soon learned. In 1987, Adams was voted Young Player of the Year. 'If we had that boy,' one Division One manager said privately, 'we'd conquer the world.'

Over a period of 19 years Adams played 421 League games at the heart of the Arsenal defence. A cult hero at Highbury, tickets for his testimonial sold out in two days.

On his arrival as manager at Highbury, in May 1986, George Graham quickly realised the potential of the young players on the staff, most notably his centre-half. 'With the likes of Tony around I could afford to feel optimistic about the future,' Graham said in 1995.

Graham founded his challenge for the championship on a sound defence, with Adams at its core. In training, Graham worked tirelessly coaching a zonal marking system.

As a 'flat back four', the Arsenal defenders pushed up in a line as a unit, compressing the play, in a bid to restrict space to opponents in midfield, and with the aim of catching opposing forwards offside when the forward pass was made. Hence the abiding image of Adams, standing, arm raised, appealing to the referee or linesman. 'I thought their goal was offside,' he said in 1991. 'But then I always do.'

The physical toll of playing for almost two

Above right A 1998 Arsenal shirt. No player has appeared at Wembley more than Adams. His international appearances together with domestic success with Arsenal, culminated in his 60th appearance at the stadium when he captained the England team against Germany in the final game to be played at Wembley in 2000.

Right An England training top from 2000. Adams captained England for the first time in 1994 and took part in his one and only World Cup in France in 1998.

decades finally caught up with Tony Adams. 'I have degeneration in the bones,' he said, announcing his retirement in 2002, at the age of 35. 'I want to walk in a few years' time. The body has packed up on me, really.'

'He does everything 100 per cent,' Ian Wright, his Arsenal team-mate, said. 'He's not one to shirk a challenge.'

Such qualities made Adams an automatic choice for England at Euro '96. 'Tony was magnificent in that tournament as both a defender and a leader of the team,' Terry Venables said.

Adams had not yet fully recovered from a knee operation the previous January when he played in Euro '96. Soon after the tournament, he had to undergo further surgery.

Injuries like these increasingly sidelined Adams in later years. Like all footballers, he took longer to recover as he aged; healing can take longer still if the player drinks excessive alcohol.

Immediately after losing against Germany in the semi-final of Euro '96, Adams embarked on a seven-week drinking binge. Only at the end of it did he 'reach rock bottom'. At this point he contacted Alcoholics Anonymous.

While dealing with his addiction, Adams played on. The effects of long-term drinking were becoming increasingly evident, however, in Arsenal's second 'Double' season, 1997–98, injuries restricted Adams to 26 League appearances. He was fit, though, to play in the final home game of the season when Arsenal clinched the championship. He was even on hand to score the fourth goal against Everton.

In 2001–02, Adams played only ten games, but again he was there to lift the Premier League trophy at Highbury, just as he had been in Cardiff when the FA Cup was won the week before.

The first name in the index of the official club history, published in 1986, sums it up. It reads: Adams, Tony.

TALKING POINT

Tony Adams proved his remarkable capacity to recover from setback and adversity during an eventful season of fluctuating fortunes in 1990–91.

In the space of 12 months, Adams was first overlooked by England for the World Cup in Italy and then jailed for drink-driving. By the end of the season, however, he was lifting the championship trophy for the second time as Arsenal captain.

George Graham, the Arsenal manager, said: 'No one has more will to win and bloody-mindedness in the face of adversity than Tony. He is in a class of his own for tenacity and will power.'

For several seasons Adams had endured the taunts of rival supporters. Fans had been making 'ee-aw' noises at him ever since a tabloid newspaper depicted him as a donkey following his scoring an own goal.

'No other player in the League had been under the sort of pressure Tony faced virtually every time he ran onto the pitch,' Graham said.

There was more bad news in December. Two days after being charged with reckless and drunk driving, Adams became the first player to be sent off under the new professional foul law.

On a brighter note, Adams regained his place in the England squad. Then another blow: he was convicted in court. He would eventually serve two months in prison.

When he returned to action 7,000 fans turned up to watch a reserve team match. His first-team recall in the League, for the away game at Liverpool, followed soon after. Arsenal won the game 1-0, consolidating their lead at the top of the table. The Gunners eventually won the title by a margin of seven points.

Above A Sparta Praha Football Club pennant presented to Arsenal in 2000. Despite Arsenal winning two 'Doubles', in 1998 and 2002, success in the Champions League has eluded the club. For a time they played their Champions League home games at Wembley, but it did little to improve their results.

Left The 1988 Barclays League Division One Trophy. Adams picked up this trophy twice by leading Arsenal to the Division One Championship in 1989 and 1991.

ERIC CANTONA (1966–)

Player • Inducted 2002 • 43 Caps • 1 Division One Championship • 4 Premiership titles • 2 FA Cups

Eric Cantona, the Frenchman nicknamed 'Le King' by the Stretford End, added the final, vital ingredient to the mix that made Manchester United the best team in England, ending 26 years of frustration.

When Cantona arrived at Old Trafford in November 1992, for a modest fee of £1 million, Manchester United were lying in sixth place in the Premier League. The following May they were crowned champions, for the first time since 1966–67.

'We were an inspired and transformed team,' Sir Alex Ferguson, the manager, said. 'Eric had a priceless presence.'

Remarkably, Cantona had managed a repeat of his earlier, equally dramatic experience at Leeds United. The previous year he had arrived at Elland Road in mid-season and they, too, went on to win the title. 'Eric Idol,' one newspaper called him. 'Ooh, Aah Cantona,' chanted the delighted Leeds fans.

'I was a hit with everyone,' Cantona said, referring to his brief spell in Yorkshire, after coming out of self-imposed retirement. 'Eight goals for Leeds. I had become the leader.'

Once he had crossed the Pennines on completing his transfer, Cantona immediately impressed Roy Keane: 'Collar turned up, back straight, chest stuck out, Eric glided into the arena as if he owned the place.'

'Straightaway, he illuminated Old Trafford,' Ferguson said. 'The place was a frenzy every time he touched the ball.'

Cantona formed a partnership with Mark Hughes. In the 20 games they started together in 1992–93, Manchester United scored 39 goals. The team had managed barely a goal a game before his arrival. 'It had the best defence, but not the best attack,' Cantona said.

In the mid-1990s, Nike ran a poster campaign featuring Cantona's image. Referring to the World Cup win of 30 years earlier, the caption read: '1966 was a great year for English football. Eric was born.'

KEY MATCH

Liverpool 0 Manchester United 1, FA Cup final, Wembley, 11 May 1996

Roy Keane was thankful that the ball fell to Eric Cantona. If it hadn't, Manchester United might not have completed their second 'Double' in three seasons.

'That winning goal,' Keane recalled, 'No one else would have been capable of scoring that goal. His knack of scoring important goals always stood out. As an individual, Eric was a legend.'

He was also underrated for his ability in the air, according to Alan Hansen, the television pundit. So when Manchester United were awarded a corner late in the game, Hansen looked for Cantona at the far post. He wasn't there. For some reason he'd withdrawn himself to the edge of the penalty area.

'Looking back, it seems inevitable that the ball would somehow to come to him,' Alex Ferguson recalled. 'But when it did, the ball bounced up at quite an awkward height. Eric needed good foot movement and perfect body position to execute a scoring shot.'

Since signing Cantona, Ferguson had been impressed by the Frenchman's commitment to individual skills practice during training. 'That vital volley was a dramatic demonstration of the value of all Eric's devotion to practice,' said Ferguson.

Cantona, the first foreign player to captain a Cup-winning side, had also influenced the team's tactics. Before the game, Ferguson had sought the views of senior players; Cantona, conscious of the threat posed by the Liverpool forwards, suggested Keane be deployed in a defensive role just in front of the back four. The manager agreed. 'It was a good idea,' Ferguson said.

Left Manchester United's captain Eric Cantona scores the game's only goal, in the 1996 FA Cup final on 11 May against Liverpool, securing the club's second Double in three years.

KEY MUSEUM ARTEFACT

This *Spitting Image* puppet of Eric Cantona from the 1990s epitomises the rich tradition of caricature in English football. Before the early 1900s, when photography became a regular means of capturing the quick action of a football match, the only way to record games was through etchings and engravings. Many newspapers and magazines continued to print humorous cartoons of famous players even after photographic images were readily available. The huge growth in the popularity of football after the launch of the Premiership saw players like Cantona being treated in the same way as politicians and film and pop stars.

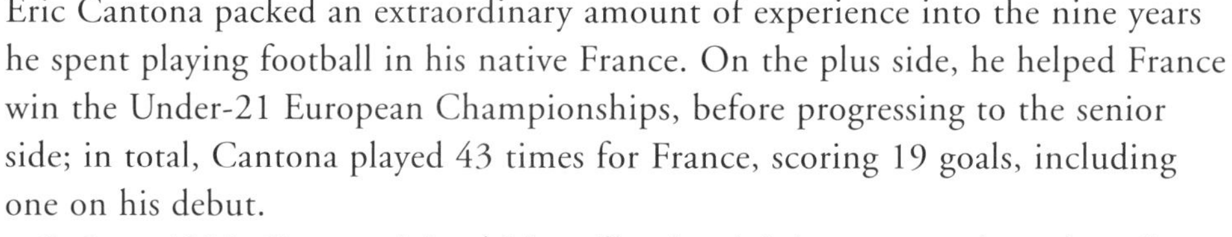

Eric Cantona packed an extraordinary amount of experience into the nine years he spent playing football in his native France. On the plus side, he helped France win the Under-21 European Championships, before progressing to the senior side; in total, Cantona played 43 times for France, scoring 19 goals, including one on his debut.

In June 1988, Cantona joined Marseille, the club he supported as a boy, from Auxerre for a French record fee of £2.3 million. In 1989–90 he won a French Cup-winner's medal with Montpellier.

So much for the highlights. The list of negative experiences was appreciably longer. Cantona was suspended from international football for 12 months for insulting Henri Michel, the France coach.

On another occasion, he was sent off for throwing a football at the referee and banned for four weeks. When Cantona heard the ruling, he called each member of the disciplinary panel an idiot to their face. The suspension was doubled to two months.

Marseille also suspended him, this time for throwing his shirt to the ground in protest after being substituted, while at Montpellier, Cantona was disciplined following a dressing-room fight with a team-mate. By now his career was in crisis. Cancelling his own contract in a mix of frustration and despair, he announced his retirement, at the age of 25, in 1991.

"I sometimes have the impression that if Eric can't score a beautiful goal he would rather not score at all."

– Michel Platini

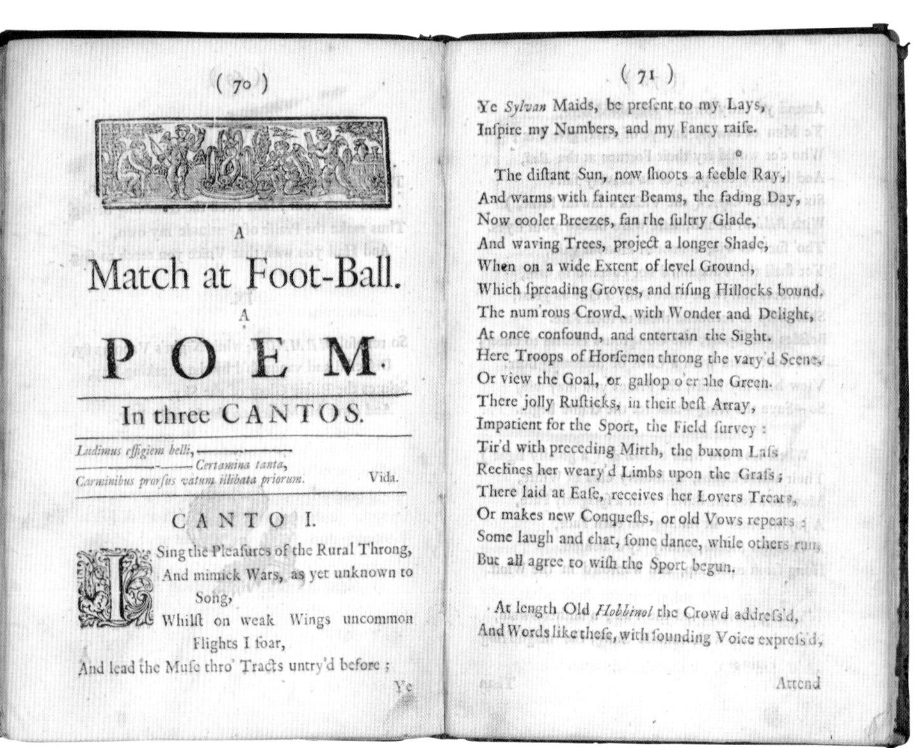

(70)

A

Match at Foot-Ball.

A

POEM.

In three CANTOS.

Ludimus effigiem belli, ——————
—————— *Certamina tanta,*
Carminibus prorſus vatum illibata priorum. Vida.

CANTO I.

I Sing the Pleaſures of the Rural Throng,
And mimick Wars, as yet unknown to Song,
Whilſt on weak Wings uncommon Flights I ſoar,
And lead the Muſe thro' Tracts untry'd before;

Ye

(71)

Ye *Sylvan* Maids, be preſent to my Lays,
Inſpire my Numbers, and my Fancy raiſe.

The diſtant Sun, now ſhoots a feeble Ray,
And warms with fainter Beams, the fading Day,
Now cooler Breezes, fan the ſultry Glade,
And waving Trees, project a longer Shade,
When on a wide Extent of level Ground,
Which ſpreading Groves, and riſing Hillocks bound,
The num'rous Crowd, with Wonder and Delight,
At once confound, and entertain the Sight.
Here Troops of Horſemen throng the vary'd Scene,
Or view the Goal, or gallop o'er the Green.
There jolly Ruſticks, in their beſt Array,
Impatient for the Sport, the Field ſurvey:
Tir'd with preceding Mirth, the buxom Laſs
Reclines her weary'd Limbs upon the Graſs;
There laid at Eaſe, receives her Lovers Treats,
Or makes new Conqueſts, or old Vows repeats;
Some laugh and chat, ſome dance, while others run,
But all agree to wiſh the Sport begun.

At length Old *Hobbinol* the Crowd addreſs'd,
And Words like theſe, with ſounding Voice expreſs'd,

Attend

Right This poem, 'A Match at Foot-Ball', was published in an 18th-century collection by Concanen. Although many thought that Cantona was the first football poet, history appears to tell us otherwise.

Left *Le Rouge Devil*, a sculpture by David Hughes made in 2000.

Michel Platini, who once said he had 'the impression that if Eric can't score a beautiful goal he would rather not score', eventually persuaded Cantona to return.

Platini rated Cantona highly, recalling the Montpellier player during his time as France manager. Now he suggested a new start elsewhere: 'What about a move to England?'

By the age of 25, Eric Cantona had been employed by six clubs in France and one club in England. For the remaining five years of his football career he put an end to his nomadic ways. 'I value truth, honesty, respect for one another, sincerity, compassion and understanding,' he said. 'These qualities are found at Manchester United.'

Roy Keane, the United captain, attributes the success of Cantona at Old Trafford to the man-management of Alex Ferguson. 'The manager gave Eric the freedom to be himself without undermining his own authority,' Keane said.

Cantona felt valued and wanted in Manchester. 'The other players accepted this special treatment because he could justify it with his brilliance on the field,' Keane said.

Only once did Cantona threaten to walk out. In 1995, he was suspended for eight months for an infamous 'kung-fu' attack on a supporter of Crystal Palace. Convicted of common assault, the Frenchman was eventually sentenced to 120 hours' community service.

When he subsequently fled the country, threatening to quit the game, Ferguson made a special trip to Paris in a bid to dissuade him. The manager kept faith with Cantona, offering him a new three-year contract and later, in 1996, the captaincy. Cantona responded by leading the club to a second 'Double' in three seasons.

'Eric had done more than any other player to deliver success for the manager,' Keane said. 'Loyalty is a cornerstone of the gaffer's character. He defied everyone outside the club to rescue Eric's career and rehabilitate him.'

TALKING POINT

Eric Cantona spoke of a deep and abiding respect for the history and rituals of English football.

The experience of playing at Wembley for the first time, in 1992, fulfilled all the expectations the Frenchman had harboured since childhood.

On 8 August, Cantona lined up for Division One champions Leeds United against Liverpool, the FA Cup winners, in the Charity Shield. As a boy growing up in France, Cantona had been entranced by the traditions surrounding the old stadium.

'To play at Wembley, for a footballer, in terms of the prestige and the honour that emanate from playing there, is a little like Wimbledon for a tennis player,' Cantona said, describing the pitch as 'the most wonderful playing surface in the world'.

'I will never forget that day in what I call the temple of football. I scored three goals, and Leeds won. All in all, it was one of the best days of my career.'

'The national anthem, the chants and shouts of the supporters, the stadium full of the colours of both teams playing against each other, the presentation of the trophy – I remember everything,' he wrote later.

Left The 1997 Football Writers' Association, Managers' Award presented to Cantona's manager and mentor, Alex Ferguson, after the club's fourth Premiership title in five years.

Above The October 1994 Manager of the Month award, which was presented to Alex Ferguson. A Cantona-inspired hat-trick of Championships eluded the club in 1995 after he was banned for assaulting a spectator. Ferguson convinced Cantona to return to his career after he received a lengthy suspension.

UMBRO
UMBRO

HOPE POWELL (1966–)

Player • Inducted 2003 • 66 caps • 1 National League title • 2 FA Cups • 1 League Cup (as of end-May 2005)

Hope Powell, a former England international and Double-winning captain with Croydon, broke new ground by becoming the first woman in the world to gain the UEFA Pro Licence, the highest qualification in the game.

On her retirement as a player in 1998, Powell was appointed England women's national team coach, with responsibility for the senior, Under-19s, Under-17s and Under-15s sides. At the age of 31 she was the youngest ever person to be given the job.

A football prodigy, Powell made her debut for England at the age of 16. 'As soon as Hope joined the squad she stood out as an exceptional talent,' said Gill Coultard, the former England captain.

'As a creative player she had this outstanding technical ability, and it was obvious to everyone that she would make the step up into the England team,' Coultard said.

In a career disrupted badly by injury, Powell played 66 times for her country as an attacking midfield player or occasional striker between 1983 and 1998, scoring 35 goals at a ratio of more than one goal every two games.

At club level, Powell enjoyed her greatest success in 1996 when, in addition to being appointed England vice-captain, she lifted both the League and FA Cup with Croydon.

She spent nine years of her career with Millwall Lionesses, winning the women's FA Cup in 1991. Earlier, during a two-year stint with Friends of Fulham, she ended up on the losing side in the 1989 final, despite scoring twice.

In 2002, Powell was awarded an OBE in the Queen's birthday honours list in recognition of her services to women's sport. 'This is a great honour for women's football,' she said. The following year she gained the UEFA Pro Licence at the end of a 12-month programme.

KEY MATCH

England 1 Sweden 0 aet (Aggregate 1-1, Sweden won on penalties), European Championship final, second leg, Kenilworth Road, 27 May 1984

Hope Powell was still a teenager when she helped England match the best team in the world in the final of the inaugural Women's European Championship, only to suffer the bitter disappointment of losing in a penalty shoot-out.

One year after making her international debut as a 16-year-old, Powell played in the two-leg final against Sweden, then regarded as the number one team in the rankings.

'Playing in the 1984 final was one of the highlights of my career as a player,' Powell said. 'It was a great experience for me at that early stage of my career. I was only disappointed that we did not get the result we wanted.'

England were delighted to return from the first leg in Sweden with only a one-goal deficit. 'They were easily the better side over there, and they could easily have won the game by a two- or three-goal margin, but we stuck at it well,' Coultard said.

It rained heavily for several days before the return leg in Luton, turning the pitch into a quagmire. The heavy conditions suited the English players, who fought tenaciously to level the scores on aggregate. 'The weather did us a favour,' Coultard said. 'We were able to get the goal to take the game into extra-time.'

Lennart Johannsson, the President of UEFA, watched the game at Kenilworth Road. 'The conditions were really bad on the day,' he said. 'The two teams did well to play such good football in the circumstances.'

Left Hope Powell playing for England.

KEY MUSEUM ARTEFACT

This trophy was made to commemorate the first FIFA World Championship for women, which was held in China in 1991. Although England failed to qualify for the tournament, and have yet to win a major international trophy, there is a rich history of women's football in England. One of the earliest trophies to be presented to a women's team was the Harry Weldon Cup. It was won by the great Dick, Kerr ladies team at Anfield in 1921. The game was played in front of 35,000 spectators. The trophy was named after the music hall star, who presented it to the winning team.

Above A programme from the Liverpool v Arsenal Women's FA Cup semi-final in 1996. Liverpool won through to the final only to be beaten by Croydon 4–2 on penalties after drawing 1–1 after extra time.

Right A sample of the kit worn by women footballers in the 1890s. Women began to play football in public schools and universities at this time when their emancipation was also becoming a prominent social issue.

Hope Powell made her debut for England in a 6–0 thrashing of the Republic of Ireland at Reading in a European Championships qualifier on 11 September, 1983. England went on to the reach the final of the competition, losing in the final against Sweden the following year.

It was the closest Powell came as a player to winning a major honour with England. The squad reached the semi-finals in the tournament in 1987 and 1995 and the quarter-finals in 1991 and 1993.

For most of her time in international football Powell formed a central midfield partnership with Gill Coultard, the most capped female England player

> **"She had this rare quality of being able to know where the other players were without even looking, and to find them with a perfect pass."** – *Gill Coultard*

in history. The team tactics were formulated in order to take best advantage of Powell's attacking ability and finishing talent. 'Of the three of us in midfield, Hope was the one who was given the freedom to break forward more often,' Coultard said.

'Hope's skill set her apart as an England player,' said Coultard, who played 119 games for England between 1981 and 2001. 'She was a creative player in the mould of Paul Gascoigne. She was two-footed and a good dribbler. Hope could see a pass and she could also score goals.'

Powell took up football seriously at the

age of 11. 'I've had a passion for the game ever since I was a young girl,' she said. 'It was in my heart from the very start. All I wanted to do was play.'

Hope Powell faced a difficult challenge when she took over as England national team coach in 1998. Her first task was to restore confidence: England had lost ten of their previous 12 games, including two heavy defeats against the United States of America the previous summer.

Powell immediately set out to tighten a defence that had conceded ten goals in those two games on tour in the US. Her influence was soon apparent: in her second game in charge, England restricted Norway, one of the three major powers in women's football at the time, to a single-goal victory in an away friendly in Lillestrom in August 1998.

Gradually, as Powell has brought in a new generation of younger players, results have improved. In 2005 England won six games in a row, the team's best run for 18 years.

'The average age of the squad is below 25,' Powell said in 2005. 'The future is very exciting for the England women's team.'

Their improvement was confirmed with a 1–0 victory over Norway in a friendly at Barnsley in 2005. A goal from Anita Asante, the Arsenal midfield player, after 34 minutes gave England their first ever victory 12 attempts against the Scandinavians, who were third in the FIFA rankings at the time.

The game was organised as part of England's preparations as hosts for the European Championships in the summer of 2005.

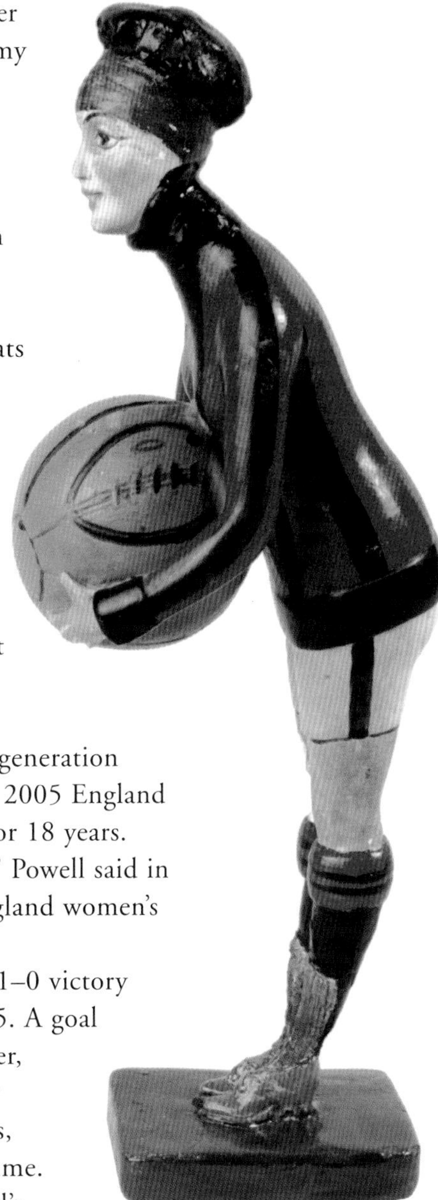

Above This glamorised representation of a woman footballer from 1900 did not reflect the truth about the women's game. It is indicative of the attitude towards women who played football from many quarters during the period.

TALKING POINT

Hope Powell is the first ever full-time national team coach of the England women's team. She is the also the first woman to do the job. 'I consider it a tremendous privilege to have this role and I feel very fortunate to do this work for a living.'

'When I am working with the players, my approach is to be relaxed, open and direct,' she said. 'I believe that it is vital to establish a relaxed atmosphere for players in the squad. The important thing is to bring your own style to the job. It would be foolish to do it any other way. If you try to be someone different, the players see through that.'

Powell has the handicap of working with players who cannot commit full-time to the sport.

'I would obviously prefer for the England players to be full-time professionals, but that is not the case,' Powell said. 'My players strive to be professional in their attitude, but they have to work full-time as well as train at football. As a squad, we get together five days ahead of a match and we build something into the calendar every month.'

Since taking over as England national team coach in 1998, Powell has been willing to put her faith in younger players, bringing down the average age of the side.

'This does influence how I do the job,' Powell said. 'I try to give the younger players as much confidence as possible. Sometimes nerves get the better of them, but I let them know I have total faith in them, and I tell them to enjoy it.'

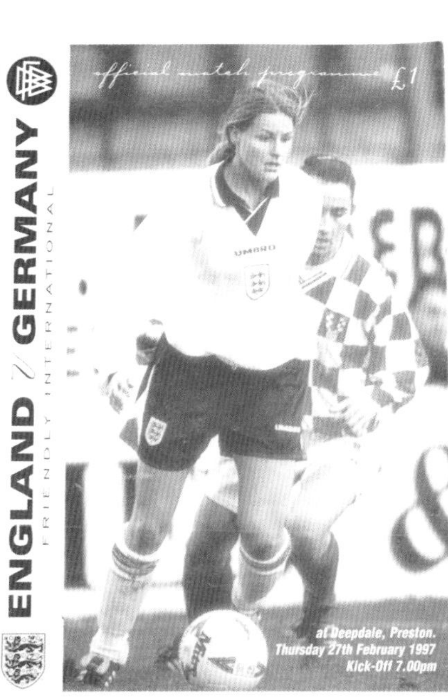

Right A programme from the 1997 England v Germany international game. This international at Deepdale was not the first women's game to be played at the ground: Dick, Kerr Ladies first played there in 1917.

MANCHESTER
UNITED
UMBRO
SHARP

PETER SCHMEICHEL (1963–)

Player • Inducted 2003 • 129 caps • 1 European Champions League • 5 Premiership titles • 3 FA Cups • 1 League Cup

Sir Alex Ferguson has described the £505,000 transfer fee that Manchester United paid Brondby in 1991 for a goalkeeper he nicknamed 'The Viking' as the buy of the century.

'At his best, I don't believe a better goalkeeper than Peter Schmeichel has played the game,' Ferguson said. 'He is a giant figure in the history of Manchester United and our debt to him will never be forgotten.'

When Schmeichel arrived at Old Trafford, the club were still chasing their first championship title since 1967; when he departed seven years later, Manchester United were crowned the best team in Europe in what was his last game in their colours.

'During most of his time with us, Peter was the best goalkeeper in the world, and it was fitting that his eight years with us should climax perfectly with the treble,' Ferguson said.

Before the quarter-final second leg in 1999, Inter players tried to intimidate their opponents before the game in Milan. In response, Schmeichel rallied his team-mates in the tunnel: 'When the great Peter raises his voice, the walls shake,' Ferguson said. 'The Inter players certainly got the message.Psychologically, it was an important moment for us.' Manchester United went through.

A member of the Denmark side that unexpectedly won the European Championships in Sweden in 1992, Schmeichel began his career at Brondby, where he won four championship medals in five seasons.

Football was not the only sport he played as a boy. Schmeichel was also an exceptional handball player, developing useful skills that he would one day introduce to English football. The best handball goalkeepers are expert in the 'star-jump', the spread-eagling of arms and legs in an attempt to block a shot from close range. Schmeichel used the same technique in football in one-against-one situations. 'He blocks so much of the goal,' Alan Hansen said. 'His ability in these situations must be worth 12 points a season. He is in a class of his own.'

KEY MATCH

Manchester United 2 Arsenal 1, FA Cup semi-final, Villa Park, 14 April 1999

Peter Schmeichel had lost sense of time as Dennis Bergkamp readied himself to take the last-gasp penalty that would determine whether Manchester United created history. It would only be later that he understood the full implications of the moment.

Instead of there being seven minutes left to play, as Schmeichel believed, only seconds remained in normal time. The score was 1–1. If Bergkamp scored, Manchester United would be knocked out of the FA Cup and their bid for the Treble would be over.

'Looking back,' Schmeichel said later, 'I can see that, at that point, I was facing one of the most important moments in my career.' It was, he believed, a moment that would also decide the outcome of the Premiership run-in between the two teams.

'If we had been knocked out of the Cup, I don't think we could have gone on to win the Premiership, as we did. If Bergkamp had scored, the momentum would have all been with Arsenal in the closing stages.

'When it comes to a penalty, as a goalkeeper you have to take a chance and gamble on the outcome.'

Bergkamp strode up and hit a firm shot, about waist high, to Schmeichel's left. 'I gambled correctly and hit the jackpot,' he said. In extra time, a wonderful individual goal by Ryan Giggs settled an engrossing tie that had lasted four hours.

Left Peter Schmeichel shouts instructions to his defenders in United's 1–1 draw with Internazionale at the San Siro Stadium in the second leg of the UEFA Champions League quarter-final on 17 March 1999.

KEY MUSEUM ARTEFACT

This shirt was worn by Peter Schmeichel in the inaugural season (1992–93) of the Premier League. Its bright, distinctive pattern was not something new in the history of the football shirt. In the early days of kit design, during the mid-1880s, clubs often experimented with exotic, bizarrely-coloured shirts. In their previous incarnation, as Newton Heath, Manchester United wore shirts of yellow and green. Local rivals Blackpool once wore red-, yellow- and navy-blue-striped tops, whilst Bolton Wanderers, rather embarrassingly, wore the most unusual shirt in British football history when they donned white tops emblazoned with red polka dots in 1884.

Right A pair of padded Umbro shorts worn by Peter Schmeichel in the late 1990s.

Roy Keane, the Manchester United captain, described Peter Schmeichel as 'a poser who fancied himself in a big way and played to the crowd'. Keane wasn't being critical; he realised it was part of the Dane's 'act' as a goalkeeper. 'His pose was part of what he had to do to gee himself up,' Keane said.

All the mannerisms, the finger-pointing and gestures of frustration, were a deliberate attempt to build his self-confidence. Keane acknowledged, 'To be fair, Peter did the business. He was as good a goalkeeper as anyone in the world. That, rather than the antics, was what mattered,' said Keane.

> **"It is of huge importance to me that my opponents are intimidated by my presence between the posts."**
>
> *– Peter Schmeichel*

Schmeichel used his temper to his own advantage, to stay alert and focused, 'so that I feel that I am constantly part of the game, which is essential for me to perform at my best'.

'If you take my on-field presence, both visual and verbal, away from me, I would be a quite ordinary goalkeeper,' he wrote. 'Trust me, I've tried to restrain myself and it just didn't work.'

Schmeichel said that his arrogant behaviour 'in some aspects of his football life' was part of a deliberate match strategy, with only one aim: to win.

'You cannot underestimate the power of psychological strength in the midst of a football match,' he wrote. 'It's of huge importance to me that my opponents are intimidated by my presence between the posts.

'Everything I do in goal is aimed at undermining the self-confidence of my opponents. Even a fraction of a second delay in shooting can make all the difference.'

In 22 of the games he played in his second season as a Manchester United player, Peter Schmeichel did not let in a goal, earning him the nickname 'Mr Clean Sheet'. 'As you can imagine, I made no attempt to prevent anyone from using it,' he said.

His goalkeeping was a crucial factor in Manchester United winning the title in 1992–93. The following season they became only the fourth club to achieve the feat of successive championships. In the process, Schmeichel beat the club record of 76 consecutive League appearances set by Alex Stepney in the 1960s. His consistent presence provided vital stability.

After coming to England, Schmeichel changed his style as a goalkeeper.

In eight seasons he played 292 League games, conceding goals at a rate of 0.834 per match. In almost half of the games, he kept a clean sheet. After a spell in Portugal, Schmeichel had stints with Aston Villa and Manchester City before retiring.

Schmeichel earned the nickname 'Mr Clean Sheet'. 'As you can imagine, I made no attempt to prevent anyone from using it.'

TALKING POINT

Sitting on the bench at the Nou Camp Stadium, Alex Ferguson turned to Steve McClaren, his assistant, and said: 'What the hell is he doing?'

Peter Schmeichel was sprinting the length of the field to add his weight and height to the attack at a corner in the dying moments of the Champions League final.

Roy Keane, who missed the game in Barcelona because of suspension, was equally taken aback. 'I've never seen this work before,' the Irishman muttered to himself.

Manchester United were losing 1–0 as the game entered injury-time. There were only two minutes left in what was Schmeichel's last game for the club. As he crossed the half-way line, he ignored the manager's 'vigorous body language which signalled unmistakably that I should get back in my goal immediately'.

'I knew that my green goalkeeper's jersey would cause considerable confusion,' he recalled. Several Bayern players were drawn to him. 'It was the kind of chaos defenders dread, and the ball eventually fell to Teddy Sheringham to score. We were never going to lose after that.'

Above A rosette worn at the 1999 FA Cup final when Manchester United beat Newcastle United 2–0 in their quest for the Treble.

Below A commemorative mug celebrating the 1999 Treble picturing, from left to right, Peter Schmeichel, David Beckham and Ryan Giggs.

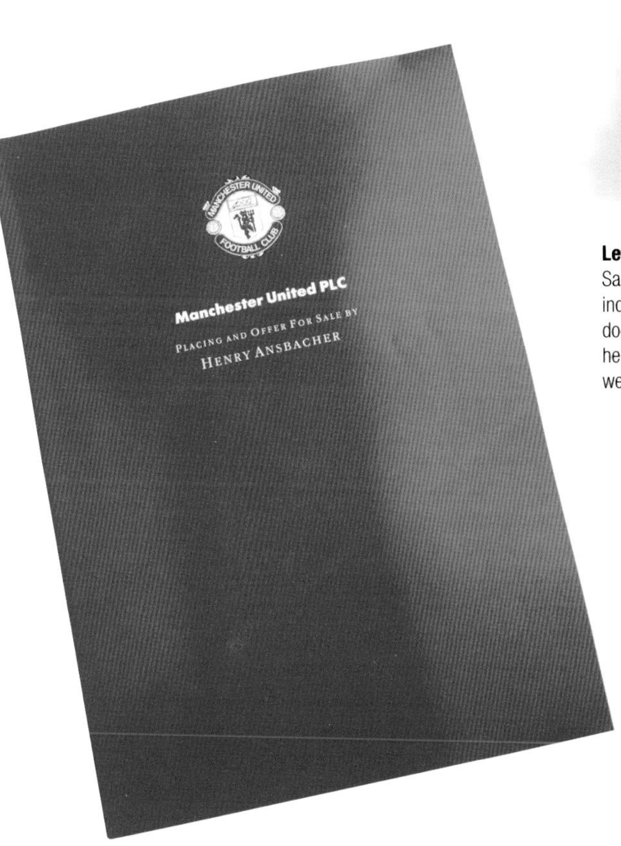

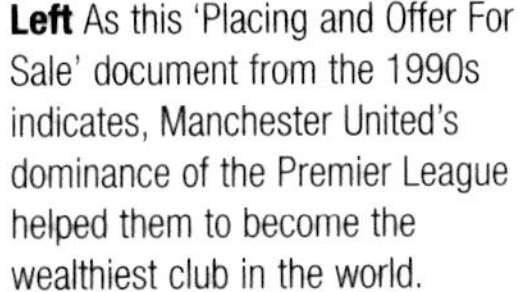

Left As this 'Placing and Offer For Sale' document from the 1990s indicates, Manchester United's dominance of the Premier League helped them to become the wealthiest club in the world.

JVC

IAN WRIGHT (1963–)

Player • Inducted 2005 • 33 caps • 1 Premiership title • 2 FA Cups • 1 League Cup

Ian Wright made himself an instant idol at Highbury on the back of his showmanship, commitment and finishing ability. A hat-trick for Arsenal on his League debut set him on his way to becoming the leading goalscorer in the club's history.

George Graham, the Arsenal manager, considered him indispensable to the Gunners side which reached four major Cup finals in three seasons in the 1990s. 'No successful Arsenal side had ever been so dependent on one man,' Graham said. In a last hurrah at Highbury, Wright helped the club win the Premier League title in 1997–98.

Graham rated him as 'one of the top-dozen strikers I have ever seen', as an instinctive finisher in the mould of Jimmy Greaves and Denis Law. 'Just like them, Ian is a natural,' Graham said.

Following his £2.5 million transfer from Crystal Palace in 1991, Wright finished the season as the leading goalscorer in Division One, with a total of 29 goals. Three years later he scored for Arsenal in 12 consecutive games, a club record, between 15 September and 23 November 1994. 'Ian had all the qualities you want from a striker: lightning pace, sharp reflexes, courage, and an eye for goal,' Graham said.

Wright played in two FA Cup finals, both of which went to a replay, scoring four times. Two of those goals were for Crystal Palace in their final against Manchester United in 1990, a game which Palace eventully lost. He also netted in both finals against Sheffield Wednesday in Arsenal's FA Cup and League Cup 'double' success in 1993.

In European competition, Wright experienced mixed fortunes. In 1993–94, he missed Arsenal's victory over Parma in the final of the European Cup-winners' Cup because of suspension. The following season he scored in every round of the competition up to the final, only for Arsenal to lose against Real Zaragoza.

KEY MATCH

Arsenal 4 Bolton Wanderers 1, Premier League, Highbury, 13 September 1997

In his understandable excitement, Ian Wright made one miscalculation on the day he broke the Arsenal goal-scoring record that had stood for half a century, a feat that reinforced his status as a hero at Highbury.

Having meticulously planned his celebration beforehand, Wright got ahead of himself when he scored the first of his three goals against Bolton.

Running away from the goal, his arms aloft, Wright then lifted his Arsenal shirt over his head to reveal a t-shirt with the slogan: '179 – Just Done It.'

Actually, he had only equalled the record set by Cliff Bastin, a flying left-winger for Arsenal during the inter-war years.

Four minutes later he put the record straight, scoring his second goal of the game and his 179th in total for the club. It was a simple tap-in. 'It was such an easy chance that I was actually happy before I put the ball in the net,' he said later.

At the age of 33, Wright made history in typically flamboyant fashion. Going into the game he had not scored in the Premier League for a month, but he now found his touch, completing a hat-trick in the second half with a fine volley.

At 4–1 Arsène Wenger, the Arsenal manager, could afford to substitute Wright, allowing the veteran striker to leave the field to a standing ovation.

Left Ian Wright turns away to celebrate after scoring against Sheffield Wednesday in the FA Cup final on 15 May 1993.

KEY MUSEUM ARTEFACT

It is claimed that Arsenal, under their original name of Dial Square, received their first set of shirts from Nottingham Forest. Playing in red jerseys, the club soon became known as the Woolwich Reds. It was the great Herbert Chapman, who managed the club from 1925 to1934, who changed the sleeves to the distinctive white that we recognise today. This shirt was worn by centre-forward Ian Wright in the season that he broke the club's long-standing goal-scoring record set by Cliff Bastin. On 13 September 1997, he scored a hat-trick to take his tally to 180 League and Cup goals.

Ian Wright was already 21 years of age before he made his breakthrough into full-time professional football. He would make up for lost time in spectacular fashion.

Wright had been working as a plasterer when Crystal Palace invited him for a two-week trial in 1985. After three days Steve Coppell, the Palace manager, offered him a three-month contract on £100 a week.

'On his first day at Selhurst Park, Ian told me that he wanted to play for England, which was quite a bold statement for someone who had just walked in off a building site,' Steve Coppell, the Palace manager, recalled.

Less than five years later Wright fulfilled his ambition, winning the first of his 33 caps for England, and scoring a total of seven goals. In his six seasons at Palace, Wright scored 90 League goals in 225 appearances, helping the club to promotion from Division Two in 1988–89.

Right An Arsenal Christmas card from 1947. The memories left by Ian Wright and his predecessors at Highbury will never be forgotten as the club move to a new stadium at Ashburton Grove in September 2006.

Wright had been working as a plasterer when Crystal Palace invited him for a two-week trial in 1985. After three days Steve Coppell, the Palace manager, offered him a three-month contract on £100 a week.

Soon after making his international debut in the victory over Cameroon at Wembley in February 1991, Wright was on his way to Highbury.

George Graham went to great lengths to secure his transfer. To keep his interest secret, and ensure his rivals were not tipped off about Wright's availability, Graham attended the Football Writers' Association's annual golf tournament on the day the deal was finalised. 'I didn't want anyone to guess what we were up to,' he said.

At Highbury, Wright's scoring rate increased dramatically. In his first 79 games for Arsenal, he scored 56 goals. Within two years of his arrival, he became the quickest player to register 100 goals for the Gunners, beating the record set by Ted Drake six decades earlier. In total, Wright scored a club-record 185 goals for Arsenal.

'Throughout my life I have always been caught up in the emotion of the game,' Ian Wright said in 1997. 'Sometimes my mouth runs away with me.'

The force of his character had an immediate impact at Arsenal. 'Ian lit up the pitch and the dressing room with the electricity of his performances and his personality,' George Graham said.

On the downside, Wright also found himself at odds with opponents and referees, a behavioural trait that is reflected in a blemished disciplinary record. 'That same competitive edge got me into fights at school, even at primary school,' Wright said. 'Sometimes I just can't help myself; I just have to tell referees where they are going wrong.'

'He has a touchpaper temper to go with his fizzing spirit,' Graham said. 'I had to douse the fire that was always burning within him. His bubbling enthusiasm could run away with him, but while getting him to control himself I had to be careful not to rob him of his natural desire to compete.'

Graham always highlighted the positive aspects of Wright's character. 'There is not a thimbleful of cowardice in him. He is barely five feet nine inches tall which, by modern standards, is quite small for a striker, but there is a lot of power packed in his muscular frame. He also has the courage to go in where it hurts if he feels his reward might be a goal,' Graham said in 1995.

'You could not ask for a more genuine, honest professional than Ian Wright,' he added.

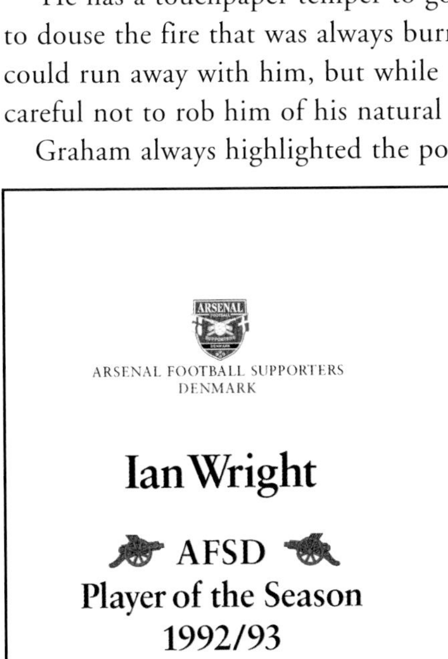

ARSENAL FOOTBALL SUPPORTERS
DENMARK

Ian Wright

AFSD
Player of the Season
1992/93

SØNDRE BANEVEJ 19, 1. SAL · 3400 HILLERØD · DENMARK
TELEPHONE +42 260 007

Left This programme is from the official celebration that took place after Wright was named 'Arsenal Football Supporters Denmark, Player of the Season' in 1993.

TALKING POINT

As a boy Ian Wright lived for the FA Cup final. He would be sitting in front of the television from the moment coverage began in the morning. 'I loved it all,' Wright recalled. 'The build-up, everything. It was a brilliant, special day.'

Wright fulfilled an ambition when he played in his first Cup final, against Manchester United in 1990. 'If the only medal from my whole career was an FA Cup winner's medal, I'd be happy to look back and say I had a great time,' he said.

Wright was substitute for the game. Palace were losing 2–1 with 20 minutes to go when he was told to warm up. His instructions from Steve Coppell were simple: 'Just go on and do anything you like to spark something. Try and make a difference.'

As he ran on, Wright thought to himself: 'If I get the ball anywhere near goal I'm going to shoot.' With virtually his first touch, he did just that, after a run into the penalty area. 'I knew it was in as soon as I hit it,' he said. He was so overjoyed, tears began streaming down his face.

During extra time, Wright scored again, this time with a volley at the far post. 'It was such an amazing moment that I didn't know how to celebrate,' he said. 'So I just started running.' Palace led 3–2.

Manchester United equalised late on, and went on to win the replay. 'We were just seven minutes away from the greatest dream of our lives,' Wright said.

Three years later Wright did get his hands on a winner's medal, as an Arsenal player.

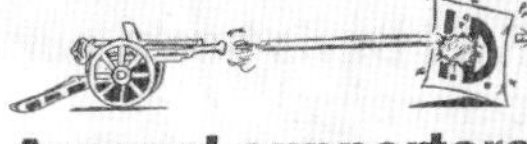

Arsenal supporters against I.D. cards

Hillsborough - Never Again!

The tragedy at the FA Cup semi-final between Liverpool and Notts Forest, in which 95 innocent fans were crushed to death came as a terrible and personal shock to all football supporters. It is not unusual to stand in similar conditions to those at Hillsborough. Many fans will be thinking: 'It could have been me.'

Our campaign has sent a message of condolence via the Liverpool supporters club and would ask you to donate generously to the appeal fund.

The crass insensitivity of Thatcher in pushing through the ID Bill no matter what evidence emerges has angered millions. Not only will crushes outside grounds intensify, but it is another example of the attitude of the Tories and the police that all football fans are potential thugs.

We demand that the ID scheme be withdrawn and that the government finances improvements in the grounds. This means tearing down the cages, more safety measures, better facilities, toilets and food. Last but not least the first aid equipment at Hillsborough was a disgrace – with few stretchers, little or no oxygen and no heart reviving machines.

★ No more Hillsboroughs!
★ Join our campaign.
★ Chant Anti-ID slogans during the match (today v Norwich).
★ Demand that the fans' voice be heard.

Say no to I.D. cards!

Left Ninety-six supporters lost their lives in the disaster at Hillsborough, Sheffield in 1989. As a result of the changes that were implemented after the official report into the disaster, Ian Wright belonged to a new generation of players who benefited from newer, safer stadiums in the 1990s.

Top left Ian Wright played in the first all-seated FA Cup final in 1990. He came on as substitute and scored two goals for Crystal Palace against Manchester United. The game ended 3–3, but United won the replay 1–0.

DARIO GRADI (1941–)

Manager • Inducted 2004 • Two promotions from Division Four
2 promotions from Divsion Three (as of end-2004–05)

Sir Bobby Robson believes that Dario Gradi works at the difficult end of professional football with great determination, skill and integrity.

Since 1983, Gradi has worked for Crewe Alexandra, making him the longest serving manager in the game, ahead of Sir Alex Ferguson of Manchester United. During that time he has lifted the modest club in Cheshire from the bottom of the old Fourth Division to a place in the Championship, competing against clubs whose support base dwarfs the average 7,000 home attendance at Gresty Road.

'Dario is honest, diligent and remarkable,' Sir Bobby Robson said. 'He has done a great job at Crewe and proved himself to be one of our best managers.' Arsène Wenger, the Arsenal manager, describes Gradi's working relationship with Alex as 'a great marriage'.

Before Gradi took over, Crewe had spent the entire 20th century languishing in the bottom two divisions of the Football League. In contrast, in seven of the eight seasons up to the end of 2004–2005 the club has been one promotion away from the Premier League.

He arrived to find a club lacking a coaching system and youth team, so he set them up himself. Since then Gradi has coached 21 youngsters who have gone on to play for their country at full, Under-21 or Under-18 level. Danny Murphy, Robbie Savage, Neil Lennon, Seth Johnson,Geoff Thomas and, most notably, David Platt, all came through the system at Crewe before graduating to Premier League clubs.

Gradi is a chairman's dream manager: since 1983, he has brought in £20 million in transfer fees, ten times the outlay on new players; the team has won promotion four times, and average crowds at Gresty Road have more than tripled.

KEY MATCH

Crewe 1 Brentford 0, Second Division Play-offs final, Wembley, 25 May 1997

One by one, having collected their winner's medal, the players passed the trophy down the line in the Royal Box to the manager who had guided them to promotion against the odds.

Dario Gradi carried the trophy down the famous steps at Wembley before the team embarked on the traditional lap of honour.

In the final moments of normal time, Gradi had turned to Danny Murphy, the future England international standing beside him: 'Danny, can you believe it, we're one minute away from playing in the First Division?'

Crewe won the game with a goal from the long-serving left-back Shaun Smith in the 34th minute. Smith scored at the back post after Steve Macauley, the centre-back, headed down a free-kick taken by Murphy.

'We murdered them 1–0,' Gradi recalled. 'A couple of efforts were cleared off the line. We should have won easily but in the end it didn't matter.'

The goal marked one of the last contributions made by Murphy to the Crewe cause. Troubled by a hamstring problem, Murphy was only passed fit an hour or so before kick-off. He lasted 70 minutes before being replaced.

It was his final appearance for Crewe. Within a matter of weeks Murphy was on his way to Liverpool for a fee of £3.5 million. Remarkably, the substitute who took Murphy's place at Wembley was another future England midfield player.

Seth Johnson stayed at Crewe until until his £3.6 million transfer to Derby County in 1999.

Left Dario Gradi patrols the touch line at Gresty Road. His notepad is used to record tactical observations.

KEY MUSEUM ARTEFACT

Gradi began his managerial career at Wimbledon in 1978. During his spell at Plough Lane, he took them from the old Fourth Division to the Third. Finding it difficult to adjust to life in a higher league, the Dons were relegated the following year. Gradi left the club in 1981, but the Wimbledon fairytale had begun. By 1988, they were FA Cup winners, becoming the first club to win both the FA Cup and the FA Amateur Cup. The Amateur Cup (below) was launched in 1893 as a response to the domination of the FA Cup by professional teams. It was won for the last time in 1974.

When Dario Gradi started his project at Crewe, he had no contract. It meant that the board could sack him with two weeks' notice. He is now nearing the end of his second ten-year deal with the club.

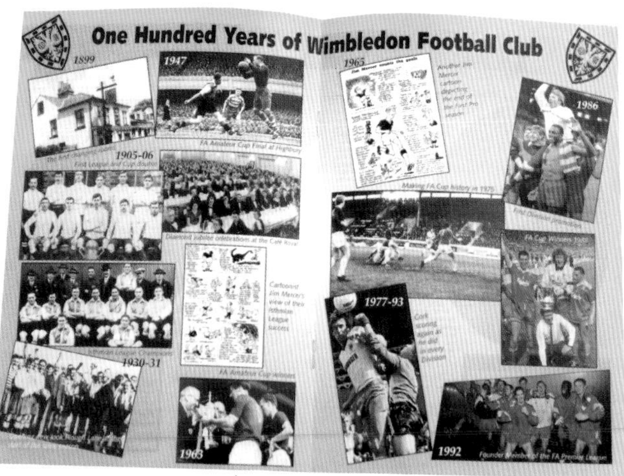

Crewe had finished the previous season in 91st place in the Football League, above the bottom club only on goal difference, and that represented a big improvement on 1981–82 when the club ended 15 points adrift at the wrong end of Division Four.

“The ground is a lasting legacy to my work here, and perhaps they might name some part of the ground after me when I'm dead and gone, but I'd be too embarrassed if they did it while I was still around.” – *Dario Gradi*

Above This double-page spread from a Wimbledon match-day programme in the 1990s features 100 years of the club's history.

Right A 1985 Crewe Alexandra match-day programme. When Gradi took over at Gresty Road, the club had been floundering in the old Fourth Division for 14 years.

'The team was struggling and the ground was a dump,' Gradi recalled. 'But that was just what I wanted when I applied for the job. There was only one way to go, and that was up.'

Almost half of the transfer funds injected into the club have been spent on facilities at Gresty Road. A new main stand cost £5 million, with £500,000 spent on the rest of the ground. The training ground took up another £2 million.

The people of Crewe rewarded Gradi for his work: in 2003, he was given the Freedom of the Borough of Crewe and Nantwich.

'I am a teacher,' Dario Gradi said. 'I am not a coach for the players at the very top level. I'm all about helping players improve. I try to develop skilful players. We always try to play good football; none of this whack and chase stuff.'

His first task was to find a permanent training ground for the nine players who were still on the books. They also had no training kit.

The sports teacher at a nearby school offered use of the school fields, in return for a promise to present the prizes at the annual sports day.

> "I organised a sponsor for the team minibus and I also had a room under the stand refurbished to give the players somewhere to relax. I think I was the first manager to put in a real effort to make something happen."
>
> – *Dario Gradi*

TALKING POINT

Dario Gradi has made a habit of finding young players who have been rejected by other clubs and helping them develop into potential internationals. David Platt, an England captain and once the most expensive footballer in Britain, is the most striking example of many successful Crewe graduates.

Gradi offered Platt a new start in the game in 1984 when he was released by Manchester United at the age of 18. Four years after arriving at Crewe on a free transfer, Platt was sold to Aston Villa for a fee of £200,000.

'David can go on to become a truly great player,' Gradi said at the time. Platt proved him right. In July 1991 Bari invested £5.5 million, a record sum for a British player, to take him to Italy. He went on to play for Juventus and Arsenal, winning 62 caps for England along the way.

'When David arrived at Crewe he was a decent all-round player without being truly outstanding at one aspect of the game,' Gradi recalled. 'We gave him an opportunity and the surroundings in which to develop.

'His breakthrough was largely down to nature. One summer he suddenly developed physically. He was stronger and his stamina improved significantly.

'He had always said that central midfield was his best position, and now he was able to prove his point. Early on in his career we put him on the wing to keep him out of trouble, but he had developed the strength to cope with a central role and the stamina to play box-to-box.

'David had also played some games at centre-forward and his natural goal-scoring ability made him really stand out as a midfield player. He was a good finisher. It was no surprise when Villa took an interest in him.'

Above At the time of Crewe Alexandra's celebrations of the 1977 Jubilee, the club had not played football at a level higher than Division Three since they failed to be re-elected to Division Two in 1896.

Left David Platt, one of Dario Gradi's many protégés, scores for England in their 1-0 victory over Belgium in the 1990 World Cup second round.

UMBRO
TELE +
26

ROY KEANE (1971–)

Player • Inducted 2004 • 60 caps • 7 Premiership titles • 4 FA Cups (as of end-May 2005)

Roy Keane can properly be described as the heart and soul of the Manchester United side that enjoyed an unprecedented dominance in English football during the 1990s.

Sir Alex Ferguson, the Manchester United manager, attributes the rise of the club to the Irishman who has driven on both himself and his team-mates relentlessly, culminating in the club's victory in the Champions League final in 1999.

During his time as manager of the Republic of Ireland, Jack Charlton rated Keane the best midfield player in Britain. 'Roy has a competitive instinct that is phenomenal. The lad is a marvel.' Graham Taylor, the England manager, said: 'I just wish he was English.'

By the end of the 2004–05 season Keane had won seven Premiership winner's medals.

'If I could have any individual player in the world in my team, money no object, it would be Roy,' Brian Clough, the former Nottingham Forest manager said. It was Clough who gave Keane his break, signing him as a teenager from Irish semi-professional side Cobh Ramblers in 1990.

Ferguson quickly identified him as the player who could lead Manchester United to the ultimate club prize in Europe. When Keane eventually became available for transfer, in the summer of 1993, Ferguson acted swiftly. 'Roy, Manchester United are going to dominate the domestic game with or without you,' he argued. 'With you, we can win in Europe.'

The following season Keane was voted Footballer of the Year by both the football writers and his fellow professionals, winning 53 per cent of the vote in one poll, the highest figure on record. It was a typically defiant and determined response to his bitter disappointment at missing out on playing in the Champions League final against Bayern Munich because of suspension.

Bryan Robson, whose leadership role Keane assumed at Old Trafford, said: 'I haven't seen him have an average game yet. He is outstanding. He is a Manchester United legend, and if I had to pick a World XI, Roy would be in it.'

KEY MATCH

Juventus 2 Manchester United 3, Champions League semi-final, second leg, Turin, 21 April 1999

Sir Alex Ferguson believes that the reaction of Roy Keane to the bitter disappointment of realising he would would miss the Champions League final defines him as a player.

'I didn't think I could have a higher opinion of any footballer than I did of the Irishman but he rose even further in my estimation against Juventus,' Sir Alex recalled, referring to Keane's performance in the semi-final, second leg.

Keane had already reduced the deficit on the night with a near-post header when he was booked for a mistimed tackle on Zinedine Zidane. It was his second caution of the tournament and meant an automatic suspension for the final.

'Once it happened he seemed to redouble his efforts to get the team there,' Ferguson said. 'It was the most emphatic display of selflessness I've seen on a football field, inspiring all around him.'

A sense of numbness came over Keane when Juventus went 2–0 up after 11 minutes, giving them an aggregate lead of 3–1, but he quickly realised that the circumstances had created the kind of situation he relishes most: a test of mental strength.

'Anybody seeking to prove that they were worthy of playing for Manchester United also had the chance to prove it,' Keane recalled.

The momentum gradually shifted. When Andy Cole scored a third goal, Keane knew that Manchester United would play in the final, even if he would not. At that moment he did not care. Only later, his job done, did the regret come.

Left Roy Keane in action during the Champions League semi-final against Juventus on 21 April 1999.

KEY MUSEUM ARTEFACT

These shin pads, manufactured by Umbro, are called Armadillo pads because their design mimics the burrowing mammal's protective plates. As a destructive midfield player, Keane's physical style of play makes this type of equipment a necessity. Sam Widdowson, who played for one of Keane's former clubs, Nottingham Forest, invented shin-guards in 1874. Initially they were worn outside the sock and fastened around the back of the calf with a strap and buckle. As playing kit developed, the pads became shorter and were worn under the socks.

Sir Alex Ferguson set his sights on signing Roy Keane within 15 seconds of first seeing him live in action.

In 1990, Keane was playing in his first season for Nottingham Forest in a First Division fixture against Manchester United. 'I always remember the kick-off,' Ferguson recalled. 'The ball went back to Bryan Robson and Roy absolutely cemented him! I said to myself: "Bloody cheek of him! How dare he come to Old Trafford and tackle like that."'

Roy Keane loathes complacency; in himself and in others. Relentlessly, over the years, he has driven his team forwards.

The childhood boxer relished the challenge of top-flight football. 'During my time in the ring as a lad I developed a certain confidence when confronted by physical aggression,' he said.

Boxing also made Keane incredibly fit. Training in the gym developed his stamina, giving him an 'exceptional engine', to coin Jack Charlton's phrase. Working 'box to box', Keane earned a reputation at Forest as a goalscorer. Gradually, following his transfer to Manchester United, he modified his game, accepting greater responsibility. However, it took the intervention of Robson, the player he had once flattened, to bring about the change.

Robson, then nearing the end of his playing career, took Keane aside for a quiet chat. He urged the Irishman to drop deep in order to initiate attacks. It was a task Keane had previously left to others. 'Bryan was right about me copping out,' he said later. 'I still lacked confidence in my ability in possession.'

The message from Robson was direct: 'Trust your own talent. Get involved'. Keane took the advice. At the end of the season Manchester United had won the 'Double'.

Roy Keane loathes complacency. Relentlessly

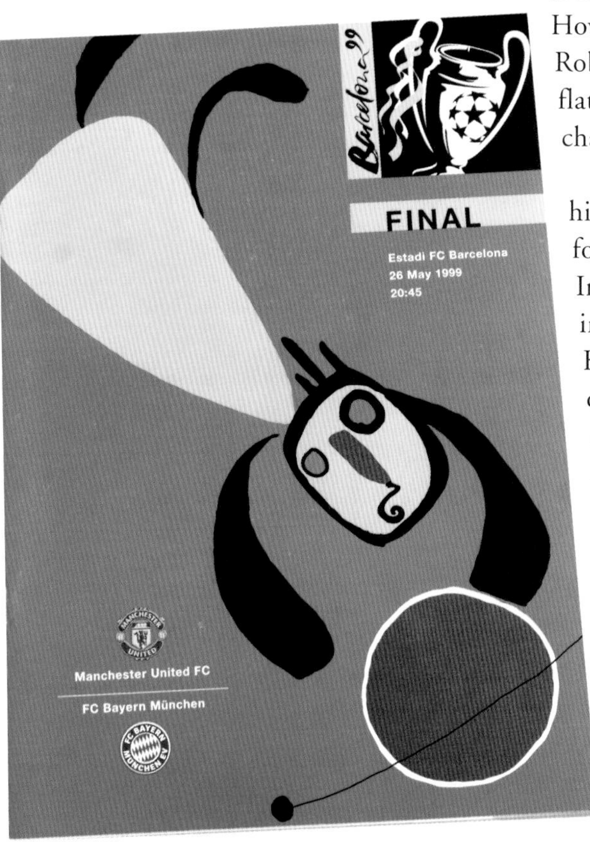

Right The programme of the 1999 European Cup final. Keane was the catalyst for United's amazing comeback from 2–0 down in the Champions League semi-final, second leg, against Juventus. His goal helped United secure a 4–3 victory. Unfortunately, he was booked in the game and so missed the final through suspension.

over the years, he has driven both himself and his team-mates forward. Alex Ferguson has identified this fierce will to win as perhaps the most positive factor in the rise of Manchester United.

'I worked for every second with complete determination and absolute concentration,' Keane said of himself as a youngster. 'The determination was obvious. It was my trademark.'

The constant striving for improvement has led to problems with authority. He walked out of the Republic of Ireland training camp before the World Cup in 2002, charging FAI officials of being unprofessional in their organisation.

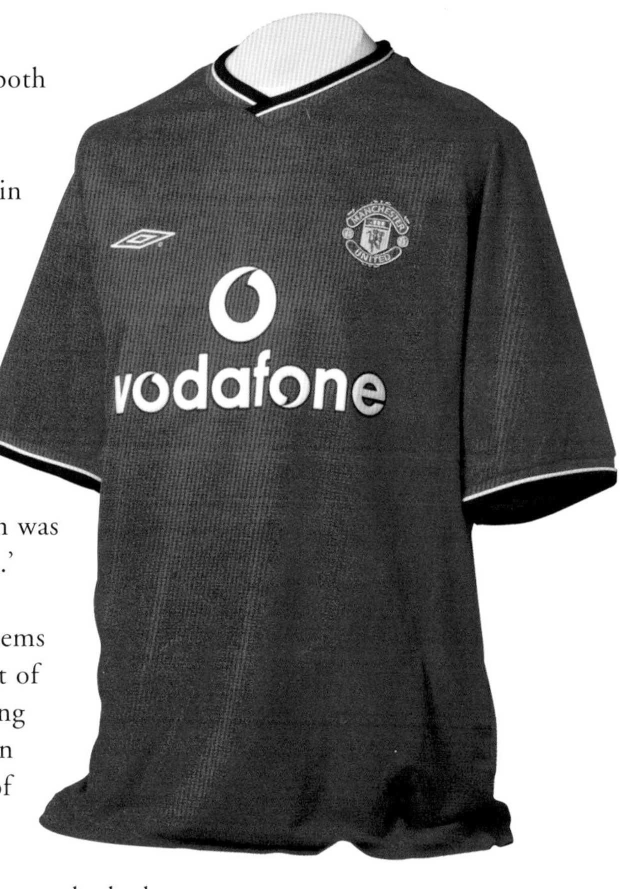

At the age of 30, all the pressure he had placed upon himself and his team-mates over the years to win suddenly caught up with him. He decided to quit. 'I'd had enough,' Keane later recalled. 'Driving, always driving. Putting myself and everyone else through it all. I thought to myself: "There's only so much people can take."'

Keane had a history of red cards and confrontations with referees. One infamous incident involving Andy D'Urso shocked him. 'The psycho in the middle with veins bulging in his head is me,' he said, referring to a photograph of the incident.

The combined persuasive power of his wife and his manager changed his mind about retirement. He later vowed to calm down, a commitment reflected in an improved disciplinary record.

In recent years, Keane has been used more sparingly, his influence saved for more important games. 'Roy is a legend,' Ferguson said. 'He will always be revered by fans of Manchester United.'

Left The 1994 World Cup Mascot. Keane played in all the Republic of Ireland's games in the 1994 tournament. After defeating the Italians in their opening group game, the Irish progressed to the second stage where they were knocked out by Holland.

TALKING POINT

Roy Keane was rejected as a teenager by scouts working for a host of English clubs. In 1990, at the age of 18, he looked lost to top-level football. Nobody had bothered to offer him even a trial.

Yet 12 months later, this apparent failure had journeyed from the obscurity of semi-professional, lower division football in Ireland to a starting place in an FA Cup final at Wembley.

The turning point came when Noel McCabe, a scout working for Brian Clough, saw something that his competitors had missed. 'You're a Forest player, son,' McCabe told Keane. 'You can pass the ball simply, work the two boxes and score goals.'

After playing one reserve match, Keane was offered a contract. The transfer fee paid to Cobh Ramblers was £47,000. Three months later, Keane travelled to Liverpool in the belief he'd be looking after the first-team kit. Just before kick-off, Clough told him he was playing. Keane was a virtual unknown. Warming up on the pitch, several of his own Forest team-mates had to ask him his name.

On his home debut he was substituted near the end of the game. The Forest fans gave him a standing ovation.

At the end of 'this fairytale season for me', Clough selected Keane for the FA Cup final in May 1991, at the expense of Steve Hodge, an England international. A few days later, he made his international debut. 'I had exceeded my wildest dreams,' Keane said.

Above A Manchester United shirt from 2000. Keane captained United to the second of their three, back-to-back Premiership titles in 2000.

Left Yellow and Red Cards from1990. In his early career at Manchester United, Keane was often shown a yellow card for either persistent infringement or dissent. The use of cards to signal a booking or a sending-off was the idea of the English referee Ken Aston in 1966, but the cards were not introduced into the English game until 1976.

ALAN SHEARER (1970–)

Player • Inducted 2004 • 63 Caps • 1 Premiership title (as of end-2004–05)

Alan Shearer has justified the status he once held as the world's most expensive footballer by scoring more goals than anyone else since the launch of the Premier League in 1992.

Shearer is the first player since the 1930s, the heyday of the bustling, robust English centre-forward, to score more than 30 goals in the top division in three successive seasons.

His tally of 34 goals in 1994–95, the middle season of his outstanding run, helped Blackburn Rovers win the championship title for the first time in 81 years.

'Alan is a player in a class of his own,' Kenny Dalglish, the then Blackburn manager, said. 'He lifts the whole team and turns draws into victories. In a word: priceless.' John Barnes, the England winger, described Shearer's value to his team as 'incalculable'.

Shearer stands alone as the leading goalscorer in the history of Premier League. Between 1992–93 and the end of 2004–05, he scored 250 league goals for Blackburn and Newcastle United.

His outstanding form during the mid-1990s had raised his value in the transfer market seven-fold in the space of five years: from £2.2 million, the fee Dalglish paid Southampton in 1992, to the £15.6 million fee Newcastle United invested in 1996.

Shearer has been transferred twice in his career: the first of his transfer fees was a British record; the second was a world record sum for a footballer.

It was widely reported that Blackburn refused to sell Shearer to Manchester United earlier in 1997 for fear that his arrival at Old Trafford would make Alex Ferguson's side unbeatable.

Jack Walker, the millionaire benefactor at Ewood Park, even offered to make Shearer the player-manager of Rovers, at the age of just 25, in a last-ditch effort to keep him at the club, but the lure of Newcastle United proved too strong for a player who had supported the club as a boy.

KEY MATCH

England 4 Holland 1, European Championship group game, Wembley Stadium, 18 June 1996

When the newspapers criticised Alan Shearer over his lack of goals in the build-up to Euro '96, his response was always the same: 'I'm certain that when it starts for real at the tournament I will start scoring again.'

It was a bold statement, perhaps even foolhardy, he later admitted. If he had failed to find the net, he knew he would have left himself open to criticism. He had, in effect, put his international career on the line.

By the time it was all over, Shearer was the tournament's top scorer with five goals. Two of those goals – a penalty and a shot at the end of 'a scintillating move' – came in the game against Holland; the 'finest performance I have been involved with for England.'

'The atmosphere at Wembley before this game was the best I have ever known. The backing of the fans had reached great heights,' he recalled.

The Blackburn Rovers forward had gone almost two years without finding the net for England. The England manager, however, never contemplated dropping Shearer. Privately, Terry Venables went even further, assuring him that, barring injury, he would be first choice for the tournament, regardless of his goal-scoring record in the remaining warm-up games.

When a chance fell to him in the opening game of Euro '96, against Switzerland, he recalled, 'My only thought was to smash it ... When it went in, I was delirious.'

Left Alan Shearer shoots for goal against Switzerland in Euro '96.

KEY MUSEUM ARTEFACT

This shirt was worn by Newcastle United's Jimmy Stewart in the 1911 FA Cup final. Shearer's home-town club had an excellent record in the early years of the competition. They won the FA Cup in 1910, 1924, 1932, 1951, 1952 and 1955. Shearer has appeared in two FA Cup finals with Newcastle, picking up two runners-up medals in 1998 and '99. He can consider himself a little unfortunate in that the two teams who defeated Newcastle, Arsenal and Manchester United, went on to win the Double and the Treble respectively.

Within minutes of the opening of the London Stock Exchange on Monday, 28 July 1997, the shares of Newcastle United dipped eight pence, wiping millions off the club's value. The explanation for the sharp dip in value was obvious: two days earlier Alan Shearer was seriously injured in a pre-season friendly. He would be sidelined for six months, and the reaction of the market highlighted his importance to the team.

> **"Alan is a nightmare to defend against because if a cross comes in he will always be there."** – *John Barnes*

John Barnes, a team-mate at Newcastle said: 'Alan is a nightmare to defend against because if a cross comes in he will always be there. He is very clinical at hitting the target, and he can also drop his shoulder and score from 30 yards.'

Fully aware of Newcastle United's long tradition of great centre-forwards, he made one demand of Keegan before signing: Shearer wanted to wear the number nine shirt. Hughie Gallacher, Jackie Milburn, Wyn Davies and Malcolm Macdonald, and now Shearer. 'As a Newcastle fan, I knew what it meant,' he said.

On 9 April 1988, Alan Shearer made a stunning impact on top-flight football, scoring a hat-trick on his debut for Southampton as a raw youngster aged 17 years and 240 days. It made him the youngest player ever to score a hat-trick in the top division. But the next phase of his education proved a little more difficult: he managed only 20 more goals in 117 League appearances over the

Right An engraving from the FA Cup final between Blackburn Rovers and Notts County in 1891. When Shearer moved to Rovers in the early 1990s, he joined a club that had dominated the FA Cup in its early days. They had won the trophy in three successive seasons from 1884 to 1886.

following four years. It was a modest return even at a club struggling at the wrong end of the table.

His potential, however, was obvious. In 11 games for the England Under-21s, he scored 13 goals. He then graduated through the ranks to England 'B' and full international level. On his England debut, he scored a goal in the 2–0 win over France at Wembley in February 1992.

It was a signal for his career to take off. Following his transfer to Blackburn Rovers, his scoring rate rose sharply. In 138 appearances for Rovers, he scored 112 goals, an exceptional return to the top division.

In 1995–96 he needed one more goal to record his third 30-goal haul for the third successive season, a record in the Premiership. Despite being troubled by a groin injury that needed surgery, he was determined to achieve his target, and with only four weeks remaining before the start of Euro '96, he took a risk. He delayed the operation for several days to allow him one more chance. Shearer scored the goal he needed against Wimbledon, and then worked tirelessly to get himself fit for England. We all know what happened next.

TALKING POINT

Alan Shearer was staggered by the sight of an estimated 15,000 fellow Geordies standing in the rain outside St James' Park to greet him on his homecoming to the club that he supported as a boy.

He was introduced to the crowd as a returning hero. 'The whole scene at the ground brought a lump to my throat,' he said later, 'and I am not normally an emotional person.' The Newcastle supporters had amended the lyrics of England's anthem for Euro '96: 'Shearer's Coming Home,' they chanted.

As a boy, Shearer, a product of the proud Wallsend Boys Club, had queued for four hours to witness Kevin Keegan's debut as a Newcastle player in 1982. During the press conference, Shearer said, 'The money and the attention have not changed me. I'm still a sheet metalworker's son from Newcastle.' He later recalled: 'And that was just how I felt.'

Keegan, who had returned to the club as manager, said: 'This is the signing for the people of Newcastle. Everything about Alan made him worth the money – his character, his stability, the fact that he is a winner.'

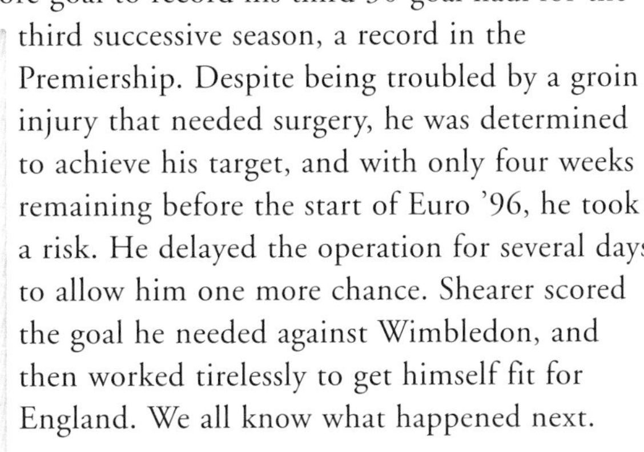

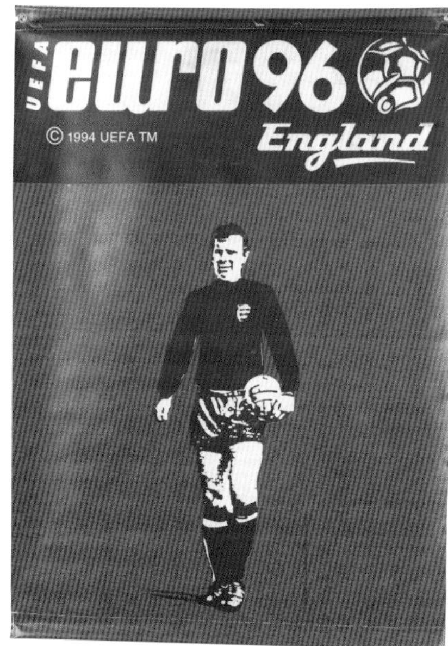

Left This cigarette card, issued by John Player & Sons, features the Newcastle United side that eventually lost to Bradford City in the 1911 FA Cup final replay. Newcastle's fine record in the competition helped to create the passion for the game on Tyneside.

Above left A Euro 96 CD rom, showing how Shearer's success on the field at Euro '96 resulted in commercial success off it.

Above One of a number of Euro '96 banners that featured players from the past. This one celebrates the career of Bobby Moore. Shearer was the tournament's leading scorer with five goals.

adidas
SHARP

RYAN GIGGS (1973–)

Player • Inducted 2005 • 50 Caps • 1 European Champions League
8 Premiership titles • 4 FA Cups • 1 League Cup (as of end-2004–05)

The longest-serving player during the Alex Ferguson era at Manchester United, Ryan Giggs is the most successful footballer in the history of English football in terms of individual honours.

Since making his debut for Manchester United as a 17-year-old in 1991, he has won eight championship medals. As of the end of 2004–2005, Giggs had also claimed four FA Cup winner's medals.

'I can say honestly that whatever Manchester United have paid me in my time as manager at Old Trafford was justified at a stroke by securing Ryan Giggs as a player for the club,' Ferguson later recalled. 'When he runs at people, he can leave the best defenders in the world with twisted blood.'

Roy Keane said: 'When I joined the club in 1993, Ryan was light years ahead of me in terms of ability and maturity. He is funny, cheeky and blessed with extraordinary talent.'

'Giggs will tear you apart again,' the Manchester United supporters were soon chanting, re-working the lyrics of the cult Joy Division song.

'In his position on the left wing he is amongst the best players in the world,' Ottmar Hitzfeld, the Bayern Munich manager once said. Raul, the Real Madrid striker, said: 'He can open up the game because he is very fast and very direct.'

At international level, Giggs became the youngest man to play for Wales when he made his debut as a substitute against Germany at the age of 17 years and 321 days in 1991. When fit, he has been an automatic choice for his country of birth ever since.

Since 1991, Giggs has played more than 600 games for Manchester United in all competitions, a longevity matched only by Bill Foulkes, a defender during the Matt Busby era, and Bobby Charlton. 'A great player for this football club over many years,' Charlton said.

KEY MATCH

Manchester United 1 Manchester City 0, Division One, Old Trafford, 5 May 1991

Ryan Giggs wasn't sure if he'd heard correctly. It was an hour and a half before the start of the Manchester derby, and Alex Ferguson had just read out the names on the team sheet.

'I had been expecting to be one of the substitutes, but the gaffer had read out my name in the first eleven,' Giggs recalled. 'That is my biggest memory of the day: sitting in the dressing room listening to the team-talk.'

Giggs had made his first appearance for the club as a substitute against Everton two months earlier. Now he was about to make his full debut. 'I was pretty nervous up to the kick-off,' he recalled.

He marked the occasion by scoring a goal, although to this day he thinks it should have been registered as an own goal. His shot took a massive deflection on its way into the net for the winning goal of the game. 'The record book has my name again, so I'll take it.'

Ferguson was delighted by Giggs' performance. 'Even in those early games, Ryan was obviously a great player in the making. The supporters had all heard about this outstanding young player on the books, and there was a great sense of anticipation.'

George Best, the player with whom Giggs has been compared throughout his career, watched the Welshman's progress. 'One day they might even say that I was another Ryan Giggs,' Best said in 1992.

Left Manchester United's Ryan Giggs goes past Wimbledon's Warren Barton in a game at Old Trafford in 1992.

KEY MUSEUM ARTEFACT

This programme from the Under-15 schoolboy international between England and Germany features, among others, Ryan Wilson. Wilson subsequently adopted his mother's surname of Giggs. The first international schools fixture was between England and Wales at Walsall in 1907 and England won 3–1, while England's first game against Scotland was in 1911. Giggs could play for England Schools because he was educated in England. Although he was born in Cardiff, he grew up in Swinton, Salford. Another notable name on the team sheet is Nick Barmby, who went on to star for Spurs, Everton, Liverpool and Middlesbrough.

MARVIN HARRIOTT
20.4.74 Marvin gained his early experience with Barking and Dagenham Schools' F.A. and Essex County S.F.A., for whom he appeared as a Central Defender or Full-back. Since September he has been a pupil at the F.A. (G.M.) National School. He enjoys playing a variety of sports and in his spare time likes to listen to 'pop' music. His ability was also recognised by West Ham United F.C. for whom he has signed Schoolboy Forms. His ambition is a career with the 'Hammers', and, perhaps, the full England Squad.

RYAN WILSON

RYAN WILSON
27.11.73 Moorside High School, Salford. Ryan gained his initial experience of Representative Football with the City of Salford Schools' F.A. Under 14 squad as a Left-winger and has gained further honours by his selection for Greater Manchester

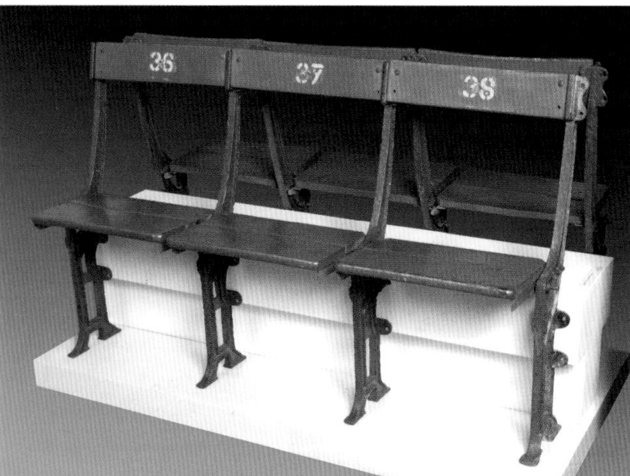

Above These are six of the original, wooden, folding seats from Wembley Stadium in 1923. Giggs has played regularly at Wembley throughout his career winning the FA Cup on three occasions and the League Cup once. He has also appeared in one losing final and four Charity Shields at the stadium.

Right This Geomerlin ball was used in the Premier League in the 2000–01 season. Giggs has won eight Premiership titles, including three back to back between 1999 and 2001.

Alex Ferguson watched with increasing excitement, as a young, wiry teenager played in a trial match at the Manchester United training ground.

Giggs had been training at the Manchester City school of excellence until the age of 14. All that changed on his 14th birthday, when the Giggs family received a visitor at their home in Swinton: Alex Ferguson had made a special journey to persuade the teenager to sign schoolboy forms at Old Trafford.

> **"When I saw Ryan in that trial match he gave one of those rare and priceless moments that make all the sweat and frustration and misery of management worthwhile."** – *Alex Ferguson*

Two years later, Giggs signed amateur forms, turning professional in November 1990, soon after his 17th birthday. Within four months he made his first-team debut.

'The only honest reaction to Ryan as a young player was feverish excitement,' Ferguson recalled. 'He had made the transition from schoolboy to senior football with absolute ease and by the end of 1990 he was lighting up the place. Leading players at the club raved about him.'

Ryan Giggs was the first player to embrace Alex Ferguson after the final whistle of the Champions League final against Bayern Munich at the Nou Camp in Barcelona in 1999.

It was an emotional moment for Giggs. 'When the game ended I just went,' Giggs recalled. 'I just started crying, and there was nothing I could do about it.'

Manchester United had scored two late goals to win the game. 'I can remember the game quite clearly, but those last five minutes are a blur,' he said.

So fearful were Bayern Munich of his threat on the wing that they lobbied successfully for the pitch to be narrowed for the match. Giggs played a crucial role in the victory, according to Ferguson. Selected on the right wing, Giggs faced Michael Tarnat, the Bayern left-back. 'Ryan was a constant threat and Tarnat was making regular demands to the bench looking for back-up,' Ferguson

> “He carried his head high and he looked as relaxed and natural on the park as a dog chasing a piece of silver paper in the wind. From that moment we protected Ryan like the treasure he was.” – *Alex Ferguson*

said. ‘The strain Ryan put on the opposition was one of the factors that steadily drained them in the second half.’

Giggs had been working for the previous three years on broadening the scope of his game in terms of his passing, vision and positional play.

‘I believe I am a better player now than I was ten years ago,’ Giggs said in 2004. ‘I am more relaxed as a player these days, and I cherish things a lot more. I probably ran twice as much a decade ago but that was often because I was out of position. Now I instinctively know where I should be.’

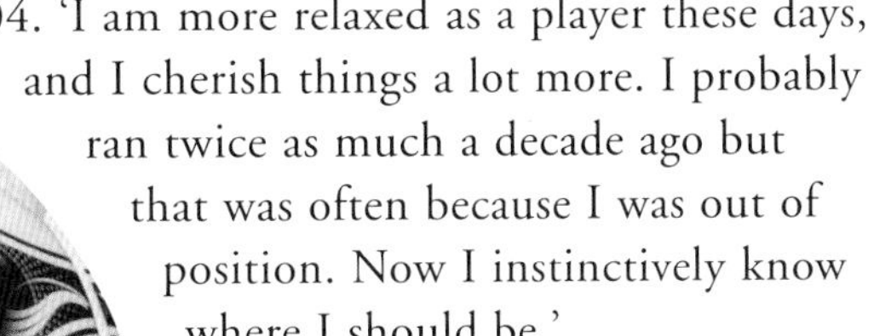

TALKING POINT

‘When the ball came to me just inside my own half in extra-time at Villa Park, my first thought was simply to get into their half. We were down to ten men against Arsenal and I wanted to relieve some pressure. I just got the ball and set off.’

‘I didn’t realise at the time just what type of goal it was. I thought I was much nearer the goal when I got the ball, say 30 yards out, and maybe beat one, perhaps two defenders. It was instinct. I didn’t realise that I started in my own half and beat three or four players until I got home and watched a replay on television.’

‘When I found myself near goal, all I thought about was hitting it hard and making sure it was on target. I did cringe a bit when I saw the celebration. I took off my shirt and whirled it over my head: sometimes when you score you just don’t know what you’re doing.

‘It was a night of mixed emotions for me. I was obviously very proud to have scored an individual goal like that, but I also suffered an ankle injury and had to leave the ground on crutches.

‘That victory in the FA Cup semi-final in 1999 gave us the belief to go on and eventually win the Treble,’ Giggs told the official Manchester United website.

‘It was not just a special goal, it was historic,’ Alex Ferguson said. ‘Given the context, this has to be one of the best goals ever scored in major football.’

Above When Giggs won the FA Youth Cup as captain of Manchester United, in 1992, he was following in the footsteps of the great Busby Babes. United’s Youth Team won the trophy every year from its inception in 1953 until 1957. This 1958 magazine features the original ‘Babes’ in their last game before eight of them lost their lives in the Munich air disaster.

Left A football that was used in the 1998 World Cup finals. Like his Manchester United predecessor, George Best, Giggs has so far been unable to parade his talent at the World Cup finals because of his country’s lack of success.

PHOTOGRAPHY ACKNOWLEDGEMENTS

Photographs on pages 6, 14, 18, 22, 26, 30, 34, 38, 42, 46, 50, 54, 58, 62, 65, 66, 69, 70, 74, 78, 82, 86, 90, 94, 98, 102, 106, 110, 113, 114, 118, 122, 126, 130, 134, 138, 142, 146, 150, 154, 158, 161, 166, 170, 174, 178, 182, 186, 190, 193, 194, 198, 202, 210, 214, 218, 226, 230, 234, 237, 238, 242 and 246 copyright © **Popperfoto.com**, a photographic agency whose sports department is one of the world's largest and most comprehensive, with particular breadth and depth in football, cricket, rugby, golf, tennis, World Cup and Olympic games. With grateful thanks for both their unique collection and excellent service; page 162 copyright © Mirrorpix; page 206 copyright © Action Images.

All other photographs copyright © The National Football Museum, produced by Norwyn Photographic and Pete Lucas Photography.

INDEX

References in italics are to captions.
References in bold are to main entries.

A

B

D

E

F

G

H

I

J

K

L

M

N

O

P

Q

R

S

T

U

V

W

Y

Z